Education for Sustainable Development

In 2005, The United Nations launched its Decade of Education for Sustainable Development, which recognises that education, including Higher Education is the key to the change in social attitudes that will be needed to protect the welfare of future generations. This involves helping learners to live as though the future matters and to achieve ecoliteracy. This includes the understanding that personal lifestyle decisions may have consequences, ranging from climate change, through loss of biodiversity, to pollution and resource depletion that may permit environmental degradation on a planetary scale. It also involves helping them to develop the skills needed to cope with such challenges. This international collection of research papers and position statements from special issues of the Journal of Geography in Higher Education and Applied Environmental Education and Communication, written by many of the leading practitioners in the field, aims to provide resources and practical guidance for all seeking to promote and engage in education for a sustainable future. Rabindranath Tagore encouraged each learner to make their actions demonstrate a harmonious union between education and environment. David Orr argued that the world needs people who live well in their places to make the world both habitable and humane and that the main challenge for education is to help learners make their minds fit for life on Earth. This book tries to chart a practical route towards these objectives.

This book was previously published as special issues of the *Journal of Geography in Higher Education* and *Applied Environmental Education and Communication.*

Brian Chalkley is Director of the Higher Education Academy Subject centre in Geography, Earth and Environmental Sciences at the University of Plymouth, UK.

Martin Haigh and **David Higgitt** are Co-Editors of the *Journal of Geography in Higher Education* and Professor at Oxford Brookes University, UK and Associate Professor at the National University of Singapore, respectively.

Education for Sustainable Development

Papers in Honour of the United Nations Decade of Education for Sustainable Development (2005-2014)

Edited by Brian Chalkley, Martin Haigh and David Higgitt

Routledge
Taylor & Francis Group
LONDON AND NEW YORK

First published 2009 by Routledge
2 Park Square, Milton Park, Abingdon, Oxon, OX14 4RN

Simultaneously published in the USA and Canada
by Routledge
270 Madison Avenue, New York, NY 10016

Routledge is an imprint of the Taylor & Francis Group, an informa business

Transferred to Digital Printing 2009

Typeset in Times by Value Chain, India

British Library Cataloguing in Publication Data
A catalogue record for this book is available from the British Library

ISBN 10: 0-415-46005-0
ISBN 13: 978-0-415-46005-7

CONTENTS

Approaching the UN Decade of Education for Sustainable Development: Prospects and Challenges

DAVID HIGGITT

The 'United Nations Decade of Education for Sustainable Development' came into existence on 1 January 2005. UN Resolution 57/254, proposing the decade, was tabled by Japan at the 57th Session of the United Nations General Assembly in December 2002. The resolution itself is the culmination of a long and winding journey through high level international commissions that can ultimately be traced back more than quarter of a century to the UN Conference on the Human Environment in Stockholm in June 1972. Considerable momentum was generated during the 1992 Earth Summit in Rio de Janiero with consensus intensifying after the 2002 World Summit on Sustainable Development at Johannesburg. UNESCO is the designated lead agency for the promotion of the Decade. Education for Sustainable Development is centred around an assumption that humanity must dramatically shift its present course of development to ensure a healthy, just and secure world for future generations. As such its focus is on a combination of environmental, social and economic development, though much of the dialogue about the initiative, including this book, has been largely from the environmental education sector. In the words of the Draft Implementation Scheme: "Education for Sustainable Development has come to be seen as a process of learning how to make decisions that consider the long-term future of the economy, ecology and equity of all communities. Building the capacity for such futures-orientated thinking is a key task of education" (UNESCO, 2003).

This book volume reproduces two collections of papers, prepared and presented as the UN Decade of Education for Sustainable Development (UNDESD) got underway. The papers reflect on the successes, challenges and obstacles confronting academics and practitioners seeking to deliver on the goals and ambitions of the Decade. Contributors share hopes, aspirations, frustrations and skepticism, through critical review of the ambitions of education for sustainable development (ESD) and through case study examples of ESD in practice.

The two paper collections in question were originally published in the *Journal of Geography in Higher Education* and in *Applied Environmental Education and Communication.* The original editorial introductions to the papers (Higgitt et al., 2005; Monroe & Fien, 2005; Chalkley, 2006) have been removed and replaced with a new entrée and a prospective which summarizes more recent developments. Section 1 contains twelve papers from a symposium published in two parts in the *Journal of Geography in Higher Education* (JGHE) in March 2005 and July 2006, respectively. These papers represent the proceedings of two conference sessions convened by Martin Haigh with the assistance of David Higgitt and Brian Chalkley. The first session, "Geography and Sustainability in Higher Education," was organized on behalf of the journal and the Royal Geographical Society's Higher Education Research Group (HERG) at the Annual Conference of the Royal Geographical Society with the Institute of British Geographers (RGS-IBG) in London, September 2003. The second meeting, "Towards the UN Decade of Education for Sustainable

Development," took place during the International Geographical Congress, in Glasgow, August 2004, and represented collaboration between HERG, the IGU Commission for Geographic Education and the journal itself.

The antecedent event for the conference sessions was a joint UK-Russian symposium, partly funded by the Geography, Earth and Environmental Sciences (GEES) Subject Centre, which took place in Moscow in June 2002. In the UK, subject centres were established under the Learning and Teaching Support Network (LTSN) and subsequently incorporated into the Higher Education Academy. The GEES Subject Centre is at the University of Plymouth and produces its own journal, *Planet,* to disseminate examples of innovative teaching practice and pedagogy. A Special Edition of *Planet* (LTSN-GEES, 2002), compiled and edited by Brian Chalkley, introduced a series of short papers setting the scene for ESD initiatives within the GEES disciplines.

JGHE was established in 1977 under a conviction that the importance of teaching and learning in higher education had been consistently undervalued and under-represented. It therefore developed to provide a forum where practitioners could discuss educational interests, present educational research and advocate new ideas relevant to the teaching of geography (and cognate disciplines) in all institutions of higher education. During the subsequent three decades JGHE has carved out a distinctive niche for presenting full length papers concerned with pedagogic and institutional issues confronting the discipline of geography in Higher Education Institutes (HEIs). Reflecting its origins, JGHE is an international journal with a strong British influence. The editors and commissioning editors represent four continents and the Editorial Board has become increasingly internationalized as electronic communications have replaced conventional mail. The sequence and location of events leading up to the symposium also suggest a dominant British perspective. However, grant support from the GEES Subject Centre, the RGS-IBG and *JGHE* itself enabled major international participation in both conference sessions. Indeed, the eight papers presented in Glasgow represented eight different countries and four continents, while five nations and three continents were represented in London. Of the 14 papers that made it through the peer review process to publication, eight originate in the UK and the remainder is from Austria, Italy, New Zealand, Russia, Singapore and USA.

Applied Environmental Education and Communication (AEEC) was founded in 2002. The focus of the journal is the fields of environmental social marketing, environmental journalism, environmental education, sustainability education, environmental interpretation, and environmental health communication. It is a multidisciplinary journal aimed at both academics and practitioners with a mission to help readers solve real environmental problems through a synergistic relationship between research and practical information. As such the objectives of the two journals have a number of commonalities in terms of providing practitioners with specific advice to implement ideas, frank reporting about the pros and cons of innovative approaches and an aversion to jargon. The blend of academic and practitioner perspectives is reflecting in the composition of the editorial board. Two thirds of the Editorial Board is based in USA. Section 2 of the volume contains 16 papers which were originally published as a special issue of *AEEC* in October 2005. The volume was edited by Martha Monroe and John Fien, both editorial board members of *AEEC*, who describe the concept arising from a conversation about the challenges that environmental educators face in adjusting their programmes to support the ethos of ESD at the start of the UN Decade. An international team was assembled and invited to write about the ways environmental educators could respond to the opportunities and challenges that the Decade might usher in. The papers are short commentaries and in order to allow invited speakers a free opinion, the regular peer review process was stream-lined. Whereas the *JGHE* symposium is mainly focused on the role of HEIs responding to ESD, with a specific focus on the role of Geography, the *AEEC* collection draws more widely from interdisciplinary environmental education at different levels from community learning through to university teaching. Nevertheless, the theme of promoting sustainability literacy among students, communities and policy makers is prevalent throughout both sets of papers.

Logistical reasons require that the papers are presented in the same order as their original publication. The division of the *JGHE* collection into two halves was partly determined by the speed with which papers passed through the review process but broadly speaking the collection is topped and tailed by papers that are concerned with the responsibility of HEIs in promoting environmental awareness and a consciousness of sustainability issues. This embraces the role of universities in educating future generations of leaders, in supporting life-long learning and professional development, in interacting with communities, civil society and Non-Governmental Organizations. In between, papers provide overviews of the context of environmental education in relation to institutional constraints and policies, reporting from several different countries. The *AEEC* collection is similarly organized with the first four papers providing philosophical discussion about the perceived trajectory of ESD and its relationship with Environmental Education. Next, links with other areas of the educational agenda, most notably citizenship and natural resource management, are explored before embarking on a global tour of ESD case studies from nine countries. Three important themes criss-cross through the book. First, the Decade for Education for Sustainable Development is widely held to offer the best opportunity to date to implement lasting and radical changes to educational programmes. Indeed it is hard to imagine any disagreement with UNESCO's principal objectives to facilitate networking and interaction between ESD stakeholders, encourage improved quality in ESD learning and teaching and associated educational reform and to align ESD efforts towards targeting the Millennium Development Goals. The questions of how to get there, which routes to take, how to track the journey and how to recognize the destination are much more contentious. In short, the pathways to ESD invite vigorous debate. Second, many of the papers in the collection are explicitly about ESD initiatives in the tertiary sector. UNDESD invites critical reflection about the role of HEIs and the responsibilities of the sector create a better world. To some critics, however, HEIS are embedded in a conventional educational structure that panders to consumerism and reinforces the machinery of resource destruction. The role of HEIs in greening curricula is a key theme. Third, the role of academic disciplines is scrutinized. Not surprisingly, a key concern is the role of Geography in positioning itself as an instinctive provider of ESD. A brief review of academic writing on ESD and related topics suggests that few academic disciplines have acted decisively in this regard while the (small g) geography of academic writing reveals the usual degree of Anglo-American domination.

Pathways to ESD

The conventional definition of sustainable development derived from the 1987 Bruntland Report is "development which meets the needs of the present without compromising the ability of future generations to meet their own needs" (WCED, 1987). In practice, sustainable development is a nebulous concept, a chimera that can be adapted, contradicted and contested, and caricatured as a "large, diverse and rapidly expanding field of enquiry populated by heterogeneous discourses, multiple approaches and a variety of recommendations as to the ways forward" (Williams & Millington, 2004, p. 99). In view of the voluminous discussions about the language of sustainability, neither set of editors expressly invited authors to focus exclusively on the issue of defining ESD. Contrasting narratives of the history of international initiatives that led up to UNDESD are provided by Haigh (Chapter 1.2) and Combes (Chapter 2.1), the former reporting form the context of connected initiatives in Higher Education and the latter an inside, but unofficial, view from within UNESCO. The short contribution by Paden (Chapter 2.7) includes the text of the Ahmedabad Declaration proposed on the end of the first international conference of UNDESD hosted by the Centre for Environment Education in Ahmedabad, India. The text captures the urgency and enthusiasm of educators embarking on the Decade and the recognition that the pathway is a learning journey for all involved. Eloquent appraisals of the meaning of education for sustainable development can be found elsewhere (e.g. Huckle & Sterling, 1996; Tilbury et al., 2002; Scott & Gough, 2004; Gough & Scott, 2008). Nevertheless conceptual fuzziness about the meaning and objectives of ESD is a legitimate concern. As Monroe & Fien (2005, p. 204) note, "not only will a definitional murkiness make it difficult to communicate ESD to the public, it will also make it challenging to operationalize objectives, to measure value, and to know what it is that we seek."

Initiatives intended to bolster environmental education are, therefore, beholden to some institutional definition of sustainable development. There are implicit limits to strategies imposed by such frameworks, boundaries that demarcate the extent to which prevailing systems can be questioned, hidden political subtexts. Many of these system constraints are evident in the papers in the collection. Broadly, these boundary conditions can be characterized by the distinction between weaker and stronger sustainability. Weaker sustainability can be considered to adopt environmental initiatives within an orthodox narrative of economic growth, where actions to alleviate environmental problems are seen as the forebears of sustainable economic development. Not only can sound environmental practice improve efficiency and therefore drive further growth, but the environmental technology industry itself becomes a lucrative growth area. At the other end of the scale, stronger sustainability challenges the prevailing optimism that technological advance or improved efficiency is the basis for future economic growth. Rather it argues for reduced demand, predicated on recasting attitudes to nature and notions of development. Such an approach demands a critique of concepts of economic growth, development and the meaning of 'progress.' David Selby in the closing paper of the *JGHE* symposium (Chapter 1.14), adopts a parable form to visualize the search for pathways towards ESD. Selby argues that the " the meteoric and seemingly inexorable rise of the idea of sustainable development … provided a means of paving – some critics would say 'papering' – over the ongoing rift between the environmental lobby of the metaphorical North of the planet and the development lobby of the metaphorical South of the planet. Confronted by a need to act given the increasingly evident confluence of multiple environmental and social crises, it allowed for consensus around a theme persuasive enough to be attractive to both and also vague and diffuse enough to enable everyone to invest it with their own meanings." UNDESD, imbued with national and international momentum, presents a pathway beckoning environmental educators. Whether the path leads to the realization of the objectives of the Decade or is just a detour on the business-as-usual route to economic growth is a question troubling the critics. Sauvé & Berryman (Chapter 2.4) set out the arguments for pursuing alternative 'pathways', particularly through challenging the dominant market economy conceptions of environment evident in much of the language of UNESCO and by adopting a "pedagogy of uncertainty and humility."

At the same time, the rapid institutionalization of ESD provides an opportunity for greater recognition of environmental education. Many authors are at pains to point out the two terms are not identical (e.g. McKeown & Hopkins, 2003) and, hence, there is more to increasing awareness of sustainable development than exposing students to information about environmental processes. Nevertheless, in many nations, initial responses to ESD have been built on strong foundations of environmental education. McKeown & Hopkins (Chapter 2.2) emphasize the shared goal and strong foothold that has already been achieved in setting the agenda for ESD. A concern not to miss the bandwagon is thinly disguised. Thus Gonzales-Gaudino (Chapter 2.14) expresses apprehension that the long and difficult fight to raise the profile of environmental education in Mexico could be side-tracked by a reinvention of concepts under an ESD banner. On the other hand, an institutional shift towards ESD brings opportunities to refocus narrow definitions of environmental education and address issues of social change, inequality and social justice and community development. Elsewhere in Latin America, Andelman (Chapter 2.8) and Malhadas (Chapter 2.10), relating ideas from Argentina and Brazil, respectively, see the established link between environmental programmes and community networking as a clear opportunity to gain increased awareness under the UNDESD flag. Similarly, a strong shift towards community-based initiatives in environmental education programmes is reported in Australia (Lang; Chapter 2.9), Austria (Hama et al.; Chapter 1.4), Japan (Ninmiya-Lim; Chapter 2.11) and Kenya (Malakwen; Chapter 2.12). Meanwhile, in Malaysia (Lim; Chapter 2.13) the success of fieldwork as a stimulus for sensitizing students to environmental issues, but the generally limited progress of environmental education in the formal curriculum of schools and universities. The role of HEIs in driving an ESD agenda is emphasized. It is worth noting that not all environmental educators see ESD as a panacea. Jickling & Wals (2008), for example, sees ESD as a globalizing force propelled by UNESCO to subvert the original – and valuable – remit of EE. This is further reflected in the "closing circle" and "firm and shaky ground" analogies of Sauvé & Berryman (Chapter 2.4) and Selby (Chapter 1.14) respectively. The more optimistic scenario is presented by Cloud (Chapter 2.3) who advocates systems thinking as the underlying mental model for sustainability education. He argues, quite simply, that regardless of stance on where environmental education and sustainability education should be deemed to start and finish, the infusion of systems thinking and competencies associated with ESD will enhance educational experience in any case.

The worldwide examples illustrate a number of similarities in ambitions and frustrations. Monroe & Fien (2005) note that ESD has the potential to span the gap between North and South but the role of ESD takes on different dimensions. Gambini (Chapter 1.8) conducted questionnaires to determine students' environmental attitudes in Australia, China, Sri Lanka and Italy. Variations between the countries, and to some extent between the disciplinary backgrounds of the students, identify interesting cultural influences on attitudes such as faith in progress and the role of science and technology. Such cultural influences permeate many of the institutional settings of environmental education programmes. For Allen (Chapter 2.16) writing from Swaziland, the alignment of ESD with Millennium Development Goals is of utmost significance. These goals include eradication of extreme poverty, universal primary education, gender equality and empowerment of women and elimination of diseases, especially HIV/AIDS and malaria epidemics. Elsewhere, Allamano (2008) argue that across southern Africa ESD needs to be adapted to recognize the ways which HIV/AIDS profoundly weakens the education sector. Bourn (Chapter 2.5) pushes for a higher profile of the development agenda in the UK's approach to ESD, calling for a reduction in the emphasis on the environmental agenda and a clearer awareness of the Millennium Development Goals. Davidson et al (2009) provide an interesting example of how this might be put into practices in the university classroom describing a role-play activity to simulate the implication of trying to survive in a marginalized and poverty-stricken African community.

The Role of Universities: Greening the HE Curriculum

Most HEIs are keen to promote their environmental credentials and terms such as sustainable development regularly feature in mission statements. On one hand, an increased presence of sustainability strategies and statements of intent are positive indications of some action towards the quest for sustainable development that was formally adopted at the Rio de Janiero Earth Summit in 1992. On the other, it is clear that for many institutions the well-meaning rhetoric does not penetrate very far into policy implementation. Just as inter-governmental progress on environmental issues has been disappointing slow, so the profile of HEIs in promoting sustainability development has been patchy.

Progress towards sustainability by HEIs is most typically expressed in terms of the implementation of campus environmental policies, typically focused around waste reduction, recycling initiatives and energy efficiency. Many of the environmental initiatives adopted by HEIs might be regarded as examples of weak to moderate sustainability as they tend to address issues of efficiency rather than challenge the dominant orthodoxy of the institution engaged in the production of skilled graduates to enhance regional / national economic growth. While a handful of modules that present ideas from 'deep ecology' may be tolerated, initiatives must be compatible with the institutions other missions. For example, Higgitt (Chapter 1.7) reports on student attitudes towards sustainability in Singapore and contemplates the dilemmas facing promotion of ESD in a university ethos highly geared towards entrepreneurship and economic growth. Chapman and colleagues (Chapter 1.8) turn this concern into a question whether New Zealand's schools and universities are in a position to respond programmatically to UNDESD. Their sobering conclusions highlight the mismatch between the grand visions and rhetoric of political support for UNDESD and the institutional impediments that hinder action. Among their conclusions they identify the operational obstacles of timetable and curriculum constraints in schools and of disciplinary boundaries in universities; the difficulties of aligning sectoral initiatives given the already weak coordination between schools and universities; and the lack of a realistic assessment of the present status of ESD. A similar analysis of the New Zealand situation is provided by Law (Chapter 2.15).

The first two papers from the *JGHE* symposium focus on the broad challenges and obstacles confronting ESD within the HE sector. Martin & Jucker (Chapter 1.1) lament the inadequacies of political leadership in responding to the challenges of sustainability and suggest that the shortcomings reflect poorly on the universities through which world leaders graduated. They argue that to produce a future generation of earth-literate graduates, universities have responsibilities to increase awareness and tools for a sustainable future to all graduates. In tracing the recent history of declarations that paved the way for the UN Resolution 57/254, Haigh (Chapter 1.2) identifies a series of obstacles that threaten the route to increasing awareness of sustainable development across HE curricula. These barriers include departmental and disciplinary boundaries, academic reward structures which encourage short-term targets and an institutional mindset spawned from an industrial model of progress.

Despite skepticism of a yawning chasm between rhetoric and action, the sector has made some progress towards mobilizing consensus in line with the objectives of UNDESD. The Talloires Declaration, signed by 280 universities in some 40 countries (USLF, 1990), urges universities world-wide:

> <numbered points>(1) to seek, establish and disseminate a clearer understanding of Sustainable Development ...at the local, national and global levels, in ways consistent with their missions;
>
> (2) to utilize resources of the university to encourage a better understanding on the part of Governments and the public at large of the inter-related physical, biological and social dangers facing the planet Earth, and to recognize the significant interdependence and international dimensions of sustainable development;
>
> (3) to emphasize the ethical obligation of the present generation to overcome those practices of resource utilization and those widespread disparities which lie at the root of environmental unsustainability;
>
> (4) to enhance the capacity of the university to teach and undertake research and action in society in sustainable development principles, to increase environmental literacy, and to enhance the understanding of environmental ethics within the university and with the public at large.

The Association of University Leaders for a Sustainable Future (ULSF), a non-profit organization promoting sustainability and environmental literacy within the HE sector, act as the secretariat for signatories to the Talloires Declaration (Calder & Clugston, 2005). The ULSF are major partners (with the International Association of Universities and Europe's Copernicus-Campus) in the UNESCO-led consortium GHESP (Global Higher Education for Sustainability partnership) (IAU, 2004). Some individual institutions who had signed up to Talloires are able to demonstrate considerable progress towards the multipronged objectives of ESD. For example, Tufts University, who hosted the conference which led to the declaration at their European campus in Talloires, has made considerable progress towards an integrated policy and curriculum on climate change (Rappaport & Creighton, 2007). Koester et al. (2006) report on the experience of Ball State University, Indiana whose whole-systems approach to greening the campus stems back over 15 years. Such examples illustrate that the path towards greening HE is long and complicated. Some aspects of the institutional setting enable immediate changes at minimal expense, while others require significant capital investment or transformation requiring structural change. Many of the world's leading universities are only at the beginning of the greening process. The tricky issue of greening the curriculum remains a considerable challenge. Two initiatives from the UK are described in the book. Scott & Gough (Chapter 1.10) provide a critical review of the ESD within British Higher Education, highlighting some of the partnerships which have formed between HEIs and government task forces. Particular attention is given to the Higher Education Partnership for Sustainability (HEPS) toolkit designed to assist institutions integrate sustainability into their educational programmes. Dyer et al. (Chapter 1.11) report on the inauguration of the Centre for Sustainable Futures, one of 74 Centres for Excellence in Teaching and Learning funded by the Higher Education Funding Council for England (HEFCE).

It is worth noting at this point that the first statement within the Talloires Declaration calls for HEIs to develop a clear understanding of Sustainable Development "in ways *consistent* with their missions" (emphasis added). This raises issues about the roles and responsibilities of the environmental disciplines and environmentally-minded academics to instigate 'mission-drift' during the unfolding Decade of Education for Sustainable Development.

A Role for the Environmental Disciplines?

Although the earlier discussion identifies that ESD is not, or should not be the sole responsibility of environmental educators, there is a clear expectation that the environmental disciplines will take some sort of lead towards greening HE curricula.

One focus of the conference from which the JGHE symposium derives, addressed the role of geography, often assumed to be at the vanguard of environmental and sustainability issues. What influence does the discipline have in terms of driving environmental initiatives within both individual HEIs and across the broader HE sector? As such does the UN Decade of Education for Sustainable Development offer a significant opportunity for geographers and the discipline to make a concerted an overt contribution, has the boat been missed already, or is a disciplinary viewpoint on ESD itself contradictory to an all embracing HE curriculum infused with sustainability concepts?

Geography would appear to be the discipline that is most readily associated with the subject area of sustainable development. There is, of course, enormous variation in the coverage of sustainability concepts within individual degree courses and there are even a few degree programmes that have incorporated sustainability into the degree title (Chalkley, 2002). From a disciplinary perspective, UNDESD may not only present an opportunity to push for a greening of curricula but also propel Geography into the limelight. There appears to be little evidence that the subject has yet acted decisively to recognize ESD as a central concern. Recent debates about the future of geography (Thrift, 2002) highlight the allure (to physical geographers at least) of the 'big science' model of earth systems science and the aspirations to participate in large scale, government-mandated global change research projects. Slaymaker & Spencer (1998) contend that the research capable of addressing issues of sustainable development exists in a sparsely inhabited niche between traditional small scale reductionist science and earth system science. Ultimately, "a discipline that does not have sustainability as a goal at all scales of analysis may itself be unsustainable" (Slaymaker & Spencer, 1998, p. 257).

A strong affiliation between Geography and ESD would appear to offer a ready made agenda for geography, but herein lies a paradox. The disciplinary boundaries constructed to lay claim a particular subject area are seen as a major obstacle to ESD which needs to be interdisciplinary and infiltrate across all aspects of the HE curriculum. Just as weak sustainability is criticized as being more concerned with sustaining economic development rather than the environment, so the path taken by the discipline must be focused on promoting ESD and not merely as a pretext for sustaining the discipline. On the other hand, the prognosis for a discipline that does not seize the opportunity is equally bleak. Writing about the role of Geography in promoting environmental education and research in the USA, Bednarz (Chapter 1.6) laments the lack of activity. He partly attributes the sluggishness to the comparatively small size and low status of university geography and partly to the controversial nature of environmental issues in the US context. Any claims that Geography is the key discipline that bridges the human-environment divide are dampened by most practitioners having a primary interest firmly entrenched on one side or other of the 'divide'. For Bednarz, the danger is that if Geography does not respond to the opportunities presented by ESD, other disciplines will move in and capture the market.

Related to the struggle for academic territory are the important questions of providing sustainability literacy for the university population as a whole. After all, Martin & Jucker's (Chapter 1.1) vision of educating earth-literate leaders requires some mechanism to ensure that all students have an opportunity to gain the kind of environmental awareness that will inform future decision-making. On this point, educators may be divided on the wisdom of force-feeding all comers as opposed to providing the necessary courses for those with genuine interest. Baillie et al. (2007) writing from the disciplinary background of Chemical Engineering report on the contrasting success of two compulsory courses designed to provide students with an appreciation of environmental sustainability. A common first year course for 600 students taught as an intensive module ran into problems as students grasped for understanding of concepts. A second year course for 35 students in a geological engineering programme, structured around enquiry-based learning, fared much better. Fighting for whole-systems campus greening to deliver compulsory ESD is one thing; delivering effective and socially transformative teaching is a greater challenge yet. MacGregor (Chapter 2.6) proposes a "curriculum for the bioregion" as an integrative mechanism to connect the abstract concepts of sustainability with the grounded experience of "life places". This provides an impetus for involving university students in environmental projects with local communities. A number of papers in the book consider the role of university education beyond the immediate student cohort. Haigh (Chapter 1.13) explores the relationship between universities and Non-Governmental Organizations (NGOs). A case study considers an Earthwatch programme "Reclaiming the Land". Such NGO projects provide informal environmental sustainability education which can contribute to lifelong learning. Martin *et al.* (Chapter 1.5) consider another form of outreach activity – continuing professional development (CPD). The rapidly changing requirements of the labour market for environmental professional dictates both a need for CPD but also a stimulus for curriculum design in the environmental disciplines.

A final area of service for HEIs concerns the role of teacher training. Higgins & Kirk (Chapter 1.12) reflect on the challenges of reorientating teacher education towards sustainable futures, using examples from the Scottish experience. Part of the challenge concerns the balance between sustainability as part of the formal discipline-based content of teacher training (and in the UK context this means Geography) and as cross-cutting informal opportunities such as citizenship education or outdoor education. Elsewhere, teacher-trainers and educational researchers have noted the tensions arising from the sustainability agenda. Oulton et al. (2004) argue that teachers need far greater preparation to incorporate ideas of controversy into citizenship education, while Huckle (2002) provides some foundations of political ecology to assist teachers to consider the construction and representation of nature in the context of citizenship education.

Given such a wide ranging remit of higher education, the role of environmental disciplines in promoting ESD can be investigated to some extent by a bibliometric analysis of journal writing. The Web of Science database was used to determine data on the quantity, disciplinary background, origin and impact of writing on ESD-related issues. The search term is tracked in the title and abstract of all ISI-listed journals. Of course, a limitation of such a search is that there are many reputable journals which are not ISI-listed (*AEEC* is just one example) and therefore the bibliometric data is biased to some extent. Nevertheless the analysis shows that the term "Education for Sustainable Development" has only featured in 43 journal articles, while the term "Education for Sustainability" occurs in even fewer. Table 1 reports results of search terms ranked by disciplines. The disciplines are determined by the classification of the journal and not by the background of authors. A journal may be listed in more than one disciplinary category. For example, *JGHE* is listed under both Geography and under Education and Educational Research. Environmental Science journals dominate writing, typically accounting for a quarter of the occurrences of the search terms. In the case of the term "Environmental Education" almost 40 per cent of the 777 records are from environmental science journals, well over double the contribution from educational research outlets. But curiously, "Education for Sustainable Development" is the one term where environmental science does not dominate, lying third behind educational research and geography. It should be noted that environmental sciences and educational research are far larger fields than geography (both in terms of number of listed journals and total number of papers published). Geography features in the top five except for search terms centred on "Environmental Sustainability" and ranks second specifically on ESD. Table 2 then plots the data by country of origin. Despite the inclusiveness promoted by UNDESD and the worldwide examples provided in this book, the search terms reveal Anglo-American domination so typical of academic writing in general. A curiosity here is that USA dominates every category but does not appear at all under ESD. England (the database collates results for Wales and Scotland separately) is in the top two for all categories. Brazil and Mexico challenge the domination of the orthodoxy.

Search Term	No.	Ranking					Geography Rank
		1	2	3	4	5	
Environmental Education	777	Env Sci	Educ	Ecol	Ed Sci	Geog	5
Environmental Education + Sustainability*	131	Env Sci	Educ	Ecol	Geog	Env Eng	4
Environmental Sustainability	659	Env Sci	Env Stud	Econ	Ecol	Plan	10
Environmental Sustainability + Education	29	Env Sci	Econ	Educ	Env Stud	Agric / Env Eng	—
Sustainable Development + Education	329	Env Sci	Educ	Env Eng	Water	Geog / Ecol	5=
Education for Sustainable Development	43	Educ	Geog	Env Sci	Env Eng	Water	2
Education for Sustainability	25	Env Sci	Env Eng	Educ	Geog	Water	4

Table 1 Distribution of ISI-listed journal publications by discipline for subject area of environmental education, environmental sustainability and related themes.

Note: Searches are conducted on exact phrases. The + sign indicates combined search for two terms. * indicates a wildcard search on sustain* rather than exact term sustainability. Search period covers publications from 1980 to March 2008.

Key: Agric = Agriculture, Multidisciplinary; Ecol = Ecology; Econ = Economics; Educ = Education & Educational Research; Ed Sci = Education, Science Disciplines; Env Eng = Engineering, Environmental; Env Sci = Environmental Sciences; Env Stud = Environmental Studies; Geog = Geography; Water = Water Resources

Search Term	No.	Ranking (and per cent share)				
		1	2	3	4	5
Environmental Education	777	USA	England	Brazil	Canada	Germany
		34	13	4	4	4
Environmental Education + Sustainability*	131	USA	England	Brazil	Canada	Australia
		24	19	5	4	4
Environmental Sustainability	659	USA	England	Australia	Canada	Italy / Netherlands
		29	15	11	9	7
Environmental Sustainability + Education	29	USA	England	Australia	—	—
		38	24	7		
Sustainable Development + Education	329	USA	England	Australia	Canada	Italy / Netherlands
		21	12	9	6	5
Education for Sustainable Development	43	England	Canada/ Netherlands		Australia / Mexico	
		32	14		7	
Education for Sustainability	25	USA	England	Canada	Mexico /Netherlands	—
		36	16	12	8	

Table 2 Distribution of ISI-listed journal publications by country of origin for subject area of environmental education, environmental sustainability and related themes.

Note: Searches are conducted on exact phrases. The + sign indicates combined search for two terms. * indicates a wildcard search on sustain* rather than exact term sustainability. Search period covers publications from 1980 to March 2008.

The impact of writing on Educational for Sustainable Development is far from overwhelming, at least as far as ISI citation statistics measure impact. Only one of the 43 articles returned by a search yielded ten or more citations. In this article, Huckle (2002) focuses on the role of ESD in the teaching of 11-14 year olds in the national curriculum in schools in England. It can only be hoped that the wave of writing on ESD is having real impact in terms of informing practitioners and prompting policy makers to ask critical questions.

The thirty papers in the volume provide an overview of the remit of the UN Decade of Education for Sustainable Development, identify many obstacles that impinge on the progress of sustainability thinking and also provide examples of the sweep of ESD-related activity from a diverse range of national settings.

References

Allamano, E. (2008) HIV and AIDS: Responding to a threat to education for sustainable development, *Natural Resources Forum*, 32(2), pp.142-151.

Baillie, C. & Remenda, V. (2007) Education for sustainability, *Journal of Biobased Materials and Energy*, 1(1), pp. 163-170.

Calder, W. & Clugston, R. (2005) Editorial: Education for a sustainable future, *Journal of Geography in Higher Education*, 29(1), pp.7-12.

Chalkley, B. (2002) Introduction: setting the sustainability scene, *Planet*, 4, p. 3.

Chalkley, B. (2006) Education for Sustainable Development: Continuation, *Journal of Geography in Higher Education*, 30(2), pp.235-236.

Davidson, J.H., Du Preez, L. Gibb, M.W. & Nel, E.L. (2009) It's in the Bag! Using simulation as a participatory learning method to understand poverty, *Journal of Geography in Higher Education*, in press.

Gough, S. & Scott, W. (2008) *Higher Education and Sustainable Development: Paradox and Possibility* (London: Routledge).

Higgitt, D., Haigh, M. & Chalkley, B. (2005) Towards the UN Decade of Education for Sustainable Development: Introduction, *Journal of Geography in Higher Education*, 29(1), pp13-17.

Huckle, J. (2002) Reconstructing nature: towards a geographical education for sustainable development, *Geography*, 87(1), pp. 64-72.

Huckle, J. & Sterling, S. (1996) *Education for Sustainability* (London: Earthscan).

IAU (2004) GHESP: Global Alliance to promote higher education for sustainable development (International Association of Universities). Available at http://www.unesco.org/iau/sd/sd_ghesp.html (accessed November 2004).

LTSN-GEES (2002) Special Edition on Education for Sustainable Development, *Planet* 4.

Jickling, B. & Wals, A.E.J. (2008) Globalization and environmental education: looking beyond sustainable development, *Journal of Curriculum Studies*, 40(1), pp. 1-21.

Koester, R.J., Eflin, J. & Vann. J. (2006) Greening of the campus: a whole-systems approach, *Journal of Cleaner Production*, 14(9-11), pp. 769-779.

McKeown, R. & Hopkins, C. (2003) EE ≠ ESD: defusing the worry, *Environmental Education Research*, 9(1), pp 117-128.

Monroe, M.C. & Fien, J. (2005) The role environmental education might play in the Decade for Education for Sustainable Development, *Applied Environmental Education and Communication*, 4, pp.203-206.

Oulton, C., Day, V., Dillon, J. & Grace, M. (2004) Controversial issues – teachers' attitudes and practices in the context of citizenship education, *Oxford Review of Education*, 30(4), pp. 489-507.

Rappaport, A. & Creighton, S.H. (Eds) (2007) *Degrees that Matter : Climate Change and the University* (Cambridge, MA: MIT Press).

Scott, W. & Gough, S. (2004) *Sustainable Development and Learning* (London: RoutledgeFalmer).

Slaymaker, O. & Spencer T. (1998) *Physical geography and environmental change* (Harlow: Longman).

Thrift, N. 2002 The future of geography. *Geoforum*, 33(3), pp. 291-298.

Tilbury, D., Stevenson, J.B., Fien, J. & Schreuder, D. (Eds) (2002) *Education and Sustainability: Responding to the Global Challenge* (Gland, Switzerland and Cambridge: IUCN).

ULSF (1990) *Programs: Talloires Declaration* (Washington, DC: Association of University Leaders for a Sustainable Future).

UNESCO (2003) *United Nations Decade of Education for Sustainable Development 2005-2014: Framework for a Draft Implementation Scheme* (Paris: UNESCO).

WCED (World Commission on Environment and Development) (1987) Our Common Future (Oxford: Oxford University Press).

Williams, C.C. & Millington, A.C. (2004) The diverse and contested meanings of sustainable development, *Geographical Journal*, 170(2), pp. 99-104.

Educating Earth-literate Leaders

STEPHEN MARTIN & ROLF JUCKER

Introduction

> We are now citizens of the Earth joined in a common enterprise with many variations. We have every right to insist that those who purport to lead us be worthy of the task. Imagine such a time! *(Orr, 2003)*

Universities and colleges the world over are facing some serious challenges as demand grows for a better qualified and more flexible workforce in an increasingly complex and dynamically changing world. Globalization and further expansion of the European Union require new types of knowledge and new forms of professional expertise. And nowhere is this need for new competences and capacity building more crucial than in the area of sustainable development where problems transcend national boundaries and call for new forms of cooperation and ways of learning (Sterling, 2001; Jucker, 2002).

Whilst there are a small number of examples of emerging good practice in meeting this challenge, the sustainability agenda has not had a major impact on the thinking and practice of the majority of staff who teach in universities. And yet the very survival of our species is threatened by the world consuming goods and services at an unsustainable pace, with serious consequences for the well-being of people and the planet (Worldwatch Institute, 2003).

This paper explores some of the key challenges facing universities as they embrace the sustainability agenda.

The Changing Professional Landscape in the EU

For nearly three decades education policy has been driven principally by the perceived need to equip people with the skills and knowledge required to produce goods and services capable of competing in an increasingly aggressive global market. In the UK, the existing policy framework for sustainable development is currently under review, and will be influenced by a number of individual policy papers on, *inter alia*, energy, sustainable communities, proposals for substantial reforms of agriculture (the Curry Report) and planning regulations. More recently, a sustainable development action plan for education and skills, published by the Department for Education and Skills (http://www.dfes.gov.uk/sd/) will also have to be taken into account. The sustainability agenda has already had a major impact on the labour or occupational market for those who have taken part in educational courses and training programmes in the environmental field. The scale and range of the so-called eco-industries in the European Union (EU) is summarized in Table 1.

In a global context, the market for eco-industries is estimated at around €550 billion which means that the EU has approximately one-third of the overall market, equal to the USA (ECOTEC, 2000). Whilst this ECOTEC report focused mainly on pollution and resource management, other sources indicate that job opportunities for those with an environmental education have tended to spread from the public to the private sector as well as into the rapidly growing non-governmental sector of public interest organizations, not-for-profit consulting firms and various publication, media and information outlets. New posts are emerging within the agencies of the EU itself as well as inter-governmental bodies. There is clearly an increasing range of new and demanding career trajectories that universities will need to reflect in reviewing and updating their undergraduate and postgraduate programmes.

The qualifications that are now required for the growing and diverse range of jobs in this emerging labour market are significantly different from those that previously characterized the environmental professions in Europe. Most of those employed in an environmental capacity within local authorities at a national level, including research and teaching staff, were primarily from a natural science discipline, whereas the new positions call for new kinds of competences in business, economics, law, politics, sociology,

Table 1. The market for goods & services in the eco-industries in the EU (includes the EU 15 and candidate countries for enlargement (ECOTEC Research and Consultancy, 2000))

Total Goods and Services	€183 billion/year
Direct employment	2 million FTEs
Investment	€54 billion/year
Renewables market	€5 billion/year

communications and computer science as well as in environmental ethics, human ecology and environmental management. Some sources predict that in the future courses will need to include conflict management and an understanding of cultural differences in international contexts (Essence, 2001).

In addition, there is strong evidence of a greater emphasis being placed on interdisciplinary, problem-solving capability rather than a traditional and overly specialized scientific competence. Geography, with its long tradition of multidisciplinary approaches, should be well placed to lead this shift towards problem-centred, rather than discipline-centred education. In particular, geography, earth and environmental sciences will be challenged to significantly contribute to the growing emphasis in the UK and Europe on developing sustainable communities (see for example the Egan Review, 2004). In the UK and Holland these issues are being addressed by the creation of a number of new interdisciplinary professional groups, such as the Sustainability Alliance, the Society for the Environment in the UK, the Dutch Association for Environmental Professionals and the Professional Practice for Sustainable Development (PP4SD) initiative (see Martin & Hall, 2002; Martin 2002; and http://www.sustainabilityalliance.org.uk; http://www.vvm.to; http://www.ies-uk.org.uk).

Educating Earth-literate Leaders

As we look back on the World Summit for Sustainable Development (WSSD) in Johannesburg and reflect on its impact, it seems apparent that political leadership the world over has so far failed to rise to the challenge of sustainability (UNED-UK, 2002). And yet in all likelihood most of the hundred or so leaders who attended will have a higher education degree from some of the world's most prestigious universities.

This raises some serious questions for our university administrators and the governance structures. Why, as David Orr once remarked, is it that the people who contribute most to exploiting poor communities and the Earth's ecosystems are those with BAs, MScs and PhDs and not the 'ignorant' poor from the South (Orr, 1994)? Why is the illiteracy amongst the world's politicians as to how the world works as a living system so widespread? Why is it so rare that we encounter in our leaders the qualities needed to enable sustainability: humility, respect for all forms of life and future generations, precaution and wisdom, the capacity to think systemically and challenge unethical actions? And more worryingly on the basis of current performance, what hope of improvement is there for future leaders?

The fact that the higher education sector is seriously failing society by producing leaders incapable of addressing our most pressing problems should trigger some critical consideration about the fundamental role of universities in society, based on three key assumptions:

- If universities are the nursery of tomorrow's leaders and educate most of the people who develop and manage society's institutions, then the sector bears "profound responsibilities to increase the awareness, knowledge, technologies, and tools to create a sustainable future", as the *Talloires Declaration* (signed by many of the world's university leaders) stated in 1990 (ULSF, 1990). This clearly implies that graduates of *every* discipline (whether as engineers, teachers, politicians, lawyers, architects, biologists, banks managers or tourism operators, etc.) will need a sound working knowledge of sustainability.

- Universities the world over are regarded as centres of the most advanced knowledge. They should therefore, through their teaching and their institutional practice, embody role models for the wider society and be microcosms of best practice for the future.
- "Higher education institutions are allowed academic freedom and a tax-free status to receive public and private resources", says Anthony Cortese from Second Nature, a leading US institution in education for sustainability (Cortese, 1999). In exchange for this privileged position, society rightly expects from universities that they contribute as much as possible to the solution of society's problems.

To these reflections should be added the fact that sustainable development is now a mainstream policy issue in the UK and the EU and that there is an increasing demand for graduates with a broad interdisciplinary training in sustainable development and problem solving (Essence, 2001). All of this suggests that we should develop strategies on how to turn the universities into sustainable institutions.

Such strategies would need to be concerned with all aspects of higher education and find answers to the following questions: How is the ecological footprint (impact) of these institutions shaping up to sustainability criteria? Is the sector promoting education for sustainable development across the curriculum? Do universities fulfil their role in communities and promote sustainable development through outreach and collaboration with industry? What value has the research done in universities when considered in a sustainability framework (i.e. does it contribute to solving the most urgent problems or does it boost unsustainable practices)? And lastly, what do the graduates of these institutions do in the world? Are they contributing to the building of a sustainable society or are they, as one leading commentator says, 'part of the rear guard of a vandal economy' (Orr, 1994)?

An analysis of the university system based on these questions shows relatively little progress. University systems have not been at the forefront of implementing sustainability and have even lagged behind developments within school systems (UNESCO, 1997). The main reason cited for the inability of our universities to engage in this transdisciplinary endeavour called sustainability is that "the frontiers between academic disciplines remain stoutly defended by professional bodies, career structures and criteria for promotion and advancement" (UNESCO, 1997). The university system ignores this issue at its peril because, as the International Association of Universities has stated, "Universities must not forfeit their natural claim to leadership. If we do not get involved ... to help solve the overwhelming problems of our global society ... we shall be ignored" (IAU, 1993).

Sustainable Universities?

There is a growing and in some senses an overwhelming range of tools and techniques available to any institution or organization setting out on the sustainable development journey (see for example, http://www.projectsigma.com; www.naturalstep.org.uk; www.unesco.org/education/tlsf). Whatever the approach, the action taken should be based on a number of important guiding principles (Bartel *et al.*, 2001; Jucker, 2003). One of the most useful approaches is based on the five capitals model (SIGMA, 2003) because sustainable organizations need to actively manage five types of assets that they rely on and contribute to. They are:

- Natural capital (the environment);
- human capital (people);
- social capital (social relationships and structures);
- manufactured capital (fixed assets);
- financial capital (profit, loss, revenue, etc.).

It is important to stress that these assets also need to be managed for the long term not just for the immediate future, thereby building up stocks of capital and living off the interest. They are also interdependent because changes in one will probably cause an impact on another. However, in this model, one form of capital cannot simply be traded against another.

Universities, like any other organization, play a significant role in how these various forms of capital are used, developed and maintained. The most obvious one is exploiting the flows of energy and resources from the earth's biophysical systems (e.g. land, air, water and natural systems). They also contribute to the other major form of capital that flows from the hands and brains (i.e. human capital) of the academics who work in them and the students they teach. These are the only two real sources of wealth in the world; everything else—money, machines and institutions—is derived from these primary sources. Sustainability can only be achieved if the stock of capital is kept intact or increases over time. If our universities deplete or consume more than they build up or invest, then their and others' opportunities to consume in future will inevitably be reduced. At the heart of the current environmental crisis is the way in which our levels of consumption and production contribute to the unsustainable depletion of the Earth's natural capital to the extent that the ability to support the projected human population levels is seriously questioned (Wilsdon & Porritt, 2000).

Even a cursory assessment of how our universities currently operate demonstrates the significant and serious gap between the aspiration of becoming more sustainable and current practice (Jucker & Martin, 2003).

Ecological Footprint of Universities

A useful measure of sustainability within an institution is through a technique called ecological footprinting (EF). This is a simple aggregate indicator of human impacts and is usually defined as the bio-productive area (of land or sea) that would be required to maintain current consumption using prevailing technology (Wackernagel & Rees, 1996; Chambers *et al.*, 2000). The authors behind the EF concept have come up with the notion of 'Earthshare', which is the bio-productive area of the Earth divided by its total population. This concept is helpful in providing a comparison between the consumption patterns of the countries in the North and those in the South and helps to put in context the actions required in support of global inter-generational equity and justice. The most recent literature on EF and universities is based on an Earthshare of 1.92 ha/head of population (Flint, 2001; Venetoulis, 2001; Griffiths, 2002; Dawe *et al.*, 2004).

A recent comparison of EFs derived from a number of universities and colleges highlights some of the issues (see Table 2; Dawe *et al.*, 2004). Although the data available are limited and in some instances the absence of particular figures makes comparisons difficult, it reveals in broad terms the highly variable extent to which institutions are living

Table 2. Ecological Footprint comparisons between some colleges and universities. (Redlands analysis excluded food.)

University/College	Total EF (ha)	No. of staff	No. of students	Campus area (ha)	EF/staff member	Spatial multiplier†	Proportion of earthshare*	EF/student
Newcastle, Australia[1]	3,211	2,200	17,000	135.00	1.46	23.79	0.76	0.19
Redlands, CA, USA[2]	2,375	2,727	[no data]	133.50	0.87	17.79	0.45	[unknown]
Swansea (Univ. Wales)[3]	10,004	2,316	10,314	19.66	4.32	508.85	2.25	0.97
East Anglia, UK[4]	2,499	2,500+	13,000+	41.40	1.0	60.36	0.52	(est.) 0.19
Holme Lacy College, UK[5]	296	64	460	240.00	4.63	1.23	2.41	0.64

*This figure is based on earthshare being equal to 1.92 ha (as given in Chambers *et al.*, 1996, pp. 150–151).
†Spatial multiplier is an estimate of how many times the actual college/university land area would need to be multiplied to cater for the institutions actual Ecological Footprint.
Sources: [1]From Flint (2001); [2]from Venetoulis (2001); [3]from Griffiths (2002); [4]estimates supplied within Griffiths (2002), and some figures (+) estimated by Mel Pascoe (personal communication); [5]from Vetter and Dawe (2001) and this paper.

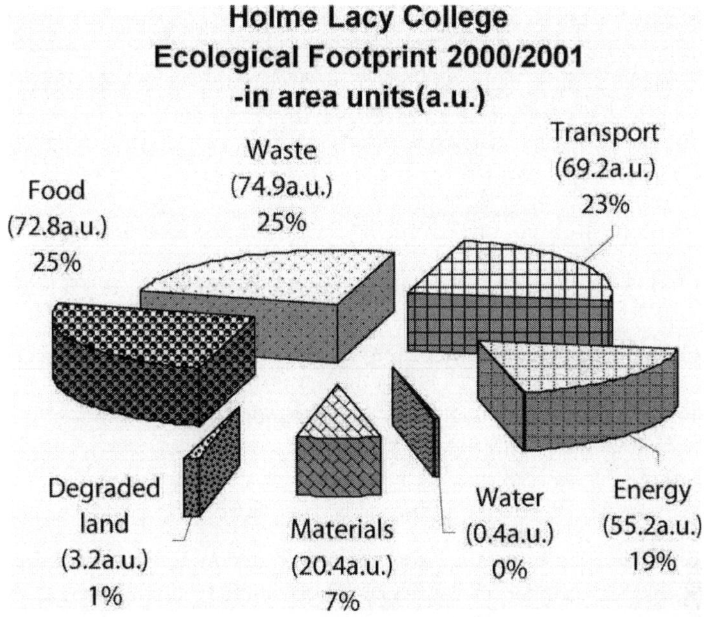

Figure 1. Holme Lacy College's Ecological Footprint (EF) totalled 296.07 area units.

beyond their 'Earthshare'. In two cases the EF is more than twice the 'Earthshare' and might be even higher if the consumption patterns of all employees outside work hours were included (see Dawe *et al.*, 2004). Whilst it is difficult to draw too many conclusions from this limited data, in the case of Holme Lacey College it is clear that a small rural college with only 64 staff is consuming 2.4 times its 'Earthshare', simply within work time. Estimates by Chambers *et al.*, (2000) suggest that the 'Earthshare' may diminish to 1.4 ha by 2050. In effect this would make the implications of this level of consumption even more worrying because staff at Holme Lacey would be consuming approximately 330 per cent of their global entitlement.

Disaggregating the various components of the EF reveals that food, transport, waste and energy contribute by far the largest component of the footprint of an educational institution (Figure 1).

Education for Sustainable Development Across the Curriculum

Universities also need to address the sustainability agenda through their curriculum. This is arguably a university's most important contribution to the sustainability agenda, but probably the least developed. There are a number of reasons why this has arisen. Sustainable development education has evolved as a process that is consistent with the holistic view of sustainable development. It has its roots in other cross-curricular themes such as environmental education, development education and education for citizenship. Recent debate centres on two contrasting approaches to curricular reform (Sterling, 2001). The first argues for the incorporation of sustainable development knowledge, skills and concepts into existing curricula; the second promotes the idea of changes in the concept and processes of education and learning as a whole. In short, the curriculum response to sustainability might be primarily piecemeal, affecting isolated parts of institutional practice, or systemic where whole system change becomes the agenda (Baines & Sterling, 2001). A recent study carried out as part of the EU Socrates Thematic network for Agriculture, Forestry, Aquaculture and the Environment (Bor *et al.*, 2000) has identified some of the key issues institutions face in systemic change (Table 3).

In contrast with this analysis, much of the existing practice in universities in the UK can be summarized as follows:

1. Much of the curriculum is discipline based and often highly technical and specialized.
2. The impact of human activity on the environment is generally under-represented in the university curriculum, except in the narrow context of health and safety.
3. Curriculum change is largely driven by economic policy, which emphasizes vocational outcomes.
4. Where sustainable development is taught, it is not fully integrated as a core element.

There are relatively few examples of a university tackling the sustainability curriculum issue in a systemic manner. Hawkesbury Agricultural College in Australia is widely regarded as one of the best-documented examples of developing an alternative curriculum. The Hawkesbury experience was a far-reaching and bold experiment, which developed an expanded view of the curriculum based on process and real-world problems, rather than as prescribed content and set outcomes (Bawden, in Bor *et al.*, 2000). The action research approach adopted is based on a process by which knowledge is created through the

Table 3. Key challenges for educational institutions seeking to integrate sustainability concepts and practices

i.	Integrating sustainability presupposes the rethinking of institutional missions
ii.	The imprecise nature of sustainability can be seen as an advantage or disadvantage in evoking dialogue on implications for curriculum, pedagogy, etc.
iii.	Sustainability is complex. The concept touches all aspects of our existence, involves deep questions about human responsibility and destination, and can be seen at different levels from micro to global and through different perspectives. Therefore, curriculum review based on sustainability is essentially a holistic and interdisciplinary exercise.
iv.	Planning for sustainable development education will lead to questions about purpose, content and method and the role of teachers in the institution. It requires teachers to also see themselves as learners, and to work with uncertainty and open outcomes.
v.	There is no blueprint for institutional and curriculum reform. Successful change depends on an inclusive and communicative process.

transformation of experience. Such an approach needs students to be involved in experiencing real situations, which through appropriate thinking and planning they could act on. This approach is the basis of a number of new courses being piloted in the UK (see University College Worcester/Pershore Group of Colleges—Advocacy Programme, http://www.projectcarrot.org).

Conclusion

There is no question that universities and colleges need to embrace sustainability as urgently as the political and economic sectors and society as a whole. This is highlighted, for example, in the UK by the significant influence that the oil and gas industries have on academic research priorities and the extent to which public funding is supporting the extraction of fossil fuel and climate change, while only 2 per cent of the total funding goes towards researching the environmental impacts of the industry (NEF, 2003).

Undoubtedly, there is some good work already under way. In the UK, the Environmental Association for Universities and Colleges (http://www.eauc.org.uk) has been a pioneering group in supporting a growing and influential programme of activity along with the Learning and Skills Development Agency; the Environment Agency and Forum for the Future through its HEPS (Higher Education Partnership for Sustainability) programme (http://www.forumforthefuture.org.uk). Studentforce for Sustainability (http://www.studentforce.org.uk) has also pioneered an innovative programme of graduate work placements in organizations focusing on sustainability. The higher education funding councils are increasingly considering sustainability issues, and some of the largest professional bodies have recently set up a Sustainability Alliance, which will put greater emphasis on the need to include sustainability criteria in their accreditation procedures for degree programmes. Some professional bodies are also including sustainability in their Charters.

At an international level, the Global Higher Education Sustainability Partnership (GHESP) is creating a sustainability toolkit to help universities tackle this important agenda (http://www.ulsf.org/toolkit) whilst UNESCO has produced an online learning resource to help educators teach sustainability issues (UNESCO, 2004). Also, in 2002 the United Nations General Assembly proclaimed the 10-year period 2005-2014 as the United Nations Decade of Education for Sustainable Development.

What we really need is a review of the situation in the sector and a strategy to achieve effective change in mainstream educational thinking, policy and practice. We should not only determine where the sector is at present but also engage as many institutions as possible in the review process, making sure that it is driven by their needs. A lot of expertise has been built up over the past decade, in geography and many other HE departments, even though it might only be visible in small pockets of good practice. To multiply these efforts we need cooperation and partnership, not only between universities but also with industry, local authorities and society at large. But this bottom-up approach has to be complemented by government commitment to a sustainable university sector, and there is no better way of doing this than linking funding to performance measured against sustainability indicators. When ministers of education start to ask Vice-Chancellors and Principals tough questions about sustainability, we might just stand a chance of making a difference to the education of our future leaders. Sustainable development needs to be at the core of the education system and disciplines such as geography need to play a prominent role in ensuring that HE curricula are attuned to sustainability issues. In this way university systems and disciplines can help to create societies and workforces more sensitive to sustainability agendas, and to produce political and business leaders with levels of earth-literacy appropriate to the challenges of the twenty-first century.

Acknowledgements

This paper is based on a keynote address presented at an International Conference on Education for a Sustainable Future: Shaping the Practical Role of Higher Education for Sustainable Development, at Charles University, Prague, Czech Republic, September 2003, organized by the International Association of Universities.

References

Baines, J. & Sterling, S. (2001) *Project Carrot -Curriculum Development: A Report for Project Carrot to Inform the Further Development of a Sustainable Curriculum for Agriculture and Land Management at Holme Lacy and the Pershore Group of Colleges* (Chorleywood: Bureau for Environmental Education and Training).

Bartel, M., Sheldon, C. & Martin, S. (2001) The Sigma Project: sustainability in practice, *Journal of Institution of Environmental Sciences*, 10(6), pp. 1–4.

Bor, W., Holen, P., Wals, A. & Filho, W. L. (Eds) (2000) *Integrating Concepts of Sustainability into Education for Agriculture and Rural Development* (Frankfurt a.M: Lang).

Chambers, N., Simmons, C. & Wackernagel, M. (2000) *Sharing Nature's Interest. Ecological Footprints as an Indicator of Sustainability* (London: Earthscan).

Cortese, A. D. (1999) *Education for Sustainability: The Need for a New Human Perspective*, (Boston: Second Nature). Available at http://www.secondnature.org/pdf/snwritings/articles/humanpersp.pdf (accessed April 2004).

Dawe, G., Martin, S. & Vetter, A. (2004) An overview of ecological footprinting and other tools and their application to the development of sustainability process: audit and methodology at Holme Lacy College, UK, *International Journal of Sustainability in Higher Education*, 5(4), pp. 340–371.

ECOTEC Research and Consultancy (2000) Analysis of the Eco-Industries, their Employment and Export Potential, Available at http://www.europa.eu.int/comm/environment/enveco/industry_employment/ecotec_exec-sum.pdf (accessed July 2003).

Egan Review (2004) *Skills for Sustainable Communities* (London: Royal Institution of British Architecture and the Office of the Deputy Prime Minister), Available at http://www.odpm.gov.uk (accessed April 2004).

Essence (2001) Thematic Network of Environmental Sciences. Available at http://www.essence.vsnu.nl (accessed July 2003).

Flint, K. (2001) Institutional ecological footprint analysis: a case study of the University of Newcastle, Australia, *International Journal of Sustainability in Higher Education*, 2(2), pp. 48–62.

Griffiths, A. (2002) An ecological footprint analysis of the University of Wales Swansea's Singleton campus, unpublished BSc thesis, Swansea Institute of Higher Education.

IAU (International Association of Universities) (1993) Sustainable Development and the Universities: IAU's position, Available at http://www.unesco.org/iau/sd/position.html (accessed April 2004).

Jucker, R. (2002) *Our Common Illiteracy. Education as if the Earth and People Mattered* (Frankfurt a.M.: Lang).

Jucker, R. (2003) A vision of a sustainable university. Available at http://www.swan.ac.uk/environment/VisionforasustainableUniversity.doc (accessed April 2004).

Jucker, R. & Martin, S. (2003) Une vision pour une université durable, *La Revue Durable*, 8, pp. 48–52.

Martin, S. (2002) Sustainability, systems thinking and Professional Practice, *Planet*, 4, pp. 20–21.

Martin, S. & Hall, A. (2002) Sustainable development and the professions, *Planet*, 3, pp. 17–18.

NEF (2003) *Degrees of Capture. Universities, the Oil Industry and Climate Change* (London: New Economics Foundation).

Orr, D. W. (1994) *Earth in Mind: On Education, Environment, and the Human Prospect* (Washington, DC: Island Press).

Orr, D. W. (2003) The case for the Earth, *Resurgence*, No. 219, July/August, pp. 16–19.

SIGMA (2003) *The SIGMA guidelines—An Overview. Putting Sustainable Development into Practice—A Guide for Organisations* (London: British Standards Institute). Available at http://www.projectsigma.com (accessed April 2004).

Sterling, S. (2001) *Sustainable Education—Re-Visioning Learning and Change* (Dartington: Green Books).

UNED-UK (2004) UK Report Back from the World Summit on Sustainable Development, Available at http://www.johannesburgsummit.org/html/documents/summit_docs.html (accessed April 2004).

UNESCO (1997) *Educating for a Sustainable Future—a Transdisciplinary Vision for Concerted Action*, document EPD.97/CONF.401/CLD.1 (Paris: UNESCO).

UNESCO (2002) *Teaching and Learning for a Sustainable Future. A Multimedia Teacher Education Programme* (Paris: UNESCO). Available at http://www.unesco.org/education/tlsf/ (accessed April 2004).

ULSF (1990) *Programs: Talloires Declaration* (Washington, DC: Association of University Leaders for a Sustainable Future), Available at http://www.ulsf.org/programs_talloires.html (accessed April 2004).

Venetoulis, J. (2001) Assessing the ecological impact of a university: the ecological footprint for the University of Redlands, *International Journal of Sustainability in Higher Education*, 2(2), pp. 180–196.

Vetter, A. & Dawe, G. (2001) *Towards a Sustainable Holme Lacy College* (Hereford: Caleb Management Services, Holme Lacy College (Pershore Group of Colleges) and Bulmer Foundation).

Wackernagel, M. & Rees, W. (1996) *Our Ecological Footprint: Reducing Human Impact on the Earth* (Gabriola Island, BC: New Society Publishers).

Wilsdon, J. & Porritt, J. (2000) Making sense of sustainability, *Journal of the Institution of Environmental Sciences*, 9(6), pp. 6–9.

Worldwatch Institute (2003) *Vital Signs 2003–2004: The Trends That Are Shaping Our Future* (London: Earthscan in association with Worldwatch Institute).

Greening the University Curriculum: Appraising an International Movement

MARTIN HAIGH

Introduction

In February 2003, Resolution 57/254 for a 'United Nations Decade of Education for Sustainable Development', proposed by Japan, was adopted by the Second Committee of the 57th Session of the United Nations General Assembly. Education for Sustainable Development (ESD) will have its decade from January 2005 (UN, 2003). The Decade offers academe's best chance to date for making the deep and radical changes that will be necessary if the world's higher education institutions (HEIs) are to enact their responsibilities for creating a better and self-sustainable world. Hopefully, the Decade will allow time for some deep thinking, critical introspection and constructive change across the whole academic enterprise (Tilbury & Goldstein, 2003). Many agree that changes must be made because, as David Orr has commented, "the crisis of the biosphere is symptomatic of a prior crisis of mind, perception and heart. It is not so much a problem in education but a problem of education" (Orr quoted in Viederman, 2001, p. 2). In brief, many believe that our present educational structures are less appropriately geared to meeting the needs of the future than to reinforcing the destructive characteristics of our current age (Berry, 1999; Sterling, 2001). The first part of this paper aims to sketch out the evolution of ESD in international declarations—a story with which few HE academics (including geographers) are familiar. The paper then goes on to consider the obstacles within academic systems that inhibit the 'Greening of our Universities' and their curricula.

International Movements

UN Resolution 57/254 culminates a long and diverse international process. The Resolution invites governments to promote and improve the integration of education for sustainable development in their respective educational strategies and action plans at the appropriate level (UN, 2003). UNESCO is designated the lead agency and the Dakar Action Framework is given priority (WEF, 2000). The Dakar Framework for Action, which emerged from World Education Forum in Dakar, Senegal, April 2000, reaffirmed commitment to UNESCO's 'Education for All', a programme that stresses basic rather than higher education (WEF, 2000). The framework urges nations to provide both stronger leadership and resources. It targets sub-Saharan Africa, South Asia and the less developed countries (LDCs) in general, as well as gender and health (especially HIV) issues. Environmental education, sustainability and teacher education are mentioned in passing. Nevertheless, ESD in HEIs, the 'greening of the universities', which has often been the subject of international aspirational declarations, will benefit from the declaration of the Decade.

The Higher Education movement traces its roots back to the 'Stockholm Declaration on the Human Environment' adopted at the United Nations Conference on the Human Environment, June 1972. This contains little about greening the curriculum or ESD but it may have provided a 'wake-up call' to HEIs (Kiss & Shelton, 1993). However, five years later, mitigated through the Belgrade Charter of the International Workshop on Environmental Education (1975), delegates from 68 states, eight UN agencies and 20 NGOs (international non-governmental organizations) emerged from the world's first 'Intergovernmental Conference on Environmental Education', Tbilisi, Georgia, October 1977, with the Tbilisi Declaration (McKeown & Hopkins, 2003). This urged education to consider the environment in its totality: natural and built, technological and social (economic, political, cultural-historical, ethical, and aesthetic); to be a continuous lifelong process, and to be interdisciplinary in its approach (UNESCO, 1977).

Concerns about the barriers to ESD, provided by the internal disciplinary orientations of academe, have been echoed many times. In December 1991, the Halifax Declaration, which emerged from the 'Conference on University Action for Sustainable Development' held at Dalhousie University, Halifax, Nova Scotia, urged HEIs to place far more weight on the value of interdisciplinary work. In support of the 'Green' mantra, 'think globally, act locally', the declaration urged HEIs to be more proactive for sustainable development and emphasized concrete actions at home (Halifax, 1991). It also supported the UNCED process.

Agenda 21, the landmark report of the United Nations Conference on Environment and Development (UNCED), Rio de Janeiro, Brazil, June 1992, includes ESD as Chapter 36: Promoting Education, Public Awareness and Training (Information Habitat, 1993). The chapter accepts Tbilisi as its major precedent along with recommendations from the 'World Conference on Education for All: Meeting Basic Learning Needs', Jomtien, Thailand, 1990' (World Conference on Education for All, 1990). Costed at $1.2 billion (1993–2000), Chapter 36 covers many aspects of education, formal and non-formal, higher and basic, while emphasizing 'education for sustainable human development'. The chapter's three strands concern the reorientation of all education towards sustainable development, increasing public awareness of sustainable development and promoting training that assists sustainable development. For example, it advises that universities should enrich pre-service curricula for journalists by increasing the emphasis on environment and development topics. The Chapter worries about the general lack of awareness of the interrelated nature of all human activities and the environment. It commends the fuller development of open and outward-looking universities. It also urges countries to strengthen or establish centres of excellence in interdisciplinary research and higher education in environmental and developmental sciences, as well as in law and the management of environmental problems (Information Habitat, 1993).

However, UNCED and the UN-UNESCO intergovernmental juggernaut are far from being the only processes at work. In October 1990, the University Leaders for a Sustainable Future (1990) met at the Tufts University European Center, Talloires, France, October 1990 (ULSF, 1990), The resulting Talloires Declaration, an influential document, is endorsed by some 280 universities in 40 nations. Admittedly, this is a tiny proportion of the world's HEIs, and amongst these, only a fraction of those aspirational HEIs have seriously addressed implementation. However, Talloires argues that "in creating an equitable and sustainable future for all humankind in harmony with nature, Universities have a major role in the education, research, policy formation, & information exchange necessary to make these goals possible" (USLF, 1990, p. 1).

The USLF now promotes ESD based on the Earth Charter. This emerged in the Rio + 5 Forum, March 1997, and was conceived as unfinished business from UNCED Rio, 1992. The Earth Charter was launched in 1994 by Maurice Strong and Mikhail Gorbachev, President of Green Cross International. The Earth Charter Initiative was the product of an open consultation process involving thousands of individuals and hundreds of organizations from around the world. Its proponents claim that it is evidence of a growing worldwide popular movement seeking to ensure a better future for all. Corcoran (2002) calls the Charter a recipe for 'good globalization' (cf. discussion between Jackson, 2003 and Haigh, 2003). The Charter argues that humanity is one family with a common destiny that shares mutual responsibility for the community of life and for future generations. Principle 8 urges us to advance the study of ecological sustainability and the free exchange of knowledge. Principle 14 urges us to integrate, into formal education and lifelong learning, the knowledge values and skills needed for a sustainable way of life (Earth Charter, 2000).

A second US-led initiative, the Campus Earth Summit, 1995 at Yale University, produced the influential 'Blueprint for a Green Campus'—an action plan for campus greening. According to the sponsors of the 'Blueprint for a Green Campus':

> A green campus is one that integrates environmental knowledge into all relevant disciplines, improves environmental studies course offerings, provides opportunities for students to study campus and local environmental problems, conducts environmental audits of its practices, institutes environmentally responsible purchasing policies, reduces campus waste, maximizes energy efficiency, makes environmental sustainability a top priority in land-use, transportation, and building planning, establishes a student environmental center, and supports students who seek environmentally responsible careers. (Heinz, 1995, p. 2)

The Campus Earth Summit's 10 recommendations begin with two that emphasize teaching and with the argument that environmental knowledge should be integrated into all relevant disciplines and go on to argue that the quality of environmental course offerings should be improved (Campus Earth Summit, 1995). They end with two recommendations that urge support for students during their time on campus through the establishment of a student environmental centre and through additional support for students seeking environmentally responsible careers (Campus Earth Summit 1995). In between are a series of recommendations that are designed to ensure that the ecological footprint of higher education is as small as possible.

In Europe, the lead has been set by COPERNICUS, the '*CO*operation *P*rogramme in *E*urope for *R*esearch on *N*ature and *I*ndustry through *C*oordinated *U*niversity *S*tudies', which traces its origins back to Bologna and the Magna Carta of European Universities 1988. The sponsor, the CRE, later Association of European Universities, has over 520 HEI members in 41 states, while its charter is endorsed by 306 HEI heads in 37 nations. The COPERNICUS Campus Charter, 1993, charges Universities with the duty to propagate environmental literacy and promote the practice of environmental ethics in society (COPERNICUS, 1993). It asserts:

> Education at all levels, especially university education for the training of decision-makers and teachers, should be oriented towards sustainable development & foster environmentally aware attitudes ... it must become environmental education in the fullest sense of the term. (COPERNICUS, 1993, p. 1)

In the same period, the Swansea Declaration, released by the Association of Commonwealth Universities' 15th Conference, University of Wales, Swansea, August 1993 (ACU, 1993), and the more influential 'Kyoto Declaration on Sustainable Development 1993' produced by the International Association of Universities (650 members) Ninth Round Table in Japan (IAU, 1993), urged HEIs to disseminate a clearer understanding of sustainable development, to respect the ethical obligations of "development which meets the needs of the present without compromising the needs of future generations" and to enhance their capacity of universities to teach and research in sustainable development. Kyoto, especially, focuses on ethical issues. It aims:

> To emphasize the ethical obligation of the present generation to overcome those practices of resource utilization and those widespread disparities which lie at the root of environmental unsustainability ... and to enhance the understanding of environmental ethics within the university and with the public at large. (IAU, 1993, p. 1)

Both Declarations emphasize the need for environmental literacy, which supplants earlier pronouncements in support of interdisciplinarity, while Kyoto, like the later 'Blueprint for a Green Campus', sketches out a University Action Plan for its implementation (ACU, 1993; IAU, 1993; Campus Earth Summit, 1995).

Action, or rather the lack of it, becomes an increasing concern in later documents. The Thessaloniki Declaration, adopted in December 1997, begins by noting lack of progress (MIO-ECSD, 1998), namely that the recommendations and action plans of the Belgrade 'Conference on Environmental Education' (1975), Tbilisi (1977), the Moscow 'Conference on Environmental Education and Training' (1987), and the Toronto 'World Congress for Education and Communication on Environment and Development' (1992) "are still valid and not fully explored", which translates as 'largely forgotten'. The Thassaloniki Declaration argues that special emphasis should be given to the reorientation of teacher training programmes, hoping that teachers will spread the word through the community. It also starts to think about a core problem: Who is going to pay for this work? Its suggestion is that all involved reinvest a portion of the savings from the greening process into strengthening of environmental education (MIO-ECSD, 1998).

The new millennium has seen a degree of coalescence in the international movement. The Global Higher Education for Sustainability Partnership (GHESP) combined the: International Association of Universities, ULSF, COPERNICUS Campus and UNESCO (UNESCO, 2001). A key concern of its Lüneburg Declaration of October 2001 was globalization. Here, higher education for sustainable human development is painted as a critical component of efforts to humanize globalization (Corcoran, 2002). The declaration states that:

> Education in all its forms plays an indispensable role in addressing the critical challenges of sustainable development. The interconnected issues of globalization, poverty alleviation, social justice, democracy, human rights, peace and environmental protection require inclusive partnerships to create a global learning environment ... Higher education has ... a special responsibility ... to generate the new knowledge needed and train the leaders and teachers of tomorrow, as well as communicate this knowledge to decision-makers and the public-at-large. (UNESCO, 2001, p. 1)

The action orientation continues. The Lüneburg organizers commit to the following five-year targets:

> a. Create a global learning environment for higher education for sustainable development; b. Promote expanded endorsement and full implementation of the Talloires, Kyoto and Copernicus declarations; c. Produce an action-oriented Toolkit for universities, managers, administrators, faculty and students designed to move from commitment to concrete action. (UNESCO, 2001, p. 2)

In fact, several such toolkits exist already (cf. Campus Earth Summit, 1995; Ashmole 1996; Second Nature, 2001; McKeown, 2002).

Meanwhile, the final stage of the UNCED process ahead of the UN Resolution that convened the 'Decade of Education for Sustainable Development' from 2005 (UN, 2003) was the 'Ubuntu Declaration on Education and Science and Technology for Sustainable Development', September 2002. This was issued at the 'World Summit on Sustainable Development' (WSSD) in Johannesburg on behalf of "the education and scientific organizations of the world" led by the United Nations University and UNESCO (UNESCO, 2002). The Ubuntu Declaration confirms that greater emphasis on education, especially in science and technology, is essential to reaching sustainable development goals and seeks a global alliance to promote these ends. The Declaration calls on:

> Governments of the World Summit for Sustainable Development and the Post-Summit agenda to: Designate educators as the tenth stakeholder group in the WSSD process [and] calls on educators, Governments and all relevant stakeholders to: review the programmes and curricula of schools and universities, in order to better address the challenges and opportunities of sustainable development, with a focus on: creating learning modules which bring skills, knowledge, reflections, ethics and values together in a balanced way. (UNESCO, 2002, p. 1)

Across the board, the pattern of international agreements has evolved from general concerns about environmental sustainability, through recognition that disciplinary barriers were inhibiting the world's capacity to cope with environmental problems, to the notion that every educated person should possess 'environmental literacy' and that HEIs should provide good role models for sustainable development. Later documents stress the ethics of environmental sustainability, increased emphasis on the interactive nature of the relationships between society and environment, the notion that ESD should permeate the whole HE curriculum and an increasing frustration with the lack of progress and change in the global educational system. Gradually, the emphasis has shifted from the statement of ideals to the elaboration of ways, means, models and the financial resources needed to drive the process forward.

Implementation remains the major challenge. MacNeill (1996, p. 12) asks Canada's University Presidents "Why do we keep signing more declarations and doing less?" Introducing the 2002 Conference on Environmental Management for Sustainable Universities, Charles Hopkins, points out that while ESD has become a "priority of mention" in sustainability declarations and national planning documents, there is a large gap "between the recognition of the need for education's contribution and the reality of actual delivery" (Hopkins, 2002, p. 1). Greening education has remained a "forgotten priority" when it comes to funding, actual programme delivery, and the struggle for the hearts and minds of the students and their communities is very far from won.

Curriculum Greening and ESD: Obstacles and Opportunities

The United Nations' Earth Summits, UNCED, Rio 1992 (including Agenda 21 and WSSD,) Johannesburg 2002 (including its WEHAB projects) have done a great deal to change the global approach to environmental problems and to provide a major showcase for environmental thinking. However, the rate of change on the ground remains very slow and not all of the changes that occur are positive. The question, asked at all levels, is what is the cause of the delay?

Greening the Curriculum: What Does it Mean?

One problem is that there is no general agreement, yet, on what the remit is for 'greening the curriculum', 'education for sustainable development', 'sustainability education' and 'environmental education' (McKeown & Hopkins, 2003). Are these concepts really so similar and what, if any, may be their hidden political, value-laden subtexts? There is also confusion about whether these ideas can or should apply across all disciplines or be restricted to some areas or some types of institution (Thomas & Nicita, 2002, p. 486; Parkin *et al.*, 2004, p12; Kasimov *et al.*, 2005). McKeown & Hopkins (2003, p. 7) also note that many respondents regarded ESD as an 'addition' for their curricula, rather than a change of orientation.

Funding and Perverse Subsidies

Certainly, there are sound managerial reasons why relatively few ESD/Green Curriculum programmes have been implemented effectively and, on a day-by-day basis, top of the list is funding. Accepting the UK as a case study, there have been useful initiatives, including the Higher Education HE21 Project and HEPS partnership scheme, organized through 'Forum for the Future' (HE21, 1999; HEPS, 2003; Parkin *et al.*, 2004) and also the work done by the excellent UK system of 'Learning and Teaching Support Networks' (LTSN), notably the University of Plymouth-based LTSN for 'Geography, Earth and Environmental Sciences' (e.g. LTSN-GEES, 2002). However, in the UK, as in North America, education is too often regarded as a secondary function for faculty in most universities. University leaders place far greater value on research, especially when that brings in additional external funding. This means that most HEIs organize themselves with an eye to the advancement of research and, as a result, teaching activities tag along behind. In the case of research, the UK Government has offered, inadvertently, what Myers in another context calls 'perverse subsidies'. These are subsidies that reward unproductive practices (Myers, 1998). ESD, by definition, demands practical, applied, interdisciplinary, holistic, problem-solving thinking—global thinking but local action. However, the UK's Research Assessment Exercise (RAE), which aims to concentrate UK research funding in a small number of elite institutes, has equally encouraged research concentration in highly specialized, discipline-based research clusters. In reifying the kind of research performed by traditional elite universities, RAE procedures have also strengthened academic 'blue sky', 'international' research against applied and locally relevant research, and because of the 4–6 year RAE funding cycle, projects with a short-term paybacks have been prioritized against those longer-term works needed to promote sustainable development.

In mitigation, however, the teaching arm of UK Government policy, which has already sponsored the LTSNs, is now sponsoring a series of Centres for Excellence in Teaching and Learning (CETLs). Here, ESD competes with a plethora of other pedagogic concerns for attention—but there remains hope that a heavily funded ESD-CETL could provide another spark for better cross-disciplinary practice and communication—at least in its home university (HEFCE, 2003).

Academic Tribes, Benchmarks and Disciplinary Barriers

The problem of achieving cross-disciplinarity may be incidental to the UK system for research funding but it is absolutely central to the way in which all HEIs are organized. HEIs' academic teams are fragmented into quasi-independent departments—each charged with concern for a disciplinary body of knowledge. In this context, environmental issues are treated by most HEIs as the property of a select few disciplines (particularly geography and the environmental sciences), which often lock their offerings away behind the barriers of specialization. As a result, the discussion of environmental issues, sometimes even particular aspects of single environmental issues, becomes seen as the property of different academic tribes. Heinz (1995, p. 6) complains: "Engineering, chemistry, biology, physics—they are all sovereign and heaven forbid that we should ask them to knock down their ivy walls and build bridges instead". Canada's University Presidents (NRTEE, 1996, p. 24) affirm, as Common Principle 4, that the temptation to entrench certain subsets of skills and knowledge as 'environmental' must be avoided. Cortese (2001, p. 2) proposes that interdisciplinary systems thinking should replace the disciplinary focus, lateral rigour replacing vertical rigour, in order to address environmentally sustainable action on all scales. This is an important issue, which often is lost amidst the other arguments. Meanwhile, the Copernicus Campus Charter wryly advises universities, while encouraging interdisciplinary and collaborative education and research on sustainable development, to strive to overcome "the competitive instincts between disciplines and departments" (COPERNICUS, 1993).

Appreciating these issues, Canada's University Presidents argue that the way ahead is to involve students directly and actively in problem-based learning and practical work—fieldwork, placements in the community, group-work, etc. (NRTEE, 1996). It is said that educational psychologists note that we retain 80 per cent of what we do and only 10–20 per cent of what we hear and read (Cortese, 2001, p. 2). Moreover, few real-world problems rest comfortably within individual disciplines. Different environmental problems require inputs from a different array of disciplines. These University Presidents argue and emphasize that the problem should define the disciplinary expertise that is required (NRTEE, 1996, p. 24). Meanwhile, Canada's universities remain as academic in approach and fragmented by discipline as HEIs elsewhere.

A related problem for many disciplines, including geography in many nations, is the proscribed curriculum. National benchmarking and syllabus-setting documents are created in many nations in an attempt to make sure that the teaching offered by HEIs covers the heartlands of each discipline (Tikhonov *et al.*, 1995; Simmons *et al.*, 2000). Once created, these prescriptions for education, geographical or otherwise, may persist for many years and much reduce the scope of individual HEIs for innovation. Equally, once a change is embedded in such a benchmark, it quickly affects the whole system (cf. Kasimov *et al.*, 2005).

Ecoliteracy Courses or Curriculum Greening?

In many HEIs, attempts to circumvent these problems have resulted in the addition of short, usually introductory-level, courses to the early stages of the undergraduate core curriculum. Such courses present learners with a small package of ideas on environmental literacy or the needs of sustainable development. They aim to give students a grounding in ESD's core issues and encourage them to consider how their actions affect the environment (Ashmole, 1996). The problem is that these packages are often seen as something apart from the learner's main education, a discrete package of knowledge, another course to be passed and forgotten, but not something generally relevant to their main course of study.

So, if the creation of specialist environmental degrees and diplomas risks the ghettoization of environmental learning, and if the creation of environmental literacy modules risks tokenism in both provision and learning, there remains only one solution. This is full-scale 'curriculum greening' (Ashmole, 1996). This means suffusing the whole academic enterprise with 'green issues' and ESD topics (Ali Khan, 1991). Every programme from Arts to Engineering would include opportunities for learners to explore the fundamental messages of ESD. The COPERNICUS Campus Charter urges universities to incorporate an environmental perspective in all their work and to set up environmental education programmes that expose teachers and students to the global challenges of environment and development, irrespective of their field of study (COPERNICUS, 1993). Edinburgh University's 'Student Declaration for a Sustainable Future', endorsed by the Students' Representative Council in November 1995, agrees that:

> We, as learners, will seek to ensure that issues of environmental sustainability are addressed throughout the curriculum, [and continues] education should enable all individuals to make informed decisions concerning their responsibilities towards the environment and the communities. (Ashmole, 1996, p. 1)

Hence, ESD issues may be integrated into the teaching of all subject areas with appropriate areas developing explicitly environment and ESD-related modules. Several excellent curriculum greening resource packs contain multiple case studies of this process at work in various disciplines and many more examples are to be found in individual university websites (Campus Earth Summit, 1995; Ashmole, 1996; HE21, 1999; Second Nature, 2001; McKeown, 2002; HEPS, 2003).

There has been much debate about the role and responsibilities of the educator in promoting ESD and related 'Green' ideas and much squeamishness about the intrusion of educators into an increasingly politicized arena. The sanguine William Scott (2002) identifies four kinds of responsibility: to demonstrate to learners why sustainable development is important to them, to help learners gain plural perspectives from a range of 'cultural stances', to provide learning opportunities through appropriate curricula, and to help learners understand what they need to do to keep their own and other peoples' 'options open'. Scott (2002, p. 6) suggests that to do less would seem neglectful and to do more runs the risk of indoctrination.

The Academic Value System

Unfortunately, ESD is not simply a technical matter, no more is 'Greening the Curriculum': their propagation requires changes in value systems, first in HEIs, and second in society at large. Viederman (2001) launches his thoughts on such matters with the following quotation from a lecture 'On Global Education' in which Nobel Laureate Elie Wiesel speculates on the education of those who commit war crimes. Weisel notes:

> They did not come from the underworld; some came from the best and most prestigious universities ... they had degrees and even doctorates in medicine, philosophy, jurisprudence and theology. In other words, they were not shielded by their education. What was wrong with it? It emphasized theories instead of values, concepts rather than human beings, abstraction rather than consciousness, answers instead of questions, ideology and efficiency rather than conscience. (Weisel 1990, quoted in Viederman, 2001, p. 1)

Viederman (2001) continues with a litany of the failings of an education system that subscribes to the myth of technology as saviour, that conflates growth with development, that equates abundance with well-being, that relies on the market to achieve equity and social justice and that ignores the rights, not merely of other species but of humanity's future generations (cf. Berry, 1999; Jucker, 2002). Educational philosopher Smith reflects that the current structure does not just fail to nurture a learner's appreciation for the systems of this living world but provides an "encouragement to disdain them" (Smith, 2002, p. 7).

Nobel Peace-prize winner Payutto (1995) argues along similar lines in a much reprinted chiding of Thailand's academic elite:

> Science learns the truths of nature, but only on the material side, and then uses the knowledge gained for technology, with the objective of a life of abundance... (Payutto, 1995, p. 80)

> ... desire has no end and so the need for material resources is endless. Because material goods are obtained through the exploitation of nature, it follows that the manipulation of nature is also without end and without check. Ultimately, nature will not have enough to satisfy human desires, and in fact the exploitation of nature in itself gives humankind more misery than happiness. (Payutto, 1995, p. 60)

There are limits to growth and to the continuing obsession with material abundance is not helpful (Capra, 2002). Universities help perpetuate the myth of eternal progress, endless growth and expanding personal consumption, despite the self-evident truth that the global resource base and the capacities for self-renewal in natural systems are limited (Bowers, 2001). Years ago, Gandhi proposed his 'economy of limited wants' and it is certain that self-restraint will be essential to any sustainable approach to the planet's resources (Doctor, 1967). Indeed, there is a need to encourage learners to rethink the categories by which society interacts with the non-human world (Gough, 2002).

Equally, there is a need to rethink our current educational practices, which have been characterized by managerialist, materialist, exploitative, techno-rationalism and short-termist attitudes (Sterling, 2001; Smith, 2002). Smith continues to suggest, with Gandhi, that our education splits mind from body and ignores the latter (Smith, 2002). This is a problem that arises from the way that learning is delivered (Gough, 2002). Dispassion and objectivity are central to the value systems of many of the environmental disciplines. Payutto notes:

> Science does not connect the truth to ethics, but instead, because it deals only with the material world, connects it to technology ... science concerns itself solely with the question "what is" shrugging off any concern for "what should be". (Payutto, 1995, p. 80)

The consequence is that when such programmes are delivered they often share the characteristics of those courses designed to introduce Western students to different cultures but which manage to treat these cultures as objects of study, 'fossils in a museum case' rather than living, alternative ways of world-making (Bowers, 2001; Haigh, 2003). Most university courses on the environment and sustainable development treat these matters as academic subjects, something external to the learner (Jucker, 2003). Geographers, too, have more often than not resisted the arguments of those who have suggested to them that they should become involved—with the environment, with communities and with their problems of both, and, on the whole, settled into the more comfortable role of outside commentator (Haigh, 2002).

Learners obtain their understandings in many other ways than the ingestion of instructional materials. Bowers (2001) writes:

> . . . the taken-for-granted attitude toward commoditized relationships, knowledge, activities is given explicit legitimation in only certain university departments. It is daily reinforced through the use of textbooks, computers, tuition fees and the general ethos that equates a university education with increased economic success. Bowers (2001, p. 2)

Students absorb many implicit attitudes from their HEIs, which may include their approach to the world. These views are learnt by example—what is done as much as what is said. No doubt, universities like to conceive themselves as the leaders of society and social change. In fact, they function rather more as its followers and as servants for its dominant ethos or perhaps mythos (Berry, 1999; Jackson, 2003). Even the 'Greening Campus' movements have tended to focus on the less difficult material and managerial aspects of making university operations more sustainable. Hence the 'Universities of Australia Ecologically Sustainable Development Charter of May 1998', which was sponsored by the National Union of Students, argues that:

> We, the Vice-Chancellors of universities in Australia, acknowledge that protection of the environment is an area of critical concern for, not only the education community, but the entire community . . . a range of environmental problems have beset the Australian ecosystem. These problems range from climate change to species extinction; from water, soil and air degradation to toxics accumulation; from natural resource depletion to non-sustainable development practices; and realize that these problems require the urgent attention of the research, teaching and administrative sections of all Australian universities. (ASEN, 1998)

Nevertheless, the action targets are the library, photocopiers, university-wide recycling systems, catering outlets' waste reduction, energy auditing, and ethical investment rather than curriculum enhancement and reform (ASEN, 1998). Certainly, promoting the sustainability of campus operations is important work. Great things are being done by organizations, which include the UK's Environmental Association for Universities and Colleges (http://www.eauc.org.uk) and others internationally, and this work will do a great deal to change the subliminal messages about sustainable development that HEIs transmit to their students. However, these measures do not change the qualities of the formal education that is delivered.

Contribution from Geography

In theory, geography, which seeks to combine the study of environments and societies, could play a key role in 'greening the curriculum' (Chalkley, 2002). Geographical education has long sought "to prepare people to take their place on the world stage" (Lidstone, 2001, p. 2; citing "the world's first university post-holder in Geography and Education"—James Fairgrieve). However, in fact, the special contribution of geography and geographers is not yet very great. At the time of writing, no geography programme is listed in the Institutional Section of the GHESP toolkit (ULSF, 2004) although, cheered on by the American National Council on Geographical Education, geographer McKeown has published her own ESD Toolkit (McKeown, 2002). In the UK, HEPs involved 15 HEIs but geography contributed to just three of the 26 curricula listed, although the UK geography subject benchmark is mentioned as a model of good practice (Simmons *et al.*, 2000). However, in the UK, Geography for 11- to 14-year-olds is a major vehicle for ESD and so has a key role to play (Reid *et al.*, 2002). In Russia, Kasimov (2005), introducing an eight-volume compendium that scopes the range of past and present geographical research, calls the search for the solutions to environmental problems one of the great integrating themes in Russian geography. In Brunei, under-utilized channels for environmental education are used by geographers to help communities preserve their own habitats (Odihi, 2001). In India, where, like the USA, physical geography is less developed and the discipline leans towards the social sciences, greening the curriculum is led by pressures from outside the academy (Jackson & Pande, 2000). The role of Australia's geographers, their departments all now merged within larger groupings, may be typical. Their contribution is described as important, if uncoordinated, but awake to the valuable opportunities offered by ESD at a time when traditional disciplines are under threat (Jones, 2002).

The multi-authored pioneering IUCN survey of ESD worldwide includes many authors who have geographical training (Tilbury *et al.*, 2002). Stevenson (2002, p. 187) sums up a book that offers an alternative to a "hegemonic Western worldview" that seems to demand "a detached posture of objectively observing the external natural and material environment, commodifies knowledge and culture, delineates education and schooling as serving primarily an economic function, and assumes human control over nature and elite groups having power and control over other people". By contrast, the radical position of the IUCN contribution "emphasizes: the integration of different knowledge systems (indigenous and modern, local and global, cross-disciplinary); education and schooling that serves cultural, civic and liberating, as well as economic, purposes; human connectedness with nature and with each other; and distributed power through participatory democracy" (Stevenson, 2002, p. 187). Meanwhile, the editors of *International Research in Geographical and Environmental Education* worry that few geographers yet debate the radical ESD agenda, "the conventional wisdom that the main purpose of geographical education is to promote an environmental ethic and that this is of such importance that other educational intentions must be subservient" (Lidstone & Gerber, 1998, p. 87; cf. Davidson, 2003).

Paradigm Shift

It has long been realized that ESD/Greening Education will require a paradigm shift in the way that education itself approaches the Earth and its future welfare (Berry, 1999; Rest, 2002). Sterling (2002) suggests that our problems are mainly the result of the way we approach the world and the solutions require redesigning our thought and actions rather than the world around us. Frequently, our problem-solving efforts fail since the solutions that are adopted are, in fact, more closely allied to the source than the cure of the problem.

For example, in land reclamation research, traditional solutions are framed by civil engineering approaches that tackle individual symptoms rather than the general state of ecological imbalance and the health of the geoecological system (Haigh, 2002).

Equally, the ESD toolkits recently developed by HEPS (Parkin *et al.*, 2004) and to a lesser degree by GHESP (ULSF, 2004), are all firmly anthropocentric. Sustainability is defined in human terms. One curriculum, commended by the HEPS document, asks readers to 'consider what kind of society they require for the future' and mention of environmental security is hard to find (Parkin *et al.*, 2004). Elsewhere, the message is that 'we will take charge, do this, engineer that'. Missing is the fact that humans are not the only created beings and that, even today, they are a small part of a very complicated, biological, life-support system about which they know distressingly little. Missing is any real sense of humans-in-context or of our species' "part-ness" in something rather larger. Missing is a sense of real humility. In fact, barely concealed within their 'ecology-equity-economy' rubric (Fien, 2002), is that old 'Industrial Age' myth that 'we know what we are doing and we know best'. The present state of our habitat is a testimony to the reality of this popularly held assumption. Equally telling is the following quotation: "one of the most important drivers for sustainability literate graduates will be the demand from employers" (Parkin *et al.*, 2004, p. 6 but cf. Berry, 1999, p. 85).

Jackson and Pande (2000) propose that India's educators should begin some serious questioning of deeply ingrained worldviews inherited from the West. These include present notions of 'progress', top-down 'government', the negative aspects of 'conservation', and 'development' that is only 'economic'. Sterling (2001) charts a shift from the materialist mechanistic worldview of current Western thinking towards an ecological worldview based on systems thinking. Sue Greig and team try to help schools break free of a current 'fragmentalist' outlook, which recognizes the differences between the objects of the observed world, and to assist them in replacing this with a holistic ESD worldview, which recognizes the mutuality and integration of all aspects of society and nature (Greig *et al.*, 1989). Joanna Macy provides a handbook for educators that begins with a series of holding actions in defence of natural systems, includes a wealth of teaching methods, and targets a new worldview that extends from the theory of living systems deep into the realms of spirituality (Macy & Brown, 1998). This last also makes many academics squeamish, but others agree that a prerequisite to understanding the meaning of ESD is a spiritual appreciation of 'wholeness' (Sterling, 2002). Macy points out that the main challenge within ESD/Curriculum Greening is to reconnect learners with the reality of their world; learners need to identify themselves as a part of the large wholeness of the Earth System (Macy & Brown, 1998). Reconnection of the learner, first with the wholeness of humanity, in all of its multicultural richness through internationalization of the curriculum, then with the wholeness of life and the living planet—these are the key goals for ESD and greening the curriculum (Naess, 1987).

Unfortunately, our present HEIs are more set up to teach knowledge in discrete fragments, often from a reductionist and analytical perspective, rather than as holistic interacting systems (Greig *et al.*, 1991; Sterling, 2001). If ESD is to effect the 'greening of the whole curriculum', ultimately and inevitably, this must involve a major shift in the priorities and structures of higher education and its delivery (Cortese, 2001, p. 1). There is a need to overcome the 'culture of denial' that presently inhibits the curriculum reform but it is questionable whether this can be achieved without external leadership (cf. Bowers, 1997).

In the UK, the course of HEIs tends to be determined by two external drivers, the decisions of governments and the decisions of 17-year-olds about which course they will select and which HEI they will attend. The decisions of these would-be students are affected by many factors but they include their previous experience in education. The disciplinary barriers that fragment environmental understanding and inhibit ESD are strongest in the HE sector. There may be greater scope for effecting change further down the system, creating new systems of study in primary and secondary schools, and, using our contemporary zeitgeist, allowing the resulting student choices to in turn change the HEIs. In this respect, the basic education thrust in UN Resolution 57/254 (UN, 2003), the pointers to teacher education in the Dakar Declaration (WEF, 2000), the Earth Charter (Earth Charter, 2000) and UNCED's Agenda 21, Chapter 36—with its additional advice for the training of journalists and other media writers (Information Habitat, 1993)—all seem entirely apt. However, Daniella Tilbury notes that, across Europe, schools struggle to introduce this innovative form of education into the mainstream curriculum (Tilbury, 1999). Her research suggests that the existing curriculum culture and structures of European schooling conflict with the nature and principles of environmental education.

Of course, HEI students also have a constructive role to play. Mansfield (1998) proposes that, in the USA, HEI environmental programmes are shifting college education, away from learning based in disciplinary specialization towards interdisciplinary experiential learning. Anecdotally, he cites examples of students challenging campus administrators to make operations more sustainable and hopes that students gain a better understanding of abstract global issues through working on manageable local ones involving recycling, energy conservation, greening transportation, catering, water conservation and waste management (Mansfield, 1998).

Conclusion

It is difficult to imagine that the societal changes required to create a sustainable future will occur without assistance from higher education (Cortese, 2001). Equally, it is difficult to imagine higher education making the changes needed to affect ESD, even the 'greening' of their own offerings, without outside help. Even in academe, the voices that speak for the future and for green issues are few, often marginal. Additionally, these days, such ideas are challenged by a powerful mindset that still regards the world as boundless, economic growth as endless, technology as the solution to all problems and material abundance as the key to human welfare and happiness. Given a finite world, until self-restraint becomes a factor in human affairs, there is little or no hope that sustainable development can be achieved. However, at the highest levels, awareness is growing that changes must come and this thinking is becoming better developed in the advice prepared by the international community.

This article has sketched out the background to the Declaration of the United Nations 'Decade of Education for Sustainable Development' in February 2003 (UN, 2003). This declaration grows from the Dakar Framework for Action (WEF, 2000) and owes strong allegiance to UNESCO's 'Education for All' basic education programme. However, it will also benefit the cause of ESD in HEIs. Unfortunately, evaluation of the internal problems within HEIs suggests that their ability to transform themselves to address the ESD agenda by curriculum greening is limited by their internal structures, especially the way they fragment knowledge with disciplinary barriers, and an ethos that seeks to divide the learner from reality through the objectification and externalization of the subjects of study. Changing this situation is a key problem and here the route may well involve both governments and the transformation of primary and secondary education, where disciplinary barriers are less rigid. Clearly, HEIs can assist this process through teacher training. Later, the HEIs may perhaps be transformed by the choices of the new generation of college-bound youngsters.

Meanwhile, the further declarations of the international communities of higher education chart a more gentle evolutionary approach to greening their curricula. Since Tbilisi (UNESCO, 1977), general concerns about environmental sustainability have evolved through recognition of the negative effects of disciplinary barriers to the notion that every HEI should imbue its students with 'environmental literacy'. In the process, many HEIs have accepted that they should provide good role models and have struggled to make their own physical operations less profligate. Later documents have stressed the ethics of environmental sustainability—ecology, equity and economy—and the notion that ESD should permeate the whole HEI curriculum. Meanwhile, there have been signs of increasing frustration with the slow rate of progress (Thessaloniki Declaration, 1997: MIO-ECSD, 1998), as well as an elaboration of handbooks that illustrate examples of best practice. Implementation remains the major challenge and it is just possible that, from January 2005, the United Nations Decade of Education for Sustainable Development may facilitate and accelerate the changes that are needed. Certainly it will be interesting during this Decade to observe how far geography and geographers commit themselves to this agenda.

Acknowledgements

Thanks go to Dr Rolf Jucker, University of Wales, Swansea, for helpful comments on the draft of this text and to Oxford Brookes University for funding this project through their Teaching Fellowship Scheme.

References

Ali Khan, S. (1991) *Greening the Curriculum* (London: World Wildlife Federation with the Committee of Directors of Polytechnics).

ACU (1993) *The Swansea Declaration (from) People and the Environment—Preserving the Balance*, Association of Commonwealth Universities' 15th Conference, University of Wales, August 1993, Swansea, Wales (London: Association of Commonwealth Universities). Available at http://www.unesco.org/iau/sd/swansea.html (accessed August 2003).

ASEN (1998) *The Universities of Australia Ecologically Sustainable Development Charter* (Canberra: National Union of Students). Available at http://www.asen.org.au/campaigns/unis.html (accessed August 2003).

Ashmole, A. (1996) *Curriculum Greening: A Resource Pack for Integrating Environmental Perspectives into Curses* (Edinburgh: University of Edinburgh Centre for the study of Environmental Change and Sustainability). Available at http://www.cecs.ed.ac.uk/greeninfo/gcpack/index2.htm (accessed August 2003).

Berry, T. (1999) *The Great Work, Our Way into the Future* (New York: Belltower).

Bowers, C. A. (1997) *The Culture of Denial: Why the Environment Movement needs a Strategy for Reforming Universities and Public Schools* (Albany: SUNY Press).

Bowers, C. A. (2001) *Greening the University Curriculum* (Boston: Second Nature: Education for Sustainability Resource Guides). Available at http://www.secondnsture.org.guides..ulty_writings/writings_bowers.html (accessed May 2001).

Campus Earth Summit (1995) *Blueprint for a Green Campus: The Campus Earth Summit Initiatives for Higher Education* (New York: Heinz Family Foundation), Available at http://www.envirocitizen.org/blueprint/blueprint.pdf (accessed August 2003). See also http://www.princeton.edu/ ~ rcurtis/earthsum.html and the critique by Sevin, J. (1995) Conference reveals Yale's shades of Green. *Yale Herald*, 3 February 1995. Available at http://www.yaleherald.com/archive/xix/3.2.95/news/conference.html (accessed August 2003).

Capra, F. (2002) *The Hidden Connections* (London: HarperCollins (Flamingo)).

Chalkley, B. (2002) Introduction: setting the sustainability scene, *Planet*, 4, pp. 3.

COPERNICUS (1993) *COPERNICUS University Charter for Sustainable Development* (Brussels: European Universities Association / CRE). Available at http://www.copernicus-campus.org/sites/charter_index1.html (accessed June 2003).

Corcoran, P. B. (2002) The Earth Charter: An ethical framework for 'good' globalization (Draft Version), *Environmental Management for Sustainable Universities (EMSU) 2002 Conference*, pp. 80–85 (Grahamstown, South Africa: Rhodes University).

Cortese, A. (2001) *Education for Sustainability: the University as a Model for Sustainability* (Boston: Second Nature—Education for Sustainability Resource Guides). Available at http://www.secondnsture.org.guides..gs/writings_cortese_univ_modl.html (accessed May 2001).

Davidson, J. (2003) Editorial: The challenge of education for sustainable development and global citizenship, *Journal of Geography in Higher Education*, 27(3), pp. 235–238.

Doctor, A. H. (1967) *Sarvodaya: A Political and Economic Study* (London: Asia Books).

Earth Charter (2000) *The Earth Charter and Earth Charter Handbook*. Available at http://www.earthcharter.org; http://www.earthcharter.org/files/charter/charter.pdf (accessed August 2003).

Fien, J. (2002) Reorienting education for a sustainable future, *Teaching and Learning for a Sustainable Future*, Module 4 (Paris: UNESCO). Available at http://www.unesco.org/education/tlsf/pdf/pdf_list.htm (accessed June 2004).

Gough, S. (2002) Right answers or wrong problems? Towards a theory of change fro environmental learning, *Trumpeter, Journal of Ecosophy*, 18(1), pp. 1–15. Available at http://trumpeter.athabascau.ca/content/v18.1/gough.pdf (accessed August 2003).

Greig, S., Pike, G. & Selby, D. (1989) *Green Prints for Changing Schools* (London: World Wide Fund for Nature & Kogan Page).

Haigh, M. J. (2002) Land reclamation and deep ecology: in search of a more meaningful Physical Geography, *Area*, 34(3), pp. 242–252.

Haigh, M. J. (2003) Internationalising the curriculum: response to M.G. Jackson, *Journal of Geography in Higher Education*, 27(3), pp. 331–340.

Halifax (1991) *Creating a Common Future: An Action Plan for Universities. Follow up to the Halifax Conference on University Action for Sustainable Development, December 97–11, 1991* (Halifax: Dalhousie University, Lester Pearson Institute for International Development). Available at http://iisd.ca/educate/declarat/halifax.htm; and http://www.unesco.org/iau/sd/halifax.html (accessed August 2003).

HE21 (1991) *HE21 Archive: Best Practice Guides* (London: Forum for the Future), Available at http://www.forumforthefuture.org.uk/aboutus/default.asp?pageid = 367 (accessed August 2003).

HEFCE (2003) *Centres for Excellence in Teaching and Learning* (London: Higher Education Funding Council for England). Available at http://www.hefce.ac.uk/learning/TInits/cetl/ (accessed May 2004).

Heinz, T. (1995) Preface, *Blueprint for a Green Campus: The Campus Earth Summit Initiatives for Higher Education*, pp. 7–8 (New York: Heinz Family Foundation). Available at http://www.envirocitizen.org/blueprint/blueprint.pdf (accessed Aug. 2003).

HEPS (2003) *Higher Education Partnership for Sustainability* (London: Forum for the Future). Available at http://www.forumforthefuture.org.uk/aboutus/default.asp?pageid = 361 and http://www.theforumelab.org.uk/uploadstore/Curriculum%20toolkit%20–20sep%2002.doc (accessed August 2003).

Hopkins, C. (2002) The role of education in attaining a sustainable future, *Environmental Management for Sustainable Universities (EMSU) 2002 Conference*, pp. 1–3 (Grahamstown, South Africa: Rhodes University).

IAU (1993) *Kyoto Declaration on Sustainable Development* (Geneva: International Association of Universities). Available at http://www.unesco.org/iau/sd/position.html#THE%20KYOTO (accessed July 2003).

Information Habitat (1993) *Agenda 21 and the Earth Summit Agreement*. Available at http://habitat.igc.org/agenda21/; Agenda 21—36: Promoting Education, Public Awareness and Training, Earth Summit, 1992 at http://habitat.igc.org/agenda21/a21–36.htm (accessed August 2003).

Jackson, M. G. (2003) Internationalising the curriculum, *Journal of Geography in Higher Education*, 27(3), pp. 325–331.

Jackson, M. G. & Pande, G. P. (2000) *Environmental Education in India: A Critical Assessment of Developments to Date and Suggestions for the Future* (Almora: Uttarakhand Seva Nidhi Paryavaran Shiksha Sansthan/Uttarakhand Environmental Education Centre).

Jucker, R. (2002) *Our Common Illiteracy: Education as though the Earth and its People Mattered* (Frankfurt a.M.: Lang).
Jucker, R. (2003) UNESCO's 'Teaching and Learning for a Sustainable Future': a critical evaluation of underlying unsustainable myths, *Trumpeter, Journal of Ecosophy*, 19(2), pp. 07.1–7.25. Available at http://trumpeter.athabascau.ca/content/v19.2/07_Jucker.pdf (accessed August 2003).
Kasimov, N. S. (2005) *Foreword, Geography Society and Environment* (Moscow: Moscow State University Publishing), [in Russian].
Kasimov, N. S., Malkhazova, S. M. & Romanova, E. P. (2005) Environmental education for sustainable development in Russia, *Journal of Geography in Higher Education*, 29(1), pp. 49–59.
Kiss, A. & Shelton, D. (Eds) (1993) *Manual of European Environmental Law* (Cambridge: Grotius).
Lidstone, J. (2001) A global antidote based on established disciplines: antidote to fatalism in a globalized world, International Geographical Union, Commission on Geographical Education, Helsinki Conference, unpublished paper.
Lidstone, J. & Gerber, R. (1998) Theoretical underpinnings of geographical and environmental education research: hiding our light under various bushels, *International Research in Geographical and Environmental Education*, 7(2), pp. 87–89.
LTSN-GEES (2002) Special Edition on Education for Sustainable Development, *Planet*, 4, Available at http://www.gees.ac.uk (accessed May 2003).
MacNeill, J. (1996) Keynote address, *University Presidents' Workshop: Learning and Sustainability, Summary Report*, pp. 12–14 (Ottawa: National Round Table on the Environment and the Economy).
Macy, J. & Brown, M. (1998) *Coming Back to Life: Practices to Reconnect our Lives, Our World* (Gabriola Island, BC: New Society).
Mansfield, III, W. H. (1998) The greening of the campus: students are beginning to hold their institutions of higher learning to a higher standard, *Worldwatch*, 11(3), pp. 24–30.
McKeown, R. (2002) Education for Sustainable Development Toolkit (vers.2), Available at http://www.esdtoolkit.org/authnote.htm (accessed June 2004).
McKeown, R. & Hopkins, C. (2003) EE ≠ ESD: defusing the worry, *Environmental Education Research*, 9(1), pp. 117–128.
MIO-ECSD (1998) *Environment and Society: Education and Public Awareness for Sustainability: The Thessaloniki Declaration* (Athens: Mediterranean Information Office for Environment, Culture and Sustainable Development). Available at http://www.mio-ecsde.org/Thess/declar_en.htm (accessed August 2003).
Myers, N. (1998) *Perverse Subsidies* (Winnipeg, Manitoba: International Institute for Sustainable Development).
Naess, A. (1987) Self-realization: an ecological approach to being in the world, *Trumpeter, Journal of Ecosophy*, 4(3), pp. 128–131, (reprinted in: Drengson, A. & Inoue, Y. (Eds) (1995) *The Deep Ecology Movement, An Introductory Anthology* (Berkeley: North Atlantic Books)).
NRTEE (1996) *University Presidents' Workshop: Learning and Sustainability, Summary Report* (Ottawa: National Round Table on the Environment and the Economy).
Parkin, S., Johnston, A., Buckland, H., Brookes, F. & White, E. (2004) *Learning and Skills for Sustainable Development: Developing a Sustainably Literate Society: Guidance for Higher Education Institutions* (London: Higher Education Partnership for Sustainability, Forum for the Future). Available at www.heps.org.uk; www.forumforthefuture.org.uk (accessed May 2004).
Odihi, J. O. (2001) Environmental education: beckoning roads for Brunei Darussalam, *International Studies in Geographical and Environmental Education*, 9(3), pp. 197–210.
Payutto, P. A. (1995) *Towards Sustainable Science: A Buddhist Look at Trends in Scientific Development* (Bangkok: Buddhadhamma Foundation), (trans. B. Evans, from *Buddhasasana ny Thana Pen Rahk Than Korng Wityasaht* (Chiang Mai: University of Chiang Mai, Science Faculty, 1992).
Reid, A., Scott, W. & Gough, S. (2002) Education and sustainable development in the UK: An exploration of progress since Rio, *Geography*, 87(3), pp. 247–255.
Rest, A. (2002) From 'environmental education' to 'education for sustainable development'—the shift of a paradigm, *Environmental Policy and Law*, 32(2), pp. 79–85.
Scott, W. (2002) Educations and sustainable development: challenges, responses and frames of mind, *Trumpeter, Journal of Ecosophy*, 18(1), pp. 06.1–6.12. Available at http://trumpeter.athabascau.ca/content/v18.1/scott.pdf (accessed August 2003).
Simmons, I. G., Agnew, C. T., Bradford, M., Birkhill, S., Buckingham, Hatfield, S., Chalkley, B., Chapman, K., Clark, G., Gilbert, D., Healey, M. J., Matthews, J. A., Richards, K. S., Unwin, D. J., White, P. E., Craig, L. &

Gardiner, R. (2000) *Geography Benchmarking Statement* (Gloucester: Quality Assurance Agency for Higher Education). Available at http://www.qaa.ac.uk/crntwork/benchmark/geography.pdf (accessed May 2004).

Smith, R. (2002) Sustainable learning, *Trumpeter, Journal of Ecosophy*, 18(1), pp. 07.1–7.8. Available at http://trumpeter.athabascau.ca/content/v18.1/smith.pdf (accessed August 2003).

Sterling, S. (2001) *Sustainable Education: Revisioning Learning and Change* (Bristol & Dartington: Schumacher Society & Green Books).

Sterling, S. (2002) A Baker's dozen—towards changing our loaf, *Trumpeter, Journal of Ecosophy*, 18(1), pp. 1–14. Available at http://trumpeter.athabascau.ca/content/v18.1/sterling.pdf (accessed August 2003).

Stevenson, R. (2002) Conclusion—education and sustainable development: perspectives and possibilities, in: D. Tilbury, R. B. Stevenson, J. Fien & D. Schreuder (Eds) *Education and Sustainability: Responding to the Global Challenge*, pp. 187–196 (Gland, Switzerland and Cambridge, UK: Commission on Education and Communication). Available at http://www.gse.mq.edu.au/units/sus_dev/ESDBook.pdf (accessed June 2004).

Thomas, I. & Nicita, J. (2002) Sustainability education and Australian universities, *Environmental Education Research*, 8(4), pp. 475–492.

Tikhonov, A. N., Sadovnichy, V. A. *et al.* (1995) *Geography: Program 'Universities of Russia' Block 2: Universities as Centres of Fundamental Research* (Moscow: Moscow University Publishing House).

Tilbury, D. (1999) Sustaining curriculum policy and development in environmental education: a European action research project, *European Environment*, 9(1), pp. 24–34.

Tilbury, D. & Goldstein, W. (2003) *Supporting the United Nations Decade on Education for Sustainable Development, 2005—2015* (Gland, Switzerland: International Union for the Conservation of Nature, Commission in Education and Communication). Available at http://www.lut.mah.se/nms/forskarnatverk/ESDstatementdoc6.pdf and http://www.iucn.org/cec/documents/ACF8B55.pdf (accessed September 2003).

Tilbury, D., Stevenson, R. B., Fien, J. & Schreuder, D. (Eds) (2002) *Education and Sustainability: Responding to the Global Challenge* (Gland, Switzerland & Cambridge, UK: IUCN Commission on Education and Communication), Available at http://www.gse.mq.edu.au/units/sus_dev/ESDBook.pdf (accessed June 2004).

ULSF (1990) *Programs: Talloires Declaration* (Washington, DC: Association of University Leaders for a Sustainable Future). Available at http://www.ulsf.org/programs_talloires.html (accessed July 2003).

ULSF (2004) *Global Higher Education Sustainability Toolkit*, Available at http://www.ulsf.org/toolkit/designframework.html (accessed May 2004).

UNUN (2003) Resolution 57/254. United Nations Decade of Education for Sustainable Development; Resolution adopted by the General Assembly. United Nations General Assembly, 57th Session, 21 February 2003, Agenda item 87 (a) 02 55612; Document: A/RES/57/254 (New York: United Nations). Available at http://www.unesco.ch/pdf/UNDekade.pdf (accessed August 2003)2003.

UNESCO (1977) *Tbilisi Declaration, Intergovernmental Conference on Environmental Education, 1977* (Paris: UNESCO). Available at http://www.gdrc.org/uem/ee/tbilisi.html (accessed August 2003).

UNESCO (2001) *The Lüneburg Declaration on Higher Education for Sustainable Development of 10 October 2001* (Paris: UNESCO), Available at http://www.unesco.org/iau/ghesp/LuneburgDeclarationFinal.html (accessed August 2003).

UNESCO (2002) *Ubuntu Declaration on Education and Science and Technology for Sustainable Development* (Paris: UNESCO). Available at http://www.unesco.org/iau/sd/unbutu.html#UBUNTU-Declaration (accessed August 2003).

Viederman, S. (2001) *Ecological Literacy: Can Colleges Save the World?* (Boston: Second Nature—Education for Sustainability Resource Guides). Available at http://www.secondnature.org/guides. . .y_writings_viederman.html (accessed May 2001).

WEF (2000) *Dakar Framework for Action: 'Education For All': Meeting Our Collective Commitments*, text adopted by the World Education Forum, Dakar, Senegal, 26–28 April 2000 (Paris: UNESCO). Available at http://www.unesco.org/education/efa/ed_for_all/dakfram_eng.shtml (accessed, August 2003).

World Conference on Education for All (1990) *Final Report of the World Conference on Education for All: Meeting Basic Learning Needs*, Jomtien, Thailand, 5–9 March 1990 (New York: Inter-Agency Commission (UNDP, UNESCO, UNICEF, World Bank)).

Environmental Education for Sustainable Development in Russia

N. S. KASIMOV, S. M. MALKHAZOVA & E. P. ROMANOVA

Introduction

Education, professional training and public information concerning environmental problems were recognized at the World Conference on the Environment in Rio de Janeiro (1972) and at the Summit in Johannesburg (2002) as among the prerequisites for the transition to sustainable development and for dealing with the problems of the future survival and prosperity of mankind. It is essential that key decision-makers and also a significant part of the general public have appropriate environmental knowledge. However, just 10 years ago there was no common understanding in Russia as to what kind of training was necessary for experts dealing with the diverse and complex problems of the interrelations between society and nature. Environmental education was not prescribed by legislation, although there have always been links between education in general, environmental education and education for sustainable development (ESD) (Kasimov *et al.*, 2002a, 2002b).

Creation of a System of Higher Environmental Education in Russia

Levels of Environmental Education

Sometimes it is said that we still do not have a system of environmental education in Russia, but it is not true (Kasimov *et al.*, 2002a). At present environmental education is an integral part of the triad 'Environmental upbringing, environmental education, and environmental training'. All its parts are closely interrelated and indispensable for the creation of environmental consciousness among the public, based on the awareness of the necessity to achieve the best possible state of the environment at global, regional and local levels. In practice, this means the necessity to optimize the interrelations in the 'society–nature' system by reducing or, whenever possible, eliminating harmful influences. It also means replacing existing waste-abundant and resource-exhausting technologies with low-waste and environmentally safe ones and creating social, legal and economic mechanisms providing for the sustainable existence of particular groups of the population (countries) and for mankind as a whole.

At present there are five basic levels of environmental education and training for the Russian population.

- The *Preparatory* level includes elements of pre-school environmental education.
- The *General* level is environmental education in primary and secondary schools and in non-specialized colleges, technical and higher schools.
- The *Specialized* level is environmentally oriented training in biological, geographical, agricultural, chemical and other faculties of universities.
- The *Special* level is the training of master's and postgraduate students in environmental specialities at classical and technical universities.
- The fifth level is the *retraining* of experts in the different branches of the environmental sciences (continuing professional development).

At each level there are specific requirements, purposes and approaches to the organization of environmental education. So, within higher schools it is obligatory to include special courses (for example, 'Ecology' or 'Nature Conservation') in the curricula; a number of general environmental and nature conservation subjects are compulsory at non-specialized technical schools, colleges and higher schools. More profound training is carried out in the natural sciences' faculties of the universities. According to the new state educational standards adopted by the Russian Federation Ministry of Education, the block of fundamental natural sciences disciplines includes 'Ecology' as an obligatory course, and for some specialities there is also a course in 'Nature Conservation' as well. However, it should be noted that environmental education remains a significant problem in Russian secondary schools.

Structure of Higher Environmental Education

According to the Law on Education approved by the State Duma of the Russian Federation, a multi-level system of environmental education is provided in Russian universities. This system is conceptually in line with the main principles of the European Union's Bologna Declaration on the organization of Higher Education.

In 1994 the Russian Ministry of Education approved two strands of environmental education, namely fundamental environmental education within the framework of both

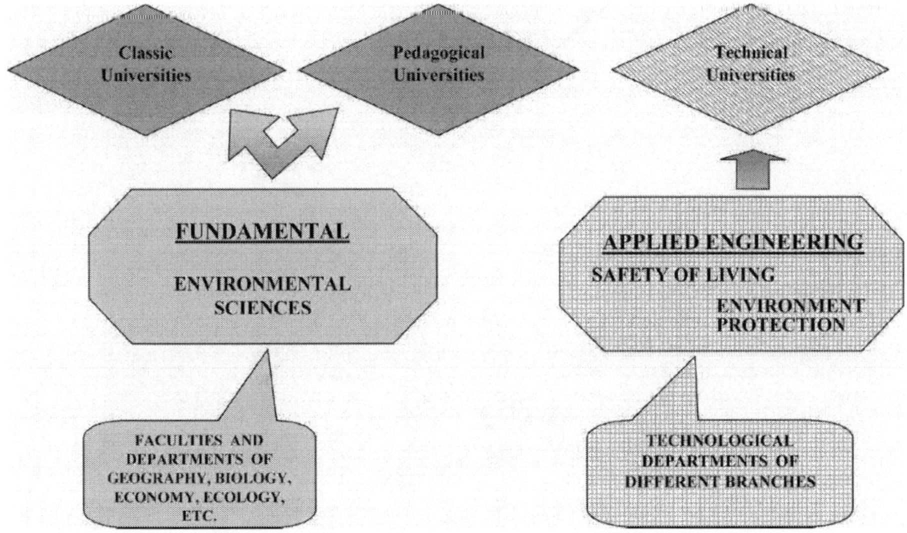

Figure 1. Fundamental and applied lines of higher environmental education in Russia

the natural and social sciences; and applied engineering environmental education delivered by technological colleges (Figure 1).

Fundamental environmental education is delivered by geographical, biological, economic, ecological and other faculties of state and private universities. The universities of the country train bachelor's and master's students in areas such as ecology, nature management, geoecology and bioecology (see below). Over 10 years the number of such departments and faculties has increased 15 to 20 times and by the end of 2003 about 130 Russian universities were training students in the environmental sciences (Figure 2).

Applied engineering environmental education is focused on the needs of various branches of the economy. In technical colleges there are two groups of specialities, i.e. Safety and Health (65 higher schools) and Environment Protection (also approximately 65 higher schools).

This article deals in more detail with the structure and the content of fundamental or classical environmental education, which is based on the following principles. The first is an interdisciplinary approach. Russian environmental education is in essence interdisciplinary as it is based on different spheres of education dealing with environmental problems, such as geography, biology, chemistry, geology, economics, law etc. This means it operates at the junction of the natural and social sciences. An interdisciplinary approach is essential for the training of experts who will be able to occupy professional positions in business, industry, management and academe, and to tackle problems related to the assessment of air, water and soil pollution and landscape deterioration, as well as the identification of a broad range of adverse factors affecting human and environmental health. The leading role of geography in the development of education for sustainable development in Russia is mainly due to its unique position at the interface between the natural and social sciences. Unlike other environmental sciences, geography already has a concept of nature management based on both physical-geographical and socioeconomic-geographical principles. Since the 1970s Russia's

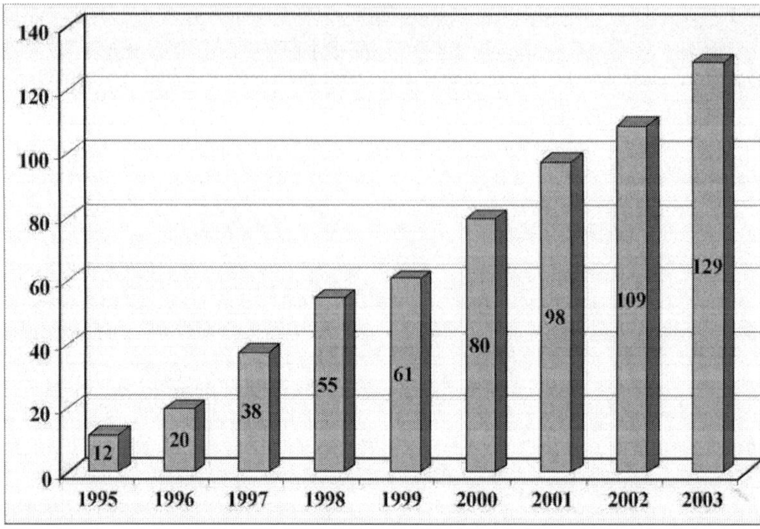

Figure 2. Number of RF universities providing training in Environmental Sciences. *Source*: Kasimov *et al.* (2002a, with additions)

traditional strength in physical geography has been complemented by a new emphasis on the discipline's environmental and human dimensions. This has provided a favourable basis for the development of ESD.

Second, the vast size of Russia and the diversity of its regions make it necessary to combine the federal and regional components of environmental education. The Federal component builds on the disciplines that are obligatory for all higher schools which are necessary for future environmentalists to master. It is a compulsory component of training accounting for about 50 per cent of the curriculum and includes basic courses in social sciences, mathematics, physics, chemistry, information science, general geography and ecology. Curricula and learning materials for the Federal component are developed by the Scientific Methodological Council on Environmental Education and Sustainable Development of the Educational Methodological Association for classical university education (see below). The regional component, accounting for another 50 per cent of the students' curricula, is specified by the individual universities themselves so that they can train experts able to solve local and regional problems in environmental management and protection.

In line with the modern multi-stage system of higher education, bachelors, specialists and masters are trained in four environmental sciences at Russian universities (Figure 3).

Ecology in a general sense deals with the functioning of ecosystems under economic stresses and the promotion of their sustainable development. It is an interdisciplinary science studying man-induced changes in the natural environment and the responses of the environment as a whole, and its abiotic components, to human impact.

Nature management deals with the problems of natural resources management and sustainable development. It focuses on a set of productive activities aimed at the utilization of natural resources in order to meet the needs of society. It also includes the management and control of these activities to prevent resource depletion and the adverse effects of

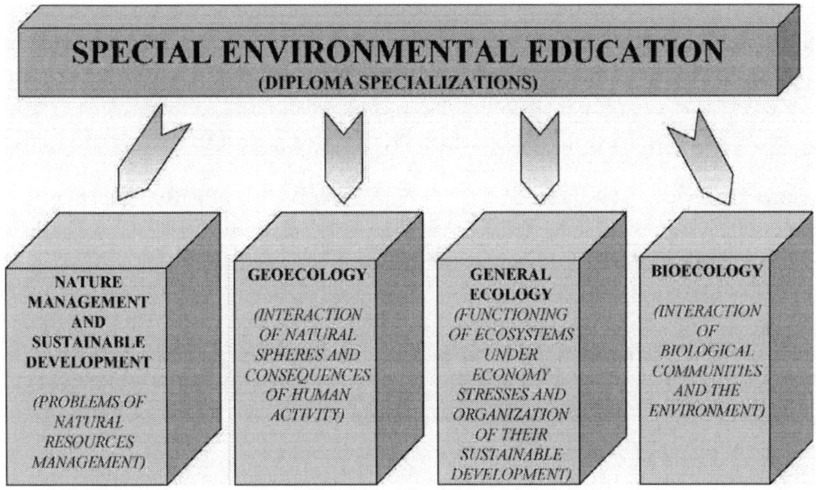

Figure 3. University specialities in Environmental Sciences

inappropriate resource utilization. As follows from this interpretation of nature management, the courses tend to operate at the junction between geography and economics.

Geoecology studies various human impacts on the environment and stems from the evolution and integration of a number of geographical, geological, pedological and related disciplines. Unlike proper traditional ecology, geoecology focuses on the interactions of society with the natural and transformed environment. It is a field of action for geographers, geologists, soil scientists etc.

Bioecology studies the interaction of biological communities and the environment and it is mainly the sphere of biologists.

In addition to these four main areas of environmental education, many fundamental sciences, including chemistry, physics, mathematics, biology, geology, geography, soil science etc., and also agricultural, medical, military and other sciences, have environmental sections in courses taught in dozens of universities across Russia.

Thus, it is safe to say that over the past decade an up-to-date system of higher environmental education has been created in Russia, which is implemented now at universities in all regions of the country.

Management of Environmental Education

Guidance on the curriculum and the elaboration of the state educational standards are provided by educational methodological associations (EMAs) created under the Russian Federation's (RF) Ministry of Education, (Kasimov *et al.*, 2002a). The largest of them is the EMA on classical university education headed by Moscow State University. The EMA comprises 20 scientific methodological councils which coordinate the content of education in particular sciences, such as mathematics, physics, chemistry etc. One of the councils supervises education in the field of environmental sciences; its members total about 100 professors drawn from all Russian universities training students in environmental sciences. About 4000–5000 ecologists, geoecologists and experts in nature management are graduated annually in Russia and, as we know, they are much needed in both public and private sector organizations in many parts of the Russian Federation.

From Environmental Education to Education for Sustainable Development (ESD)

The concept of Education for Sustainable Development calls for the transition from professional environmental training to an economically and socially focused model of education based on wide interdisciplinary knowledge and a complex approach to the development of society, economy and environment. This approach has been reflected in the Environmental Doctrine of Russia adopted in the autumn of 2002 by the Government of the Russian Federation. Decisions of the World Summit in Johannesburg and the Ministerial Conference on the Environment (Kiev, May 2003) suggest that education for sustainable development is to be considered among the basic priorities for the world community. The UN General Assembly has declared a Decade of Education for Sustainable Development beginning from 2005. However, at the same time, the level of environmental, cultural and social responsibility of the population is far behind the present-day challenges. To overcome this gap it is essential to update the existing education system and develop new education programmes in the field of sustainable development.

Given that the achievement of sustainable development is an integrated natural, social and economic target, education for sustainable development should also integrate natural, social and economic knowledge.

In accordance with the goals of sustainable development, the content of ESD also has three aspects (Figure 4):

- *Environmental*—protection of the integrity of ecosystems, the carrying capacity of the biosphere, biological diversity, and the quality of the environment.
- *Economic*—providing the imperative of sustainable development for economic management (efficient use of natural resources, strategic sustainable management of territories, resources and economic sectors).
- *Social*—education in the sphere of human rights, health, safety, conflict studies, ethnology, anthropology, etc.

Over recent years the authors have supervised and implemented several programmes aimed at the improvement of the system of environmental education. With support from the World Bank, the US Institute of Sustainable Communities (the Soros Foundation) and the GEF the leading professors at Moscow University have designed and introduced new courses with a strong emphasis on sustainability. These include the Economics of Nature Management, Nature Management, Environmental Auditing, Environment and Population Health Assessment, Evaluation and Conservation of Biological and Landscape Diversity, etc. Computer-based and published textbooks and manuals have been issued for these courses, which are incorporated into the federal educational standards.

Russia's Contribution to the Strategy of Education for Sustainable Development

As is widely acknowledged, the concept of sustainable development in its present-day understanding was formulated for the first time in the 1987 Report of the World

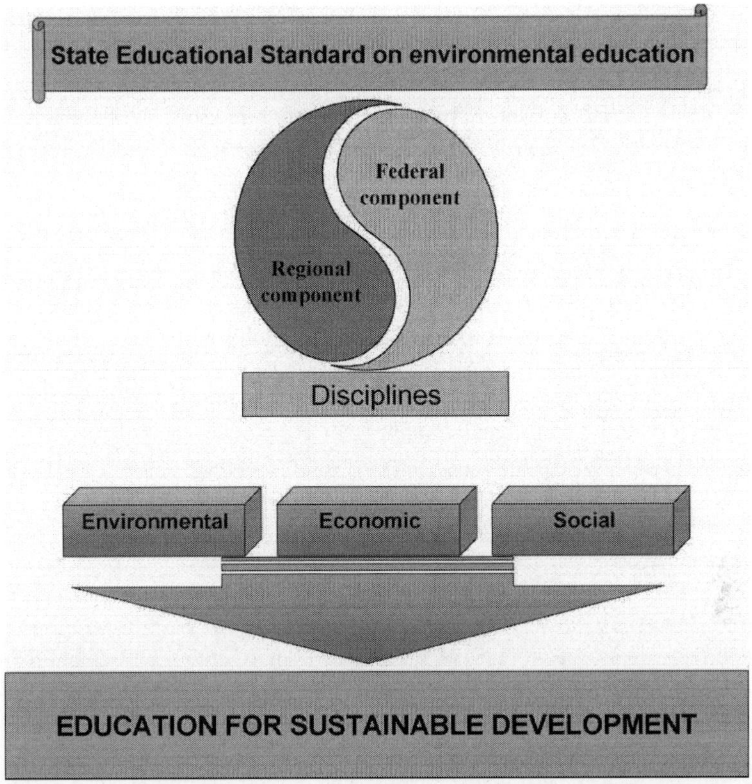

Figure 4. From environmental education to education for sustainable development. Transformation of federal and regional components of the State Educational Standard, increasing emphasis on environmental-economic and social disciplines

Commission on the Environment and Development (the Brundtland Commission). In 1992 it already appeared as a basic functional category in the Rio Declaration on the Environment and Development. At the same time the Brundtland Report said little about the theoretical basis and scientific preconditions of the concept of sustainable development. Taking into account the goals of the authors of the Report and the extremely short time available to them, the above-mentioned limitations should not be interpreted as serious shortcomings. Nevertheless, the question of the origin and nature of the concept of sustainable development is of indubitable academic and practical interest. In this connection it is useful to examine more attentively the theoretical achievements of Russian scientific schools in the environmental aspects of development and their contribution to the concept of sustainable development.

Of special interest in this context in Russia is the concept of nature management formed in the period from the mid-1960s to the early-1970s. Among the founders of the concept of nature management in our country was a remarkable Soviet scientist, David L. Armand, a physical geographer and landscape scientist engaged in the practical implementation of nature management principles. In 1964 he published his book significantly named *For Us and For Our Grandchildren*, which became for Soviet readers practically the equivalent of the Swiss Jean Dorst's *Before Nature Dies* for Western people.

The book *For Us and For Our Grandchildren* was the first one in Russian to put forward the scientific approach to use of natural resources as eternal values for the human community. In this way Armand's book is conceptually very close and in many respects even identical to the Brundtland Report 'Our Common Future'. Let us note that the very title of the book, which is its principal proposition stated and defended by the author, could be regarded as a brief and aphoristic interpretation of the concept of sustainable development: 'development which meets the needs of the present without compromising the ability of future generations to meet their own needs'.

This similarity is by no means accidental, as is shown in the last paragraph of the conclusion of the book *For Us and For Our Grandchildren*. Here Armand writes: "The moral duty of each generation is to leave more and better natural wealth to the next one than it has received from the previous one." As we see, the dominating idea is that of a fair distribution of natural resources in relation to our descendants.

Curiously, the above-mentioned statement of the Soviet scientist is almost repeated word for word in the Brundtland Report (*Our Common Future*). In the section 'Preservation and strengthening of resource base', we read: "It [protection of the environment] should be regarded as a part of our moral debt in relation to other people and the future generations." The similarity, both in meaning and in words, is quite evident. It will be remembered, however, that Armand's book was published 23 years before the Brundtland Report.

It is well known that the progress of ESD received particular attention at the Ministerial Conference 'Environment for Europe', which was held in May 2003. Among other major environmental problems in Europe it was stressed that the ideas of environmental education and education for sustainable development should penetrate educational systems and spheres at all levels—from elementary education to the professional retraining of experts and decision-makers. The Kiev Conference also called for the development and delivery of an ESD strategy. Within the framework of the UN Economic Commission for Europe, Russia together with Sweden supervised the elaboration of such a strategy. During 2004–2005 the emphasis is on the preparation of national concepts and action plans for the development of this line of education in European countries. In this process Russia represents the interests of transition economy countries and supported the adoption in the strategy of a range of dispositions, which take into consideration the economic situation and education traditions of Eastern European, Caucasian and Central Asian countries. The Representative of Russia (Prof. N.S. Kasimov), as one of the leading countries of this process, is the vice-chairman of the Task Force and the Working Group for strategy development.

Russia welcomes and contributes to this kind of international cooperation. Under the aegis of the RF Ministry of Education, in 2002 a project was implemented called, 'Development of a uniform system of integral social and economic indicators for a cycle of teaching disciplines on the sustainable development of territories using the UNECE experience' (the Project leader being Prof. Svetlana M. Malhazova). In the same year an International Conference on 'Environmental Education in Russia and Italy' was held in Italy, and in 2003 Russian–Italian summer schools on the problems of environmental education were organized in Russia and then in Italy.

These schools also gave attention to the examination of the ESD strategy in Great Britain, its experience being of considerable interest for the Russian experts. A Russian–British conference 'Environmental Education and Sustainable Development' was held in

Moscow in 2002 (Organizers: Faculty of Geography, Lomonosov Moscow State University, Dean Prof. Nikolay Kasimov and LTSN Subject Centre for Geography, Earth and Environmental Sciences, University of Plymouth, Director Prof. Brian Chalkley). The decisions and outcomes of the conference appeared to be very important for understanding the relationships between environmental education in Russia and the all-European educational space. The results of these activities have become the subject of several joint publications (Kasimov *et al.*, 2002a; LTSN-GEES, 2002). In 2003–2004 the project 'Environmental education for sustainable development in classical universities' (Project leader—Prof. Nikolay S. Kasimov) was implemented under the aegis of the British Embassy (Moscow) within the framework of the Environment Project Fund (http://www. geogr. msu.ru/ESD). The above-mentioned joint initiatives have all been aimed at the adoption of the European experience of environmental education and education for sustainable development and its possible application in Russian universities.

As a national leader of university education, Moscow State University (MSU) has already actively promoted the incorporation of ESD into existing educational systems and the coordination of activities in this sphere. In 2002 the Scientific-Methodological Council on Ecology was transformed into the Scientific-Methodological Council on Ecology and Sustainable Development. In late 2002 the all-Russia meeting 'Environmental Education for Sustainable Development' was held at Moscow State University to discuss the National Action Plan for ESD. This deals primarily with the use of available resources on environmental education and with ideas of nature management as a natural-scientific and economic-social basis for education in the field of sustainable development (Draft UNECE Strategy Education for Sustainable Development, 2003; Kasimov, Mazurov & Tikunov, 2003).

Ideas of sustainable development are being incorporated into many disciplines and courses by the method of so-called 'embedded education': the material in existing courses is used to provide a vehicle for teaching the ideas of sustainable development and is subsequently built up into independent educational blocks or courses in sustainable development.

In the Faculty of Geography of MSU, for example, a meeting of the Methodological Commission was held in July 2003 to discuss the integration of the sections on Sustainable Development into the programmes of the following courses: 'Fundamentals of Ecology', 'Natural and Recreation Resources of the World', 'Environmental Problems of the World Economy', 'Recreation Geography', 'Economy of Tourism with the Basics of Statistics', 'Tourism Marketing' and 'Geography of the Global Tourist Market'. The Commission examined the experience of the MSU Department of Socio-Economic Geography of Russia in the integration of Sustainable Development into general and specialist courses, such as 'Introduction to Geography' (for first-year students), 'Social and Economic Indicators of the Development of Countries and Regions' and 'Environmental Basis of National Production' (for second-year students), 'Economy of Nature Management' (for fourth-year students) and 'Ecology of a City' (for fifth-year students).

In late 2003 the group of experts of the MSU Faculty of Geography elaborated the addenda to the state educational standards and curricula of three existing environmental specialties. According to the addenda the subject 'Sustainable Development' should be included in the federal component of all three specialties and thereby become compulsory for the training of specialists in ecology, nature management and geoecology throughout the system of higher education in Russia.

Draft programmes outlining ESD curricula and materials were elaborated by the MSU professors and then offered to 120 universities. The universities, in their turn, submitted some ESD programmes and ideas of their own. All these teaching and learning materials are to be issued as a separate publication.

Throughout 2004 the MSU Faculty of Geography continued its work on extending and enhancing its ESD teaching. The work focused on changes in the content of summer field training and professional training of students. The general geographic field training of the first-year students at the Training and Research Station of the Faculty of Geography in the Kaluga oblast (the village of Satino) now deals with the issues of sustainable development of territories from the geoecological and socioeconomic points of view. For example, during geological-geomorphologic field training the students are given a number of tasks with the aim of assessing the environmental effects of certain economic activities (quarry operation, increase of arable lands, etc.) and of suggesting alternative methods for the implementation of sustainable development of a geographical area. The assessment should be based on practical knowledge of the area's geological-geomorphologic features and theoretical knowledge of relief dynamics and evolution. Particular attention is given to sustainable development issues during socioeconomic field training for students taking the programme on Regional Policy and International Tourism. They become aware of recent socioeconomic changes and the problems facing both private enterprises and the government authorities in the sphere of sustainable development at the regional level.

The specialized field training for second-year students also emphasizes issues regarding the sustainable development of territories. For example, these issues are discussed during field training in the MSU Departments of Nature Management, Socio-Economic Geography of Foreign Countries, Socio-Economic Geography of Russia, World Physical Geography and Geoecology, and many others.

To diversify educational provision and make use of modern scientific knowledge, including the theory of sustainable development, a programme of additional training and retraining of geography and geoecology specialists is now available at the MSU Faculty of Geography, i.e. The Geographical Basis of Sustainable Development. The start of the programme in November 2003 was preceded by the detailed design and elaboration of the curriculum (for details see http://www.geogr.msu.ru/ESD).

Contacts with other universities and the analysis of their curricula and learning materials have shown that the concept of sustainable development now forms an important element in the structure of education in practically all Russian universities. It is reasonably safe to suggest, therefore, that sustainable development has become a core part of teaching programmes within modern environmental education. The creation of a truly national strategy for ESD is among the major tasks for the years to come.

Conclusion

Although the achievements of Russia in the sphere of reducing environmental problems still fall short of many Western countries, progress in environmental education in Russia has already been rapid and reasonably successful. A characteristic feature of ESD in Russia is its derivation (in part) from the original concept of nature management elaborated by Russian geographers in the twentieth century and in particular from the work of David Armand.

There is an obvious interrelation between education in general, environmental education and education for sustainable development. It is evident that any true education, by definition, works to the benefit of sustainable development. It is also important that the introduction of ESD provides a unique opportunity for reviewing and strengthening education as a whole, especially in Russia. This realization provides an opportunity to incorporate ESD into modern training; a chance to reintegrate the post-Soviet educational space; and a chance to restore the traditional values of education as part of our culture and at the same time to introduce the most recent innovations in this sphere.

And, finally, a brief word on the question: 'Is it possible to develop ESD in a country like Russia with a rather unstable economic situation?' The evidence presented in this paper strongly suggests that substantial progress in ESD can be achieved. Indeed, the balanced sustainable development of a country and the ensuring of a sufficiently high quality of life for its population are possible only through education, which should acquire support at all levels, preserve its historic achievements and yet be permanently in a quest for progress. In relation to sustainability, this quest is urgent. Rapid and substantial changes are needed if education is to play its full role in the development of more sustainable economic and social systems. In Russia, our education system has now begun to address this task but there remains much to be done.

Acknowledgements

The authors wish to thank Prof. Brian Chalkey, Director of the UK's LTSN Subject Centre for Geography, Earth & Environmental Sciences, University of Plymouth, for collaboration and valuable suggestions on the first draft of this article.

References

Armand, D. L. (1964) *For Us and for Our Grandchildren* (Moscow: Mysl), [in Russian].

Dorst, J. (1970) *Before Nature Dies* (Boston: Houghton Mifflin).

Draft UNECE Strategy for Education for Sustainable Development (2004) available at http://www.unece.org/env/wgso/SustainableDevelopment/ESD/welcomeESD (accessed April 2004).

Kasimov, N. S., Malkhazova, S. M., Romanova, E. P. & Chalkley, B. (2002a) Environmental education in Russian universities, *Journal of Geography in Higher Education*, 26(2), pp. 149–157.

Kasimov, N. S., Malkhazova, S. M. & Romanova, E. P. (2002b) The role of Environmental Education for Sustainable Development in Russian Universities, *Planet*, 4, pp. 24–25.

Kasimov, N. S., Mazurov, J. L. & Tikunov, V. S. (2003) Vector of innovation: from environmental education to education for sustainable development, in: N. S. Kasimov & V. S. Tikunov (Eds) *Education for Sustainable Development: Materials of the All-Russia Meeting*, pp. 15–32 (Moscow: Smolensk), [in Russian].

Kasimov, N. S. & Tikunov, V. S. (Eds) (2003) *Education for Sustainable Development: Materials of the All-Russia Meeting* (Moscow: Smolensk), [in Russian].

LTSN-GEES (2002) Special Edition on Education for Sustainable Development, *Planet*, 4. Available at http://www.gees.ac.uk (accessed April 2004).

Mazurov, Yu. L. (2003) Education for sustainable development, its contents and macrostructure, *Vestnik Mosk.Un-ta*, Ser. 5 Geography, No 4, pp. 3–9 [in Russian].

An Environmental Education Concept for Galtür, Austria

ANGELA MICHIKO HAMA, MICHAEL SEITZ, ANJA SANSONE
& JOHANN STÖTTER

Introduction

The village of Galtür is a small Alpine community, located 1600 m above sea level in the Paznaun valley, Tyrol. Originally a rural and agricultural settlement, the village has undergone tremendous socioeconomic and ecological changes in the last century. As elsewhere in the Eastern Alps, these changes were mainly triggered by the growing economic wealth in Europe and the onset of mass tourism in the 1950s (Bätzing, 2003). The transformation of the village into a ski and hiking resort with agriculture as a minor sideline reflects the shift from farming to service industry as the main source of income. Today, Galtür is characterized by a monostructural economy, which is based solely on tourism. However, the community has always pursued its own course and tries to keep tourist activities and infrastructure from growing uncontrollably. In 1976, the population of Galtür

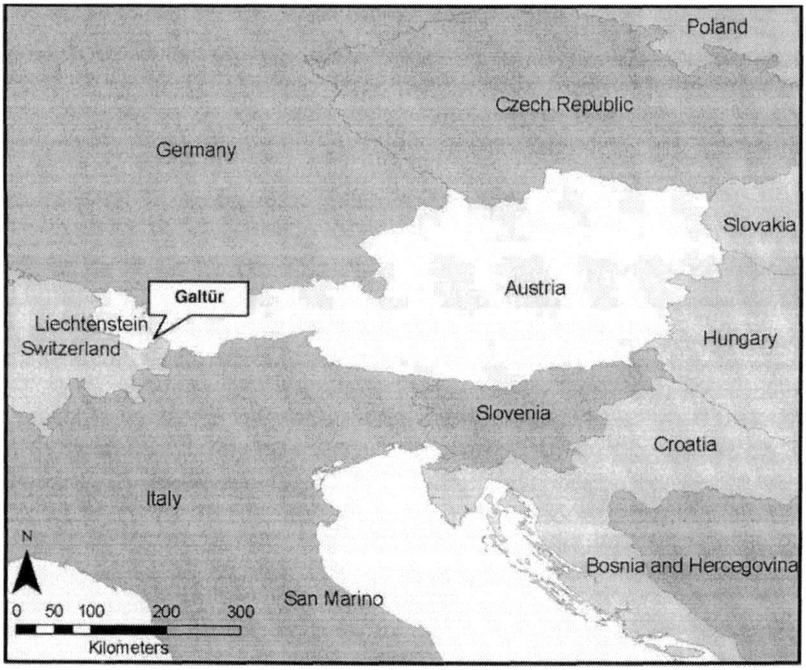

Figure 1. Geographical location of Galtür. (*Source*: ESRI)

voted against the establishment of a glacier ski resort on Jamferner, one of their community-owned glaciers, which was a unique decision at the times and made way for a more gentle and sustainable form of tourism (Lorenz, 1999). Galtür therefore differs considerably from ski resorts like Ischgl or Sölden, whose primary goal is economic benefit (Figure 1).

In February 1999, the village of Galtür gained tragic publicity worldwide, after it had been hit by an avalanche of catastrophic dimensions with 31 fatalities. Extraordinary meteorological conditions characterized the winter of 1998–1999, and record amounts of snow led to numerous avalanche events all over the Alps, cumulating in the avalanche catastrophe at Galtür (Mair, 2000) on 23 February. Before the disaster, the whole valley had been cut off from the outside world, which had made prior evacuation of the settlements impossible. Owing to adverse weather, rescue efforts were hampered by complications. The damage to persons and infrastructure was immense. In addition to the 31 fatalities, 11 people were injured and property damage ranged around €5 million (Heumader, 2000). The direct effects on the tourism industry were devastating, especially as the winter season accounts for an average of 70 per cent of overnight stays. The number of visitors slumped to virtually zero in the weeks after the avalanche event, and a drop of more than 20 per cent in overnight stays was recorded for the winter season of 1998–1999 (Stötter *et al.*, 2002a). The following winter and summer seasons showed a significant upswing, but the total long-term impact on the reputation of the resort cannot be anticipated. To date, Galtür has not fully recovered from the shock, in both an emotional and a financial sense.

In the immediate aftermath of the avalanche disaster, a set of security measures was devised, which have been carried out since the summer of 1999. Even though the recurrence probability of the Galtür avalanche is said to be longer than 150 years, additional avalanche fences are under construction in the starting zones of avalanche-prone mountain faces, and new galleries and tunnels have been built for the main road in the Paznaun valley. An avalanche dam (of almost 400 m in length) has been erected to protect Galtür from future avalanches (Gemeinde Galtür, 2000). The dam was designed as a building, housing an underground garage, a civil defence centre and the 'Alpinarium'. The latter institution reflects the change in perception of natural hazards, which was triggered by the catastrophe. This led to the wish to establish an institution that focuses on the interaction between people and the Alpine environment and aims to contribute to sustainable development. The Alpinarium comprises an exhibition centre, an academy that offers seminars on Alpine issues, and is a meeting place for local inhabitants and tourists. So far, a small exhibition has opened as a pilot project, but in 2005, the Tyrolean state exhibition (Tiroler Landesausstellung) with the provisional title 'The future of nature' will take place in the Alpinarium. The state exhibition will draw up scenarios of future strategies for life in the Alps. In this study, an environmental education concept with an emphasis on geography and sustainability is being developed in order to render the Alpinarium a unique environmental education centre that sets an example in Austria's west (Figure 2).

The Institute of Geography of the University of Innsbruck and the alpS Centre for Natural Hazard Management are conducting this project in cooperation with the Alpinarium Dokumentation GmbH Galtür. Some 60 per cent of the €400,000 budget is funded by public authorities; the remaining 40 per cent is company-funded. Four postgraduate geographers are working full time on the development of the environmental education concept for a maximum duration of 29 months. Their work

Figure 2. View of the Alpinarium. *Source*: Seitz

and the Alpinarium as a whole illustrates the way in which geography and geographers can play an important role in promoting the public understanding of sustainability and environmental issues.

Reasons for and Goals of the Environmental Education Concept

Global change is an ecological, economic, social and political issue, with both society and nature contributing to all aspects of these changes. Omnipresent in all spheres of life, global change has a high impact on every individual and ought to be of great concern to society. For example, the number of disasters caused by natural hazard events (Munich Re Group, 2002), such as the drought of 2003 and the floods of 2002 in Europe, are increasing at an intimidating speed. Therefore, management strategies have to be developed with regard to a sustainable future.

Agenda 21 deals with the problems of global change and calls for sustainable development in ecological, economic and social terms (United Nations, 1992). The Agenda acknowledges the importance of high mountain regions and devotes chapter 13 to them: 'Managing Fragile Ecosystems: Sustainable Mountain Development'. Two programme areas were agreed upon (United Nations, 1992; Funnel & Parish, 2001):

1. Generating and strengthening knowledge about the ecology and sustainable development of mountain ecosystems.
2. Promoting integrated watershed development and alternative livelihood opportunities.

Thus, Agenda 21 strengthens the case for securing the Alpine environment in a sustainable way and providing the public with knowledge concerning mountain-related global change issues. Furthermore, Chapter 36 of Agenda 21 advocates promoting education, public awareness and training, and its programme areas include reorienting education towards sustainable development and increasing public awareness (United Nations, 1992). The 2002 World Summit on Sustainable Development in Johannesburg reaffirmed the importance of education for sustainable development, which led to it adopting the 'United Nations Decade for Sustainable Development 2005–2014' (UNESCO, 2002). On account of this, environmental education in the Alps is to be considered essential and has to be made a top priority, especially as the Alps have always been of global interest due to their natural and cultural diversity and are presently the number one tourist destination worldwide. Geography should play a more important role in disseminating knowledge and creating environmental awareness and responsibility for this area. Its manifold aspects make it an integrative discipline, and so geography can contribute substantially to environmental education and education for sustainable development by 'going public' with the results and conclusions from geographical research (Figure 3).

As often postulated, global change research needs to become the core and trendsetting topic of academic geography curricula. This issue has to be addressed in geography teaching programmes in further and higher education, and students need to be trained as 'future multipliers', too. The environmental education concept of Galtür incorporates an academic programme, which also aims at providing skills on dissemination and raising public awareness.

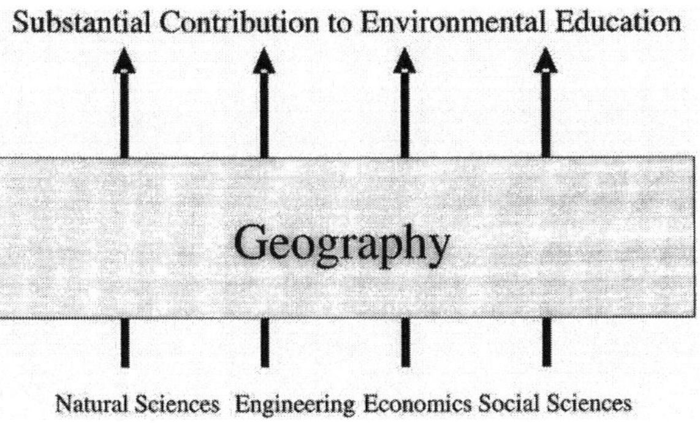

Figure 3. The integrative nature of geography

The Alpinarium intends to implement Agenda 21 on a local level. Mountain communities like Galtür often experience global change at first hand. They are at higher risk of being affected by natural hazards resulting from a rapidly changing human environment and from climate change processes (Stötter *et al.*, 2002b). The geographical and historical situation of Galtür enables the Alpinarium to exemplify global change processes and highlight strategies for sustainable development in the Alps. Moreover, the community's attention, which is a precondition for any successful Local Agenda, was called to these issues after the avalanche catastrophe of 1999. By implementing a fully-fledged environmental education programme based on Agenda 21, public consciousness can be raised and a change in attitudes towards the Alpine environment initiated. In addition, the Alpinarium and its environmental education concept intend to attract a new clientele of tourists and thereby diversify Galtür's economy. This might be strategic for a sustainable future for the village.

In order to communicate and operationalize the ideas of Agenda 21 comprehensibly and effectively in the context of the Alps, the environmental education concept needs to concentrate on a manageable number of themes. As potential themes are numerous, it was necessary to employ a selection modus, which is based on six equally important principles. The themes under consideration have to be target-group oriented, should have an interdisciplinary character, need to be relevant to current affairs and issues, and must regard the spatial context. Moreover, the themes have to be experience-based and also feasible. These principles were chosen as they are all prerequisites for arousing people's interest in a specific topic (Haubrich *et al.*, 1997). Interdisciplinarity makes it possible to approach themes from different points of view. If a theme does not connect to current affairs and issues as well as personal experiences, it is unlikely to be significant for environmental educational matters. Naturally, the implementation of a theme needs to be accomplishable, and a theme must include narrative aspects to be teachable. The spatial context is especially noteworthy for the environmental education concept developed for Galtür, because a connection to the region and its landmarks is essential (Figure 4).

Having met all six requirements, four themes were shortlisted. These were the fields of natural hazards, water, biodiversity and, finally, a complex of farming, tourism and traffic. Additionally, an extensive literature compilation of more than 5000 titles was conducted, which had the highest 'hit rates' for these four themes. Thus, the literature compilation supports the choice of topics. The themes, selected on a preliminary basis, reflect issues

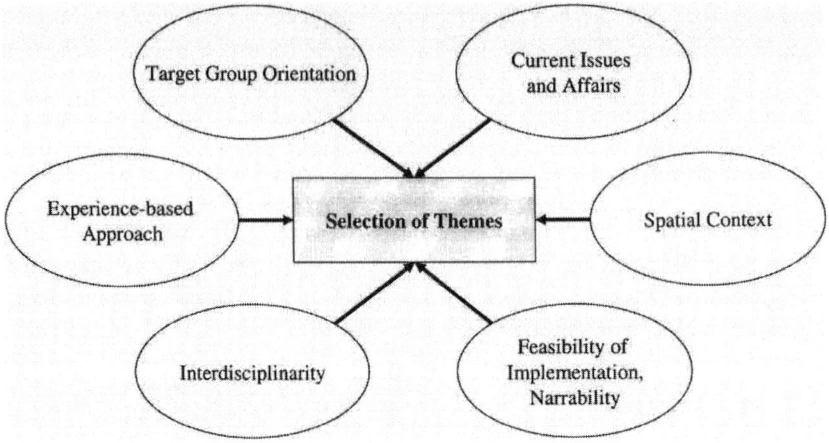

Figure 4. Selection modus for themes

that are of great concern for the population of the Alps and the future development of this mountain region. By dealing with themes of this kind in the environmental education concept of the Alpinarium, it should be possible to implement some of the aspects of Agenda 21 and contribute to a sustainable future for the Alps.

The Environmental Education Concept and its Research Methodology—How Can the Goals be Reached?

The environmental education concept must endorse the idea of holism, be unique, be tailored to the needs of the Alpinarium and has to disseminate the vision of sustainable development in the Alps. Incorporating the two main protagonists of environmental education, the approach analyses and evaluates society and landscape with a blend of geographical and sociological, as well as pedagogic and didactic methods. The intertwining and adaptation of ideas and methodologies from various disciplines renders the concept integrative and innovative. Additionally, new methods are being developed and applied for the first time in the course of concept development. It is hoped that the concept as a whole will become standardized and thus transferable to other Alpine regions.

The approach is split into three integral parts, comprising the analysis and evaluation of the educational potential of the Alpine landscape, the educational interest in the landscape and implementation strategies. These three studies give answers to the central research problem, which is: 'What *can* society, what does society *want to,* and what *should* society learn from the Alpine landscape?'

The assessment of the Alpine landscape of Galtür with regard to its educational value deals with the 'can' side of the question and takes the importance of the spatial context into account. The recording and analysis of the educational interest of society in Alpine landscapes illuminates the 'want' side, gaining insight into people's wishes, expectations and needs concerning the Alpine environment. Combining the results of the potential of and interests in the landscape and including aspects of current environmental issues as well as logistical matters will lead to the development of implementation strategies. These

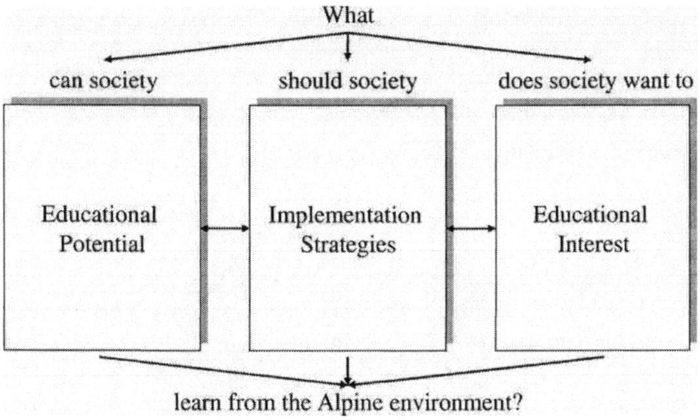

Figure 5. The three pillars of the enviornmental education concept for Galtür

address the last aspect, the 'should' side of the research problem. The three pillars introduced above constitute the framework of the environmental education concept of the Alpinarium (Figure 5)

Some basic principles of the environmental education concept originate from various fields of research, such as general didactics, applied and regional geography, pedagogy and psychology. The 'Hamburg Model' provides the didactic guidelines for the environmental education concept (Schulz, 1981, in Gudjons, 1999). Originally developed for classroom teaching, this successful didactic theory is transferred to the environmental education sector for the first time (according to our knowledge). It had to be altered only slightly in order to meet the requirements of the more outdoor-based learning environment of the Alpinarium. Following Schulz (1981), four factors are essential for successful and interesting teaching of knowledge and skills: goals, students' backgrounds (i.e. abilities, interests and experiences), content, and the methods and media. By setting the transmission of the sustainability idea as the main goal and analysing the public interest in the landscape, the factors 'goals' and 'background' are incorporated into the environmental education concept of the Alpinarium. Assessing the educational value of the Alpine landscape contributes to identification of the contents, and the development of implementation strategies allows for the application of methods and media appropriate for environmental education. Additionally, the idea of inductive and deductive teaching procedures, dating back to Comenius (Gudjons, 1999), can be taken up in an ideal way, as the landscape and science centre are adjacent to each other and interlinked.

A field of application of regional geography is heritage interpretation. This approach tries to 'translate' research results in the field of natural and cultural heritage into a comprehensible language by provoking thought, and by revealing and relating the attractions of a site (Carter, 2001; Gee *et al.*, 2002). Heritage interpretation is conducive to the advancement of tourism based on experiences of nature, the identification of the local population with their natural and cultural environment, and the promotion of ecological and social issues (Lehnes & Glawion, 2000). The ideas of heritage interpretation, which try to bring landscape to life, serve as a basis for the environmental education concept. In this study, the approach is being further developed and its actual interpretation procedures are specified. Although the existing procedures convey the importance of the analysis of landscape and of potential visitors, as well as bearing teaching practices in mind, they still lack elaborate didactic elements and more precise tools for the analysis and evaluation of landscape and society. In addition, the procedures have to comply with the distinctiveness of the Tyrolean Alps. Finally, the fundamentals of pedagogic psychology (e.g. Mietzel, 1998; Tücke 1998; Edelmann, 2000), environmental psychology (e.g. Kaplan & Kaplan, 1989; Kaplan *et al.*, 1998) and pedagogics (e.g. Blankertz, 1982; Kron, 1991; Gudjons, 1999) play a vital role in forming the principles of the environmental education concept of the Alpinarium.

In the following section, the three pillars of the concept for Galtür will be described in more detail, addressing their inherent principles, methods and expected results. First, the educational potential and its underlying evaluation method will be explained; second, the procedure for analysing the educational interest of the people will be introduced, and third, the process of developing implementation strategies for the Alpinarium will be outlined.

Educational Potential

The educational potential is defined as the informative value and meaningfulness of a landscape in respect of educational issues. Its analysis and evaluation represent key elements of the environmental education concept. The study provides answers to the questions 'What *can* society learn from the Alpine landscape?' and 'What are the educational values of the Alpine landscape?'. In order to examine this landscape adequately, a tool for the assessment of its educational potential is being developed and applied. The method draws on aspects of physical and human geography, landscape ecology, spatial planning and didactics, and allows for the inclusion of logistical factors (Figure 6).

This study endeavours to reveal the characteristics and processes of the Alpine landscape of Galtür, as the spatial context is most relevant for environmental education purposes. Most existing environmental education institutions do take the role of landscape into consideration but there are still major deficits in thorough landscape screening as the prerequisite for scientifically and pedagogically sound environmental education concepts (Giesel *et al.*, 2002). This screening process needs to encompass diverse aspects of the biotic and abiotic environments in order to capture the essence of a place (Carter, 2001).

Landscape evaluation for land-use options has its roots in geography and is nowadays an established field in landscape ecology, too. Two approaches, the potential concept and the function concept, deal with the assessment of various values of landscape.

The term 'potential' was introduced by Bobek & Schmithüsen (1949; in Bastian, 1997). Neef (1969) developed it further, and it was his idea to determine the overall potential of a region. This generalized approach was operationalized by differentiating the potential into several partial potentials, which include the biotic yield potential, water supply potential, waste disposal potential, biotic regulation potential, geoenergetic potential and recreation potential (Haase, 1978; Bastian & Schreiber 1999; Bastian & Steinhardt, 2002). All of these natural potentials "characterize the totality of landscape attributes with regard to a possible utilization by human society" (Bastian & Steinhardt, 2002, p. 214).

The second approach is concerned with the functional qualities of landscape. De Groot (1992, p. 7) defines these functions of the natural and cultural environment as: "the capacity of natural processes and components to provide goods and services that satisfy human needs (directly and/or indirectly)". He classifies the functions into four main categories,

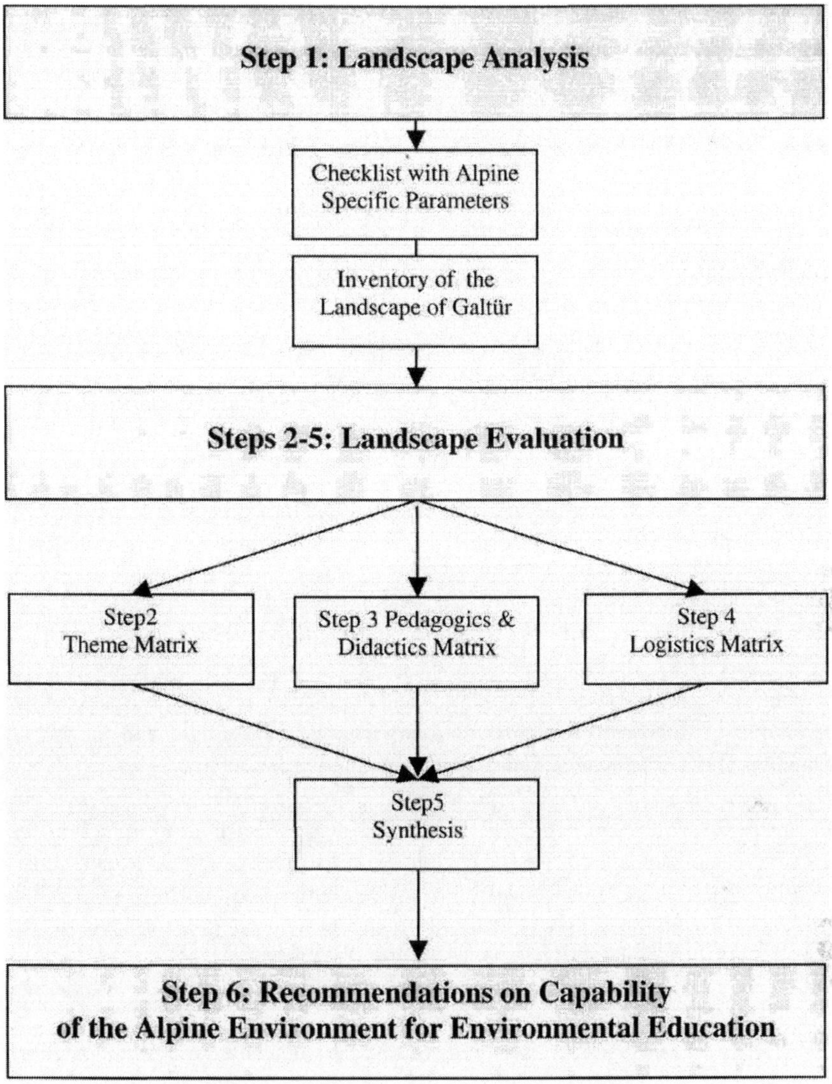

Figure 6. Tool for analysing and assessing the educational potential of the Alpine environment

called regulation functions, carrier functions, production functions and information functions. The latter include the function of providing educational and scientific information. Similar classifications for landscape functions are provided by, for example, Marks *et al.*, (1989); Grabaum (1998); and Bastian & Schreiber (1999). Even though most function classifications include educational functions, no explicit methods for the evaluation of this functional aspect of nature have been devised up to the present.

The function approach can be understood as a more function-oriented view of the landscape, while the potential approach is more natural resource-oriented. However, both concepts engage with the idea of characterizing the capability and usability of a landscape. The terms 'potential' and 'function' are, therefore, interchangeable, and a mixture of both concepts forms the theoretical background of the method developed for the Alpinarium. The term 'educational potential' was deduced from these two concepts and created while developing the environmental education concept for the village of Galtür.

As mentioned above, no studies concerned with the precise analysis and evaluation of the educational value have been conducted so far. Moreover, only a few studies in landscape research deal with the special evaluation requirements of Alpine regions, with most of these studies examining the recreational potential or function (cf. Degenhardt, 1980; Dollinger, 1998). Therefore, a new method to analyse and evaluate the educational potential of Alpine landscapes needs to be developed. On the one hand, it has to consider the unique features of this specific landscape type; on the other hand, aspects of other evaluation methods in landscape ecology ought to be adapted and incorporated. Furthermore, it has to be applicable on a mesoscale level.

The following procedure for analysing and evaluating the educational value of the Alpine landscape was developed. It comprises six steps, ranging from defining parameters to decision-making (Riedel & Lange, 2001).

- *Analysis.* In a first step, a general checklist of Alpine-specific parameters with geographical relevance is generated. The checklist includes the categories geomorphological processes and features, rock, water, soil and vegetation, as well as land use and infrastructure, and ensures the integrative approach of the method. These categories are further differentiated, which leads to a total of *c*. 50 parameters. On the basis of the checklist, an inventory of the landscape of Galtür is made, using thematic maps, aerial photos, orthophotos and digital data on various aspects of the community. Additionally, missing data are mapped in the field and the whole collection of data are managed, visualized and analysed in a GIS.
- *Evaluation.* Steps two to five represent the phase of evaluating the landscape characteristics with regard to their educational value. Attributing values to the descriptive parameters is considered the crucial step in landscape assessments, as the scientific findings are transformed to social categories (Poschmann *et al.*, 1998; Bastian and Steinhardt, 2002). In this study, matrices are used for the evaluation, and an ordinal point scale with five ranks is applied.
    - *Themes.* In step two, each parameter is evaluated with reference to the themes outlined above;
    - *Didactics and pedagogics.* In step three, the parameters are assessed according to didactic and pedagogic criteria. These criteria incorporate, among others, age groups of students, activity forms and social forms in the context of teaching (e.g. games, experiments, group work), and teaching principles such as student orientation and science orientation (Apel & Seibert, 1996; Haubrich *et al.*, 1997);
    - *Logistics.* Step four evaluates the parameters with regard to logistics, such as accessibility, time requirements, activities (e.g. walking, bicycle riding, mountaineering) as well as meteorological and seasonal requirements. By applying thematic and pedagogic/didactic criteria, the theoretical educational potential of the landscape can be assessed. The actual educational potential can, however, only be extracted when logistical factors are included;
    - *Synthesis.* In the fifth step, the results from the previous three evaluation steps are synthesized and verbally interpreted. Moreover, the whole evaluation phase is analysed in a GIS, in order to be able to test different options.

Decision-making. Finally, recommendations on the capacity of the Alpine landscape of Galtür for educational usage can be given in step six and then implemented.

This tool will deliver important results for the environmental education concept of Galtür, and it reflects the importance of basic research in the field of environmental education. With the method being divided into a manageable number of six steps, it is easy to apply and handle. By combining qualitative and quantitative evaluation modes, the results become more significant. Even though objectivity can never be reached when individuals assess a landscape, intersubjectivity is guaranteed in this case (Günther, 1998), as all phases are documented and comprehensible. The multicriteria-multistep procedure satisfies the requirements of modern spatial planning, takes the complexity of landscapes into account, and incorporates some aspects of the Analytic Hierarchy Process as well as cost-benefit analyses (Poschmann *et al.*, 1998). Furthermore, it specifies some of the procedures of heritage interpretation. Above all, the approach singles out the most relevant characteristics of the Alpine landscape in matters of global change and sustainability. Thus, it obtains its educational value and provides answers to the question 'What *can* society learn from the Alpine landscape?' raised in the environmental education concept described above.

Educational Interest

The analysis of the educational interest in the landscape constitutes the second pillar of the environmental education concept, whereby the term 'educational interest' is defined as the natural interest of a person to gain insight into various facets of the world and, thus, to acquire skills (Klafki, 1964; Blankertz, 1975). In this study, the educational interest in the Alpine landscape is recorded by applying methods from the social sciences. The primary objective is to answer the question 'What does society *want to* learn from the Alpine landscape?'.

The environmental education concept of the Alpinarium aims to orientate itself to the interests, needs, wishes and characteristics of its potential visitors. Therefore, a comprehensive study is needed on the recipient side of the concept. As with the educational potential, the educational interest is often not studied in depth while planning an environmental education facility. However, building a portrait of potential visitors is essential for fulfilling public expectations and avoiding serious mistakes in the development process of a concept (Carter, 2001). Recording the educational interest in the Alpine landscape fills, as mentioned, the factor 'background' in the didactic theory of Schulz (1981) and is fundamental for applying appropriate didactic and pedagogic methods when developing implementation strategies (Figure 7).

So far, no studies that focus explicitly on the educational interest in a specific landscape type or region exist. Yet, numerous studies deal either with the analysis of social structures and behaviour patterns of outdoor-oriented tourists, or assess the demand for recreational facilities in tourist regions (see Brugger, 1988; Bacher, 2002; Freytag & Hoyler, 2002). Moreover, investigations into landscape perception and assessments of the beauty of landscapes are common (e.g. Engelhardt & Weinzierl, 1976; Fairweather & Swaffield, 2002; Yamashita, 2002; De Groot & Van den Born, 2003). These findings serve as a basis for this study, as they illuminate some aspects of the attitudes of society towards nature.

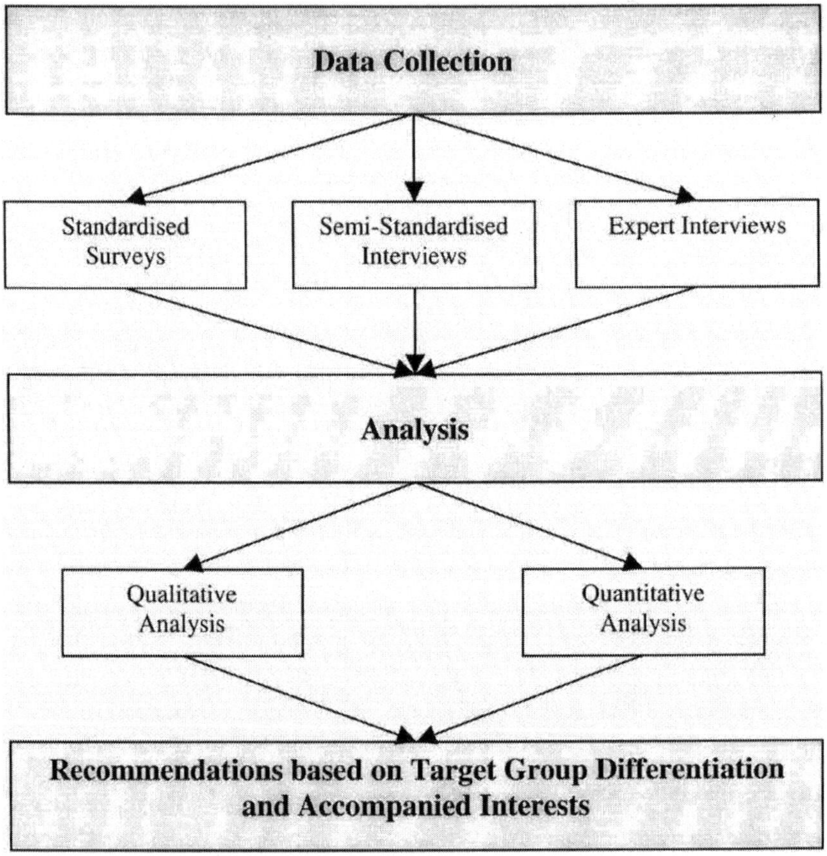

Figure 7. Method of recording educational interest in the environment

No new investigation tool needs to be developed for recording the educational interest in the Alpine landscape. Instead, established methods of empirical social research are applied and adapted to the requirements of the environmental education concept. Great emphasis is laid on the application of many different methods, in order to prevent statistical falsification of data, such as age, origin or activities of interviewees. In addition, significant correlations that were hitherto unknown can be identified by using a variety of methods (Friedrichs, 1990; Schnell *et al.*, 1992; Kromrey, 1994).

The following tools were used to collect data:

- First, a standardized questionnaire was distributed in representative accommodation facilities in the community of Galtür.
- Second, semi-standardized interviews were conducted to detect the behaviours and predilections of tourists.
- Third, a survey was launched in the Alpinarium to examine visitors' attitudes towards the Alpinarium.
- Fourth, expert interviews were conducted with individuals who represent key positions for the study. This non-standardized method helps to gather additional information, e.g. on trends and tendencies in the village and the Alpinarium.

Naturally, the educational interest cannot be defined by these methods directly. Therefore, it is necessary to deduce and interpret it from questions such as 'How do you spend your holiday?' or 'What do you expect from an exhibition with the motto "The future of nature—future life strategies"?'. In the course of the study, the survey questions needed to be revised to match the different requirements of the summer and winter seasons.

The pilot phase has now been completed and some first tendencies can already be determined. For example, people who were asked what made their holiday enjoyable answered that nice weather, peace, friendly people and fun excursions contributed to a successful holiday. These factors are also vital for a functioning environmental education concept. Furthermore, the pilot showed that most interviewees were informed about the avalanche disaster of 1999, and expressed a wish to know more about natural hazards in general and the Galtür avalanche in particular. This fact supports the preliminary selection of themes presented earlier. In addition, it indicates that the public is indeed interested in issues of global change and sustainability and also willing to acquire more knowledge, provided the information is presented in an appealing and subtle manner. Once the analyses of the results are complete, target groups with their respective interests, needs and wishes will be defined. The target groups will be carefully differentiated, since the environmental education concept intends to offer programmes for target groups from children of kindergarten age to university lecturers. This will contribute to a high outreach and multiplier effect. Finally, recommendations based on the interests of people in the Alpine landscape can be made for the environmental education concept.

Implementation Strategies

The final part of the environmental education concept is devoted to providing answers to the question 'What *should* society learn from the Alpine landscape?'. By combining and comparing the results of the previous two studies in a matrix and taking current issues relevant to Agenda 21 as well as logistics into account, the actual educational task can be deduced. This leads to the development of implementation strategies (Figure 8).

Elaborating implementation strategies is crucial for any effective environmental education concept, because the strategies are responsible for the success of the institution and its programmes. In addition to incorporating the results of the studies on the educational potential of the Alpine landscape and the educational interest of society in the landscape, this study needs to investigate further aspects of environmental education. Adequate teaching methods and media are to be applied, in order to put the principles of sustainability into practice efficiently. On the one hand, these methods and media have to highlight the information provided by the landscape, on the other hand, they ought to match the different target groups. The implementation strategies are intended to combine hands-on experience with outdoor activities and to enhance the environmental education concept with fun and adventure elements, as this fosters intrinsic motivation (Bolscho *et al.*, 1994; Beyersdorf *et al.*, 1998).

A range of existing environmental education centres, programmes and nature trails is being assessed. Priority is given to institutions in the Alps but facilities elsewhere are also being evaluated. To date, most of these centres either disregard the spatial context or the needs and interests of potential visitors, and the lack of didactic and pedagogic

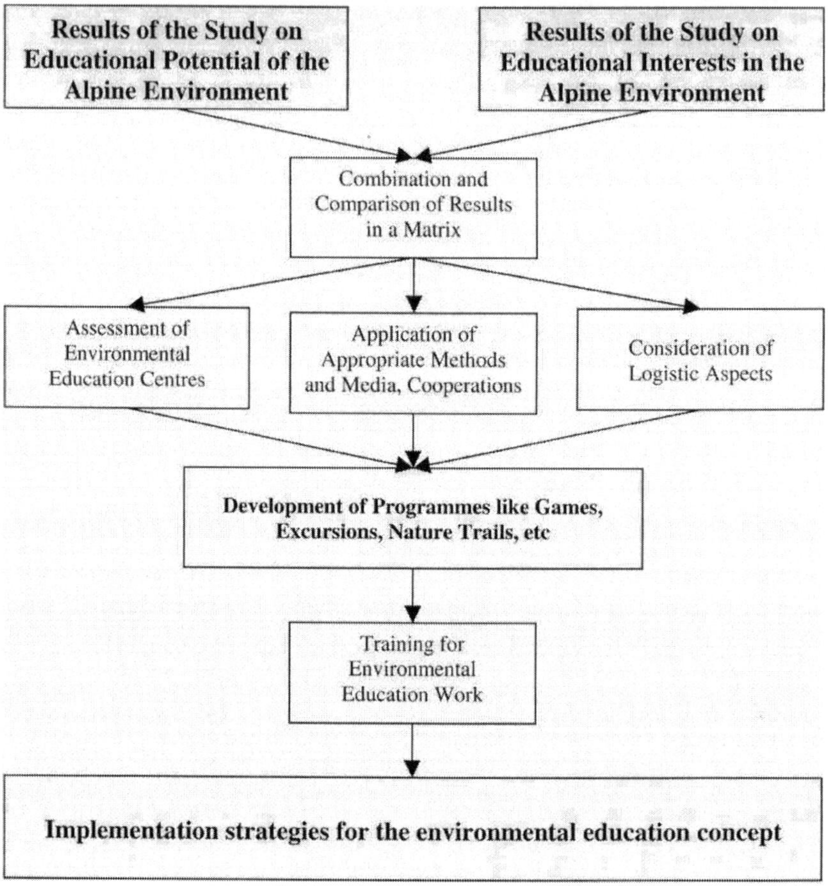

Figure 8. Implementation strategies.

principles is often evident. Moreover, successful teaching methods are being compiled and adapted to the special requirements of the Alpinarium (e.g. Kessler & Krätzschmar, 1993; Gudjons, 1998; Meyer, 2003). On the logistical side, a survey has been launched in the Tyrol, which records the requests of teachers and students concerning environmental education programmes. Furthermore, coordination with potential partners on both the scientific side and practice-oriented side has begun. Scientific institutions, such as avalanche institutes, are able to provide additional expert knowledge, while organizations like the Alpine Clubs can pass on their practical experience. Collaborating with both sides is most relevant, as one aim of the environmental education concept of Galtür is to link science and practice. Once innovative programmes, such as games, seminars, nature trails and excursions, have been developed for the target groups of the Alpinarium, local residents will be trained for environmental education work, because it benefits the community and the concept most if people from the region are involved in the Alpinarium. All these tasks need to be performed with regard to their relevance and aptitude to disseminating knowledge and skills regarding sustainability and global change issues.

Outlook

The Alpinarium in Galtür intends to offer interesting and innovative environmental education programmes. The environmental education concept is a promising approach to implementing Agenda 21, and especially Chapter 13, on a local level. The theoretical framework of this concept has been fully designed but it will always remain susceptible to alterations that might become necessary during the period of the project. The studies on the educational potential, educational interest and implementation strategies are in progress. On the basis of these results and further findings, there will be two test-runs of the environmental education programmes. The finalized version of the environmental education concept will commence in May 2005, as this is also the opening date of the Tyrolean state exhibition. Assessing the acceptance of the concept and making recommendations for the future will conclude this project by the end of 2005.

With its outreach approach, the environmental education concept for the Alpinarium creates awareness and understanding of global change and sustainability-related themes. This may lead to a more conscious attitude towards the Alps. The integrative nature of geography renders this discipline highly qualified and responsible for engaging itself in educational issues. This project combines aspects of many geographical fields and highlights the importance of geography for further and higher education and for sustainability. Exploring ways of sharing state-of-the-art results with the general public ought to be regarded as a new task in geographical research and education. The work of environmental education and education for sustainability should not be confined to academic institutions. The skills of the geographer are deserving of a much wider audience.

Acknowledgements

Many thanks go to the members of the Natural Hazards Research Group of the University of Innsbruck, especially to Margreth Keiler, for giving helpful advice and to the Alpinarium Galtür Dokumentation GmbH for the financial and personal support of this project.

References

Apel, H. J. & Seibert, N. (1996) *Prinzipien guten Unterrichts*, 4th edn (Munich: PimS).

Bastian, O. (1997) Gedanken zur Bewertung von Landschaftsfunktionen—unter besonderer Berücksichtigung der Habitatfunktion, *NNA-Berichte*, 10(3), pp. 106–125.

Bastian, O. & Schreiber, K.-F. (Eds) (1999) *Analyse und ökologische Bewertung der Landschaft*, 2nd edn (Heidelberg and Berlin: Spektrum).

Bastian, O. & Steinhardt, U. (Eds) (2002) *Development and Perspectives of Landscape Ecology* (Dordrecht: Kluwer).

Bacher, S. (2002) Akzeptanzanalyse im Nationalpark Stilfser Joch (I): Besucherbefragung (University of Innsbruck, Unpublished Master's Thesis).

Bätzing, W. (2003) *Die Alpen: Geschichte und Zukunft einer europäischen Kulturlandschaft* (Munich: C.H. Beck).

Beyersdorf, M., Michelsen, G. & Siebert, H. (1998) *Umweltbildung: Theoretische Konzepte, empirische Erkenntnisse, praktische Erfahrungen* (Neuwied and Kriftel: Luchterhand).

Blankertz, H. (1975) *Theorien und Modelle der Didaktik* (Weinheim: Juventa).

Blankertz, H. (1982) *Die Geschichte der Pädagogik: Von der Aufklärung bis zur Gegenwart* (Wetzlar: Büchse der Pandora).

Bobek, H. & Schmithüsen, J. (1949) Die Landschaft im logischen System der Geographie, *Erdkunde*, 3, pp. 112–120.

Bolscho, D., Eulefeld, G. & Seybold, H. (1994) *Bildung und Ausbildung im Umweltschutz* (Bonn: Economica).
Brugger, H. (1988) Entwicklung eines Positionierungskonzeptes für einen Winterfremdenverkehrsort basierend auf den Ergebnissen einer Gästebefragung, *unpublished master's thesis*, University of Innsbruck.
Carter, J. (Ed.) (2001) *A Sense of Place: An Interpretative Planning Handbook*, 2nd edn (Inverness: Tourism and Environment Initiative). Available at http://scotinterpnet.org.uk (accessed July 2003).
De Groot, R. S. (1992) *Functions of Nature: Evaluation of Nature in Environmental Planning, Management and Decision Making* (Groningen: Wolters-Noordhoff).
De Groot, W. T. & van den Born, R. J. G. (2003) Visions of nature and landscape type preferences: an exploration in The Netherlands, *Landscape and Urban Planning*, 63, pp. 127–138.
Degenhardt, B. (1980) *Das touristische Potential des Hochgebirges und seine Nutzung* (Innsbruck: Institute for Geography, University of Innsbruck).
Dollinger, F. (1998) *Die Naturräume im Bundesland Salzburg*, Forschungen zur deutschen Landeskunde, 245 (Trier: Zentralausschuss für deutsche Landeskunde).
Edelmann, W. (2000) *Lernpsychologie*, 6th edn (Weinheim: Beltz-PVU).
Engelhardt, W. & Weinzierl, W. (1976) *Landschaftsbewertung für Erholungszwecke: Modelluntersuchung Virgental, Osttirol* (München: Österreichische Gesellschaft für Natur- und Umweltschutz).
Fairweather, J. R. & Swaffield, S. R. (2002) Visitors' and localsapos; experiences of Rotorua, New Zealand: an interpretative study using photographs of landscapes and Q method, *International Journal of Tourism Research*, 4, pp. 283–297.
Freytag, T. & Hoyler, M. (2002) *Heidelberg und seine Besucher—Ergebnisse der Gästebefragung 2000/01* (Heidelberg: Geographical Institute of Heidelberg University).
Friedrichs, J. (1990) *Methoden empirischer Sozialforschung* (Opladen: Westdeutscher Verlag).
Funnel, D. & Parish, R. (2001) *Mountain Environments and Communities* (London: Routledge).
Gee, K., Glawion, R., Kreisel, W. & Lehnes, P. (2002) Landschaft—kein Buch mit sieben Siegeln: Landschaftsinterpretation entschlüsselt das Natur- und Kulturerbe auf unterhaltsame Weise, in: E. Ehlers & H. Leser (Eds) *Geographie heute—für die Welt von morgen*, pp. 46–56 (Gotha and Stuttgart: Klett-Perthes).
Gemeinde Galtür (2000) Online documents, available at http:www.galtuer.tirol.gv.at/l-haupt.htm (accessed July 2003).
Giesel, K., De Haan, K. & Rode, H. (2002) *Umweltbildung in Deutschland: Stand und Trends im ausserschulischen Bereich* (Berlin: Springer).
Grabaum, R. (1996) *Verfahren der polyfunktionalen Bewertung von Landschaftselementen einer Landschaftseinheit mit anschliessender Multicriteria Optimization zur Generierung vielfältiger Landnutzungsoptionen* (Aachen: Shaker).
Gudjons, H. (1998) *Didaktik zum Anfassen: Lehrer/in-Persönlichkeit und lebendiger Unterricht*, 2nd edn (Bad Heilbrunn: Klinkhardt).
Gudjons, H. (1999) *Pädagogisches Grundwissen*, 6th edn (Bad Heilbrunn: Klinkhardt).
Günther, T. (1996) *Methodische und praktische Aspekte der ökologischen Landschaftsbewertung*, IFHV-Studien, 18 (Bochum: Brockmeyer).
Haase, G. (1978) Zur Ableitung und Kennzeichnung von Naturraumpotentialen, *Petermanns Geographische Mitteilungen*, 122, pp. 113–125.
Haubrich, H. *et al.* (1997) *Didaktik der Geographie konkret*, 6th edn (Munich: Oldenbourg).
International Symposium Interpraevent Heumader, J. (2000) *Proceedings (Tagungspublikation)* (Klagenfurt: Interpraevent).
Kaplan, R. & Kaplan, S. (1989) *The Experience of Nature: A Psychological Perspective* (Cambridge: Cambridge University Press).
Kaplan, R., Kaplan, S. & Ryan, R. L. (1998) *With People in Mind: Design and Management of Everyday Nature* (Washington, DC and Covelo, CA: Island Press).
Kessler, E. & Krätzschmar, C. (1993) *Schulpädagogisches Repetitorium* (Neuwied, Kriftel and Berlin: Luchterhand).
Klafki, W. (1964) *Studien zur Bildungstheorie und Didaktik* (Weinheim: Beltz).
Kromrey, H. (1994) *Empirische Sozialforschung* (Opladen: UTB).
Kron, F. W. (1991) *Grundwissen Pädagogik*, 3rd edn (Munich: Reinhardt).
Lehnes, P. & Glawion, R. (2000) Landschaftsinterpretation—ein Ansatz zur Aufbereitung regionalgeographischer Erkenntnisse für den Tourismus, in: G. Zollinger (Ed.) *Aktuelle Beiträge zur angewandten Physischen Geographie der Tropen, Subtropen und der Regio Trirhena*, Freiburger Geographische Hefte, 60, pp. 313–326 (Freiburg: Institute for Physical Geography, Albert-Ludwigs-University Freiburg).

Lorenz, F. (1999) Die touristische Erschliessung: bewahren statt erschliessen, in: Gemeinde Galtür (Ed.) *Galtür: Zwischen Romanen, Walsern und Tirolern*, pp. 178–187 (Galtür: Gemeinde Galtür).

Mair, R. (2000) Die Katastrophe von Galtür, in: Lawinenwarndienst Tirol (Ed.) *Schnee und Lawinen 1999–2000*, pp. 107–109 (Innsbruck: Land Tirol).

Marks, R., Müller, M. J., Leser, H. & Klink, H-J. (Eds) (1989) *Anleitung zur Bewertung des Leistungsvermögens des Landschaftshaushaltes*, 1st edn, Forschungen zur deutschen Landeskunde, 229 (Trier: Zentralausschuss für deutsche Landeskunde).

Meyer, H. (2003) *Unterrichtsmethoden 2: Praxisband*, 10th edn (Frankfurt a.M.: Cornelsen-Scriptor).

Mietzel, G. (1998) *Pädagogische Psychologie des Lernens und Lehrens*, 5th edn (Göttingen: Hogrefe).

Munich Re Group (2002) *Topics: Jahresrückblick Naturkatastrophen 2001* (Munich: Munich Re Group).

Neef, E. (1969) Zur Frage des gebietswirtschaftlichen Potentials, *Forschung und Fortschritt*, 40(3), pp. 65–70.

Poschmann, C., Riebenstahl, C. & Schmidt-Kallert, E. (1998) *Umweltplanung und –bewertung* (Gotha and Stuttgart: Klett Perthes).

Riedel, W. & Lange, H. (Eds) (2001) *Landschaftsplanung* (Heidelberg and Berlin: Spektrum).

Schnell, R., Hill, P. B. & Esser, E. (1992) *Methoden der empirischen Sozialforschung* (Munich and Vienna: Oldenbourg).

Schulz, W. (1981) *Unterrichtsplanung* (Munich: Urban & Schwarzenberg).

Stötter, J., Meissl, G., Rinderer, M., Keiler, M. & Fuchs, S. (2002a) Galtür. Eine Gemeinde im Zeichen des Lawinenereignisses von 1999, in: E. Steinicke (Ed.) *Geographischer Exkursionsführer Europaregion Tirol, Südtirol, Trentino: Spezialexkursionen im Bundesland Tirol*, Innsbrucker Geographische Schriften, 33/2 pp. 167–184 (Innsbruck: Institute of Geography, University of Innsbruck).

Stötter, J., Meissl, G., Ploner, A. & Soenser, T. (2002b) Developments in natural hazard management in Alpine countries facing global environmental change, in: K. W. Steininger & H. Weck-Hannemann (Eds) *Global Environmental Change in Alpine Regions*, pp. 113–130 (Cheltenham: Edward Elgar).

Tücke, M. (1998) *Psychologie in der Schule—Psychologie für die Schule* (Münster: Lit).

United Nations (1992) *Agenda 21* (New York: United Nations). Available at http//:www.un.org/esa/sustdev/documents/agenda21/index.htm (accessed July 2003).

UNESCO (2002) *Education for Sustainability: lessons learnt from a decade of commitment*, (Paris: UNESCO). Available at http://portal.unesco.org/en/ev.php@URL_ID = 5202 and URL_DO = DO_ TOPIC and URL_ SECTION = 201.html (accessed July 2003).

Yamashita, S. (2002) Perception and evaluation of water in landscape: use of photo-projective method to compare child and adult residents' perceptions of a Japanese river environment, *Landscape and Urban Planning*, 62, pp. 3–17.

Sustainability, Systems Thinking and Professional Practice

STEPHEN MARTIN, JAMES BRANNIGAN & ANNIE HALL

Introduction

This paper sets out to explore some of the implications of the sustainable development agenda for the role and practice of professionals in a number of occupational contexts and hence has generic relevance to geographers interested in environmental education. In addition, it has specific relevance for all those teaching on undergraduate and post graduate programmes in the environmental field, such as the environmental sciences, geography and earth sciences, because it refers to some of the emerging career trajectories for graduates from such programmes. It also describes the principal learning outcomes from a sustainability workshop specifically designed to support inter-professional working. The paper reflects some of the evidence presented in the recently published Egan Review (2004), which emphasizes some of the 'skills' requirements of those seeking jobs in the built environment, local government and environmental occupations as part of the UK government's sustainable communities programme. The report describes the skills gaps in the current supply and demand levels for core occupations needed to deliver the Sustainable Communities Plan. It emphasizes *inter alia* the need for skills that meet:

> ... the diverse needs of existing and future residents, their children and other users, contribute to a high quality of life and provide opportunity and choice. They [Sustainable Communities] achieve this in ways that make effective use of natural resources, enhance the environment, promote social cohesion and inclusion and strengthen economic prosperity. (A definition of Sustainable Communities—The Egan Review (2004))

In the UK, the current policy framework for sustainable development is set out in the government's policy paper *A Better Quality of Life—A Strategy for Sustainable Development for the UK* (DETR, 1999). Currently under review, this strategy will be influenced by a number of individual policy papers on, *inter alia*, energy, sustainable communities, and proposals for substantial reforms of agriculture and planning regulations. More recently, a sustainable development action plan for education and skills, published by the Department for Education and Skills (DfES, 2003) will also have to be taken into account. The Higher Education Funding Council for England (HEFCE) is currently developing a sustainable development strategy for the HE sector, to be published in 2005. A key objective of the strategy is to build sustainable development into teaching and learning in all disciplines, with the support of the UK's new Higher Education Academy.

All of these policy changes will have a substantial impact on the education, training and employment of professionals. Indeed, amongst the 5.5 million people in the UK who call themselves professionals there is already a growing realization that they need help in understanding how to put the principles of sustainability into practice (Martin & Hall, 2002). Professionals in all sorts of roles increasingly have to demonstrate their competence in complying with complex sets of environmental, social and ethical parameters. These trends have a bearing on the curricula of higher education programmes, since many professional bodies now rely on accredited degrees as the main route for membership. As part of their accreditation procedures, several professional bodies now require undergraduate programmes to demonstrate how sustainable development is delivered as part of the curriculum. Many universities have ratified their commitment to "playing a leading role in developing a multi-disciplinary and ethically orientated forum of education in order to devise solutions to the problems linked to sustainable development" (Copernicus Charter, 1993). However, practical implementation of these principles has proved to be more difficult and progress is frustratingly slow.

There has also been a major shift in European Union (EU) policy during the past decade in respect of employment, education, training and the environment. Much of this change is encapsulated in the EU environmental policy framework, the Sixth Environmental Action Programme (EAP)—*Environment 2010: Our Future, Our Choice* (EU, 2001).

> The opening paragraph to the new framework sets out the EU's vision: A healthy environment is essential to long term prosperity and quality of life and citizens in

Europe demand a high level of environmental protection. Future economic development and increasing prosperity will put pressure on the planet's capacity to sustain demands for resources or to absorb pollution. At the same time, high environmental standards are an engine for innovation and business opportunities. Overall, society must work to de-couple environmental impacts and degradation from economic growth. Business must operate in a more eco-efficient way, in other words producing the same or more products with less input and less waste, and consumption patterns have to become more sustainable.

Throughout the new EAP, greater emphasis is placed on the integration of environmental concerns into wider economic and social policies through the new policy doctrine of sustainable development. Consequently, there has been a shift toward so-called 'preventive' measures.

Much of the thinking underpinning the Sixth EAP is based on the EU strategy for sustainable development. This contains some wide-ranging proposals including a commitment to including sustainable development as the *core concern* of all EU policies; the establishment of a sustainable development 'Round Table' of about 10 independent experts; and the establishment of a two-yearly Stakeholder Forum.

Issues for the Professions

Some of the issues and implications of the new sustainable development policy framework and its impact on professional practice (and by implication the undergraduate curriculum) are summarized below (Essence, 2001):

(1) Throughout the EU there have so far been relatively few attempts to relate environmental higher education to the changing needs of the labour market, but this will change.
(2) The qualifications required for many jobs in the emerging labour market are very different from those that have previously characterized the environmental professions in Europe.
(3) New kinds of competences in business, economics, law, politics and public administration, sociology, communications, ethics, human ecology, environmental management as well as more traditional natural sciences are being sought by employers.
(4) There is a need for people with an interdisciplinary problem-solving capability, rather than a traditional and often overly specialized scientific competence.
(5) Graduates from existing environmental programmes are finding employment difficult, largely because their curriculum is insufficiently directed at meeting the needs of employers (see the Egan Review, 2004 and Martin *et al.*, 2004).
(6) The issue of academic quality is closely connected to the more general issue of professional competence in the new and emerging environmental labour market.
(7) Many of the tasks of company/organization environment officers and managers are often company or brand specific, hence general education programmes are difficult to devise.

(8) The skills most often required by employers are of the softer kind—communication, leadership, organizational, etc. These are notoriously difficult to teach in a formalized university setting.
(9) Future qualifications will need to include conflict management and an understanding of cultural differences in an international context.
(10) The role of professional institutions needs to be strengthened to help graduates into environmental employment sectors.
(11) No state within the EU currently recognizes 'environmental consulting' as an official and hence legally binding profession.
(12) Only Belgium and France offer vocational training in environmental consulting (e.g. the Institut Eco-Conseil, Strasbourg, leading to a Mastéres specialisé named 'Eco-conseillor: analyse et gestion de l'environnement'). The Institut Eco-Conseil has attained legal protection in France for the title 'Eco-conseiller' it offers to its graduates. The Association Française des Eco-conseillers (AFEC) is the umbrella organization for environmental consulting in France.
(13) There is relatively limited inter-professional cooperation across the EU. Hence it is difficult to establish common requirements across disciplinary boundaries (one exception is the Dutch Association of Environmental Professionals).

Professional bodies are increasingly being asked to review their traditions and practice—radically and urgently—with far-reaching implications for those higher education courses for which they control or influence the curricula. The challenge of sustainable development has potentially profound implications for professions across a range of disciplines—whether engineering, geography, urban design and planning, environment science, accounting, manufacturing or whatever profession—in both the practice and role of the professional. Engineers, for example, in designing solutions to meet modern needs, are not only responsible for the safety, technical and economic performance of their activities, but they also have responsibilities to use resources sustainably; to minimize the environmental impact of projects, wastes and emissions; and to use their influence to ensure their work brings social benefits that are equitably distributed. Similar considerations are an integral part of the professional training of town planners, a career path for which geography graduates are particularly well suited. These sustainability responsibilities heighten the importance of ethics in curriculum design and require greater emphasis on codes of conduct and the role of the professional as social change agent.

The Changing Employment Sectors

Recent data (ECOTEC, 2002) on the market for goods and services produced by the so-called 'eco-industries' in both the European Union (EU) and the Candidate Countries (i.e. EU proposed enlargement) indicates that they supply approximately €183 billion of goods and services a year. In a global context the market for eco-industries is estimated at around €550 billion, which means that the EU has approximately one-third of the overall market, equal to the USA. The waste-management industry has seen the most growth in recent years and has the largest annual expenditure. Direct employment in the EU eco-industries is over 2 million full-time equivalents, with 1.5 million jobs in pollution management and 650,000 in resource management. There has been a shift in employment from the public to private sectors, particularly in waste management. Whilst parts of the environmental sector (e.g. consultancy and research) comprise highly educated and skilled individuals, there is a continual need for improvement in skills and training given some of the rapid technological changes taking place in recovery and recycling and other aspects of resource use and environmental management.

It is also important to recognize the rapidly growing non-governmental sector of public interest organizations, not-for-profit consulting firms and various publications, media and information outlets. New posts are emerging within the agencies of the EU itself as well as in inter-governmental bodies. There is clearly an increasing range of new and demanding career trajectories, all of which will influence the future curriculum of environmental and other educational programmes.

Professional Practice for Sustainable Development (PP4SD)

It was in this wider context that a new initiative, Professional Practice for Sustainable Development (PP4SD; see www.pp4sd.org.uk), was launched in 1999 (Martin & Hall, 2002). This initiative set out to work in partnership with 14 professional institutions to create a common curriculum framework for sustainable development from which to test and publish training materials. The materials developed were aimed at professionals from varying backgrounds, including business, academe and consultancy. Whilst the primary focus was on those professionals in work, we were also mindful of those 'future' professionals coming through the university system. Hence, the PP4SD process also sought to find solutions to how sustainability might be taught in undergraduate and postgraduate programmes.

The next section of this paper describes the design and delivery of a one-day PP4SD workshop in sustainable development (Baines *et al.*, 2001).

The Workshop Structure

The workshop structure is based on five overlapping themes:

(1) the principles of sustainability;
(2) an introduction to systems thinking and practice;
(3) tools and techniques for taking a future perspective;
(4) the business benefits of sustainable development;
(5) action planning.

Principles of Sustainability—A Systems Perspective

It was Tolstoy who wrote that the greatest threat to life is habit. Habit, he argued, destroys everything around us, because it familiarizes us to the point that we no longer really see things. We become incapable of bringing the familiar furniture of our lives into focus. A similar argument can be made about ideas and concepts, and about the intellectual frameworks that shape ideas and concepts. Concepts such as the environment, nature and civil society are familiar and we often take them for granted. Yet they are often difficult to define, partly because they carry with them a variety of implicit assumptions, which influence the way we think about them.

Professionals are no different. Their beliefs and values are largely defined by their long education and training in their basic discipline. Consequently, one of the first steps in designing the workshop was to create with the representatives of the professions an agreed intellectual framework within which to explore the concept of sustainability. The framework (Martin and Hall, 2002) has a number of key characteristics:

- The earth as a sustainable system is dependent on the activities of a number of well-defined bio-geo-chemical cycles.
- The earth as a sustainable system is open to flows of energy and closed to matter (based on the first and second laws of thermodynamics).
- There are four principal ways of undermining the bio-geo-chemical cycles (Porritt, 2000).
- The framework is set in a future perspective.

By setting the sustainability agenda in an 'earth as a system' context, it became much easier for professionals to engage with what needs to be done, rather than focusing on measuring, managing and mitigating downstream environmental impact, as environmental scientists tend to do (Martin, 2002). The framework provides a mental model for defining what a sustainable world might look like (Figure 1). Thus it critically supports the process of inter-professional dialogue and reflection on the issues and solutions.

In a sustainable society:

(1) Any materials mined from the earth should not exceed the environment's capacity to disperse, absorb, recycle or otherwise neutralize their harmful effects to humans and the environment.

(2) The same principles should apply to synthetic substances.

(3) The biological diversity and productivity of ecosystems should not be endangered.

(4) A healthy economy should be maintained, which accurately represents the value of natural, human, social and manufactured capital.

(5) Individual human skills, knowledge and health should be developed and deployed to optimum effect.

(6) Social progress and justice should recognize the needs of everyone.

(7) There must be equity for future generations.

(8) Structures and institutions should promote stewardship of natural resources and the development of people.

Figure 1. The PP4SD framework for sustainability

The framework was derived from a number of key sources, including: the Rio Declaration, World Business Council on Sustainable Development, the Department of the Environment Transport and the Regions (DETR), the Natural Step, the International Institute for Sustainable Development, the World Commission on Environment and Development, Forum for the Future and Natural Capitalism (see SIGMA, 2004).

Systems Thinking and Practice

The workshop begins by asking participants to draw what they understand by sustainable development. Using the drawings as an icebreaker has been an invaluable technique for promoting and facilitating the inter-professional dialogue and learning on which the course depends. It avoids the superficial and often sterile debate on definitions of sustainable development.

Drawings provide useful ways of gathering information about complex situations and are a key element of the approach to systems thinking and practice developed by Peter Checkland (1981) and Checkland and Scholes (1990). Using pictures as a way of thinking about issues is common to several problem-solving methods because our intuitive consciousness communicates more easily in impressions and symbols than words. These pictures attempt to capture the real situation through an entirely freehand, cartoon representation of all the ideas, relationships, influences, causes and effects relevant to sustainable development.

An additional dimension to this approach widely used by systems practitioners is the use of diagrams to explore the relationships or boundaries between systems of interest such as sustainability and sustainable development. Whilst these terms are often used interchangeably, they mean different things. In simple terms, sustainability means the capacity for continuance into the long-term future. Sustainable development is the journey or means of achieving the goal of sustainability. In systems thinking, both represent separate but connected systems of interest. To an individual or an organization sustainable development represents a 'sphere' of influence and action over which they have some control and direction, whereas sustainability represents a 'sphere' of concern, over which an individual or organization only exerts some limited impact indirectly through their sphere of influence. Identifying a professional's sphere(s) of influence facilitates a much more focused and productive dialogue on achievable actions and outcomes.

Tools and Techniques for Taking a Future Perspective

The workshop also applies a number of techniques to help participants to think in a future perspective because one of the challenges of sustainable development is developing resilient and adaptive decision-making tools that can cope with risk and uncertainty. These techniques include simple scenarios that exemplify the two different approaches we can take to the future and, importantly, how these approaches influence how we act. The usual way of approaching the future is through forecasting by starting from where we are and projecting trends over relatively short time intervals, e.g. 1 to 3 years. Planning based on such trends tends to lead to short-term and incremental changes. A major limitation of forecasting is that many present trends are clearly unsustainable! The alternative approach is 'backcasting', which starts by taking a 20- to 30-year perspective based on scenarios or based on the sustainability framework outlined earlier (Ison & Blackmore, 1998).

The idea is to think imaginatively about the business or organization to which you belong and seek to explore a range of fundamental changes that will make it more closely fit the sustainability framework. From each alternative future created, you then work your way backwards from the future towards the present in stages, asking such questions as—what barriers did we overcome; who helped us; whom did we need to persuade?

The differences between forecasting and backcasting are critical to how we act in response to the issues of sustainability. Forecasting at best offers a short-term future but if these trends fail us, then prediction fails us. History teaches us that sooner or later trends fail because change creates deeper more fundamental issues. In contrast, backcasting starts from your anticipated destination (most sensible climbers start planning from the summit that they wish to conquer and work backwards!) and seek to plot a course of action towards it.

Business Benefits

The next phase of the workshop uses case studies from business and industry to illustrate how sustainable development principles have been applied and to provide an opportunity for participants to develop their own thinking around practical examples. The case studies are based on ongoing businesses such as banking (the Co-operative Bank, www.cooperativebank.co.uk), construction (Carillion plc, www.carillion.co.uk) and textiles (Interface, www.interfaceinc.com). They all feature the business benefits of taking a more sustainable approach to business practice.

The project is also currently working on other case studies in land use such as farming and horticulture (www.growingforthefuture.com/start.htm). Case studies ground the systems theory of the course in real-world examples allowing participants to reflect on the progress made by some substantial businesses but also highlighting the issues surrounding organizational change. They emphasize that organizational change based on the principles of sustainability is not a steady-state process but a dynamic and complex state of affairs. There are two significant ways of embedding change in organizations, namely through procedures, tools and systems (e.g. through environmental management systems such as EMAS, ISO 14001, etc.) or through systemized organizational learning—both have their strengths and weaknesses. However, some argue that organizational learning is more effective because, unlike management systems, corporate and individual learning is inextricably linked to values (Courtice & Swift, 2002). And there is evidence that where personal and organizational values are strongly aligned there is more likely to be greater motivation to enact change (Seele, 2000).

Action Planning

Throughout the workshop an emphasis is placed on putting sustainability into practice. The final section of the workshop re-emphasizes this aspect through a short action-planning session. All participants are asked to prioritize a set of organizational and personal actions that they can set in train or influence within the next month of their work.

The priorities are based on the principles and tools outlined above. They also reflect some of the outcomes of the Environment Agency's work on organizational change carried out by their Learning and Partnership Team. Some of the key points to emerge from this work indicate that in order to embed sustainability into an organization it should:

- expect a 3- to 5-year time frame;
- stress the importance of choice and ownership at all levels;

- establish outcome-orientated working groups;
- initiate coaching and mentoring support mechanisms;
- set in place reward structures and systems;
- provide training and development;
- allocate adequate resources for innovation and change;
- make identifiable links to core business;
- accept the grand strategy but enable local flexibility.

It is often the case that organizations are willing to consider an approach to sustainable development but search for immediate benefits that are both visible and provide financial gain. Yet the true benefits of sustainable development may not be seen in the lifetime of the majority of professionals although tracking would doubtless identify significant movement and change over time.

The content and processes described above have been extensively trialled with a range of organizations and with participants at various levels of responsibility (e.g. Regional Development Agency; Environment Agency; NGOs; a utility company; European project officers). For the past two years the workshop has been run as part of the graduate training programme for Barclays Plc (for nearly 160 graduate entrants—The Business Leadership Programme). All of these examples reveal that the participants have difficulty in dealing with the environmental, social and economic contexts of their job in an integrated way. These workshops provide a stimulating set of tools and techniques to deal with one of society's most critical issues. Without exception, the workshop evaluations have been extremely positive, with participants valuing the interactive and practical activities which helped improve their ability to take decisions in the context of sustainable development and which have enhanced their readiness to put the concepts into action. The impact of the workshops in changing behaviour and practice has not been assessed in a longitudinal study. However, there is anecdotal evidence of its impact on decision-making in several organizations with which the project has a continuing relationship. The project is currently negotiating with Barclays to carry out a longitudinal study on the impacts of the workshop.

Conclusion

This paper attempts to set out some of the major issues facing professionals as they engage with and put into practice the challenging and crucial sustainability agenda. It also provides some insights into the sustainability learning needs of existing and future professionals in the workplace.

It is becoming increasingly evident from this work and contemporary experience that any approach to sustainability needs to be different from the traditional forms of education and training that are currently delivered through schools, colleges, universities and continuing professional development (CPD) (Sterling, 2001; Jucker, 2002). As many commentators are now articulating, the emphasis is more on action learning, dialogue, inquiry, participation and inter-professional partnership (Scott & Gough, 2003). Hence, the approach should not be based solely on teaching and the transmission of knowledge or just working to a national syllabus or curriculum but on allowing exploration of issues and problems through open-ended enquiry and learning, as part of an ongoing process. Consequently, effective sustainability change systems must themselves be innovative learning models aimed at changing organizational culture and behaviour.

Since the term organizational learning became popular in the 1990s, organizations have become aware of the need to develop their human capital to manage change and remain competitive. The PP4SD approach recognizes this as one of the principal ways it can engage in the process of partnership and influence behaviour and attitudes within organizations. It recognizes that many organizations, in transforming the way they work, will also have to transform they way they learn in order to sustain their competitive advantage. We even extend this argument to suggest that *sustainability learning* is a real form of competitive *advantage*. Using this kind of thinking we can apply the term *sustainability literacy* as part of a continuous organizational learning process whereby knowledge and resources regarding sustainability are shared, enhanced and utilized towards a shared goal of becoming a 'sustainable organization'. Sustainable literacy can be defined as a significant number of individuals having a basic level of knowledge and understanding about what sustainable development means for their organization and how to apply that knowledge in their working lives. Sustainable literacy does not mean that all employees need the same level of knowledge, or that any one individual needs to have a comprehensive knowledge of the field. As far as the PP4SD approach is concerned, it implies a *sufficient* critical mass of employees with at least a basic comprehension of sustainable development from its underlying principles through to the business and societal implications. They need to recognize how their knowledge and skills contribute to the organization's and society's sustainability aspirations. Professional specialists need to understand how best to interact with others in the organization as a whole in order for their knowledge and skills to become an integral part of the organizational learning process.

PP4SD has developed and successfully trialled a number of new ways of exploring how sustainable development can be a vehicle for influencing the existing cultures of organizations and the professionals who are employed in them. The PP4SD workshops demonstrate what can be done by challenging existing beliefs and values in a process based on appreciative inquiry. This in essence is a process that focuses not on what is wrong with an organization but rather on how using the principles of sustainability we can develop new and positive ways of organizing its activities sustainably. It is based on the starting point that doubt and negation undermine constructive intent. Appreciative inquiry recognizes that inquiry and change are not separate elements but are simultaneous. Inquiry is intervention. The seeds of change, that is the things people think and talk about, the things people discover and learn, and the things that inform dialogue and inspire action, are implicit in the very first question asked. Hence, rather than pursuing an organization's existing activities in a critical way, the PP4SD workshops set about questioning in a positive light new ways of doing things, by replacing existing (and reified) patterns of behaviour and discourse and creating space for new ideas and activities.

Hence the PP4SD process influences organizational culture and behaviour through interventions and facilitates conversations between professionals. It recognizes that culture is not a static thing but something that is constantly being created, affirmed and expressed within an organization as a result of all the conversations and negotiations that go on between its members. These discussions involve a continuous process of agreeing, sometimes explicitly, usually tacitly, about the 'proper' way to do things and how to interpret the events of the world around them. In order to change a culture we have to change all of these conversations, or at least the majority of them (Isaacs, 1999). And changing conversations is not the focus of most change programmes, which tend to concentrate on organizational structures or reward systems or other large-scale interventions.

The PP4SD process has a number of implications for undergraduate and postgraduate environmental programmes. The most significant is to offer more opportunities to develop the skills of dialogue and inquiry in an interdisciplinary and participatory way. Few can argue with the goals of sustainability, but many should contest and explore how sustainability can be achieved. Hence, it is critical that environmental programmes accommodate approaches to dialogue, systems thinking, principles of sustainability, and values and ethics in a professional and personal context. Above all, they should emphasize the importance of achieving systemic organizational change. These are the kinds of curriculum ingredients and approaches that, given additional prominence, will enable graduates from disciplines such as geography to benefit from the growth of interest and sustainability in business, government and the professions.

References

Baines, J., Brannigan, J. & Martin, S. (2001) *Professional Partnerships for Sustainable Development* (London: Institution of Environmental Sciences).

Checkland, P. (1981) *Systems thinking, systems practice* (New York: John Wiley & Sons).

Checkland, P. & Scholes, J. (1990) *Soft systems methodology in action* (New York: John Wiley & Sons).

COPERNICUS CHARTER (1993) Available at http://www.copernicus-campus.org/sites/uni.html (accessed December 2003).

Courtice, P. & Swift, T. (2002) Sustainability literacy and organisational learning, *New Academy Review*, 1(1), pp. 93–102.

DETR (1999) *A Better Quality of Life—A Strategy for Sustainable Development for the UK*, CM4345 (London: HMSO).

DfES (2003) *Sustainable Development Action Plan for Education and Skills* (London: HMSO). Available at http://www.dfes.gov.uk/sd/action.shtml (accessed December 2003).

ECOTEC Research and Consultancy (2002) Analysis of the Eco-Industries, their Employment and Export Potential. Available at http://www.europa.eu.int/comm/environment/enveco/industry_employment/ecotec_exec_sum.pdf (accessed December 2003).

Egan Review (2004) *Skills for Sustainable Communities* (London: Royal Institution of British Architecture and the Office of the Deputy Prime Minister). Available at http://www.odpm.gov.uk (accessed April 2004).

ESSENCE (2000) Thematic Network of Environmental Sciences, Available at http://www.essence.vsnu.nl (accessed December 2003).

EU (2002) *The Sixth Environmental Action Programme—Environment 2010: Our Future, Our Choice*, COM 31 (Brussels: The European Union).

Isaacs, W. (1999) *Dialogue and the Art of Thinking Together* (New York: Currency).

Ison, R. & Blackmore, C. (1998) *Post Graduate Programme in Environmental Decision Making: T860 Environmental Decision Making: A Systems Approach* (Milton Keynes: Open University).

Jucker, R. (2002) *Our Common Illiteracy—Education as if the Earth and People Mattered* (Frankfurt a.M: Lang).

Martin, S. (2002) Sustainability, systems thinking and professional practice, *Planet*, 4, pp. 20–21.

Martin, S. & Hall, A. (2002) Sustainable Development and the professions, *Planet*, 3, pp. 17–18.

Martin, S., Cohen, J. & Martin, M. (2004) *Opportunities for Sustainable Development in the Learning and Skills Sector: A Policy Analysis* (London: Learning and Skills Development Agency).

Porritt, J. (2000) *Playing Safe: Science and the Environment* (London: Thames and Hudson).

Seele, R. (2000) Culture and complexity: new insights into organisational change, *Organisations and People*, 1(2), pp. 2–9.

Scott, W. & Gough, S. (2003) *Key Issues in Sustainable Development and Learning: A Critical Review* (London: Routledge Falmer).

Sterling, S. (2001) *Sustainable Education—Revisioning Learning and Change*, Schumacher Society Briefing No. 6 (Dartington: Green Books).

SIGMA (2004) *The SIGMA guidelines—an overview. Putting Sustainable Development into Practice—A Guide for Organisations* (London: British Standards Institute). Available at http://www.projectsigma.com (accessed April 2004).

Environmental Research and Education in US Geography

ROBERT S. BEDNARZ

Geographers' Attitudes

Based on what geographers write about the nature of geography, it is reasonable to conclude that they see their discipline as an appropriate home for environmental or sustainability education and research. American geographers have, from the beginning, characterized a major component of geography as the study of man–land, human–environment, or environment–society relationships. When Pattison described the nature of geography in 1964 by inventorying the work geographers had done up to that time, he identified four traditions, one of which was the man–land tradition (Pattison, 1964).

In 1994, when geographic educators reached consensus on a set of standards for school geography in the United States, they identified two basic perspectives that characterized the way geographers viewed the world and solved problems. The first was the spatial perspective; the second was the ecological perspective. In discussing the importance of the second, they described Earth as being "composed of living and nonliving elements interacting in complex webs of ecological relationships which occur at multiple levels" and argued that understanding this complex interaction was fundamental if students were to realize that "human societies depend on diverse small and large ecosystems for food, water, and all other resources" (Geography Education National Standards Project, 1994, p. 58).

More recently, in a major article discussing the implications of restructuring in the academy for geography, Turner (2002, p. 53) offered a similar view of the field when he argued that two identities have dominated in geography—"geography as a spatial-chorological approach and geography as the human-environment subject". Turner asserts that although geography claimed its place in the academy on the basis of being an integrative science, both identities quickly emerged, and each dominated the discipline at various times. Although he is never quite bold enough to outline what he thinks geography's future identity should be, he implies that a merger of the two identities would be advantageous—the human environment, broadly defined, would be the subject of study and the spatial approach the method of study. The published comments of three senior geographers (Butzer, 2002; Kates, 2002; Wescoat, 2002) chosen by the editors to comment on the article reveal that although they have differences with Turner, they do not disagree with his claim concerning the importance of human-environment study within geography.

Turner's (2002, p. 53) conception of the nature of geography, that "from its modern foundation, geography has designated itself a science, and it prospers less when this role diminishes" is obviously not shared by all geographers. It should be noted, however, that he argues for a very broad interpretation of science, and he recognizes that geography embraces most ways of knowing. In fact, Turner asserts that he can group positivist, humanist, Marxist, realist and other types of geographers within the human-environment tradition because he is interested in the identity of geography, which does not limit the explanatory perspectives of the practitioners. He sees geography's openness to various explanatory realms as one of the discipline's strengths.

Geographers adopting a more critical perspective might argue with Turner's notion of geography as a science, even broadly defined, but evidence exists that these scholars also see human-environment study as a central focus of the field. At the conclusion of their chapter on new models of environment and resources in which they discuss innovative ideas brought to environmental geography by political ecology and other critical perspectives, Emel & Peet (1989, p. 72) find "an increasing engagement with what should be the central concern of geographers of all persuasions: the contradictory relations between people and Earth".

Yarnal & Neff (2004, p. 29) also assert that geography should play a major part in "complex environmental science and other approaches to human-environment studies" because geography is inherently interdisciplinary and because human-environmental science is part of geography's core. Although they tend to agree with Turner's scientific conception of human-environment geography, they note that theoretical contributions to the literature have been made by geographers with a wide variety of perspectives, including radical human geographers. With regard to geography education, they point to the calls made by Huckle (2002) for the introduction of political ecology concepts into school geography and by Diduck & Sinclair (1997) for the use of critical pedagogy in public (adult) education. Yarnal and Neff also see no conflict between geographers who advocate a complex environmental science and those who support a more critical approach because both advocate greater attention to human-environment science in schools and at university, and they agree that students and citizens must understand the natural, social, political and economic systems that are part of the human-environment tension, a tension, according to O'Riordan (1989), between exploiting and sustaining the environment.

Another example that indicates the importance of environmental studies to geography is offered by the reorganization of the Association of American Geographers' flagship journal, the *Annals*. Beginning in 2001, all academic articles were divided into four topical areas: Environmental Sciences; Methods, Models, and GIS; Nature and Society, and People, Place, and Region. This reorganization, arguably, gives half of this important journal's space to environmentally oriented content.

Finally, although this article's focus is the United States, it is apparent that geographers in other countries also see an important role for their discipline in providing environmental or sustainability education. In addressing the United Kingdom's commitment to Agenda 21, Huckle (2002, p. 64) says, "Geography has been given the major responsibility for delivering education for sustainable development" and that key ideas from radical geography can assist teachers in helping students understand humans' place in nature. In this periodical, Kasimov *et al.* (2005) report that environmental studies in Russian universities are divided into two parts, fundamental environmental education and applied engineering. The former is most typically handled by geography departments, which the authors note are more closely oriented toward the physical sciences than departments in Western Europe, the United States or Australia. Although additional evidence to support the assertion that geographers see an important place for environmental studies within geography could be presented, the examples cited are sufficient to make the case.

What Non-geographers Think

Judging by what environmentalists working outside the field of geography have written, it seems that non-geographers also think that geography has an important role to play in environmental education. The findings and recommendations of two significant recent reports support this assertion. The first was prepared by the National Council for Science and the Environment (NCSE). The Council describes its purpose as improving "the scientific basis of environmental decisionmaking" by "promoting science for the environment, enhancing programs at academic institutions, catalyzing and advancing ideas from diverse communities, communicating science-based information to society, and developing science solutions for environmental challenges". It claims the support of "over 500 academic, scientific, environmental, and business organizations, and federal, state, and local government" (NCSE, 2003, p. ii). In its major policy statement, *Recommendations for Education for a Sustainable and Secure Future: A Report of the third National Conference on Science, Policy and the Environment*, the NCSE argues that sustainability is a topic that should be included in the curricula of many disciplines at every level of education. It argues that students will learn best when educational programs use inquiry-based, collaborative, problem-solving approaches that "emphasize *systems and human–nature interactions*" (NCSE, 2003, p. 6, emphasis added), a recommendation that would seem to align well with the environmental perspective of geography.

In fact, many of the specific statements and recommendations made in the report support the notion that geography would provide an excellent disciplinary home for environmental or sustainability education. For example, featured speaker Paul Gilman, Assistant Administrator for Research and Development of the US Environmental Protection Agency, argued that spatial and temporal frames of reference are essential to understanding environmental issues. He says, "The notions embodied in this '*spatio-temporal*' theme provide guiding and orienting signals of place, context and continuity to acquired information, helping us mold that information into understanding... That is, we recognize and try to account for a '*sense-of-place*'" (NCSE, 2003, p. 8). Providing a spatial context by accounting for a sense of place is an approach that falls well within the boundaries of geography.

The report further endorses recommendations for the knowledge and skills that should be possessed by new graduates made in an article in the *Journal of Sustainability in Higher Education* (Flint *et al.*, 2000). Among the knowledge and skills listed are an understanding of: the connections between living things and their environment; how natural processes and systems affect Earth's ability to sustain life; and connections among scientific knowledge, economics, politics, historical and cultural experience, and moral, philosophical and aesthetic values (NCSE, 2003, p. 11).

The report makes other recommendations that strongly support geography's role in environmental education. In a section titled 'Geographic Learning: Designing National Programs for Local and Global Impacts', the report offers specific suggestions for teacher professional development, teaching tools, integrating geographic education (with social, environmental, science and economic content), and the geography curriculum (NCSE, 2003, pp. 28–29). In general, this report could hardly be more supportive of geography even though it was written by a group with almost no professional geographers among its membership.

A second recent report, *Complex Environmental Systems: Synthesis for Earth, Life, and Society in the 21st Century*, published by the National Science Foundation (NSF) Committee for Environmental Research and Education, states in its foreword that its purpose is "to provide overall strategic guidance about environmental research and education" for the next 10 years (Pfirman and the AC-ERE, 2003). Although this report is aimed at a broad group of environmental researchers and educators, it makes, perhaps, an even stronger case for geography's role in environmental endeavors.

The report recommends that attention be concentrated in "three interrelated areas: (A) coupled human and natural systems, (B) coupled biological and physical systems, and (C) people and technology" (Pfirman and the AC-ERE, 2003, p. 11). All of these areas are well within geography's domain, and the first is one of the two basic perspectives that have defined the discipline. The report repeatedly mentions geography as one of the disciplines that should contribute to the three research and education areas. Among the topics identified by the report that seem most at home in geography are those dealing with land, resources and the built environment; coastal environments; environmental services and valuation; climate change; decision-making; and environmental systems and institutions.

Complex Environmental Systems also emphasizes the increasing importance of remote sensing as a data-collection method and new tools such as GIS that allow for increasingly sophisticated analysis of spatially explicit information by natural and social scientists (Pfirman and the AC-ERE, 2003, p. 5). This emphasis fits well with geography's second basic perspective, spatial analysis.

Although other evidence could be cited, what has been presented here makes it fair to claim that many educators and researchers, both geographers and non-geographers, see geography as an appropriate disciplinary home for a wide variety of environmental and sustainability education and research.

Status of Environmental Education in the United States

Given that both geographers and non-geographers see geography as an appropriate home for environmental and sustainability research and education, are these activities a major component of geography in the United States? Are geographers willing and able to meet the demand for environmental courses and programs desired by students? Unambiguous evidence is not easy to gather; the situation varies across universities; and interpretation of the data depends, to some extent, on one's point of view.

One indication of professional geographers' interest in environmental and sustainability topics is their membership in the Association of American Geographers' (AAG) various specialty groups. In 2003, the AAG offered geographers 48 specialty groups covering a wide range of topics, including some that were relatively esoteric such as 'Geography of Religion and Belief', 'Indigenous Peoples', and 'Cryosphere'. Although no environment or sustainability group per se exists, two groups are closely related to these topics: 'Human Dimensions of Global Change' and 'Energy and Environment'. In 2002, membership in these two specialty groups was 210 and 199, respectively (AAG, 2002). The mean size of specialty groups was 267 and the median 206, making the two environmental groups very close to average size (Figure 1).

The AAG Guide also allows departments to self-report their programs' specialty areas. As in the case of specialty groups, environmental and sustainability specialties are included within two broader program categories, 'Conservation, Land Use, Resource Management' and 'Environmental Studies'. Specialization in these programs was claimed by 59 and 56 percent of geography departments, respectively, and both show a modest increase since 1995 (AAG, 2002) (see the top two lines of Figure 2).

As mentioned previously, since 2001, the *Annals of the AAG* has published papers in four topical areas, each with its own editor: Environmental Sciences; Methods, Models, and GIS; Nature and Society; and People, Place, and Region. Within the first 10 issues published under this new format, 95 articles appeared. Nineteen (20 percent) and 25 (26 percent) were published in the Environmental Science and the Nature and Society categories, respectively. Environmental or sustainability issues could be addressed by papers in either of the sections. In addition to articles that deal explicitly or implicitly with environmental issues or problems, the Environmental Science section also contains some papers in geomorphology, hydrology or another sub-field of physical geography (e.g. Pease & Tchakerian, 2002). The Nature and Society section also contains a great variety of articles, ranging from those concerned with sustainability, conservation or environmental policy to those taking an environmental history or humanistic approach (e.g. Delaney, 2001; Meindl *et al.*, 2002).

By some measures, then, human-environment research is strong in US geography. Yarnal & Neff (2004, p. 28) assert that the research performed by geographers is not only well received within the discipline but is receiving recognition by scholars outside the field. They point out that about half of the geographers who are members of the National Academy of Sciences were trained in the human-environment tradition. They state optimistically that "human-environment research within geography is not only alive and well, but also growing". These optimistic views are not unique to Yarnal & Neff. Emel & Peet (1989) state

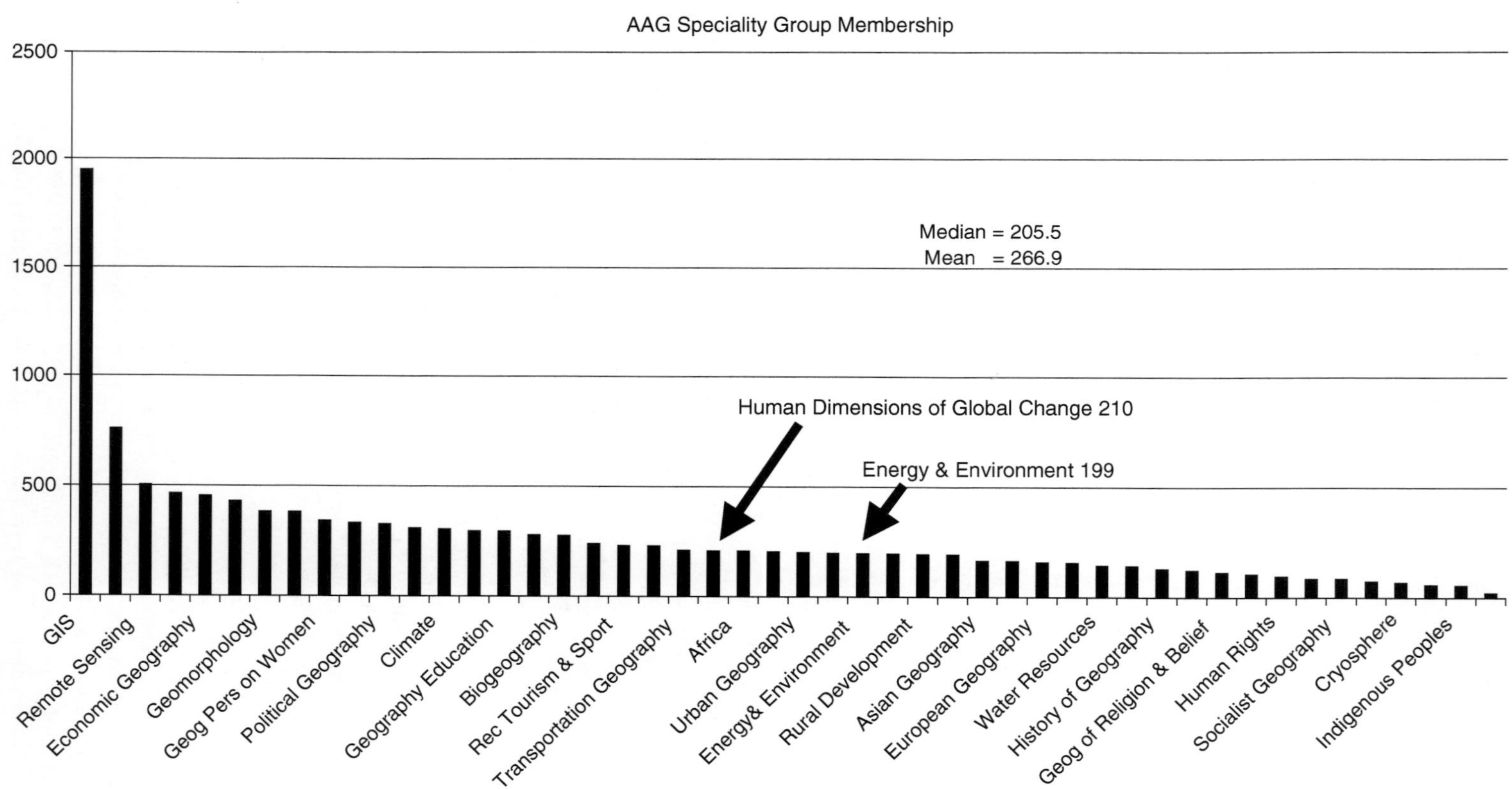

Figure 1. AAG Speciality Group Membership

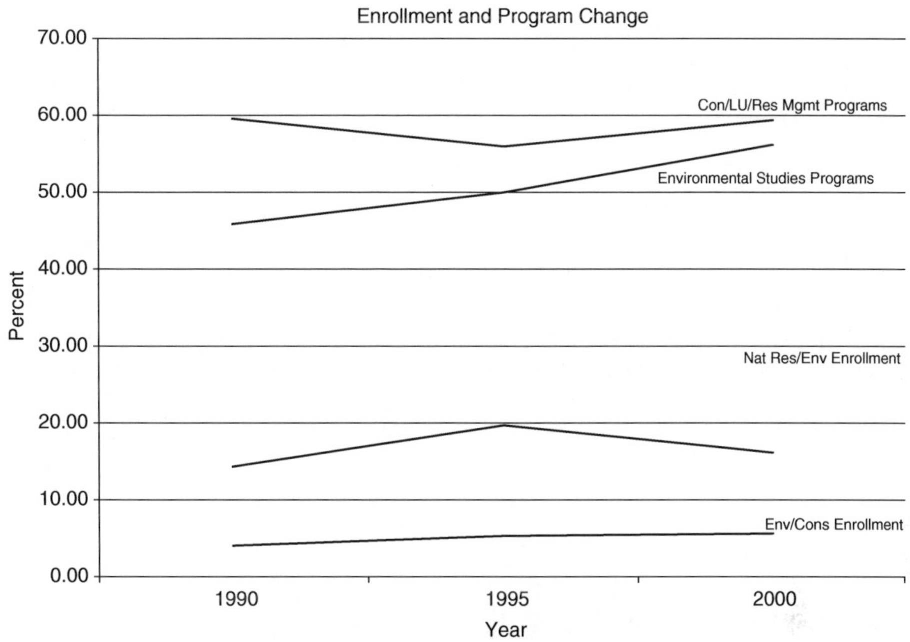

Figure 2. Enrollment and Program Change

that in reviewing the environmental work of the previous 20 years they found the development of a more mature alternative perspective on environmental questions, robust internal discussion and argument, and greater commitment to one of human geography's core areas, the relations between people and their environment. Turner (2002) also reports that human-environment geography grew significantly during the last 50 years and that environmental topics were attacked by geographers of all types including those interested in natural hazards, environmental perception, cultural ecology, agriculture, water resources, the human dimensions of global change, and political ecology.

This evidence seems sufficient to answer positively the first question posed at the beginning of this section, but what about the second: Are geographers willing and able to meet the demand for environmental courses and programs desired by students? Concerning this issue, the available information offers a less optimistic picture.

In the United States, most students come to the university having never taken a course in environmental studies or environmental science. In some states, self-standing environmental courses do exist, but for most students environmental topics are studied only in science or geography courses. Just two states, Nevada and Pennsylvania, certify or license teachers in environmental education (McKeown-Ice, 2000). In addition, earth science, which might have offered a disciplinary home for many environmental topics, has become less popular as more emphasis has been placed on comprehensive or integrated science. The material in these courses tends to be dominated by chemistry, physics and biology.

In geography the situation is not much better. Virtually all of the geography taught in United States schools is taught in courses situated in departments of social studies.

Geography is but a strand in social studies courses, which are typically taught by individuals with little or no formal training in geography or in the sciences. Because each state has almost complete control over its educational system, it is not possible to describe the previous experience that each student brings to university. Nevertheless, it is fair to say that relatively few students come with a background in geography or environmental studies, and few have had more than one course in either subject at the secondary level.

In higher education, enrollment in environmental courses and its change over time can be tracked to provide some evidence of geography's delivery of environmental education. Useful data are reported annually in *Schwendeman's Directory of College Geography of the United States.* Course enrollment numbers are compiled from questionnaires sent to virtually every geography department, and thus are self-reported data. Nevertheless, they do provide a national picture of geography education. The number and variety of courses on which Schwendemen's can collect information is limited and, unfortunately, 'sustainability' and 'environmental' are not listed as exclusive categories. Among total enrollments for introductory-level/general-education courses, the number of students enrolled in 'environmental/conservation' courses comprised 5.6 percent of the total in 2000. Enrollment in 'natural resources/environmental' courses accounted for 27.1 percent of the total number of students in 'Cultural, Economic, and Related Courses' (Walker, 2000). Environmental enrollments among lower-level geography courses have remained relatively steady over the last 10 years. It should be noted that the large increase for upper-level courses is due entirely to an increase from zero to 4000 students reported by one California university. Without those additional students, enrollment in upper-level environmental courses would represent 16.2 percent of total enrollment in 2000, a small decrease from the 19.7 percent reported in 1995 (see lower lines in Figure 2).

An examination of the course listings of the top-ten geography departments (according to the National Research Council: Pennsylvania State University, University of California at Berkeley, Ohio State University, University of Washington, University of California at Los Angeles, Clark University, University of Minnesota, University of Wisconsin, Syracuse University, and University of California at Santa Barbara), revealed that each offered at least three environmental courses. Internet course listings showed that these departments, on average, offered 120 different courses, eight of which could be said to be environmental, if courses covering physical geography with some environmental content, history of environmental thought, natural hazards, environmental social theory, resources, resource management, conservation and similar topics were counted. At seven of these universities, as many or more courses were offered by other departments. Online descriptions indicated that very few courses emphasized sustainability, a term that almost never appeared in a course title. Regardless of the emphasis, the definition used to categorize courses as environmental in this study was broadly based and very inclusive. Thus, within top geography departments, environmental and sustainability education is not absent, but neither is it abundant.

The titles of master's degree theses and PhD dissertations listed in the AAG Guide (AAG, 2002) were examined to determine the level of graduate-student study in environmental and sustainability topics. This information provides evidence beyond the presence of, or enrollment in, environmental courses. Thesis and dissertation topics were inventoried only for those departments that claimed a specialization in 'Conservation, Land Use, Resource Management' or 'Environmental Studies'. Given these departments' self-reported interest(s), it would be reasonable to expect that a significant proportion of graduate research topics would fall into the environmental or sustainability category. Of 92 dissertation titles listed, however, only 16 (17 percent) indicated some environmental connection, again, broadly and inclusively defined. Seven of these were written by students of Clark University, the only students who used the terms 'sustainable' or 'sustainability' in their titles. Of 235 theses, 27 (11 percent) contained some reference to environmental topics in their titles. Perhaps not surprisingly, many of the titles categorized as environmental had little to do with sustainable development, conservation or similar topics. Thus, although it seems that the percentages of graduate students pursuing environmental topics is probably greater than one would expect from the relatively few environmental courses offered by geography departments, the proportion is modest, especially if one contrasts the thesis and dissertation percentages with the proportion of *Annals* articles published in the Environmental Science or the Nature and Society sections (46 percent).

The difference between the active and growing environmental research activity in geography and the state of its course offerings and curricula has been noticed by others. Yarnal & Neff (2004, p. 30) agree with the evidence presented in this article when they claim that "the human-environment geography curriculum is weak in most geography departments". They point out that in the United States 55 departments offer PhDs in geography and 44 declare an interest in environmental geography, but only 17 offer an undergraduate program with a human-environment focus. Yarnal & Neff also call attention to the impact that this situation has on teacher-training programs, a problem also noted by McKeown-Ice (2000), who reports that 64 percent of those who counsel pre-service teachers advise students who are interested in environmental education to enroll in science-education programs.

Reasons for the Lack of Environmental Education in Geography

One reason for the difference between environmental and sustainability research and course offerings and curricula is that faculty interests are not necessarily reflected in the courses taught in geography departments (Yarnal & Neff, 2004). For example, the Internet home page of the University of Washington geography department indicates that sustainability and citizenship are two of the department's conceptual themes (University of Washington Department of Geography, 2004). Nevertheless only seven of the department's 148 courses are obviously environmental.

It might also be true that, because geographers of so many different perspectives have some (but perhaps not a primary?) interest in environmental and sustainability issues, they have not come together to offer a comprehensive or synthetic program to students. Indeed virtually all of the scholars cited in this article see both a challenge and an opportunity to bring geographers from various sub-fields together in order to understand contemporary environmental problems and issues. The more recent infusion of critical theory into environmental geography might also explain some of the lack of courses taking this perspective. It often takes considerable time before new theory is incorporated into courses, especially in the undergraduate curriculum.

It is also true that geography departments in the United States are typically not very large, and often their status is not high. According to the Association of American Geographers the average faculty size for departments offering bachelor's, master's and PhD degrees are five, nine and 13, respectively. Thus, offering a comprehensive environmental curriculum or even a strong focus might be almost impossible for some departments if they hope to support other geographic sub-fields.

Geography's status in the United States has almost always been threatened. Geography departments were created relatively late, 150 years after knowledge had been partitioned into natural and social sciences. Geography's human–environment interaction perspective did not fit either category of knowledge well, and in addition the partitioned academy "never truly embraced the spatial-chorological identity" (Turner, 2002, p. 61). Evidence of geography's relatively low importance in US higher education is plentiful.

Among the top 10 national universities (Harvard, Yale, Princeton, Dartmouth, Stanford, Duke, Massachusetts Institute of Technology, California Institute of Technology, University of Pennsylvania, and Washington University), as ranked by *US News and World Report* (2002), only one, Dartmouth, offers a degree in geography. At these prestigious institutions, environmental studies are offered as interdisciplinary programs for the most part. These programs typically require a student to major, and frequently earn a degree, in a traditional department. Some programs are science-based—Harvard, California Institute of Technology, Stanford and the University of Pennsylvania—whereas others are social science-based or allow an orientation toward either science or social science. Yale and Dartmouth have environmental studies departments, and MIT offers no environmental program. Therefore, in the nation's top-ranked universities, excepting Dartmouth, environmental topics are taught in multidisciplinary programs, not in geography departments. In addition, several other prestigious universities such as Northwestern University, University of Chicago and University of Michigan have closed their geography departments in the last 25 years. Of interest is that these departments were highly ranked not long before they ceased to exist.

Another indication of geography's relatively weak position is that only 60 percent of the departments listed in the AAG *Guide to Programs in Geography in the United States and Canada* (AAG, 2002) are exclusively geography departments. The remaining are hybrid departments that combine geography with a wide variety of other disciplines such as geology or earth science, planning, regional development, political science, anthropology, economics, and 11 departments that pair geography with environmental science or environmental studies.

Not surprisingly, this situation has encouraged the creation of interdisciplinary environmental programs and self-standing environmental departments, such as those noted at the top 10 universities. An Internet search using EnviroEducation.com lists 487 environmental studies programs at colleges and universities in the United States and 744 in environmental science. For purposes of comparison, the site lists 320 geography programs (EnviroEducation, 2004).

Geography's status might also explain why it has participated rather tentatively in environmental education leading to action or activism. These activities remain more controversial in the United States than in most other developed countries. Beginning with the Reagan administration, programs to increase energy production, deregulate industry and increase economic growth have been assigned higher priorities than environmental protection. The attitudes of a large majority of Bush administration decision-makers can be inferred from comments made by Vice-President Cheney to the annual meeting of the Associated Press during the California energy crisis. In an article titled, 'Cheney Promotes Increasing Supply as Energy Policy', *The New York Times* reported, "In his most comprehensive comments to date on the energy task force he is heading on behalf of

President Bush, Mr. Cheney dismissed as 1970s-era thinking the notion that 'we could simply conserve or ration our way out' of what he called an energy crisis". The vice-president went on to say, "The aim here is efficiency, not austerity. Conservation may be a sign of personal virtue, but it is not a sufficient basis for a sound, comprehensive energy policy" (*New York Times*, 1 May 2001, Sec. A, p. 1). Another indication was the content of the (still not passed) administration's energy bill. This legislation contained more than $18 billion in tax incentives to oil, natural gas, coal and nuclear power producers, deregulated the business dealings of electric utility holding companies, included a $20 billion tax subsidy to encourage construction of a gas pipeline from Alaska to Chicago but did not require improvements in auto gas-mileage or an increase in the use of renewable fuels by electricity generators (*New York Times*, 15 November 2003, Sec. A, p. 10).

Analysis of the online course descriptions of the top-ten geography departments supported the assertion that at least some geographers have made an effort to take defensible, objective environmental approaches rather than embracing more enthusiastically environmental topics that are perceived to have a controversial political component. Whereas courses in other departments very frequently mention 'sustainability', 'conservation' or 'preservation', these terms were used much less frequently in geography course descriptions. This more conservative attitude was also apparent from departmental Internet home pages. Clark University's geography department (one of the most unabashedly environmental) homepage describes its environmental component as follows:

> Geographers study the relationships between people and the environment. Geographers at Clark study how people make use of, interact with, and cause changes to environments that range from cities in the US and Asia to small holder farms in Mexico to waterways located around the world. Geographers' interest in human–environment relationships leads them to focus on location and on place. (Clark University Department of Geography, 2003)

In contrast, Clark's Program in International Development, Community, and Environment (IDCE) describes its mission as "one of the greatest challenges of the 21st century: sustaining environmental resources while promoting development" (Clark University IDCE, 2003). An examination of the articles published in the Environmental Science and the Nature and Society categories of the *Annals* shows a similar pattern. Whereas the papers published in these two sections comprise 46 percent of the total, not a single article mentions sustainability in its title, abstract, or list of key words, and 'conservation', 'resource management' and 'human dimensions of global change' are each mentioned as a key word only once. It should be noted, however, that although some might think tackling an issue such as sustainable development requires political courage, others might disagree. O'Riordan (1989, p. 93) claims that sustainable development is nothing more than a contradiction of terms in capitalist societies and "the refuge of the environmentally perplexed".

Of course there are other reasons why geography in the United States is not more active in environmental education. For example, Butzer (2002, p. 75) argues that the spatial-chorological identity dominated geography during the last part of the twentieth century serving "to marginalize physical geography… As a consequence, Earth Day 1970 found geography too emaciated to jump in and play a conspicuous role."

A short case study explicating the outcome of competition for space in the university's environmental education enterprise between geography and another department at a large public university might serve to illustrate the opportunity and challenge that environmental education presents to geography. Because geography was perceived to be unable to satisfy the demand for environmental programs and because ownership of environmental education was contested by other departments at the university, bachelor's degrees in environmental studies and environmental geoscience were created outside the geography department.

Environmental courses existed in a variety of departments at the university. Until recently, however, the only environmental program concerned with human–environment interactions, conservation and environmental policy was housed within the department of geography in the form of a degree plan concentration. The Environmental Studies Option (ESO) was created more than 20 years ago when other academic units had little interest in the topic. This attitude among university faculty was not, apparently, rare among US academics (May, 1970).

In 2001, in part because he perceived a demand from students for more environmental education, the university provost encouraged creation of a new self-standing degree program in environmental science or studies. A plan was quickly developed to convert geography's 'management and policy' and 'environmental science' degree options into standard undergraduate degree programs. Faculty from the four departments in the College of Geosciences (Atmospheric Science, Geography, Geology and Geophysics, and Oceanography) participated in the planning process. As the geosciences deans began to move the degree-plan proposals up the administrative hierarchy, they were surprised to discover that other departments objected to giving the College of Geosciences the exclusive right to grant environmental degrees. As a result, a compromise agreement was reached allowing any department to create a program and award a degree in environmental studies as long as it included a core of basic environmental courses. The department of geography, then, went from the exclusive provider of environmental degree programs to a cooperating department in a degree offered by both the College of Geosciences and the College of Agriculture and Life Sciences.

Despite US geography's inability or unwillingness to meet much of the demand for environmental education, it still has an opportunity to play a bigger role. Both geographers and non-geographers see an environmental component as a major part of the discipline. Can both human and physical geographers cooperate to provide and support environmental education, including some of the more controversial aspects? The opportunity to strengthen geography's position in the academy suggests that undertaking this task would be beneficial for both geographers and for those who look to geography for environmental education. Nevertheless, for many departments in the United States, meeting the demands of students for degree programs or concentrations will require the allocation of additional resources to environmental geography. Although departments have the freedom to hire faculty with needed specialties, the allocation of additional resources is made at a higher administrative level, and the competition for these resources is fierce.

One development suggesting that geography is moving toward a re-emphasis of its human-environment core is the recent creation of a new division of the National Academy of Sciences: Human Environmental Sciences. Geographers have moved to this division from Social and Political Sciences and, in fact, they make up the majority of the new division's membership. Perhaps this decision by the field's most prestigious scholars portends a renewal of environmental interests among all geographers in the United States, and perhaps it will raise geography's status in the academy. Nevertheless, even if human-environment topics become a more important research domain, the arguments presented here suggest that course offerings and curricula will not necessarily follow. The integration of human-environment research with geography's pedagogy is critical if geographers are to meet the challenge and exploit the opportunity that growing interest in the environment presents. The demand for courses and curricula is clear. If geography does not satisfy it, recent history suggests that other academic units move in to capture the market.

References

Association of American Geographers (AAG) (1990) *Guide to Programs in Geography in the United States and Canada 1989–1990* (Washington, DC: AAG).

Association of American Geographers (AAG) (1995) *Guide to Programs in Geography in the United States and Canada 1994–1995* (Washington, DC: AAG).

Association of American Geographers (AAG) (2002) *Guide to Programs in Geography in the United States and Canada 2001–2002* (Washington, DC: AAG).

Butzer, K. W. (2002) The rising cost of contestation, *Annals of the AAG*, 92(1), pp. 75–78.

Clark University Department of Geography (2003) Clark University Undergraduate Geography Program. Available at http://www.clarku.edu/departments/geography/undergrad/index.shtml (accessed August 2003).

Clark University IDCE (2003) Clark University IDCE Pages. Available at http://www.clarku.edu/departments/idce/index.shtml (accessed August 2003).

Delaney, D. (2001) Making nature/marking humans: law as a site of (cultural) production, *Annals of the AAG*, 91(3), pp. 487–503.

Diduck, A. & Sinclair, J. (1997) The concept of critical environmental assessment (ea) education, *Canadian Geographer*, 41(3), pp. 294–307.

Emel, J. & Peet, R. (1989) Resource management and natural hazards, in: R. Peet & N. Thrift (Eds) *New Models in Geography: The Political Economy Perspective*, pp. 49–76 (London: Unwin Hyman).

EnviroEducation (2004) Environmental Schools, Environmental Education, Environmental Colleges—The Environmental Education Directory. Available at http://www.enviroeducation.com/ (accessed December 2004).

Flint, R. W., McCarter, W. & Bonniwell, T. (2000) Interdisciplinary education in sustainability: links in secondary and higher education, *International Journal of Sustainability in Higher Education*, 1(2), pp. 191–202.

Geography Education National Standards Project (1994) *Geography for Life: National Geography Standards 1994* (Washington, DC: National Geographic Society).

Huckle, J. (2002) Reconstructing nature: towards a geographical education for sustainable development, *Geography*, 87(1), pp. 64–72.

Kates, R. W. (2002) Humboldt's dream, beyond disciplines, and sustainability science: contested identities in a restructuring academy, *Annals of the Association of American Geographers*, 92(1), pp. 79–81.

Kasimov, N.S., Malkhasova, S.M. & Romanova, E.P. (2005) Environmental education for sustainable development in Russia, *Journal of Geography in Higher Education*, 29(1), pp. 49–59.

May, J. A. (1970) *Kant's Concept of Geography and Its Relation to Recent Geographical Thought* (Toronto: University of Toronto Press).

McKeown-Ice, R. (2000) Environmental education in the United States: a survey of preservice teacher education programs, *Journal of Environmental Education*, 32(1), pp. 4–11.

Meindl, C. F., Alderman, D. H. & Waylen, P. (2002) The role of James O. Wright in promoting the drainage of Florida's Everglades in the early twentieth century, *Annals of the Association of American Geographers*, 92(4), pp. 682–701.

National Council for Science and the Environment (NCSE) (2003) *Recommendation for Education for a Sustainable and Secure Future* (Washington, DC: NCSE).

New York Times (2001) Cheney promotes increasing supply as energy policy, *New York Times*, 1 May 2001, Section A, p. 1.

New York Times (2003) Accord reached by Republicans for energy bill, *New York Times*, 15 November 2003, Section A, p. 1.

O'Riordan, T. (1989) The challenge for environmentalism, in: R. Peet & N. Thrift (Eds) *New Models in Geography: The Political Economy Perspective*, pp. 77–102 (London: Unwin Hyman).

Pattison, W. D. (1964) The four traditions of geography, *Journal of Geography*, 63(3), pp. 211–216.

Pease, P. & Tchakerian, V. (2002) Composition and sources of sand in the Wahiba Sand Sea, *Annals of the Association of American Geographers*, 92(3), pp. 416–434.

Peet, R. (1989) New models of environment and resources: Introduction, in: R. Peet & N. Thrift (Eds) *New Models in Geography: The Political Economy Perspective*, pp. 43–47 (London: Unwin Hyman).

Pfirman and the AC-ERE (2003) *Complex Environmental Systems: Synthesis for Earth, Life, and Society in the 21st Century* (Washington, DC: National Science Foundation).

Turner, B. L. (2002) Contested identities: human-environment geography and disciplinary implications in a restructuring academy, *Annals of the AAG*, 92(1), pp. 52–74.

United States (Richmond, KY: Geographical Studies and Research Center).

University of Washington Department of Geography (2004) Geography at the University of Washington. Available at http://depts.washington.edu/geog/ (accessed August 2003).

US News and World Report Staff (2002) *America's Best Colleges 2003* (New York: US News Specialty Marketing).

Walker, W. J. (Ed.) (1990) *Schwendeman's Directory of College Geography of the United States* (Richmond, KY: Geographical Studies and Research Center).

Walker, W. J. (Ed.) (1995) *Schwendeman's Directory of College Geography of the United States* (Richmond, KY: Geographical Studies and Research Center).

Walker, W. J. (Ed.) (2000) *Schwendeman's Directory of College Geography of the United States* (Richmond, KY: Geographical Studies and Research Center).

Wescoat, J. L., Jr. (2002) Environmental geography—history and prospect, *Annals of the AAG*, 92(1), pp. 81–83.

Yarnal, B. & Neff, R. (2004) Whither parity? The need for a comprehensive curriculum in human-environment geography, *Professional Geographer*, 56(1), pp. 28–36.

Finding Space for Education for Sustainable Development in the Enterprise Economy

DAVID HIGGITT

Introduction

The Decade of Education for Sustainable Development (ESD) provides an impetus and a challenge for higher education institutions (HEIs) to demonstrate leadership. The sector has affirmed its support to sustainability collectively through a series of high-level conferences, declarations and partnerships and individually through mission statements that announce environmental credentials. However, sustainability remains a nebulous concept that is variously defined, debated and deconstructed. There is no uniformly agreed definition of the scope of ESD. Consequently a major challenge for the Decade is to promote the presence of ESD from words to actions, from concept to reality and to engage in a deeper self-critical inspection of the HEIs' responsibilities.

The boundary conditions for self inspection are likely to reflect the extent to which the objectives of ESD can be constructed as compatible with other mission objectives and will reflect a variety of local contexts. The UNESCO Concept statement (2004) notes:

> There is no universal model of education for sustainable development. While there will be overall agreement on the concept, there will be nuanced differences according to local contexts, priorities and approaches. Each country has to define its own priorities and actions. The goals, emphases and processes must, therefore, be locally defined to meet the local environmental, social and economic conditions in culturally appropriate ways. Education for sustainable development is equally relevant and critical for both developed and developing countries.

A symposium inviting commentaries on the HE response to ESD provides a forum for examining those 'nuanced differences'. In this paper, a commentary is provided from Singapore. The aim of the paper is to consider the context for promoting ESD within a mission environment focused around the enterprise economy. In the first instance a survey was designed to examine student consciousness of sustainability concepts. Observations are based around surveys of three cohorts of students undertaking a module within geography at the National University of Singapore. Student experience, attitudes and perceptions provide a basis for examining the visibility of the environmental message within the institution, as well as providing the author, as a newly arrived import from a Western country, to reflect of the nuances of environmental attitudes that might inform instructional design for other environmental and physical geography modules. The survey results also raise questions about the position of the discipline of geography in relation to the challenges and opportunities present by the Decade of Education for Sustainable Development (see also Bednarz, 2006).

Reviewing the evolution of ESD through international conferences and declarations, Haigh (2005) notes that HE response has progressed from generalized statements of intent to more detailed prescriptions for activity. However, there remain many obstacles within academe on the route from intent to action. Indeed, action has rarely been louder than words. Haigh (2005) provides a critique of the many obstacles to ESD within the HE sector, identifying funding structures, disciplinary boundaries and academic value systems as problematic; evidence of the persistence, he contends, "of the obsolete mind-sets of the 'industrial age'" (Haigh, 2005, p. 31). In practical terms, the question may be crudely phrased as 'how to find room for ESD when the HEI mission is framed by the goals of economic development?' Any answers are, of course, contingent on 'local contexts, priorities and challenges' (UNESCO, 2004), contexts that provide the value-laden subtexts for concepts such as 'environmental education', 'sustainability' and 'education for sustainable development' (McKeown & Hopkins, 2003; Selby, 2006).

Furthermore, as the Talloires Declaration calls for Sustainable Development to be clearly articulated "in ways consistent with their missions" (USLF, 1990), HEIs may argue that environmental credentials can be placed to one side while the university gets on with the real business of fuelling the regional or national economy. In conjunction with the mission statement, the 'vision' on the university website, 'Towards a Global Knowledge

Enterprise: Building synergies between education, research and entrepreneurship' appears unambiguous in its pursuit of economic development. The institution's primary role is seen as fostering innovation and the spirit of enterprise in order to "apply knowledge towards social, economic and national development, for the betterment of society". This is not, of course, to suggest the environmental matters are neglected—there is an institutional environmental policy, a flourishing Campus Green Committee running activities for staff and students and a range of targets achieved for waste reduction and energy efficiency—nor to overlook that the betterment of society can be served by promoting ESD. As a newcomer to the country and the university, a survey of student perceptions of sustainable development presented an opportunity to explore the profile of sustainability and environmental issues within the prevailing institutional ethos. The survey responses provide a basis for describing joint challenges; one for mobilizing student awareness and the other for positioning the disciplinary response.

The Undergraduate Challenge: Attitudes and Awareness

The idea for examining undergraduate attitudes to sustainability was initially derived from a graduate module (GE6216: The Nature of Physical Geography), which addresses the historical development of the sub-discipline and its evolving relationship with science. The module, deriving its title from an expurgated version of the textbook by Gregory (2000), debates the remit and scope of physical geography, including the disciplines role for addressing sustainability issues.[1] Working with the five students undertaking this module as part of their research training, a questionnaire was designed to be distributed to a large class of undergraduates. The questionnaire was designed primarily to evaluate students' interpretations of sustainability, their identification (or otherwise) between the resource management and ethical dimensions of sustainability with a disciplinary home within HE, and their awareness of environmental issues in the broader region.

The undergraduate module chosen to conduct the surveys was GE3231 (Natural Hazards). This is an elective module at the 3000 level but open to qualified students at all levels and has no specific prerequisites and normally recruits between 100 and 150 students per year. Under the fully modular system, this module is also available for cross-faculty registration, each student being required to fulfil a certain number of 'breadth' modules outside her/his home faculty. While the majority registered for the module comprises second- and third-year students from within the Faculty of Arts and Social Sciences (and many of these are declared majors in geography) there are also several students from other faculties (e.g. engineering, science, computing, design and environment, business). It might be assumed that students electing a module on natural hazards would have some innate interest in environmental issues but this is not necessarily the case.

The survey was conducted on three occasions (Semester 2 of 2002–2003; Semester 2 of 2003–2004 and Semester 1 of 2004–2005). As befitting the role of the graduate module in discussing the questionnaire design there were some modifications in the scope and design of the questionnaire between the first and second surveys, but the latter design was retained for the third survey. In many pedagogic research papers it is helpful to analyse student perception and reactions for two or more cohorts, particularly to provide an objective basis for establishing the impact of some learning and teaching initiative. In this case, there has been no direct intervention in the module design and issues concerning sustainable development have only been mentioned in passing at the stage when the questionnaire is administered (approximately week 8 or 9 of a 13-week timetable). Nor has the structure or content of the module been altered significantly. The reason for surveying three cohorts of students is not, therefore, to test a claim of how the instructional method has challenged attitudes, but rather to add rigour to the empirical database and to examine to what extent external influences (i.e. campus initiatives, media reporting of environmental issues, national and international policies) have influenced perceptions.

The questionnaire survey had three broad aims. These were to gather information on general perceptions of sustainability, student awareness of environmental issues in local and regional contexts, and information on the pervasiveness of sustainability ideas within the education system, specifically its visibility within the university and wider society. Questionnaires were administered through tutorial classes (groups of about 25 students) following a brief explanation of why the information was being collected. Although it would have been useful to undertake some focus-group discussions with the undergraduate students, based on the initial survey results, this was not practical within the timeframe available. However, the survey results were discussed within the graduate module and provided some discussion points for the final lectures of the undergraduate module. A total of 291 questionnaires were completed (at a strike rate of 78 to 85 per cent for each cohort). In the following discussion any quotes used are attributed to the particular cohort (the first, second or third survey) and the declared or intended major indicated on the anonymous questionnaire. By continuing the survey each year a reasonably large longitudinal data set can be established. For the purposes of the present paper some general trends from the survey are identified but at a later stage it should be possible to conduct a more rigorous statistical analysis of changing conceptions of sustainability.

Perceptions of Sustainability

Students were asked to choose up to three phrases from a list of 10 descriptors that they would most associate with the term sustainability. The descriptors were themselves derived from a brainstorming discussion with the graduate students which identified various resource-related definitions but also some headings that reflected social justice.[2] Students overwhelmingly identified sustainability with resource status, the most popular phrases being represented in Table 1. The most frequently selected descriptor on each occasion was 'reserve resources for future'. Terms associated with personal consumption or equitable distribution scored poorly. Within a Singapore context the linking of sustainability to resources is interesting given the traditional entrepôt nature of the economy and the limited availability of land and water resources. It can be argued that such a definition externalizes sustainability beyond Singapore's borders. Coupled with the excellent performance of environmental policies in enforcing regulations and delivering a tidy 'tropical garden' environment, there is a potential for complacency, in the sense that environmental problems are thought to have been solved. Problems of resource depletion and land degradation evident in neighbouring countries may be perceived as external and unrelated to consumption patterns within Singapore. As one student (Cohort 1, Engineering) put it, "Singapore does not have any resources, so the topic of sustainability is not considered". This is a somewhat extreme view but does seem to reflect an undercurrent that environmental issues happen to *other* people in *other* places.

Table 1. Descriptors most often associated with sustainability by three cohorts of students

Descriptors selected (per cent)	*Cohort 1 (2002–2003)*[a]	*Cohort 2 (2003–2004)*	*Cohort 3 (2004–2005)*
Reserve Resources for Future	58	69	72
Balanced Use of Resources	32	55	67
Nature Conservation[b]	–	45	53
Renewable Resources	22	42	42
Long Lasting Resources	18	36	44
Number of completed questionnaires	98	85	108
Class size	115	100	138

Note: Descriptors were selected by graduate students.
[a] After the Cohort 1 survey student were asked to identify up to three descriptors;
[b] nature conservation was not listed in the original Cohort 1 survey.

Students were asked to identify what they considered to be the most pressing issue concerning sustainability in Singapore. The first survey was conducted in March 2003 at a time when negotiations regarding the transborder water supply agreement with Malaysia were taking place. Consequently, water issues dominated answers. It has continued to be mentioned frequently in subsequent surveys but in percentage terms has declined as the water debate faded from the news headlines to some extent. In the most recent survey, for example, urban regeneration is identified as a pressing issue, having received much media attention ahead of the opening of the Shaping Singapore exhibition (http://www.ura.gov.sg/shaping_spore/). Curiously, the urban haze problem, which achieved international notoriety during the 1997–1998 El Nino (Koe *et al.*, 2001), was hardly mentioned—a handful of students indicated air pollution as a pressing issue. It would therefore appear that sustainability concerns are shaped by topicality.

Regional Contexts

In the next section of the questionnaire students were asked to comment on how sustainability issues in neighbouring countries (Indonesia, Malaysia, Thailand) differed from those in Singapore. Although there are informed comments from some respondents, a large number of the remarks written indicate a limited awareness of the issues confronting neighbouring countries and a limited distinction between them. This is most apparent in the earliest survey, where there is a tendency for students to relate sustainability issues in neighbouring countries simply to abundance and availability of water supplies. A tension emerges between whether sustainability should refer to restricting resource use or to improving the efficiency of resource exploitation. For example one student commenting on sustainability issues in Thailand (Cohort 3, Geography) writes, “[they] lack knowledge and technological capabilities to fully utilize their resources”.

A concept of sustainability oscillating between ideas of environmental protection and ambitions of economic growth is apparent throughout questionnaire responses and requires consideration of prevailing perspectives in the education system. Many of the responses reflect a pragmatic, managerialist attitude to environmental issues founded on an assumption that technology and sound governance will provide solutions. Conversely, lingering problems in other Southeast Asian countries can be rationalized in terms of poor governance, inefficiency, corruption and a lack of access to technology and/or education. For the most part the identification of environmental issues in neighbouring countries is unsophisticated. Writing a decade previously about a survey of environmental awareness among secondary school students Savage & Lau (1993, p. 26) comment: "As a city detached as it were from nature and the rhythms of the natural landscape, our students are less likely to appreciate the importance of the ecological message and the dangers of environmental degradation." A similar sentiment is articulated by Kong *et al.* (1999) who concluded from focus groups with youth participants that the urbanized existence with an abundance of entertainment options limited young Singaporeans' interest in nature. They further suggest that this contributes to a passive acceptance of the privileging of development projects over nature conservation objectives. At university, such attitudes resurface as an issue in the recruitment of students to physical geography and science-based environmental modules.[3]

From a geographer's perspective a restricted personal experience of nature within a highly urbanized upbringing and a limited awareness of regional environmental issues suggest that making space for ESD is not just about competing for publicity among economic growth and entrepreneurial slogans. Rather it calls for recognition that environmental problems are spatially differentiated and multi-scaled. The geographies of environmental issues matter!

Pervasiveness of Sustainability

As noted previously, the university has a Campus Green Committee that promotes a wide range of initiatives and encourages staff and student participation. Judging from the questionnaires, however, the profile is not very visible. In each cohort, approximately 80 per cent of the respondents thought that sustainability and environmental issues did not have a high profile on campus. Sometimes students commented (inaccurately) on the non-existence of recycling facilities, but there are also many revealing comments about attitudes in this section. In particular there is a sense of frustration at the lack of emphasis and limited motivation of fellow students, as revealed in the following quotes:

> Students are continuously promoting [sustainability] through campaigns and charity drives. However, though exposure is high, participation is rather unimpressive. (Cohort 3, Geography & Sociology).

> It [environmental awareness] is not organized and visible—it feels like they are talking about it because it's a politically correct thing to do. (Cohort 1, Geography & Sociology).

> The absence of rural or suburban areas in Singapore creates a sense of apathy of these issues. (Cohort 1, Geography).

The significance of keeping one's head down and achieving good grades is a recurring theme in the questionnaires and one that has been partly explained, albeit stereotypically, in cultural terms as *kiasu* (Chang, 2004)—an anxiety not to misinterpret expectations, especially in relation to summative assessment:

> Everybody is too engrossed with results. Unless there is a tangible reward it's hard to create a profile. (Cohort 2, Geography).

> Students are more concerned about their studies, and upon graduation, their career prospects. I think Singaporeans are very dependent on the Government to solve all their problems. (Cohort 1, Chemistry).

This leads to a perceptive comment that resonates with the message from Martin & Jucker's (2005) plea in the first part of the ESD symposium:

> The only time I hear about these issues is in class and lectures. It's an irony because the future decision makers and leader of countries will come from this campus and they are not being educated and informed about it. (Cohort 3, Geography).

There are also a number of comments that imply that a sustainability message will lose out to the entrepreneurial message promoted in the university's vision statement:

> ... there's too much emphasis on how to be entrepreneurial. How can we have any business with the world on the verge of over-exploitation? (Cohort 3, Geography).

But from the perspective of undertaking some Business Studies modules comes a very different interpretation of sustainability:

> It [sustainability] is widely discussed, even in business courses which question whether the environment of a certain country is supportive enough, in terms of labour, funding, etc. to sustain a certain economic venture. (Cohort 2, Information Communication).

In the next section of the questionnaire, students were asked to comment on whether they would associate environmental issues such as sustainability with a particular subject area. Notwithstanding a number of claims for a sustainability agenda within economics, the overwhelming response, as expected, is that geography is the subject area most naturally associated with this theme, followed by biology. The potentially ambiguous role of a subject discipline representing an interdisciplinary arena is now considered.

The Geography Challenge: Responsibilities and Reactions

In debating the position of geography in higher education in relation to the ESD agenda the problematic issue of disciplinary boundaries requires elaboration. On one hand, the nature of the subject and, evidently, the expectations of HE students suggest it is the ideal vehicle for taking ESD forward. Indeed, the UNESCO ESD Statement on Quality Education presents:

> ... a new vision of education, a vision that helps people of all ages better understand the world in which they live, addressing the complexity and interconnectedness of

> problems such as poverty, wasteful consumption, environmental degradation, urban decay, population growth, health, conflict and the violation of human rights that threaten our future (UNESCO, 2004).

Geography seems to be at the heart of such a definition, but the statement continues:

> This vision of education emphasizes a holistic, interdisciplinary approach to developing the knowledge and skills needed for a sustainable future as well as changes in values, behaviour, and lifestyles. This requires us to reorient education systems, policies and practices in order to empower everyone, young and old, to make decisions and act in culturally appropriate and locally relevant ways to redress the problems that threaten our common future. In this way, people of all ages can become empowered to develop and evaluate alternative visions of a sustainable future and to fulfil these visions through working creatively with others.

At issue is whether geography, as a discipline, is best placed to preach about interdisciplinary studies or whether this can only be achieved through a radical re-engineering of disciplinary boundaries. Returning to Haigh's (2005) argument about obstacles to curriculum greening, the central concern is the way in which disciplines form 'academic tribes' that lay claim to a body of knowledge. As Haigh (2005, pp. 37–38) laments, "in this context, environmental issues are treated by most HEIs as the property of a select few disciplines (particularly geography and the environmental sciences) which often lock their offerings away behind the barriers of specialization". Intriguingly, the modular nature of the degree system described in this paper, the cross-faculty enrolment and the removal of prerequisites means that the module described is not guilty of being locked away behind the barriers of specialization. However, this raises its own problems, not least in preparing material that is suitably accessible yet sufficiently challenging for a range of backgrounds and experience. Nevertheless, many students clearly see knowledge as being a compartmentalized possession of different disciplines, typified by the comment that sustainability is a:

> ... very loose term. We have to comment/mention the particular discipline in which we want to study sustainability, such as 'sustainability of environmental protection efforts in Singapore' (Cohort 3, Engineering).

In a study of environmental education curriculum development at secondary school level in Singapore, Wong & Stimpson (2003) identify a series of tensions between the development of environmental education and the remit of the mainstream curriculum. In particular, the school system is very much examination orientated and focused more towards content knowledge than critical thinking. It is not surprising, therefore, that students arriving at university have preconceptions about where certain types of knowledge should reside. Yencken *et al.* (2002) raise similar concerns from secondary school focus groups in Asia-Pacific countries, noting the tendency for environmental knowledge to be compartmentalized into different disciplines so that although students may arrive at university equipped with cognitive appreciation of environmental issues they are poorly prepared to think systematically. Few academics would disagree that the role of HE should be to enhance critical and systematic thinking, but the issue is whether the task of producing socially critical, environmentally aware graduates should fall within the remit of geography (or cognate disciplines) or should be delivered independently of disciplinary control (and perhaps to all students).

The questionnaire asked students if they thought that sustainability should be taught as an independent module at university. Again, there is overwhelming support for such an idea (ranging from 79 to 83 per cent of each cohort). Among the positive comments in favour of such a proposal are:

> Sustainability is increasingly becoming a vital issue in today's context where emphasis is placed on consumerism and capitalism. As students it is essential that we are aware of the ecological footprints we are leaving behind. Additionally as concerned citizens of the earth, we should be fully aware of how we as individuals could contribute to a sustainable future (Cohort 3, Geography).

> ... was in the UK for exchange and I took a module called Environmental Management and was really awed by the sustainability debates which are going on now in other parts of the world (Cohort 3, Geography).

And going deeper than the pragmatic definitions of sustainability there are some thoughts about the crucial role of education:

> The issue of sustainability should be taught to all. Everyone should realize that they have a role to play and ensure that sustainability will be achieved. (Cohort 3, Geography).

> It will educate people who may create effective changes... *real* changes (Cohort 2, Geography & Sociology, original emphasis).

> It will be beneficial for students to have heightened social awareness of such issues. In particular, they can take sustainability into account in their future work/decisions. It may help them to have a more holistic view of their actions' impact (Cohort 2, Mathematics).

In one case the recommendation is tinged with realism:

> It will be an exciting and interesting addition, but only if it is an optional module. Putting it as a compulsory module is a death sentence with regards to enthusiasm (Cohort 3, Geography).

This is an interesting observation given the challenge for ESD to infuse curricula. The logistic challenge is not unprecedented. Following the SARS episode in early 2003 the university initiated a compulsory module on SARS that immediately became a graduation requirement (and also demonstrated the technical feasibility of operating an online module to all students). Similarly, a compulsory module on plagiarism has been devised.

The dissenting voices, though in a minority, provide a rationalist view of the value of environmental education:

> Environmental issues might be perceived as non-relevant to students' areas of concentration and do not have practical uses (Cohort 2, Life Sciences).
>
> It is a little too isolated to be taught in such a manner ... should be integrated into relevant modules (Cohort 2, Law).
>
> There is no marketability for its usefulness as a subject (Cohort 1, Geography).

To some extent, the situation in Singapore mirrors Bednarz's (2006) analysis of environmental education in the USA. The majority viewpoint, at least from the students' perspective, is that geography should be leading the way in promoting environmental awareness and providing sustainability literacy for future leaders, though like the USA the central geographical theme of human–environment relations is not one that has been especially prominent in module offerings. Alternative models, currently under discussion, are to develop interdisciplinary modules focused around societal engagement and service learning. These modules enable students to achieve credit from placements with voluntary organizations while providing a substantive academic component to reflect on the social and ethical issues, including, amongst other topics, environmental futures.

Summary

Repeated surveys of three cohorts undertaking a module in geography have revealed many aspects of perceptions, awareness and attitudes to environmental issues that provide impetus for considering how to develop ESD. There are some indications that students recognize the need for a critical approach to sustainability but for the most part comments appear preconditioned by the utilitarian approach to environmental management that prevails in the secondary school curriculum. Students are generally pessimistic about the interest and awareness of their colleagues in environmental issues, but very supportive of initiatives that would seek to bolster awareness, such as provision of education for sustainable development through new module(s). In a position paper on global sustainability UNESCO (2002) states:

> With respect to higher education, there will be emphasis on the role of universities in refining the concept and messages of education for sustainable development, integrating environmental, demographic, economic, social and a range of other concerns inherent in the notion of sustainability. In re-orienting their research programmes and curricula, key will be the universities' capacity for flexible interdisciplinary cooperation and for collaboration with outside institutions... Universities will have to experiment by exercising more initiative and by risking new approaches.

A comprehensive degree framework with a flexible modular system, an emphasis on cross-faculty links and an entrepreneurial culture that seeks to encourage risk-taking provides the right ingredients for exercising the interdisciplinary activities that the UNESCO statement calls for. However, student comments attest to scepticism that an environmental sustainability message can fight for air time against a pragmatic focus on obtaining good grades and a gateway to a career (as perceived in terms of practical skills and marketability). Indeed, reporting interviews with Singaporean secondary school teachers, Wong & Stimpson (2003) note the conundrum that if environmental education is non-examinable there is little incentive to take it up, but once it is made examinable students will just engage to pass the exam. Pushing the ESD agenda therefore require delicate, culturally sensitive consideration, fully conscious of the local environmental, social and economic priorities. Should ESD compete against the prevailing industrial model or seek to produce enterprising environmentalists?

Notes

[1] Ken Gregory's book *The Changing Nature of Physical Geography* (2000) is an updated edition of his 1985 *The Nature of Physical Geography*, originally conceived as the physical geography companion to Ron Johnston's highly popular *Geography and Geographers* (1983). The module's moniker adopted the later version but a bureaucratic decree limiting module titles to 40 characters resulted in 'changing' being dropped from the title—despite the implied stagnation of physical geography. Gregory's viewpoint on physical geography is fundamentally British and institutionally focused within the geography discipline, but there are plenty of critics who envisage a path for physical geography that moves towards earth system science (and by implication away from a traditional focus on human–environment relations). Such a trajectory has some implications for how the physical geography sub-discipline would present ideas about environmental issues and sustainable development and this is the focus that the postgraduate students are grappling with as they design the sustainability questionnaire.

[2] The 10 descriptors are: (a) long-lasting resource; (b) cannot be destroyed; (c) cannot be used; (d) renewable resources; (e) reserve resource for the future; (f) balanced use of resources; (g) fairness to all; (h) prevention of natural disasters; (i) personal consumption patterns; (j) nature conservation.

[3] The author has recently acted as a mentor for secondary school students conducting projects on the awareness of environmental issues among teenagers. Despite some progress in promoting environmental clubs within schools it appears that interest in and awareness of environmental issues is barely greater than the surveys conducted in the 1990s. Two-thirds of school students surveyed did not know what 'sustainable development' was though the majority were aware of the Singapore Green Plan and the Clean and Green Week initiatives.

References

Bednarz, R. S. (2006) Environmental research and education in US Geography, *Journal of Geography in Higher Education*, 30(2), pp. 237–250.

Chang, T. C. (2004) Transborder tourism, borderless classroom: reflections on a Hawaii-Singapore experience, *Journal of Geography in Higher Education*, 28(2), pp. 179–195.

Gregory, K. J. (2000) *The Changing Nature of Physical Geography* (London: Arnold).

Haigh, M. J. (2005) Greening the university curriculum: appraising an international movement, *Journal of Geography in Higher Education*, 29(1), pp. 31–48.

Johnston, R. J. (1983) *Geography and Geographers*, 1st edn (London: Arnold).

Koe, L. C. C., Arellano, A. F. & McGregor, J. L. (2001) Investigating the haze transport from 1997 biomass burning in Southeast Asia: its impact upon Singapore, *Atmospheric Environment*, 35(15), pp. 2723–2734.

Kong, L., Yuen, B., Sodhi, N. S. & Briffett, C. (1999) The construction and experience of nature: perspectives of urban youths, *Tijdschrift voor Economische en Sociale Geografie*, 90(1), pp. 3–16.

McKeown, R. & Hopkins, C. (2003) EE $\neq$ ESD: defusing the worry, *Environmental Education Research*, 9(1), pp. 117–128.

Martin, S. & Jucker, R. (2005) Educating Earth-literate leaders, *Journal of Geography in Higher Education*, 29(1), pp. 19–29.

Savage, V. R. & Lau, S. (1993) Green issues: official policies and student awareness, in: C. Briffett & L. L. Sim (Eds) *Environmental Issues in Development and Conservation*, pp. 13–28 (Singapore: School of Building and Estate Management, National University of Singapore).

Selby, D. (2006) The firm and shaky ground of education for sustainable development, *Journal of Geography in Higher Education*, 30(2), pp. 351–365.

UNESCO (2002) *Enhancing Global Sustainability: Position Paper* (New York: UNESCO). Available at http://unesdoc.unesco.org/images/0012/001253/125351e.pdf (accessed August 2004).

UNESCO (2004) Education for Sustainable Development: United Nations Decade 2005-14.Available at http://portal.unesco.org/education/en/ev.php-URL_ID=27234&URL_DO=DO_TOPIC&URL_SECTION=201.html (accessed August 2004).

ULSF (1990) *Programs: Talloires Declaration* (Washington, DC: Association of University Leaders for a Sustainable Future). Available at http://www.ulsf.org/programs_talloires.html (accessed August 2004).

Wong, F. B. K. & Stimpson, P. (2003) Environmental education in Singapore: A curriculum for the environment or in the national interest, *International Research in Geographical and Environmental Education*, 12(2), pp. 123–138.

Yencken, D., Fien, J. & Sykes, H. (2002) Environment, education and society in the Asia Pacific: Three key questions, *International Research in Geographical and Environmental Education*, 11(1), pp. 42–47.

Cultural Assumptions against Sustainability: An International Survey

BARBARA GAMBINI

Introduction

This paper presents the rationale and findings of an international survey that has been devised to provide evidence of different persons' attitudes to some key questions of sustainability. In fact, it can be argued that the visualization of the passing of time (in a line or circle, going necessarily forward or possibly backwards), the level of anthropocentrism and faith in progress all imply spatial macro-paradigms. Thus they underpin all the descriptive and prescriptive representations of a given culture, and concern both the traditional and the latest interests of geography. The same can be said about other broad taxonomic and teleological coordinates that have also been addressed, and that will be discussed below.

In an educational perspective, which is timely with the launch of the UN decade for education to sustainability, students were chosen as the main target group. "Young people form a crucial component in the process of environmental change", so much so that "we may need to await the coming of age of the younger environmentally aware generations in order to move forward significantly towards ecological sustainability" (Barrett & Kuroda, 2002, p. 238). The role of universities in providing (or failing to provide) sustainability literacy was highlighted in the first part of this symposium (Martin & Jucker, 2005). The survey was randomly distributed to and voluntarily filled in by 50 university students of geography and as many students of economics in four countries: Australia (University of Queensland), Sri Lanka (University of Colombo), China (Yunnan Normal University), Italy (University of Urbino); the language used was respectively English, Sinhalhese and English, Mandarin, Italian. The same survey was submitted to residents of an eco-village in Australia (Crystal Waters), 16 of whom accepted to respond.

These locations were chosen after a preliminary study on environmental attitudes. In his 'Discrepancies between Environmental Attitude and Behaviour: Examples from Europe and China', Yi-Fu Tuan (1974, p. 240) rightly warned against deterministically linking environmental values to environmental behaviour. He described the 'Oriental's approach to nature' as 'quiescent and adaptive', whereas the Westerner's was seen as one of 'aggressive masculinity'. But is there a direct correspondence between these sets of values and the relative environmental actions, and how tenuous is it, he asked?

Since value systems (religions, ethics, legal systems) set an ideal scenario towards which individuals are supposed to aim, actual behaviour—and environmental behaviour is no exception—tends to be more lax than the relative ethos would recommend. This is caused by numerous factors, some of which are intuitively understood, while others have long been identified by psychologists and sociologists. These include self-leniency; greed; laziness; social inertia—intended qualitatively as a natural tendency of society to perpetuate certain acquired modes, rather than a numerically expressible formula (Zaman, 2001); ignorance; lack of time, alternatives or confidence in the effects of individual actions (Barrett & Kuroda, 2002). The complex nature of ecological information (that is 'unavoidably ambiguous' in Barrett & Kuroda's words, p. 240) makes it easy to disseminate incorrect or incomplete information. Many people are convinced recycling per se is sufficient to make their lifestyle sustainable (Gambini, 2005a). Value systems are influenced by collective and individual psychology to quote Gunn (undated, p. 29): "I suspect that we focus so much on problems because we love drama, not routine", and "the moral heroism of whistleblowers stirs the blood; setting in place internal ethics agents . . . does not". The 'Not-in-my-backyard syndrome' recognizes that people often become politically active, for or against environmentally minded measures, only when their close interests are endangered. All of these circumstances convincingly explain why most people fail to seek or emulate more sustainable behaviours, but they fail to explain why many treat serious efforts in the direction of sustainability as gratuitously Spartan measures or even fanatic extremism: to express it in the vernacular, there is little sympathy, let alone admiration, for 'tree-huggers'. Nor do these factors explain why a crime against the environment, even when acknowledged as such by the legislation—for they are often legally tolerated—very rarely brings about the moral stigma that is reserved for perpetrators of other offences (embezzlement, for example, in the USA), although the 'absolute cost to society' of the former can be far superior to the cost of the latter (Moncrief, 1974, p. 85). Moral rules are investigated by theoretical and applied ethicists; crimes against the person or private property are met with 'zero tolerance' by the legislation, but the environment is notably under-contemplated by both (Gunn, undated).

This evidence suggests that there are more deep-rooted paradigms, independent of all evidence and contingency, shared by policy-makers and the people alike.

While some anti-sustainability factors can be considered universal, or at least very widespread, there exist others that are more culture-specific. Different people do not share a uniform view of the environment, and their discrepancies are not only limited to setting emergencies and priorities, which could be affected by contingency: a fair and efficacious epistemological discourse on sustainability must necessarily engage in a true intercultural dialogue among peers. Since some of the most powerful moral directives are provided by religions, the next step was to examine some of the abundant literature on religions and ecology—where religion is intended in its broadest meaning, to include similarly prescriptive systems. Some see religion as an ethos-shaping force—others see it rather as one of the various expressions of a certain ethos. Probably a bit of both, religion can be agreed to be a generally conservative force, tending to perpetuate certain mindsets and behaviours against oncoming changes.

Lynn White's controversial and thought-provoking paper in 1967 (reprinted seven years later) initiated a heated debate on Christianity's responsibility in exacerbating worldwide environmental decline. The ideological postulates that made possible this acute ecological degradation were identified in Christianity's unparalleled anthropocentrism and its active war on animism and paganism, which, by depriving nature of its soul and sacredness, "made it possible to exploit [it] in a mood of indifference to the feelings of natural objects" (White, 1974, p. 25). White's paper elicited numerous responses, some supporting his position, others mitigating it, others still confuting it altogether, mainly by looking for an alternative environmental ethos within the Christian tradition (Barr, 1974; MacQuarrie, 1974; Baird Callicott, 1994; Kinsley, 1995), or by enumerating the plentiful precedents of human-driven environmental degradation in pre-Christian Europe or in non-Christian areas (see Dubos, 1974; Tuan, 1974; Elvin, 1998 but also see Smith, 1982; Wolff, 2000; Anderson, 2002). Baird Callicott (1994) illustrates three possible interpretations of the myths of Genesis: the despotic interpretation, the stewardship interpretation and, finally, the citizenship interpretation.

On the opposite view, Buddhism would seem to have all the necessary characteristics to be a structurally eco-friendly ethic system: its basic principles of *anatman* (the non-existence of a separate self), *ahimsa* (non-violence to all living beings), the struggle to overcome desires, the middle way, all seem to be not only compatible with but injunctive of a more sustainable relationship with nature and development. Moreover, Buddhists assume we do not know how things work, and this 'presumption of ignorance' is very much in line with the sustainability principle of caution (Batchelor & Brown, 1994).

Confucianism, on its part, does not offer an explicit ecological ethos (Taylor, 1998, pp. 45–46), but several of its fundamental teachings, if properly re-interpreted and re-vitalized, could bring a unique contribution to the cause of sustainability (Kalton, 1998). Among these are inclusive humanism (Cheng, 1998, p. 212), the doctrine of *qi*, which overcomes the dualism of matter/spirit and humans/non-humans, and the very nature of Confucianism, which compensates for modern sciences' profusely descriptive and scarcely prescriptive guidance, and the sense of dissatisfaction this has caused among people (Kalton, 1998, p. 83). *Feng shui*, on the other hand, traditionally served to counterbalance the collective and self-denying pressures of official Chinese doctrines by legitimizing cumulative and exclusive interests (Bruun, 1995, p. 184).

Leading off from this interesting theoretical scenario, the idea was to submit the survey to countries where these cultures are predominant, in order to provide material, albeit of little statistical significance, to design further comparative studies on people's broad environmental paradigms. Italy and Sri Lanka were thus selected because of their predominantly Christian and Buddhist identity. China represented a challenging and widely unpredictable case because of its traditional Buddhist, Confucian and *feng shui* background, later intermingled with the dialectical materialism of communism and, more recently, with capital economy. Eco-village residents seemed a logical reference point for the previous categories: eco-villages are intentional communities set up, or modified, according to more sustainable criteria, which suggests their residents have a higher-than-average sensibility and commitment to the issues related to sustainability. The choice fell on Crystal Waters, Australia, a very famous village originally planned according to the criteria of Permaculture®. Finally, the answers of Australian students would provide a background and comparison for those of Crystal Waters residents.

Clarification is due at this point: the ecological ethos of a certain population is certainly not an eternally set, homogenous body of rules with only one determinant—religion. More likely, it varies diachronically and synchronically, depending also on history, legislation, political and economic contingencies, personal vicissitudes and education. Conversely, some mindsets and values, as formulated originally by religious thought, may be so deeply rooted in a certain culture that they are widely shared by people who do no longer recognize themselves as affiliated to that religion. By saying that "Marxism ... is a Judeo-Christian heresy", White (1974, p. 23) had already asserted that materialist philosophies that were born within the Christian intellectual ambiance had been imbued with the same basic teleological and ecological axioms: he therefore denies that there is in this respect any real difference between atheists and devotees that have been raised in countries of Christian heritage. In its concisely provocative wording, this statement implicitly hints at a very dense and crucial issue. In monotheistic religions, man has always been a variable ultimately dependent on transcendent rules. When this omnipotent factor was taken away by the growing secularization of society, in the mentality of most man became an independent variable, rather than being re-conducted to the immanent laws that are believed to regulate the rest of the cosmos: "For people who have been brought up in the monotheist tradition, it is difficult to re-gain the awe of nature that was shattered by the pronouncement of Genesis 1:28" (Toynbee, 1974, p. 147).

Within each country, the answers of geography students have been compared with those of their colleagues from economics departments, to see whether or not there are significant and consistent variations in their respective perceptions. Some economic practices are often denounced in the literature advocating sustainability, and significant dissent is to be found within the economic world itself. Noteworthy is the episode of some Paris students of economics who posted pamphlets against the exclusive teaching of an economic theory that they defined as 'autistic'—exceptionally talented for numbers, but completely detached from reality (Boyle, 2002, pp. 41–43). The author does not wish to turn all economic stances into culprits, although convinced that the systematic and accepted recourse of economy to multiform negative externalities, probably at present the main means to achieve and maintain competitiveness, is one of the greatest causes of severe environmental degradation, uneven economic distribution and social injustice all over the world, and all the more preoccupying in that it is a structural cause. Indeed, Elvin (1998, p. 15) thinks that those societies which did not resort to intensive social and environmental exploitation—in other words, externalities enforced by power relations—necessarily perished or were conquered because they lacked the relative competitive advantage.

Geography is not exempt from criticism either. According to Castree (2003), our discipline's marked anthropocentrism has prevented it from elaborating a theory on the political status of the non-human, and still makes it more reluctant even than political science to adopt an eco-centric vision. Miossec *et al.* (2004) speak of geographers' reticence to invest in the dominant, politically correct subject of sustainability, despite their unique potential insight into the issue, thanks to the wealth of material they have accumulated on most of the ecological and economic a spects of sustainability; more important even, geography constitutionally deals with scales and inter-scales analysis, and often manages to bridge the gap between the social and the natural sciences, participating as it does of both (Gambini, 2005b). This survey aims to examine some of the macro-coordinates described above, and to identify several hardly negotiable traits ('secular dogmas') that may be intrinsically incompatible with sustainability.

Methodology

A questionnaire survey was undertaken (Table 1). The questionnaire was initially piloted with a selected audience in order to collect feedback and impromptu comments. One of the respondents complained that some answers were too 'loaded' for an objective survey, but less detailed response options would have probably caused ambiguities (as happened with question 15). Open-ended questions, which would have been ideal for certain aspects, posed a great linguistic problem, and in any case they entail arbitrary decisions in the monitoring process. Although the content of the survey could possibly fit within the boundaries of phenomenography (Bradbeer *et al.*, 2004) or repertory grids, which are now

Table 1. Summary of questionnaire design and ideas

Question No.	Question/Idea	No, of options	Figure/Table reference
1–5	Personal information	–	Table 2
6	Are humans animals?	3	not shown
7	Opinion of the goal of science	3	Figure 1(a)
8	Impression of deeply altering a natural environment	3	Figure 1(b)
9	Chance of a planetary catastrophe of human origin	3	not shown
10	Chance of a planetary catastrophe of natural origin	3	not shown
11	Humankind becomes extinct while rest of planet continues its evolution	4	Figure 2(a)
12	Human life is worth more than animal and plant life	3	Figure 2(b)
13	All present day civilizations will decay and return to pre-industrial productive models	4	Figure 3
14	Opinion of progress (e.g. cars)	3	Figure 4(a)
15	Can science and technology solve environmental problems?	3	Figure 4(b)

used in risk perception evaluation (Pezzullo, 2004), these methods would not have been suitable, because the author did have an opinion about some of the issues addressed. Sandberg (cited by Bradbeer *et al.*, 2004, p. 20) argues that reliability of surveys depends mostly on their "interpretive awareness" which entails "acknowledging and managing the researcher's own subjectivity explicitly throughout the research", all of which is guaranteed by the explicitness of the survey and the personal reflections that have admittedly prompted the questionnaire, always with the caveat in mind that "one of the worst mistakes we can make in the field is to ask leading questions that tell the respondents the answer we want" (Hart, 2001, p. 325).

This study does not aim to give answers, so much as to raise questions whose investigation may prove of some help to the common cause of sustainability. The analysis presented is qualitative only: the percentage is reported for the sake of clarity (50 respondents in each group mean that one person is equivalent to 2 per cent within the same group–with the exception of eco-village residents).

The questions were deliberately worded with more communicative pragmatism than semantic rigour: the primary objective was to make questions and answers clearly intelligible; the term 'natural,' for instance, has been utilized to cover different taxonomic groups in the various questions, with common usage rather than ontological and epistemological debates in mind. In questions 9 and 10 "human origin" is opposed to "natural origin": this does not imply that the author maintains any dichotomy between humans and nature: no clearer formulation was found without resorting to over-elaborate explanations that would have probably alarmed the respondent, thus eliciting a less spontaneous answer. Similarly, questions 6 and 12 seem to have mutually contradicting formulations.

The results are presented below, followed by comments and annotations. The sum of the percentages reported will often not add up to 100, because answers left blank were not reported here, and vice versa double options (a/b, a/c etc), when they existed, were both calculated. Results are available for cross-tabulation.

Results

The first five questions were related to personal information (nationality, age, occupation, gender, religious identity). Ages ranged from 19 to 54 at the University of Queensland, with the majority in their twenties; from 20 to 27 at Colombo University, from 18 to 24 at Yunnan Normal University, and from 19 to 64 at the University of Urbino, with the vast majority in their early twenties. Nationality was very homogenous at Queensland Economics and Urbino Geography and Economics, and fairly homogenous at Colombo Economics. Some 54 per cent of the respondents of Queensland geography were of a nationality other than Australian, and Colombo geography probably also had a number of ethnic minority representatives (most students declared to be Sinhalese, with 32 per cent declaring to be Sri Lankan, Sri Lankan Moor or Muslim). Around 30 per cent of Chinese respondents were of a nationality other than Han. The religious identity declared by the respondents is given in Table 2. Some respondents, especially from among Yunnan students, chose several options together (in one case, seven of them). The total percentage, therefore, does not always amount to 100.

It was decided not to analyse the responses by gender, because all groups interviewed had a higher proportion of women respondents (varying from a 1.3:1 ratio at Queensland

Table 2. Religious identity of respondent groups, in percentages

Religious identity (%) / *Respondent groups*	*Christian*	*Muslim*	*Jewish*	*Hindu*	*Buddhist*	*Animist*	*Atheist*	*Agnostic*	*Confucian*	*Taoist*	*Other*	*No ans.*
Crystal Waters (CW)	6				6	6	19	19		6	44	
Queensland geography (Qge)	36	2	2		2	2	8	14			18	20
Queensland economics (Qec)	60						10	8			10	12
Colombo geography (ColGe)	6	18		6	66	10						4
Colombo economics (ColEc)	2				98	4	2					
Yunnan geography (YunGe)	6	2		2	34	6	44		26	10	2	8
Yunnan economics (YunEc)	6	6	2	2	34		56	4	24	6	2	4
Urbino geography (UrbGe)	68						12	2			4	14
Urbino economics (UrbEc)	74						14	4			2	6

economics to a 4:1 ratio at Urbino geography). Female students either outnumbered their male counterparts, or were more willing to complete the survey. Where the number of female and male respondents was more closely balanced (Queensland economics), the answers did not reveal any constant pattern that could support the hypothesis that one gender group has a more environmentally oriented mentality than the other, which is not to say this may not be the case, here or elsewhere. If the expression 'aggressive masculinity' does evocatively and effectively depict the Westerner's attitude to nature (Tuan, 1974), then eco-feminism may present some worthy points: it would be interesting to investigate whether or not there is a significant difference between the position of women and men on the issues raised by the present study. A survey specifically designed and delivered could bring credit in favour of or against feminist ecological theories. Similarly, no attempt has been made at operating a cross-tabulation by religious identity, but data are available for that. This decision was made due to the low statistical significance of in-group religious variations and the fact that in many cases respondents chose option I (other) or J (no answer) without specifying further.

No clear or consistent pattern could be identified in comparing the answers of geography and economics student, except in the case of the question about people being forced to give up a technological innovation in the future. In all countries, students of economics invariably seemed slightly or significantly more confident than their geography colleagues about the possibility of finding environmentally efficient alternatives to present-day technology.

The most significant comparison seems to be by respondent groups. All Crystal Waters residents, followed by more than 90 per cent of Colombo students, answered that they think humans are animals, with Urbino economics and geography students at the opposite end (36 per cent and 16 per cent respectively choosing the option that humans are not animals). Concerning the goal of science (Figure 1a), it is quite interesting to notice that none of the respondents from Yunnan University chose option b (that science is knowledge valid in its own self) in strong contrast to Crystal Waters respondents. Urbino economics and Yunnan economics students had the highest incidence of the 'human-biased' instrumental view of science, with 38 per cent and 34 per cent respectively answering that science should investigate natural laws in order to satisfy human needs (option c). On the subject of altering the natural environment (Figure 1b), CW residents (73 per cent), followed by Colombo economics (58 per cent) and Urbino geography students (52 per cent), displayed the most cautious attitude; Yunnan economics students, on the contrary, were the most 'interventionist', with 42 per cent responding that deeply altering a natural environment is dangerous but inevitable for progress.

Colombo students of both departments seemed to be the most willing to accept that humankind may become extinct (Figure 2a), with over 40 per cent thinking it a likely event, and over 35 per cent conceiving it as possible. At the other end of the spectrum are Yunnan economics students, with 38 per cent reckoning it unlikely, and 8 per cent impossible, followed by Yunnan geography and Urbino economics students (30 per cent unlikely, 6 per cent impossible in both cases). Surprisingly, the idea that human life is not worth more than animal and plant life (option a) saw the highest incidence among Urbino geography students (68 per cent) and the lowest among Colombo economics students (30 per cent) (Figure 2b), but see the comments below.

Students from the University of Colombo were the ones who most easily accepted the idea of the future decay of all of present-day civilizations (Figure 3), with 26 per cent declaring it likely, 40 per cent possible among geography students, 32 per cent likely and 28 per cent possible among economics students. In the other three universities, most students of both faculties considered the hypothesis unlikely (42 per cent to 54 per cent). Yunnan economics students had the highest record of those who declared the event impossible (30 per cent), against 18 per cent at Yunnan geography and around 13–16 per cent in all other groups.

Two-thirds of Crystal Waters respondents think it likely that one day we will have to give up some technological innovations for environmental reasons (Figure 4a), against only 2 per cent among Yunnan economics respondents and roughly one-third among geography students in Queensland, Colombo and Urbino. Most Yunnan economics students (92 per cent) reckon the event unlikely, because we will find efficacious alternatives. The same option was chosen by 74 per cent of Urbino economics students, followed by students of Queensland economics, Yunnan geography, Urbino geography, Queensland geography, Colombo economics, Colombo geography, and finally Crystal Waters residents (26 per cent).

Coming to the last question (Figure 4b), the set of responses is probably not significant, with most respondents (50 per cent in the case of Urbino geography students) uncertain as to the role of science and technology in solving environmental problems. Where they existed, comments appended to the responses were very illuminating: the most common were along the lines that science and technology can only solve environmental problems if accompanied by political will, a different set of collective priorities and a profound modification of individual behaviours. People who offered comments seemed to all agree that "Technology is not value free" (Gunn, undated, p. 15). With the specifications described above, 60 per cent of Crystal Waters respondents said they believe that science and technology cannot solve environmental problems.

Discussion

Although sample size constrains statistical analysis, it is possible to comment on certain issues addressed. With the vast majority of respondents in each country answering that they consider humans to be animals there seems to be a proportionally higher incidence of people convinced that humans are somewhat protected, or even exempt, from the risk of disappearing as a species.

One issue that is not often raised to people's critical conscience is that science and technology have a virtually unlimited destructive potential and an intrinsically limited constructive capacity—be it after accidents, natural disasters or human errors—and they are therefore non-neutral in themselves. At their present level, they cannot remedy the destruction caused by a forest fire, let alone that provoked by—say—an atomic bomb. Even within nature itself, construction takes longer than destruction, and this is a lot more so with our very partial knowledge of regulating mechanisms, which makes many of our common interventions over nature irreversible by human strength alone. We therefore usually rely on nature to rebuild degraded or destroyed environments. Our capacity to solve environmental problems is thus mainly limited to avoiding creating those problems rather than undoing them.

Some argue that a common acceptance that human life is worth nothing more than animal and plant life would pose great juridical problems, because it may imply that the killing of an animal or plant could be equated to homicide, running over a cat or deer on

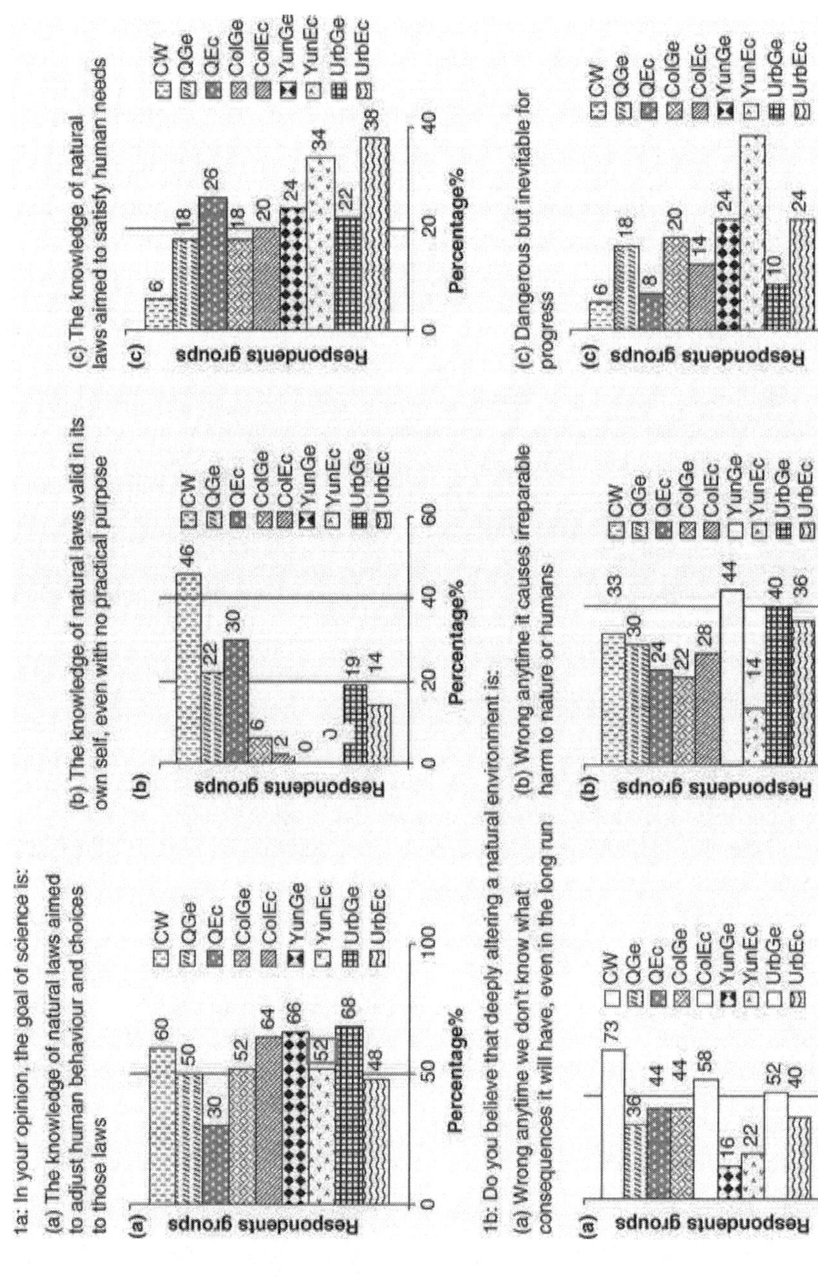

Figure 1. Responses to questions about the goal of science and alteration of the natural environment

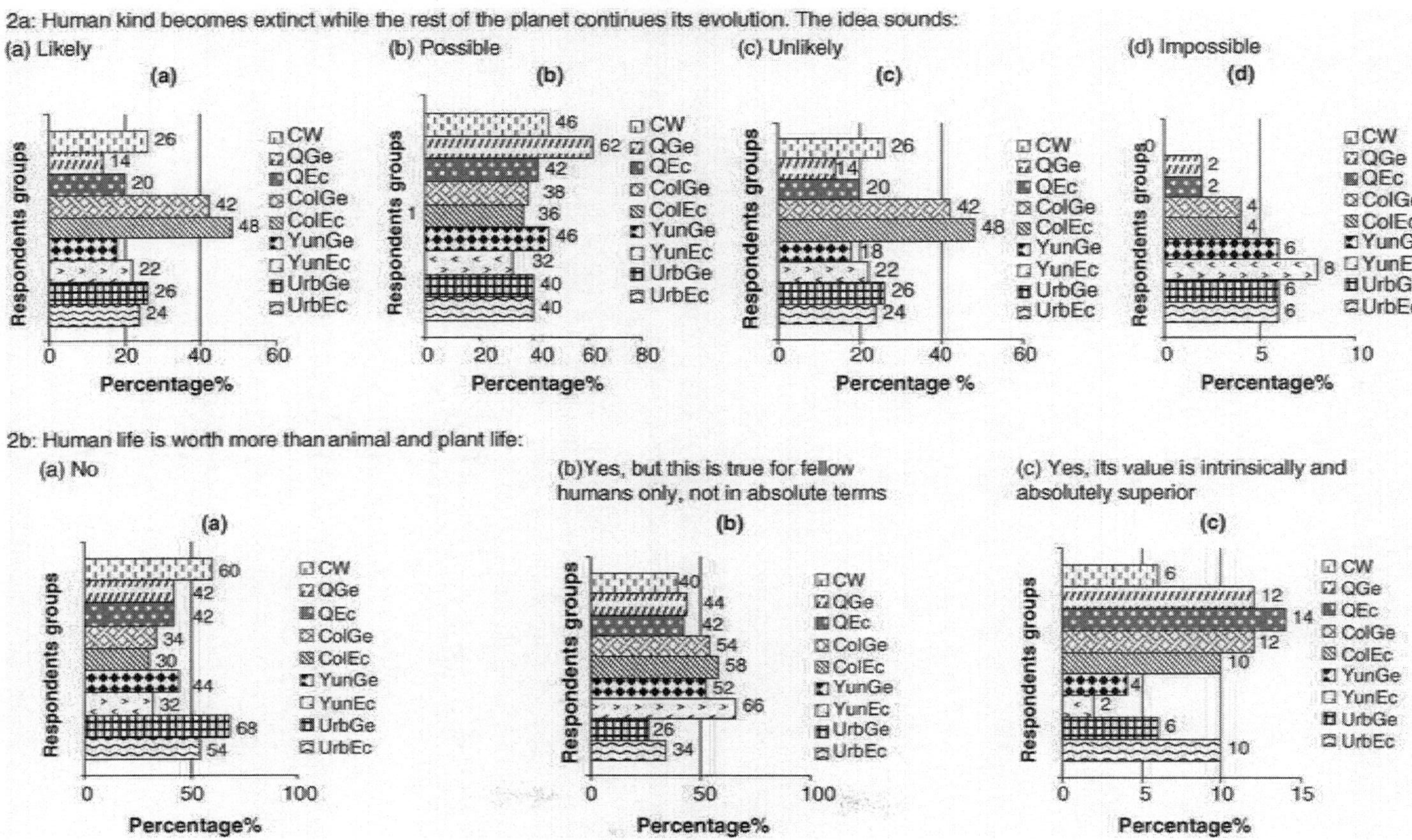

Figure 2. Responses to questions about extinction and the value of human life

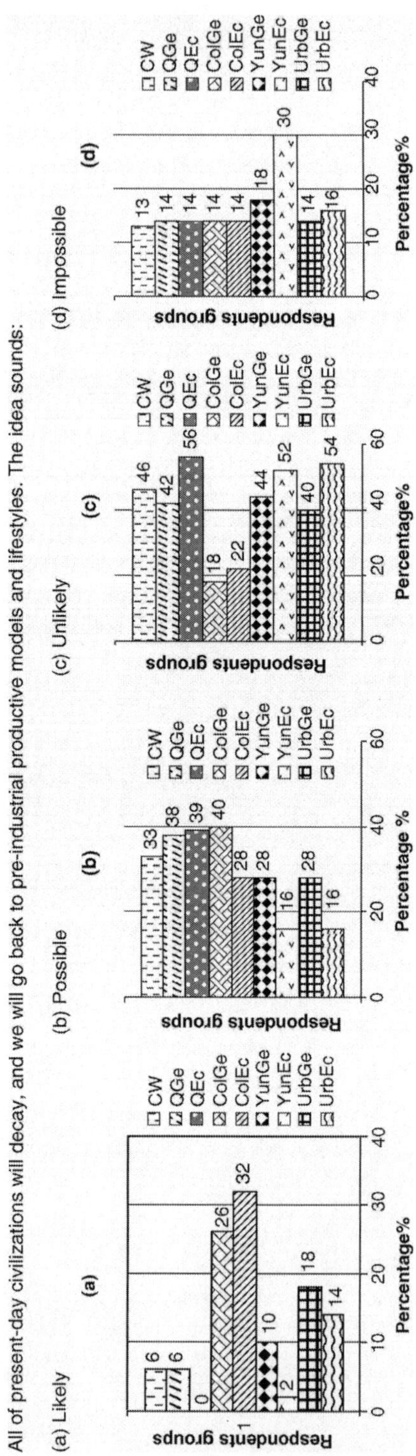

Figure 3. Responses to question about future of the civilization

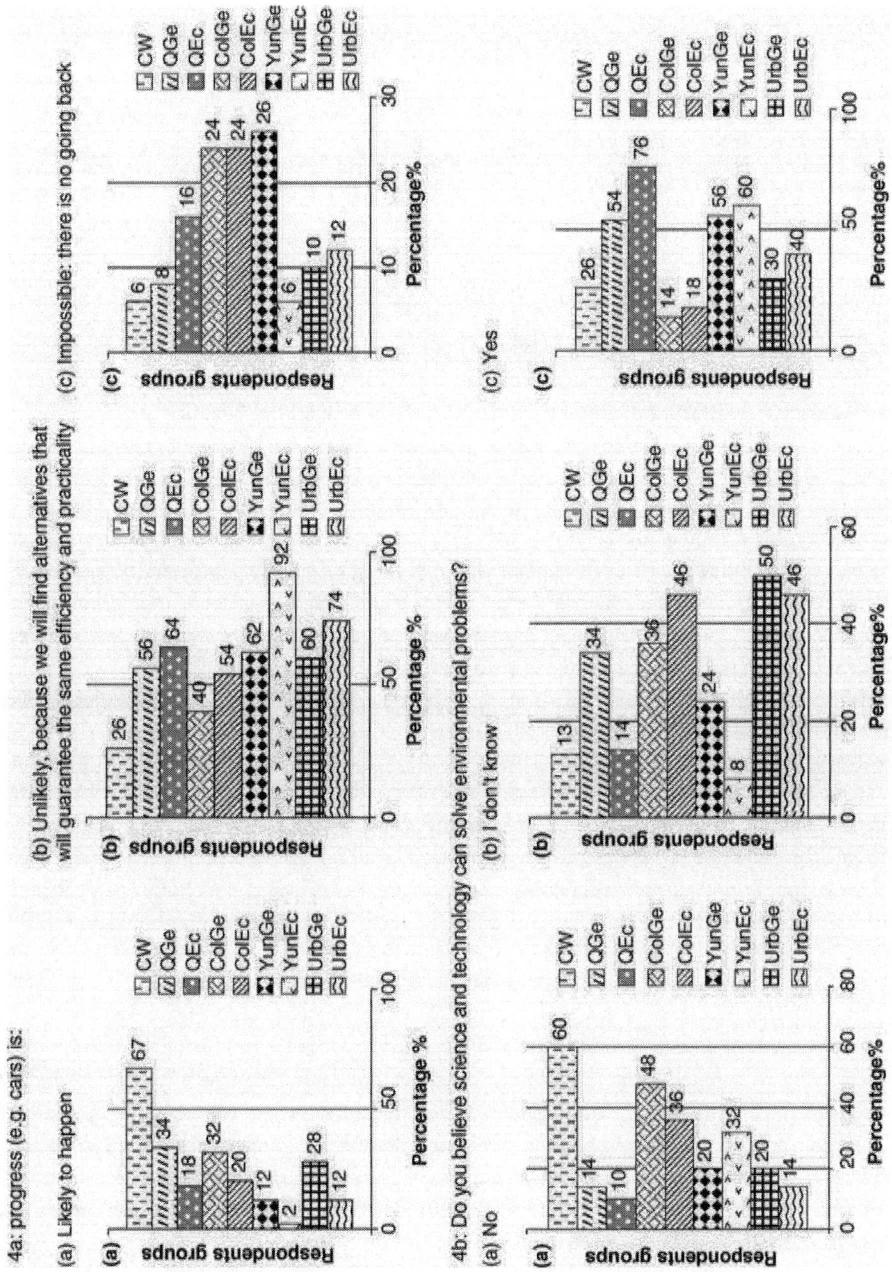

Figure 4. Responses to questions about progress and the role of science and technology

the road to manslaughter. A note must be added in this respect on Buddhism, which preaches human life as a superior state, in that humans only can attain Nirvana; this superiority is considered to be transient, though, because each being is destined to reincarnate in different living forms (Buddha himself is said to have lived 550 times under various animal and human identities before reaching Nirvana), and the existence of a separate self is considered a delusion in any case.

Apart from eco-village residents and Colombo geography students, more than half among the other groups think we will be able to find environmentally efficient alternatives to present-day technologies, and therefore will not have to give up any conquests of progress (Figure 4a). This means they either believe that science and technology can solve the problem by themselves, or that there will also be an accompanying change in consumers' behaviour and public policies. Both sources of optimism seem ungrounded to the author: the per item impact of technology—e.g. an automobile—apparently tends to diminish but the per category and global technology-induced impact has increased steadily in history. Cars, for instance, used to be the exclusive possession of a privileged elite, but they have become an ordinary commodity in rich countries. Understandably, inhabitants of developing countries are aiming to reach the same level of wealth. Also, regularly undertaking Life Cycle Assessment (LCA) may prove that, all things considered, a single technological commodity of the newer generations does not always have a diminished impact on the environment if compared with older generations. As to a change in consumers' and policy-makers' behaviour, research for more environmentally friendly alternatives is definitely not at the top of the agenda, and when such alternatives already exist (cars, energy sources, materials etc.), they do not usually receive enough attention from either consumers or policy-makers because of higher costs, lack of information, market interests and different political priorities.

Deliberately, a time frame was not specified in the questions: scientifically, over geological eras, none of the projected scenarios could be ruled out, be it a planetary catastrophe of human/natural origin, the extinction of humankind, or a return to a pre-industrial-like lifestyle. The fact that in every country some people declared these scenarios impossible may mean that they are reasoning on a biological rather than geological timescale, or that they are supported by some sort of unquestioned beliefs– the 'dogmas' that were mentioned earlier. Plausibly, both these beliefs and the habit to reason in relatively brief time frames only are crucial to the issue. Can they be negotiated, and how?

The word progress comes from a Latin verb (*progredior*) indicating movement forward, advancement (originally in physical and military terms). If progress is intended as belonging to a necessarily self-perfecting system, no matter what the symptoms are, it may overrule all other considerations and underpin all other assumptions, thus ruling out the very idea of a regression, a development line that turns back or swerves instead of proceeding linearly forward, which could seriously compromise all calls for action and change. An individual with serious and worsening health symptoms is expected to consult a physician and follow her/his recommendations. A failure to do so, based on absolute confidence that existing problems cannot but be fixed by letting the body system work, would be labelled as self-delusion, problem denial, alienation from reality.

Altogether, in many questions the view of Colombo students was closest to that of eco-village residents and ecologists. Specifically, they did not seem to have the same core belief in continual progress and advancement as the other groups and had less certainty that humans as a species are immune or protected. Would a survey of higher statistical significance confirm this impression? As for our respondents' attitudes, what is the relative importance of their Buddhist background, education, the country's policies on the matter, legislative and educational measures, spatial factors and variables (intended in a distributive and causal sense)?

Farthest from the position of eco-village residents were often Chinese students, followed by their Italian colleagues. Statistically, a sample of 100 university students may not be representative of the student population of that university, let alone the overall population of the country. However, the trends highlighted may not be insignificant, and in the case of China, the unexpected level of anthropocentrism (see questions 7, 8), faith in progress (question 13) and science (14) shown by the respondents deserve to be appreciated and further investigated. The Chinese approach to nature may no longer, or at least not always, be so 'quiescent and adaptive' as Tuan (1974, p. 240) portrayed it. An international survey conducted in the 1990s had shown that Italian respondents shared a very pronounced pessimism, a numinous-aesthetic approach combined with a moderate technocentrism (as opposed to ecocentrism), putting them in the 'Ecocydal Mysticism' quadrant (Barrett & Kuroda, 2002, pp. 243–244; see also Ayoagi-Usui, 1999). In another international research conducted in Asia-Pacific countries, Guangzhou students were the only ones to show a blend of rationalism, optimism and ecological conscience, which forms part of the 'Rational Ecologism' quadrant, whereas all other countries, with a more or less rational and more or less ecocentric vision, all figured in the 'Arcadianism' quadrant (Barrett & Kuroda, 2002, p. 257; see also Yenken *et al.*, 2000). In a personal discussion during a cruise on the Three Gorges of the Yangtze, when asked about the possible effects of the dam on people's lives and the environment, an engineer listed the priorities in the Chinese decision-making process as follows: politics, national security, national economy. The relative position of these issues in the national hierarchy of priorities probably varies in the opinion of different people, but few would disagree that individual life and the environment are not at the top of the national agenda (Gambini, 2004, pp. 9–10). The same question arises as for Colombo students: what is the weight of their cultural/religious background, personal circumstances, education, national trends and directives, and the influence of their environment?

It is not claimed that the cultural traits investigated in this paper are the only or the most relevant substrates when talking about sustainability; this is a first attempt to explore some of the cultural causes of resistance to the very understanding of sustainability. Different individuals and communities may have engendered various sets of independent assumptions that do tend to be perpetuated against all evidence and symptoms to the contrary. A failure to take them into account may compromise educational and informative efforts, and therefore, this may be a barrier to economically and ethically internalizing the environment and the very concept of sustainability, which still risks keeping the futile "charm of those notions that lend themselves to proclamations as generous as they are gratuitous, at least until jurisprudence takes hold of them and gives them some substance" (Dubois-Maury, 2004, p. 190).

Acknowledgements

The present study would not have been possible without the generous help of the faculty and students of the institutions listed below. They cannot be held necessarily to share the views expressed by the author or the very aim of this research. In alphabetic order by institution: University of Queensland: Martin Bell, Tim Brailsford, David Forster, Robert Pagan. University of Colombo: Nihal Attanayake, Jayanthi de Silva, Tissa Jayawardana, examination supervisors. Yunnan Normal University: Hu Junjing, Li Ying, Liu Rong, Xu Wei, Zhou Liang Wing. Università di Urbino: Catia Brunelli, Peris Persi. The editorial assistance of Sue Burkill and David Higgitt has been highly appreciated.

References

Anderson, A. (2002) A fragile plenty: pre-European Maori and the New Zealand Environment, in: E. Pawson & T. Brooking (Eds) *Environmental Histories of New Zealand*, pp. 19–34 (Melbourne: Oxford University Press).

Ayoagi-Usui, M. (1999) A comparative analysis of citizen's values and pro-environmental behaviour, *Asian Geographer*, 18(1–2), pp. 111–122.

Baird Callicott, J. (1994) *Earth's Insights: a Multicultural Survey of Ecological Ethics from the Mediterranean Basin to the Australian Outback* (Los Angeles: University of California Press).

Barr, J. (1974) Man and Nature: the ecological controversy and the Old Testament, in: D. Spring & E. Spring (Eds) *Ecology and Religion in History*, pp. 48–75 (New York: Harper & Row).

Barrett, B. F. D. & Kuroda, A. (2002) Ecological modernization, environmental knowledge and societal change: attitudes and behaviour of young people in Japan, *International Research in Geographical and Environmental Education*, 11(3), pp. 237–261.

Batchelor, M. & Brown, K. (Eds) (1994) *Buddhism and Ecology* (Delhi: Motilal Banarsidass Publishers).

Boyle, D. (2002) The storming of the accountants, *New Statesman*, 21 January.

Berthrong, J. (1998) Motifs for a new Confucian ecological vision, in: M. E. Tucker & J. Berthrong (Eds) *Confucianism and Ecology*, pp. 237–263 (Cambridge, MA: Harvard University Press).

Bradbeer, J., Healey, M. & Kneale, P. (2004) Undergraduate geographers' understandings of geography, learning and teaching: a phenomenographic study, *Journal of Geography in Higher Education*, 28(1), pp. 17–34.

Bruun, O. (1995) *Feng shui* and the Chinese perception of nature, in: O. Bruun & A. Kalland (Eds) *Asian Perceptions of Nature: a Critical Approach*, pp. 173–187 (London: Curzon Press).

Castree, N. (2003) Environmental issues: relational ontologies and hybrid politics, *Progress in Human Geography*, 27(2), pp. 203–211.

Cheng, C. Y. (1998) The trinity of cosmology, ecology, and ethics in the Confucian personhood, in: M. E. Tucker & J. Berthrong (Eds) *Confucianism and Ecology*, pp. 211–235 (Cambridge: Harvard University Press).

Dubois-Maury, J. (2004) Le juriste confronté au développement durable, *Historiens et géographes. Vers une géographie du developpement durable*, n.387, pp. 184–189.

Dubos, R. (1974) Franciscan conservation versus Benedictine stewardship, in: D. Spring & E. Spring (Eds) *Ecology and Religion in History*, pp. 114–136 (New York: Harper & Row).

Elvin, M. (1998) The environmental legacy of Imperial China, in: R. L. Edmonds (Ed.) *Managing the Chinese Environment*, pp. 9–32 (New York: Oxford University Press).

Gambini, B. (2004) *Ti racconto il mio paese....la Cina* (Fano: Centro Ricerche e Mediazione Interculturale).

Gambini, B. (2005a) Giochiamoci il futuro del pianeta. Esempio di un percorso di educazione alla sostenibilità, *Ambiente società territorio*, 2, pp. 34–37.

Gambini, B. (2005b) Sustainable development: Let geographers take the lead (with a little help from some friends), in: K. Donert & P. Charzyńsk (Eds) *Changing Horizons in Geography Education*, pp. 300–304 (Toruń: Heradot Network).

Gunn, A. S. (undated) Professional ethics, education and environmental law. How can we bring them together for a sustainable future?, in: A. H. Baharuddin (Ed.) *Environment and Development: Ethical and Educational Considerations*, pp. 1–50 (Kuala Lumpur: Institut Kajian Dasar).

Hart, J. F. (2001) No dead rabbits, *Geographical Review*, 91(1 & 2), pp. 322–327.

Kalton, M. C. (1998) Extending the Neo-Confucian tradition: questions and reconceptualization for the twenty-first century, in: M. E. Tucker & J. Berthrong (Eds) *Confucianism and Ecology*, pp. 77–101 (Cambridge, MA: Harvard University Press).

Kinsley, D. (1995) *Ecology and Religion: Ecological Spirituality in Cross-cultural Perspective* (Englewood Cliffs, NJ: Prentice Hall).

MacQuarrie, J. (1974) Creation and environment, in: D. Spring & E. Spring (Eds) *Ecology and Religion in History*, pp. 32–47 (New York: Harper & Row).

Martin, S. & Jucker, R. (2005) Educating earth-literate leaders, *Journal of Geography in Higher Education*, 29(1), pp. 19–29.

Miossec, A., Arnould, P. & Veyvret, Y. (2004) Développement durable: affaire de tous, approche de géographes, *Histoiriens et géographes: Vers une géographie du developpement durable*, 387, pp. 85–96.

Moncrief, L. W. (1974) The cultural basis for our environmental crisis, in: D. Spring & E. Spring (Eds) *Ecology and Religion in History*, pp. 76–90 (New York: Harper & Row).

Pezzullo, L. (2004) Repertory grids as a methodology to represent mental models for risk perception studies, paper presented at the International Geographical Congress, Glasgow, August 2004.

Smith, C. T. (1982) *Geografia storica d'Europa: dalla preistoria al 19° secolo* (Bari: Laterza).

Taylor, R. L. (1998) Companionship with the World: roots and branches of a Confucian ecology, in: M. E. Tucker & J. Berthrong (Eds) *Confucianism and Ecology*, pp. 37–58 (Cambridge, MA: Harvard University Press).

Toynbee, A. (1974) The religious background of the present environmental crisis, in: D. Spring & E. Spring (Eds) *Ecology and Religion in History*, pp. 137–149 (New York: Harper & Row).

Tuan, Y. F. (1974) Discrepancies between environmental attitude and behaviour: examples from Europe and China, in: D. Spring & E. Spring (Eds) *Ecology and Religion in History*, pp. 90–113 (New York: Harper & Row).

White, L. Jr. (1974) The historical roots of our ecologic crisis, in: D. Spring & E. Spring (Eds) *Ecology and Religion in History*, pp. 15–31 (New York: Harper & Row).

Wolff, E. W. (2000) History of the atmosphere from ice cores, in: C. Boutron (Ed.) *European Research Course on Atmospheres (ERCA)*, vol. 4 pp. 147–177 (Les Ulis: Edition Diffusion Presse).

Yenken, D., Fien, J. & Sykes, H. (2000) *Environment, Education and Society in the Asia-Pacific Local Traditions and Global Discourse* (London: Routledge).

Zaman, L. F. III (2001) Postmodern deconstruction of Newtonian science: a physical-to-social transposition of causality, *Theory and Science*, 2(1) Available at http://theoryandscience.icaap.org/content/vol002.001/05zaman.html (accessed August 2005).

A Due Diligence Report on New Zealand's Educational Contribution to the UN Decade of Education for Sustainable Development

DAVID CHAPMAN, MARY FLAWS & RICHARD LE HERON

Introduction

When Prime Minister Helen Clark arrived at the Johannesburg Sustainability Summit in 2002 she was reputedly shocked by the gap between much New Zealand practice and best practice elsewhere in the world in many spheres of sustainability activity. Two key reports released within a year of the Summit, however, the *Sustainable Development Programme of Action* (2003) and *Education Priorities for New Zealand* (New Zealand Government, 2003) failed to give education a role in sustainable development. More recently, the Parliamentary Commissioner for the Environment (PCE, 2004) argued that without some fundamental changes in education's legislative, organizational and learning frameworks, any outcomes represented as sustainable development are most likely to result from chance or be cosmetic at best. The PCE (2004) report actually confronted issues that have haunted the environmental education literature for decades. It argued that "Our dominant value systems are at the very heart of unsustainable practices" (PCE, 2004, p. 4) and that the "Culture of consumerism is ... a major barrier to getting people to think about, and to act on, sustainability issues" (PCE, 2004, p. 17). Further the PCE reported that before the 2002 World Summit on Sustainable Development, it found strong evidence that "New Zealanders cannot see how they are contributing to many problems, or how they could be contributing to solutions" (PCE, 2004, p. 33). Still optimistic about education, the PCE went on to affirm the UNESCO position that education is the most effective means that society possesses for confronting the challenges of the future... Yet despite these misgivings the PCE (2004, pp. 4–5) held that "We could, and should, be the first in the world to become a truly environmentally sustainable nation... As a signatory to the United Nations Decade of Education for Sustainable Development (UNDESD) ... New Zealand has a huge opportunity to show global leadership in this area." But as Williams (2005, p. 7) remarked after the 3rd World Environmental Conference on 'Educational Pathways Towards Sustainability' in Torino, October 2005, we "need to be challenged and concerned about New Zealand's 'low level of future-thinking for learning for sustainability' compared to other countries".

We interpret sustainability as a process or pathway towards coming to know and work on the conditions of existence for human and non-human life that is largely context specific. Thus, our interest is transformative change that moves away from unsustainable practices. We argue here that the institutional realities in New Zealand in which existing environmental education (EE) and education for sustainable development (ESD) initiatives—however interpreted—are set severely constrain any ambitions for New Zealand as a leading world example of 'educating for sustainability'.

In this paper we ask and attempt to answer two simple questions: 'What start-up conditions existed in New Zealand education in 2004' as the nation approached the UNDESD? And: 'What, if anything, has happened in Year 1 of the decade in New Zealand?' Our findings are not encouraging. Against the backdrop of *some* school and higher education sector engagement in EE and ESD prior to the UNDESD, there has been an almost complete lack of institutional recognition of the UNDESD in either sector. We then reflect on the wider implications of this situation for states becoming a signatory to the UNDESD and strategy in the New Zealand context.

Socioeducational history of EE and ESD in New Zealand

This section briefly situates the development of EE in the New Zealand education system in order to see its shadow in contemporary ESD. Broader changes over three decades have influenced school and university curricula, but in very different ways.

Changes in the schools have been informed by events in the field of environmental education, starting as far back as the UNESCO State of the Environment conference of 1972 and the subsequent formulation by UNESCO–UNEP of goals and intentions for environmental education in the later 1970s at Belgrade (UNESCO–UNEP, 1976) and

Tbilisi (UNESCO–UNEP, 1978) and by wider economic restructuring initiatives (Table 1). The 1984 Labour government initiated community consultation on curriculum, receiving over 30 000 submissions following meetings in all school communities and beyond. The draft's curriculum design matches Print's (1993) 'broad fields' design, softening traditional subject distinctions in an effort to improve links between disciplines, and included science, environment and technology as one of its learning areas. In 1989 the curriculum review was replaced by a complete overhaul of educational administration, setting up a Ministry to establish policy and devolving school governance to elected community boards. The 1990 National government also pursued educational reform, including curriculum, which was reconceptualized under an overarching Curriculum Framework (Ministry of Education, 1991, 1993). It focused on the preparation of learners for a place in a competitive global economy and reverted to a strongly subject-centred design accompanied by extensive statements of achievement objectives to structure learning. The draft statement (Ministry of Education, 1991) contained 'Science and Environment' as one heading and 'Technology' as another, in keeping with the central economic imperative. However, the final version (Ministry of Education, 1993) had no reference to the environment in its headings but in its fine print stated that environment was a theme to be found integrated into a number of curriculum statements. This was not strongly emphasized.

This period of curriculum re-conceptualization bridged the lead up to the Earth summit at Rio in 1992 at which signatories to Agenda 21 (UNCED, 1992) agreed to introduce environment and development education as a cross-cutting theme in curriculum over the next three years. New Zealand's report to Rio, 'Forging the Links' (Ministry for the Environment, 1992), declared the government's commitment to private enterprise as the most effective and efficient resource allocation mechanism and its intention to shift resource ownership from public to private hands, and noted the absence of environmental studies from the curriculum. A contract to write guidelines and policy for environmental education was let in early 1995 and a draft document circulated by the contractors. It was not published. At this time the Ministry for the Environment released its '2010 Strategy' (Ministry for the Environment, 1995) which stated that the key condition for caring for the environment was 'a vibrant enterprise economy' reflecting mainstream neo-liberal thought, and privileged the economy above all else. Finally a strategy for environmental education (Ministry for the Environment, 1998) and *Guidelines for Environmental Education in New Zealand Schools* (Ministry of Education, 1999) emerged. The latter document emphasizes that environmental education is not compulsory and its adoption is at the discretion of school boards of trustees. The release of this document in mid-1999 coincided with the lead-up to the general election in early December. Post-election a Labour coalition increased funding for teacher training related to the *Environmental Education Guidelines* and funded environmental advisers in schools.

One of the government's 2001 initiatives was to begin a 'curriculum stocktake', having seen through the final stages of the re-construction of the school curriculum. A report (Ministry of Education, 2002) identified education for sustainability as a theme that should be included in a redeveloped curriculum framework document, against which curriculum delivery should be audited. Unfortunately this commitment is not apparent in the Educational Priorities 2003–2006 (Ministry of Education, 2003), released *after* the Prime Minister's statement at Johannesburg. The priorities emphasize competition (progress will measured on international league-table standing) and are couched in the rhetoric of neo-liberalism. Most notable is that sustainability is absent from the Priorities.

Table 1. Socioeducational history of EE and ESD in New Zealand schools

Environmental movement	Curriculum developments	Political influences	Time
Stockholm 1972		Two-party system National – right of centre, rural Labour – centre left with strong trade union backing 1972 Labour in power, downturn, borrowing to maintain employment	Late 1960s, early 1970s
Belgrade 1975	Review of core curriculum published 1984 and ignored	1975 National gain power	1975–1984
Tbilisi 1977		Maintain borrowing and forced to regulate to control economic stresses Wage and price freeze	
Environment as a heading in NZ draft Curriculum Statement 1988	Public consultation and extensive review of curriculum under social democrat minister 30 000 + submissions	Labour returns 1984 in fiscal crisis, begins to deregulate economy on neo-liberal principles	1984–1989
	Review dropped in favour of educational administration reorganization under neo-liberal principles	Restructuring reaches education sector	1987–1990
Environment heading in draft curriculum framework of 1991 Earth Summit at Rio Forging the Links, NZ report to Rio 1992, 2010 Environment Strategy (1995)	Curriculum review begun again Limited consultation and heavy business influence Curriculum rewrite begun Mathematics 1992 Curriculum frameworks: Science 1993 English 1994 Technology 1995	National gain power and increase the pace and degree of neo-liberal intrusion to every sector	1990–1996
NZ draft Environmental Education Guidelines circulated (1995)	Curriculum rewrite continues Social Studies 1997	First MMP government National coalition despite mood for change Steadying of pace of reform	1996–1999

NZ Environmental education strategy (1998) Kyoto protocol proposed NZ Guidelines for Environmental Education (1999) non-compulsory	Health and Physical Education 1999		
$187 million to Bio-diversity strategy $130 million economic package in exchange for logging moratorium Johannesburg 2002 Kyoto Protocol signed	Final subject statement The Arts, 2000	Labour Coalition including Greens Some significant environmental initiatives Fallout with Greens over GE pre-election 2002	1999–2002
Sustainability included in Stocktake report but not in education priorities	10-year curriculum stocktake Publication of education priorities for 2003–2006 in response NCEA Achievement Standards driving ‘teaching to assessment’ New achievement standards written to support new courses, e.g. Sustainable Futures	Labour middle right coalition shifts balance to the right	2003–

Over the past 30 years, university sector interest in environmental questions led to a range of new programme emphases and degree structures. This, however, was a development that had far more autonomy than the school sector. Under the logic of the prevailing University Grants system the aim was not to enshrine a general curriculum but to facilitate the development of the university system with separate and distinctive components. Developments were, until the early 1990s, largely independent of restructuring pressures, shaped by competition amongst old and emerging disciplines, involved a range of approaches to environmental issues and bore no operational links to what was happening in schools. New-generation courses around the 'environment' (defined in a wide range of ways) appeared across the board, in subject areas as diverse as geography, earth science, geology, planning, economics, business, development studies, sociology, history, agriculture and law. Diplomas and degrees labelled resource management, environmental science, environmental management and environmental studies, for instance, were introduced. Sustainability was much less visible, appearing only periodically in course prescriptions and rarely in course, programme or degree titles.

In the 1990s the increasing research and postgraduate emphasis in the universities was assisted by developments in science funding in New Zealand. Of relevance is the strategic and non-disciplinary nature of the Foundation for Research Science and Technology (FoRST) investment in science. FoRST has supported sustainability research, funding 98 projects between 1995 and 2003 with 'sustainability' in the title. Most of this funding, however, went to the Crown Research Institutes; 14 projects were university based, and geographers featured as Principal Investigators in only four. While this research had an overwhelming productionist orientation, it was indicative of a substantial resource commitment to strategic research for New Zealand and as such represented a long-term funding flow that was available to the university sector. Over the past decade, however, FoRST has attempted to address how to advance this research frontier (Le Heron, 2005). In 2002–2003 it ran the Sustainable Development Investment portfolio, drawing attention to a shift in thinking: the science underpinning research needed to reflect sustainability concepts. A set of sustainability concepts was articulated: the importance of the biophysical environment; integration of environmental, economic and social dimensions; a holistic approach; a long-term view; understanding of people and values and the institutions of which they are a part; partnering with communities within the research process; and collaboration (FoRST, 2002, p. 14). Importantly, FoRST prioritized research, "that is conducive to sustainable development as a process or pathway and transitions to increased sustainable development".

Thus, at the turn of the century New Zealand's university system had choices amongst and within the universities relating to undergraduate and graduate education involving an environmental emphasis. This situation contrasted with the school system, where EE had struggled to gain a firm foothold. In both systems, ESD appeared to have had gained little traction.

Education Stock Take 2004: Some Realities of Practice

In this section we examine evidence about the actual workings of EE and ESD in the school and university systems.

Primary and Secondary Levels

A recent research project commissioned by the Ministry of Education (Bolstad *et al.*, 2004) reveals that the bulk of the initiatives are at primary school level and sadly do not go past the perennial projects of tree planting, litter schemes, worm farming and composting (see Fien, 1997; Lousley, 1999; Chapman 2003). None of the work examines causal issues or engages with the values, or the economic, social and cultural issues that shape our environmental behaviour. This work, however, constitutes exemplary practice in the eyes of officialdom. The Ministry of Education has supported school initiatives by appointing advisers, but this fails to address that EE is currently peripheral to the core curriculum emphasis on numeracy, literacy and ICT. While strong statements in support of the environment can be found distributed throughout the curriculum—developing a sense of responsibility for the guardianship of the planet is an aim in the science curriculum (Ministry of Education, 1993)—these are not prioritized. Instead the emphasis is on enterprise and preparation for the world of work in a competitive economy.

The events described above are unfortunate because the *Guidelines* do specify four key concepts: biodiversity, sustainability, interdependence, and personal and social responsibility for action, but it seems clear that very little of this comprehensive framework has so far been reflected in practice. The New Zealand Curriculum too provides considerable space for initiative. Consisting of seven curriculum statements in key learning areas, overarched by the New Zealand Curriculum Framework, the curriculum guides teaching, learning and assessment in New Zealand schools.

The Framework reminds teachers (Ministry of Education, 1993, p. 8) that environment is an important theme throughout the curriculum and also that learning experiences from different essential learning areas should be linked. With this linking in mind, the Science and Technology Statements both emphasize consideration of the impact of science and technology on people and the environment. Examination of Economic Resource allocation, of how we value place and environment, and on time, continuity and change in the social studies statement, provide contexts in which environmental issues seem crucial. Further, the language/English curriculum demands critical thinking and the analysis of text in relation to its messages and intentions.

A stern test of New Zealand's preparedness for the UNDESD is an examination of the resources available in the New Zealand education system in 2004. Most immediately, the *NZ Education Gazette* (the official record of relevant information for education) did not carry an announcement or article on UNDESD until mid-2005. It was September 2004 before the Johannesburg World Summit was covered. The *Gazette* drew attention to a wealth of sustainable development teaching and learning material on Te Kete Ipurangi (TKI), but had no reference to the decade and no link in TKI to the UNESCO website where information on the decade can be accessed in full. This said, the TKI website has considerable material on education for sustainability and related action themes, and includes online participation. At the TKI website teachers of science are encouraged to reshape the way they look at environmental education to include sustainability (but in the key words for science, sustainable development and sustainability are absent). Moreover, the Ministry of Education has commissioned only a few dedicated websites (assumed to be educationally informed resources); for social studies four of 57 listed, for geography one of eight listed.

Finally, work that critically examines our behaviour, incorporates ideas about biological and social systems and their interdependence, looks at resource allocation, rich and poor, critically analyses message systems and the interests they serve, and does this in context of planetary guardianship is rare. These statements thus stand as largely rhetorical. Environmental education is clearly a low-profile area in the curriculum and in the lived culture of schooling. Further, it is not really legitimized or valued in the structures of education (e.g. absent from Ministers' priorities) or in wider society. Nonetheless there are glimmers of change. Some new school buildings and environments are being built according to sustainable architectural principles, with the whole community involvement in decision-making. Partnerships involving museums and regional councils to provide environmental education have been funded by the Ministry of Education and the Department of Conservation has supported educational initiatives. These educational initiatives have been aimed mainly at the primary and secondary levels and been focused on environmental processes with a growing cultural inflection driven by Treaty of Waitangi obligations. Social, economic and political dimensions are generally absent. Examples include the Auckland Regional Council kids' interactive website (http://www.ecokids.co.nz), which has been developed with Tasman District Council, Hawkes Bay Regional Council and the Dunedin City Council. With the passing of the Local Government Act (2002) sustainable development has again come into focus, through the Long Term Council Community Planning process. Recent legislation aimed at upgrading building standards in the light of a national 'leaky home' controversy may shift attitudes and values towards more sustainable dwellings.

University Level

In an insightful comment, the OECD remarked that subjects in the primary and secondary schools are "legitimatized by the disciplinary structures of higher education ... the role of the university in defining what knowledge consists of in modern societies is so central that EE is seriously impaired until the universities regard it as a serious topic" (PCE, 2004, p. 74). What developments relating to sustainable development have characterized this sector over the last decade, then?

In 2004 a total of 46 courses at the undergraduate and postgraduate levels in New Zealand universities based on a survey of University Calendars from 1993–2004, included the word 'sustainability' (or similar) in the title. This was made up respectively as follows for the universities: Auckland (16), AUT (0), Waikato (5), Massey (9), Victoria (3), Canterbury (5), Lincoln (8) and Otago (0). An historical analysis over 10 years for Auckland, for instance, shows a changing menu of courses, going from a base of two in 1995 to 16 in 2004. Pioneer developments include Auckland University's Masters of Environmental Engineering that explicitly featured sustainability courses (but this was discontinued in 2005), the University of Waikato's School of Management's Sustainable Business programme (http://wms-soros.mngt.waikato.ac.nz), modules in the University of Canterbury's journalism courses and Lincoln University's Masters of Natural Resource Management and Ecological Engineering (http://www.lincoln.ac.nz/section291.html). These examples, however, do not indicate general or substantial commitment across the sector, rather a limited uptake.

Table 2 uses a different measure, the number of theses (this does not include research reports or honours or postgraduate diploma dissertations) with sustainability in the title, to gauge the level of penetration of sustainability research at the postgraduate level. The cross-university trace over 10 years shows only spasmodic research interest for the

Table 2. Sustainability in titles of New Zealand masters and doctoral theses 1993–2004

	UoA	Wai	MU	VUW	LU	UC	UoO
1993	1	0	0	0	0	2	0
1994	3	1	2	0	2	0	3
1995	0	6	3	1	1	0	3
1996	4	1	5	0	1	0	1
1997	3	3	1	1	1	0	3
1998	4	2	2	0	0	0	1
1999	5	0	5	1	2	1	2
2000	3	3	0	0	1	2	1
2001	5	2	6	2	0	0	3
2002	4	3	2	1	1	3	0
2003	4	1	2	1	1	1	0
2004	2	0	0	0	0	0	0
Total all disciplines	38	22	28	7	10	9	17
Geography	5	5	0	0	0	3	2

Abbreviations: University of Auckland (UoA), University of Waikato (Wai), Massey University (MU), Victoria University of Wellington (VUW), Lincoln University (LU), University of Canterbury (UoC), University of Otago (UoO).

Note: At least one tertiary institution, Christchurch College of Education, runs an outpost of the Griffith University (Australia) Masters of Environmental Education programme, which could account for additional theses in the area.

Sources: Brian Marshall, Subject Librarian, Science, The University of Auckland.

universities as a whole, despite the background of science funding from FoRST. Finally, an email survey of 12 academics across the universities seeking information on any local evidence about UNDESD publicity or projects was conducted in early March 2006. The survey identified appropriate staff in each university and in other organizations to contact and these personnel were approached to clarify details and obtain a view concerning the extent of activity relating to the UNDESD. The investigation revealed almost zero recognition or commitment to any aspect of the UNDESD agenda.

UNDESD in New Zealand – Year 1

Discussions with the officers in the Ministry of Education and UNESCO New Zealand responsible for coordinating New Zealand's response to UNDESD indicate, in the absence of any special or extra funding for the initiatives that the priority in the first year has been to "better communicate about sustainability and get more people engaged in taking action for sustainability. An approach is being developed using branding and social marketing ideas. The approach will be tailored to fit the resources available while being able to grow as the idea takes off. Other priorities are to work with the education sector to increase the visibility of sustainability in the curriculum and increase capacity of the media sector to report on sustainability issues" (NZRUNDESD, 2005, p. 5). Indeed, one officer commented that the New Zealand Steering Committee is constantly realizing how difficult it is to get out of our existing paradigm, or, as one member found when seeking information from the universities on behalf of the Committee, not all were interested enough to reply to queries about UNDESD activities. These frustrations and sentiments regarding inactivity were aptly captured in the keynote address title by the Chair of the

New Zealand UNDESD Steering Committee to the 2006 New Zealand Association for Environmental Education conference: 'Ten years to ingrain a sustainable mindset.'

Conclusions on and from the New Zealand Scene

Again, we are forced to conclude that most statements relating to the environment and sustainability in particular are rhetorical; actual funded programmes in either the schools or the universities are few and minimal. The New Zealand case shows how easy it would be to assume all is well. The investigation reveals four key conclusions of relevance to other UNDESD signatories. First, the context in which UNDESD arrives should not be trivialized. New Zealand has struggled to embed educational pathways involving environmental or sustainability. Second, operational parameters are major obstacles. In schools this takes the form of timetables and curriculum and assessment choices, in the universities disciplinary boundaries still inhibit wider engagement even in the larger administrative units bundling disciplines that have begun to emerge. Third, alignment of different sectoral initiatives is hard to achieve, especially when coordination between the school and university sectors has a low priority. Fourth, and perhaps most crucial, a realistic assessment of the existing situation cannot be avoided, as until this is recognized the scope for action is very limited.

We also make two further observations. First, the economic disparities between rich and poor and amongst ethnic groups are rising, both nationally (Kelsey 1999; Murphy *et al.*, 2003) and internationally (Knox *et al.*, 2003). Second, so are the educational disparities between rich and poor (Ministry of Education, 2002), and yet it is the Ministry of Education's mission to reduce disparity.

It is hard for us to avoid the conclusion that the neo-liberal assumptions informing the current social settlement, and which have informed much of the policy of successive governments since 1984, make it impossible for government to fulfil its social and educational commitments, and do not benefit the majority of citizens. The government is currently undertaking a limited web-based consultation process in response to the primary and secondary Curriculum Stocktake. We feel that this process marginalizes many citizens who have a direct interest in education. We have become cautious of the stakeholder consultation discourse, noting, for example, that learners are not considered to be stakeholders in the education process in the Stocktake Report (Ministry of Education, 2002).

Stakeholder consultation does not consider the interests of future generations or of any non-human inhabitants of the planet, and seldom addresses the concerns of those indirectly affected by changes. In moving forward, then, we would note the extensive work by Bowers (2001, 2002) which challenges the metaphors that shape our language and cognition, and the notions that humanity is entitled to dominate the earth, that all change is progress, and that the individual is the key social unit. In regard to this last metaphor, Postma (2002) argues that liberal democracy asserts second-order values of tolerance, non-violence and respect for property that enable people to pursue their individual lives under minimal first-order values restraints (you cannot tell others how to behave).

Postma argues that liberal democracy, based on the individual pursuit of fulfilment, cannot have regard for the future since reciprocity with future generations in a metaphorical market is impossible. He argues for a revaluing of public life that he describes as neo-republicanism. We are trying to be pragmatic here, but we are also trying to signal ways forward from the impasse of discursive contradiction and confusion in which we are currently mired. Our response is to propose a social visioning process that should precede the current efforts to review the school curriculum. We would suggest that the office of the Parliamentary Commissioner for the Environment would be a suitable, non-partisan site for the coordination of such a process.

It is our contention that if New Zealand as a nation intends to take the UNDESD seriously, then our response must be built on a process that explicitly examines the compromises to be faced, and develops some sort of informed collective and representative decision process to identify and work on how those challenges might be met. As a first step, it seems to us, if we do not understand the limits of our current educational frameworks, then the decade will simply be a rhetorical farce. We are optimistic that this need not be the case.

Acknowledgements

This paper has benefited from the helpful comments of the editors and anonymous referees. The authors also wish to thank everyone who provided them with information on the current New Zealand UNDESD scene. In particular, Brian Marshall, Subject Librarian, Science, University of Auckland Library, provided details for Table 2, for which the authors are very grateful.

References

Bolstad, R., Cowie, B. & Eames, C. (2004) *Environmental Education in New Zealand Schools: Research into current practice and future possibilities*, vol. 1 (Wellington: Ministry of Education).

Bowers, C. (2001) How language limits our understanding of environmental education, *Environmental Education Research*, 7(2), pp. 141–151.

Bowers, C. (2002) Towards an eco-justice pedagogy, *Environmental Education Research*, 8(1), pp. 21–34.

Chapman, D. (2003) Education for the environment – hang on a minute mate, *New Zealand Journal of Geography*, 115, pp. 21–25.

Department of the Prime Minister and Cabinet (2003) *Sustainable Development for New Zealand: Programme of Action* (Wellington: Department of the Prime Minister and Cabinet).

Fien, J. (1997) Stand up, stand up and be counted: undermining mythsof environmental education, *Australian Journal of Environmental Education*, 13, pp. 21–26.

Foundation for Research, Science and Technology (FoRST) (2002) *Investment Signals and Request for Proposals, Sustainable Development Portfolios, for Research in Sector Sustainability Portfolios, Sustainable Management of Productive Sector Environments and Sustainable Cities and Settlements* (Wellington: FoRST).

Kelsey, J. (1999) *Reclaiming the Future: New Zealand and the Global Economy* (Wellington: Bridget Williams Books).

Knox, P., Agnew, J. & McCarthy, L. (2003) *The Geography of the World Economy* (London: Arnold).

Le Heron, R. (2005) Re-constituting New Zealand's agri-food chains for international competition, in: B. Pritchard & N. Folds (Eds) *Cross-continental Agro-food Chains*, pp. 52–65 (London: Routledge).

Lousley, C. (1999) (De) Politicizing the environment club: environmental discourses and the culture of schooling, *Environmental Education Research*, 5(3), pp. 293–304.

Ministry for the Environment (1992) *New Zealand's National Report to the United Nations Conference on Environment and Development: Forging the Links* (Wellington: Ministry for the Environment).

Ministry for the Environment (1995) *Environment 2010 Strategy: A Statement of the Government's Strategy on the Environment* (Wellington: Ministry for the Environment).

Ministry for the Environment (1998) *Learning to Care for Our Environment: A national strategy for environmental education* (Wellington: Ministry for the Environment).

Ministry of Education (1991) *The National Curriculum of New Zealand: A Discussion Document* (Wellington: Ministry of Education).

Ministry of Education (1993) *The New Zealand Curriculum Framework* (Wellington, New Zealand: Learning Media).

Ministry of Education (1999) *Guidelines for Environmental Education in New Zealand Schools* (Wellington: Learning Media).
Ministry of Education (2002) *Curriculum Stocktake Report* (Wellington: Ministry of Education).
Ministry of Education (2003) *Educational Priorities 2003–2006* (Wellington: Ministry of Education).
Murphy, L., Friesen, W. & Kearns, R. (2003) The divided city and urban sustainability, in: C. Freeman & M. Thompson-Fawcett (Eds) *Living Space: Towards Sustainable Settlements in New Zealand*, pp. 95–112 (Dunedin: University of Otago).
New Zealand Government (2003) *Education Priorities for New Zealand.* (Wellington: Ministry of Education). Available at: http://www.minedu.govt.nz/web/downloadable/dl8354_v1/world-full.doc
NZRUNDESD (New Zealand Response to the United Nations Decade of Education for Sustainable Development) (2005) *Newsletter*, December, pp. 5.
PCE (2004) *See Change: Learning and Education for Sustainability* (Wellington: PCE).
Postma, D. (2002) Taking the future seriously: on the inadequacies of the framework of liberalism for environmental education, *Journal of Philosophy of Education*, 36(1), pp. 41–56.
Print, M. (1993) *Curriculum Development and Design* (St Leonards, NSW: Allen & Unwin).
UNCED (1992) *United Nations Commission for Environment and Development. Agenda 21: The United Nations Programme for Action from Rio* (New York: UN).
UNESCO–UNEP (1976) The Belgrade Charter, *Connect*, I(1), pp. 1–9.
UNESCO–UNEP (1978) The Tbilisi Declaration, *Connect*, *III*(1), pp. 1–8.
Williams, P. (2005) 'Comment': New Zealand Association for Environmental Education, *Newsletter*, December pp. 7.

Sustainable Development within UK Higher Education: Revealing Tendencies and Tensions

WILLIAM SCOTT & STEPHEN GOUGH

Introduction

In this paper, through a critical examination of developments within UK higher education, we review the agenda established at Rio (Hopkins *et al.*, 1996) and comment on issues currently affecting the UK higher education system. The targets set at Rio for education were ambitious, including: develop networks and cross-disciplinary courses; build partnerships with stakeholders; establish centres of excellence in research/education; promote the building of public awareness; identify training needs; and encourage the review of professional codes of practice. The relevance of these to the work and skills found in any higher education sector is clear.

Sustainable Development in UK Higher Education: A Snapshot

The UK higher education funding councils already promote institutional development work on sustainable development. The Higher Education Partnership for Sustainability (HEPS) (2004a) project, now drawn to a close, saw that universities might make a significant contribution towards sustainable development through their key roles as:

- places of learning and research; forming and informing the leaders and decision-makers of the future;
- major businesses; where prudent resource use not only saves money but safeguards reputations;
- key community players; as employer, purchaser and amenity provider with a major impact on the wider world of influential ideas and technological development.

The UK's Department for Education and Skills website (http://www.dfes.gov.uk/sd/learning.shtml#he) notes:

> The HEPS project is encouraging the higher education sector to adopt sustainable practices. This is a three-year, UK-wide initiative (a pioneering collaboration between Forum for the Future and 18 universities and colleges). It began in 2000 with £1 million support from the four UK funding bodies. HEPS is focused on key areas such as transport and construction and is designed to generate transferable tools and guidance, as well as inspiration for other higher education institutions.

In addition, organizations such as the Environmental Association for Universities and Colleges (EAUC: http://www.eauc.org.uk/), with a membership of two hundred further and higher education institutions, focuses on "integrating sustainability and environmental management into the business management of colleges and universities in the UK and further afield", and is involved in projects focusing on environmental performance (for example, in relation to transport, energy, effluent and waste, water use, resource procurement and the like), in the further and higher education sectors. One of these, the higher education environmental performance improvement project (http://www.heepi.org.uk/), is a project funded under the Higher Education Funding Council for England's good management practice initiative, and involves a partnership of four universities together with the joint procurement policy and strategy group with close links with the Association of University Directors of Estates. The project has four main strands of work:

- building level benchmarking of energy and water consumption;
- developing case studies of best practice in environmental performance improvement in HE;
- identifying and testing standardized measures for procurement, waste and other functions;
- developing the capacity of staff with environment-related responsibilities to achieve positive environmental change within their institutions through action workshops and other means.

The UK's Department for Education and Skills website also notes:

> Curriculum development is also an important aspect in higher education with the opportunity to create informed graduates who are knowledgeable about sustainability and can influence others. The Higher Education Funding Council for England (HEFCE) is commissioning research to establish demand by employers for sustainability knowledge, as they believe this will drive change.

However, across the sector, and over time, there would seem to have been more success in managing the environment of higher education than in engendering curriculum change (Johnston & Buckland, 2002; Reid *et al.*, 2002; Scott & Gough, 2003; 2004b; Haigh, 2005). By way of brief exemplification of these issues, Table 1 samples a range of initiatives in relation to sustainable development and higher education, both within and outside the UK. The first four issues chosen are illustrative of a very wide range of activities across the sector. The last two, which explicitly focus on teacher education, are amongst the best-documented examples of sector-specific work. For a more in-depth appreciation (and critique) of these, see Scott & Gough (2003).

It seems reasonably clear that considerable problems confront attempts to influence curriculum *alongside* changing management practices. Ashley (2005) points to one example:

> Key transferable skills are now familiar in UK higher education where *communication*, *numeracy*, and *IT* demonstrate continuity with the priorities of [schools]. However, there is no key skill such as *understanding sustainability*. (emphasis in the original)

This tension should be unsurprising as university environmental managers do not focus on curriculum, and academics do not *have* to think about sustainable development. Although a teaching or research focus on sustainable development may arise from professional choice, academic freedom militates strongly against forced curriculum change. Determinist curriculum interventions can have a negative effect. For example, in the 1997–1999 HE21 initiative UK universities were presented with documents specifying, "what sustainability learning is required by different professions" (Ali Khan, 2002, p. 15), which they all were expected to take seriously. Unsurprisingly, perhaps, little curriculum change came of this. Meanwhile, all estates/energy managers have to deal with sustainability issues whether they are enthused by the concept or not, because it is required of them by increasingly demanding legislation and regulation that would, prima facie, seem to have wide social approval.

It is not the case, of course, that nothing is happening in relation to curriculum; a prominent development in the UK is the learning for sustainable development curriculum toolkit developed through HEPS. The toolkit was developed from work done by *Forum for the Future* with the University of Antofagasta in Chile. It provides an ambitious methodology intending to inform learning activities in short courses, in whole degrees and outside higher education, for example in business. A number of ideas inform the toolkit, including that:

- universities, as noted above, are both places for learning and research and key community players with different roles that impinge on sustainable development;
- the 'triple bottom line' view of sustainable development (requiring simultaneous improvements in the environment, the economy and society) is seen as useful but over-simplistic. A more complex formulation is adopted with five kinds of capital: natural, human, social, manufactured and financial;
- 12 criteria (linked with the fivefold capital) are adduced to encapsulate a sustainable society. These relate to: non-renewable resource extraction; manufacture and use of artificial substances; the integrity of the ecological system; human health; learning and social skills; employment, creativity and recreation; governance and justice;

Table 1. Indicative initiatives in higher education in relation to sustainable development

1. **Business, the community and sustainable development**: The University of Westminster received support from the HEFCE Higher Education Reach-out to Business and the Community Fund (HEROBAC) to develop sectoral business clusters. The specific goals were to:

- engage businesses in the Greater London area with an interest in the outcome of sustainable development policies,
- identify opportunities in the areas of: climate change; logistics; and property management; and
- develop a business plan for taking forward the knowledge cluster.

⟨http://www.psi.org.uk/research/project.asp?project_id = 23⟩

2. **Energy management in higher education**. This report, commissioned by the UK Value for Money Steering Group, provides an update of the energy management study completed in 1996. It identifies key actions and future issues that need to be addressed by HE institutions in developing a strategic policy framework for sustainability that includes energy management.
⟨http://www.hefce.ac.uk/Pubs/hefce/2003/03_30.htm⟩

3. **Government action**: In May 1999 the Government published *A Better Quality of Life: A Strategy for Sustainable Development for the UK*. This strategy, which is currently being reviewed, set out a new approach to sustainable development in the UK, and key Government actions and commitments to help achieve it. The 'Framework for Sustainable Development on the Government Estate' was launched in July 2002, and is the main vehicle for systematically assessing, managing, reporting and improving performance of the Government Estate. Within education, significant improvement has been made to the environmental impact of departmental buildings. A series of initiatives aimed at reducing energy consumption across the whole education sector has been launched. The higher education (HE) sector has provided some significant examples in both estate management and teaching.
⟨http://www.dfes.gov.uk/aboutus/sd//actioncontext.shtml⟩

4. **UN Type 2 Partnerships**: These are voluntary, non-negotiated partnerships, aimed at implementing sustainable development, and are outcomes of the World Summit on Sustainable Development. More than 200 such partnerships were launched during the Summit process. The Johannesburg Plan of Implementation (JPOI) subsequently designated the Commission on Sustainable Development (CSD) as the focal point for discussion on partnerships that promote sustainable development. Partnerships relating to higher education include the international university for sustainable development, and global higher education for sustainability, which involves:

University leaders for a sustainable future ⟨http://www.ulsf.org/resources_partners.html⟩
Copernicus Campus ⟨http://www.copernicus-campus.org/⟩
International association of universities ⟨http://www.unesco.org/iau/⟩ and
UNESCO ⟨http://www.unesco.org⟩

⟨http://www.johannesburgsummit.org/html/sustainable_dev/p2_means_education1.html⟩

5. **Reorienting teacher education towards sustainability**: The purpose is to take leadership in developing an international pilot network among existing teacher training institutions, based in part on the results of the UNESCO workshop held in Thessaloniki, Greece, in December 1997. It is an instrument for facilitating collaboration between researchers and educators within the university and in other universities and teacher training institutions around the world. This network includes institutions in different countries and regions of the world. The research and demonstration focus of the network will take the form of experimentation with different approaches to reorienting teacher education towards sustainability. The experience gained through the network will be used to formulate guidelines.
⟨http://portal.unesco.org/en/ev.
php@URL_ID = 3287&URL_DO = DO_TOPIC&URL_SECTION = 201.html⟩

6. **UNESCO Teaching and Learning for a Sustainable Future programme**: This is a dissemination and training toolbox that contains guidelines and sample resources to assist in planning and facilitating workshops designed to assist participants to:

- become familiar with Teaching and Learning for a Sustainable Future;
- appreciate the value of multimedia approaches in teacher education;
- understand the many different ways Teaching and Learning for a Sustainable Future can be used in pre-service and in-service teacher education;
- relate the content of Teaching and Learning for a Sustainable Future to local curriculum and teacher education priorities;
- make a plan for conducting Teaching and Learning for a Sustainable Future training workshops.

⟨http://www.unesco.org/education/tlsf⟩

---

positive values and social cohesion; positive (for both environment and people) institutional change; safe and supportive living and working environments; resource-use efficiency and the promotion of human innovation; and accurate valuation of all forms of capital;

- to be compatible with the promotion of sustainable development, learning has to take place in a particular way. It must be learner-focused; 'holistic', draw together economic, environmental and social strands; be compatible both with the physical learning environment and with the socioeconomic characteristics of learners; be applicable at a range of degrees of complexity; and be focused on identified learning outcomes.

There is a seven-stage approach to the toolkit. First, a 'learner profile' is drawn up in order to map the world from the learner's perspective (see Figure 2 in Johnston & Buckland, 2002, p. 17 for an example of one of these). The 'learner', e.g. a particular type of professional or graduate, and the organizations or environmental aspects with which the learner interacts most are placed near the centre of the map. Those with whom interaction is infrequent and/or weaker are placed further out. Second, prospective course content is identified by listing the knowledge and skills necessary to manage each interaction in a way that is consistent with sustainable development. The categories 'ecological', 'social' and 'economic' are used to organize these lists, but it is stressed that interesting entries are likely to span categories. Third, identified knowledge and skills are scored in terms of their ability to contribute to the 12 criteria of a sustainable society. This enables, fourth, the specification of desired learning outcomes and, fifth, the design of delivery mechanisms. The sixth stage is a 'values audit', designed to check whether the course, as now designed, is compatible with the values of staff and students. Following this, a course guide can finally be prepared.

This approach recognizes the significance of the contexts in which learning takes place, and is a determined attempt to generate practical progress towards sustainable development, undaunted by difficulties of definition of terms or institutional inertia.

The toolkit emphasizes thinking originating in economics and natural science and its approach to learning is managerialist rather than emancipatory (Kemmis & Fitzclarence, 1986; Huckle, 1993) or liberal (Oulton & Scott, 1999). This is evident in:

- a target population of graduates and professionals;
- an emphasis on measurable learning outcomes informed by the '12 features of a sustainable society', rather than a pedagogy of individual and collective self-discovery;
- the idea that sustainable development is ultimately about what happens to the five kinds of capital. However, in an alternative approach (UNESCO's 'Teaching and learning for a sustainable future' programme), this is ultimately

"about the process of learning to make decisions that consider the long-term economy, ecology and equity of all communities" (http://www.unesco.org/education/tlsf/)

- learning being seen as instrumental to achieving sustainable development, rather than being, of itself, a vital and substantial *aspect* of any ongoing process of sustainable development.

(See http://www.heps.org.uk and Johnston & Buckland (2002) for further details.)

In 2004, HEPS published *Learning and Skills for Sustainable Development: Developing a Sustainability Literate Society: Guidance for Higher Education Institutions* (HEPS, 2004b). The purpose of this was "to help higher education institutions to integrate sustainability literacy into the curriculum of their learning programmes". The booklet notes (p. 5) that:

> The main part of this guide—section three—explores some of the key elements of good practice in integrating sustainability literacy into the provision of all courses in the higher education sector, and proposes a tool kit to guide practitioners. Based on existing good practice, it provides useful tools to help course designers identify and prioritize sustainability elements in any existing or new courses. This guide recognizes that there is no set model to help course procurers, designers and deliverers integrate sustainability competencies into current provision. Our hope is that it will provide sufficient balance between direction and self-discovery to enable practitioners to feel sufficiently competent to get started, to learn through the use of these tools and to feel that they are on the right track.

This curriculum design toolkit is a development of HEP's earlier ideas discussed here in response both to its own thinking and to critical external commentary.

Developing the Higher Education Curriculum: Further Issues

Though the HEPS toolkit represents valuable progress, at least three important issues remain:

- Elaborate (and expensive) pedagogies aren't always needed. Where people want to act sustainably, but cannot do so because they lack knowledge or skills, providing information may well suffice. Though the converse holds equally well—simple information provision will often not suffice, since learners may be indifferent or actively disinclined towards sustainable behaviour (Scott & Gough, 2003)—it remains the case that there is value in identifying what might be termed 'easy wins'. So, for example, management students certainly need to know where sustainable practice equates to cost reductions. Teaching this should be pedagogically straightforward *but* exploiting all such opportunities will not, by itself, be enough to achieve sustainable development. There is merit in targeting more complex pedagogies to more difficult learning challenges, but also to keeping it simple whenever you can.
- People do not necessarily learn things just because educators think them important. Learners bring important knowledge, values and skills to the learning

process, and these are productively supplemented and modified through external inputs. The question is, how far to privilege the prior knowledge of the learner, and how far that of the external expert and/or educator. *The toolkit* has a clear 'expert' focus, setting learning objectives in relation to its pre-specified 12 features of a sustainable society, which are beyond the scope of negotiation.

- Any strategy for social change needs to take account of learning that happens incidentally and independently of teaching programmes—and sometimes despite them. It is, surely, quite clear that what people learn in institutions of higher education is not the same as what they are taught.

Further, though the toolkit is admirable in that it exhibits an ingenious design aimed at respecting the learner's own context, we would argue that it does not take this far enough. O'Riordan (1989) makes a distinction between two worldviews, the one conservative and nurturing, the other radical and manipulative. The toolkit, and most other examples that could have been chosen for comparison, predominantly exhibit the former. A more complex account of the different perspectives we may have on the natural world is offered by cultural theory (Thompson, 1990), which posits mutually interdependent rationalities: the hierarchical; the egalitarian; the individualistic; and the fatalistic. On this view the toolkit inclines towards an egalitarian view, in which things make sense if they are *fair* and *just*. This is, typically, the perspective of those who are most deeply concerned with sustainable development. It is often not the perspective either of students or of the institutions for which they will one day work as graduates. On the contrary, they may think according to rules that define 'making sense', not in terms of 'being just' but in terms, for example, of 'getting a result' (the individualistic rationality) or 'complying with the rules' (the hierarchical rationality). Given that, in all societies, there will continue to be conflicts between private and collective interests, between local and national priorities (Blaikie & Brookfield, 1987, p. 83), and between now and the future (Pearce & Kerry Turner, 1990; Greenall Gough, 1993; Dobson, 2003), we should expect different perspectives to exist. Indeed, we should encourage them.

In the toolkit, worldviews and rationalities other thsn those of its designers are insufficiently explicit. A sustainable world cannot, as the toolkit would seem to suggest, only be a world of justice and collaboration. For example, when the eighth 'feature of a sustainable society' requires that: 'the structures and institutions of society promote stewardship of natural resources and development of people', this cannot be done without losers being created who, whatever the curriculum may tell them, will probably not be pleased. Such issues cannot be wished, legislated or educated away. As we have noted, the toolkit recognizes such difficult problems, and responds by offering a number of processes to prioritize course content so that it reflects the values of students and institutions. However, this leads to another problem—an example of a Bateson (1999) *double bind*: the more this is done, the less challenge to those values is offered, and the less likely learning is to accrue.

In the same way, it is important to remember that many other institutions have a bearing on the success or failure of initiatives. Universities have external responsibilities to their students and to funders, and both these are increasingly mediated through market mechanisms. Of course, many businesses now have some sort of policy relating to sustainable development, and may take account of it when recruiting staff. Similarly, research councils increasingly recognize environmental issues as a theme of research; but in both cases the relationship of sustainable development to learning may be poorly articulated, and at the margin other things are quite likely to be deemed more important. Universities have no choice but to respond to this ordering of priorities. They must also respond to the interests of governing councils, which may or may not place sustainable development high on their lists of priorities as far as the academic curriculum is concerned.

As we noted earlier, the picture is more positive in relation to the management of universities' physical resources, where potential savings from sustainable resource procurement or energy-saving measures are increasingly important, and conforming to law in relation to pollutants will remain a priority. The toolkit recognizes and seeks to address many of these difficulties, and is a sophisticated attempt to address this problem of specialization. However, the problem remains that, in any professional context, any focus on sustainable development remains essentially secondary.

There is evidence of both research and teaching taking place that relates to sustainable development. This is particularly the case with departments of geography where, in universities across the world, wide-ranging issues relating to sustainable development are not only now a major focus of teaching at undergraduate and postgraduate levels, but also key drivers of research, development and consultancy activity. There is also evidence that some institutions take sustainable development seriously as a driver of their internal management processes. There is no sense, however, that sustainable development has yet become a major strategic parameter of university life that links the business, learning, research and community functions of institutions in the way envisaged by, say, UNESCO. This is a measure of the scale of the challenge such institutions face.

It is also important to view developments in higher education in the wider national context, and to acknowledge that sectors are not freestanding. Thus what is possible in any particular institution is affected by, and affects, what is happening across the sector. In their review of progress to date, Reid *et al.* (2002) noted that work related to sustainable development continues to be seen in many cases as a costly add-on to existing programmes, rather than as a means and opportunity better to achieve existing goals, and that:

> A plethora of initiatives, however, does not amount to a national strategy, and many disparate initiatives, valuable in themselves, have not yet been linked to advantage, locally, nationally and/or farther afield. Often this is because teachers, local government officers, NGO employees, and others have lacked the understanding and/or the infrastructural support to realize such integration, particularly at the interface of bottom-up with top-down approaches.

Initiatives such as HEPs must have at least some chance of affecting curriculum because of the cultural significance of its institutional base (i.e. HEFCE, *Forum for the Future* and many prominent stakeholders/supporters) and its associated ability to mould policy. But if, for example, you are not persuaded by the seven-stage approach, the 12 criteria or the fivefold capital model, or you have your own ideas (as people in universities are supposed to have), where does this leave you? Are you to be counted amongst those who are working to help students to be "both capable and willing to accelerate change to a sustainability society" (Johnston & Buckland, 2002, p. 16), or not? Too much assertiveness might well lead the busy, the uncertain, the fearful or the naive to mistake a well-presented case for the definitive way forward.

Learning as Sustainable Development

Sustainable development, if it ever happens, will be a process in which everyone learns all the time. Its cause is unlikely to be advanced by any group that simply asserts its right and authority to teach others without learning itself. Aiding collaborators to do what *they* want to do more effectively will be more helpful than telling them they should really be doing something else. Respecting the varied institutional and professional contexts of collaborators recognizes that they not only have unique contextual insights and strategic understandings, but also have ongoing institutional commitments that demand much of their attention, and which mean that progress in relation to sustainable development will be heavily contingent.

Encouraging, facilitating and supporting sequences of small steps may well be more productive ways of exploring issues and gaining confidence than being faced with the imperative of taking giant leaps on the grounds that, for example, such sustainable development is urgent. It is particularly important that experience and confidence be achieved at a pace that makes sense to all stakeholders. As problems, failures and disappointments are to be expected, the priority must be for all to share, and learn from them. Such leadership and innovation might well include the following among its priorities:

- commissioning research, particularly into the mainstreaming of sustainable development issues into learning; and the actual and potential relationship between sustainable development and (lifelong) learning;
- better use of existing research, long-term cross-sector strategic planning, and the development of transferable skills and flexibility;
- cross-sector monitoring and evaluation of initiatives and learning in sustainable development;
- networking of practitioners in order critically to examine effective practice;
- promotion of, and leadership contributions to, international developments.

The World Summit on Sustainable Development made only two references to learning: (1) a re-affirmation of the internationally agreed Millennium Development Goals of universal primary education by 2015 and the elimination of gender disparities in primary and secondary education by 2005, and (2) confirmation of civil society's crucial role in sustainable development—with the need for the public to be (at the very least) aware of this. None of this is particularly controversial, or new. Indeed, from 1998 there has been an emerging focus on learning in the UN when the 6th session of the UN Commission on Sustainable Development (UNCSD) agreed seven priority areas for action which were all confirmed by the Summit:

- clarifying and communicating sustainable development concepts and key messages;
- reviewing national education policies and reorienting practices, including teacher education and higher education teaching and research;
- incorporating education within national sustainable development strategies and planning processes;
- promoting sustainable consumption and production through education;
- promoting investment in education;
- identifying and sharing innovative practices;
- raising public awareness.

The need for learning seems implicit in all of these, and the fact that the UN General Assembly has designated 2005–2014 as the 'decade of education for sustainable development' further strengthens higher education's role. It is also hard to see any of the UN's goals being achieved without a great deal of learning across all sectors—arising from experience, from work in schools, colleges and universities, from training, and through professional and institutional development. The Summit, however, gives learning only a supporting role in relation to a wide range of issues to do with development, health, good governance, trade and the environment (i.e. to do with sustainable development), which assumes that learning is only important *after* experts have decided what—in terms of development, health, good governance, trade, environment, and so on—should be done or learned.

This recourse to external expertise is unsatisfactory for a number of reasons. Teachers in universities know that their job is to promote learning *by* their students, rather than to promote sustainable development. Thus, if sustainable development does require learning, then *learning goals* must be a fundamental part of it. Environmental and other goals—supposedly to be achieved *through* learning—will not do by themselves just because experts with no contextual authority deem them important. Further, even where it is possible to say what needs to happen from a particular perspective (development, say) and/or a particular discipline (economics, say) such perspectives (or disciplines) are not necessarily congruent. Under these circumstances, simply seeking to promote learning without too many other preconceptions seems the only sensible way forward.

Table 2 offers an analysis of issues across sectors, drawing on ideas that have been extensively argued elsewhere (Scott & Gough, 2003, 2004a). Specifically, it comments on the rationalities underlying different perspectives on the policy options available to us in relation to various ways of viewing the problems that sustainable development purports to address. It sets out perspectives on sustainable development ranging from *denial* (A: *Problem? What problem?*) to *resignation* (D: *Humanity incapable of necessary change*), suggesting that the best perspective to take (E) is one that favours a *clumsy* approach (Thompson, 1990), which is one that entertains competing definitions of problems at the same time. Of course, such an approach can be difficult for policy-makers to explain or justify to their various stakeholder groups, who are likely not only to expect the appearance of clarity of purpose, but also to wish to promote their own particular rationality with its corresponding problem definitions. However, it is important to be clear that though this view is saying that many problems related to sustainable development are likely to continue to be characterized by uncertainty, it *is* possible (and important) to chip away at this uncertainty. It *is* possible to know things: but it is important to be absolutely honest about when we *really* know something, and when we just wish we did. There is nothing in the least bit scientifically rigorous about assuming values for unknown variables and then building these into policy prescriptions behind a screen of fine words and/or abstruse mathematics.

The ideas in Table 2 have been built up in such a 'clumsy' way; typically, such ideas (and tables) develop iteratively through thinking, discussion and critique. Of course, any such categorization has to be a simplification as the problem perspectives described here are not necessarily as fully discrete, or as unidimensional, as suggested, and the point of the clumsy approach is that value and usefulness can be found in more than one of them at the same time. The important question in all of this is to what extent they help you to think about these important issues in your own contexts. Thus, the table should be viewed

Table 2 Sustainable development: the problem–policy gap, underlying rationalities and the role of learning

Problem perspectives	Policy options	Underlying rationalities	Roles for learning
A. Problem? What problem?	1. Markets and prices (maybe with regulation and the WTO, and new technology)	Trust what works, and people; let markets enable and regulate what we do	Promote autonomy and individual responsibility
B. The problem can be addressed; it is a question of (serious) reform	2. Encourage people's actions through information and communication campaigns	Trust role models and moral leadership	Encourage responsible (environmental) behaviour
	3. Persuade people through well-targeted taxation, laws, and regulatory frameworks	Trust bureaucracy and regulation; organise behaviour through social rules	Encourage compliance
C. Although the problem is acute, building sustainable development *will* be possible	4. Technological innovation 5. A radical re-think of the human–Earth relationship	Trust experts and the hierarchies of science and nature Trust spiritual leadership and ecological design	Disseminate scientific knowledge Learn to live in harmony with other species and each other
	6. Radical change of economic structure (e.g. the overthrow of global capitalism)	Trust charismatic leaders and local participatory democracy	Learn that considerations of equity and justice should dictate how humans live
	7. Dissemble the nature of the problem; pretend a bit of reform will do	*Trust to luck*	Learning ends up being a displacement activity
D. Humanity seems incapable of the change required for sustainable development	8. Don't admit it; jolly people along or Be honest; let this understanding inform actions	*Fatalism/deception* Fatalism/ despondency	Learning ends up being a displacement activity Learn to accept the inevitable: good grace and stoicism
E. Problem? Which problem?	9. Build human capability—incrementally	A clumsy approach	Learning is integral to sustainable development

heuristically as an aid to thinking about the relationship between how we perceive problems relating to sustainable development, and how we view the adequacy of policy relating to the problems—as well as an aid to thinking about underlying rationalities and the role of learning in relation to any particular policy.

Concluding Comments

The divisions that we routinely make of knowledge into disciplines, of policy-making into ministries, and of sustainable development into economic, environmental and social components—whilst useful and necessary ways by which complex entities are made manageable—remain simplifications. For example, the economy, the environment and society are *not* separable, and sustainable development cannot arise from the independent insights of economists, environmental scientists and social scientists, working with different assumptions and methodologies. Learning is required across the institutions they represent, the constituencies they serve and the literacies they employ. Without this, there will be no sustainable development.

Lastly, how people view the world, and what they do in relation to this, matters because it makes a difference to how things turn out; that is, to how the human–environment relationship co-evolves. And what people learn matters because it informs and enables what we can do next. Reassuringly, what people learn is not always what others try to teach, which is why people, and what they learn, are crucial to (and for) sustainable development. Such factors are fundamental to higher education institutions being able to think about sustainable development, and for progress to be made in ways that make contextual and cultural sense to them.

References

Ali Khan, S. (2002) Sustainable development education in the UK: the challenge for higher education institutions, *Planet*, Special Edition 2, pp. 15.

Ashley, M. (2005) Tensions between indoctrination and the development of judgement: the case for an extended period of education for sustainable development, *Environmental Education Research*, 11(2), pp. 187–197.

Bateson, G. (1999) *Steps to an Ecology of Mind: Collected Essays in Anthropology, Psychiatry, Evolution, and Epistemology* (Chicago: University of Chicago Press).

Blaikie, P. & Brookfield, H. (1987) *Land Degradation and Society* (London: Methuen).

Dobson, A. (2003) *Economic Behaviour: Value and Values*, in: W. A. H. Scott & S. R. Gough (Eds) *Key Issues in Sustainable Development and Learning: A Critical Review*, pp. 222–224 (London: RoutledgeFalmer).

Greenall Gough, A. (1993) *Founders in Environmental Education* (Geelong: Deakin University Press).

HEPS (2004a) HEPS Key Objectives. Available at: http://www.forumforthefuture.org.uk/aboutus/default.asp?pageid=526 (accessed October 2004).

HEPS (2004b) *Learning and Skills for Sustainable Development: Developing a Sustainability Literate Society; Guidance for Higher Education Institutions* (London: Forum for the Future).

Haigh, M. J. (2005) Greening the university curriculum: appraising an international movement, *Journal of Geography in Higher Education*, 29(1), pp. 31–48.

Hopkins, C., Damlamian, J. & López Ospina, G. (1996) Evolving towards education for sustainable development: an international perspective, *Nature and Resources*, 32(3), pp. 36–45.

Huckle, J. (1993) Environmental education and sustainability: a view from critical theory, in: J. Fien (Ed.) *Environmental Education: A Pathway to Sustainability*, pp. 43–68 (Geelong: Deakin University Press).

Johnston, A. & Buckland, H. (2002) How can higher education produce graduates with the capacity to accelerate change towards a more sustainable society, *Planet*, Special Issue 2, pp. 16–17.

Kemmis, S. & Fitzclarence, L. (1986) *Curriculum Theorizing: Beyond Reproduction Theory* (Geelong: Deakin University Press).

O'Riordan, T. (1989) The challenge for environmentalism, in: R. Peet & N. Thrift (Eds) *New Models in Geography*, pp. 77–102 (London: Unwin Hyman).

Oulton, C. R. & Scott, W. A. H. (1999) Environmental education: a time for re-visioning, in: R Moon, M. Ben-Peretz & S. Brown (Eds) *Routledge International Companion to Education*, pp. 489–501 (London: Routledge).

Pearce, D. & Kerry Turner, R. (1990) *Economics of Natural Resources and the Environment* (Hemel Hempstead: Harvester Wheatsheaf).

Reid, A. D., Scott, W. A. H. & Gough, S. R. (2002) Education and sustainable development in the UK: an exploration of progress since Rio, *Geography*, 87(3), pp. 247–255.

Scott, W. A. H. & Gough, S. R. (2003) *Sustainable Development and Learning: Framing the Issues* (London/New York: RoutledgeFalmer).

Scott, W. A. H. & Gough, S. R (Eds) (2004a) *Key issues in Sustainable Development and Learning: A Critical Review* (London/New York: RoutledgeFalmer).

Scott, W. A. H. & Gough, S. R (2004b) Education and sustainable development in UK universities: a critical exploration post-Rio, in: P. Blaze Corcoran & A. E. J. Wals (Eds) *Higher Education and the Challenge of Sustainability: Problematics, Practice, and Promise*, pp. 235–247 (Dordrecht: Kluwer).

Thompson, M. (1990) Policy making in the face of uncertainty, *Concepts of the Environment in the Social Sciences: Readings 3*, pp. 161–187 (London: Wye College).

A Centre for Excellence in Education for Sustainable Development

ALAN DYER, DAVID SELBY & BRIAN CHALKLEY

Introducing the Centre for Sustainable Futures

The title 'Centre for Excellence' has been used by organizations in just about every sector of business, media, governance and education across the world. Sometimes it is simply a promotional self-aggrandizement; sometimes it is a highly prestigious award from government or an international body. Being labelled a 'Centre for Excellence' can bring enormous rewards, great professional satisfaction and enhanced credibility within the sector and with potential partners and clients. Of course, it also brings a real responsibility to consistently deliver that excellence and maintain the 'state-of-the-art' dynamic. Such a label will commonly invite intense interest, generate numerous comparisons and precipitate inevitable criticism—so it can be both a blessing and a poisoned chalice!

The idea of Centres for Excellence in Teaching and Learning (CETLs) was first announced in the UK Government's 2003 White Paper entitled 'The Future of Higher Education'. The CETL initiative was to have two main aims: *to reward excellent teaching practice, and to further invest in that practice so that CETL funding delivers substantial benefits to students, teachers and institutions*. The Higher Education Funding Council for England (HEFCE) subsequently published details of the funding and bidding process in January 2004. With a total funding of £315 million over five years from 2005, this programme represents HEFCE's largest ever single funding initiative in teaching and learning. Each CETL is in receipt of recurrent funding, ranging from £200 000 to £500 000 per annum for five years, and a one-off capital sum ranging from £0.8 million to £2 million. Following the completion of a two stage bidding process, a total of 74 successful CETL bids were announced on 27 January 2005. The new CETLs include, for example, centres focused on aspects of learning and teaching such as employability, blended learning, enquiry-based learning, assessment, undergraduate research skills, creativity and the promotion of learner autonomy. Some of the new centres will be focused entirely on these kinds of generic themes and some have links to particular disciplines. The full list of CETLs and the Institutions where they are based, can be found at the following website: http://www.hefce.ac.uk, under learning and teaching/CETL.

Many of the CETLs will be of interest to geographers, both in the UK and overseas but four in particular have a strong geographical dimension. They are:

- Sustainable Futures (University of Plymouth);
- Active Learning in Geography, Environment and Related Disciplines (University of Gloucestershire);
- Experiential Learning in Environmental and Natural Sciences (University of Plymouth);
- Spatial Literacy in Teaching (University of Leicester).

These four CETLs are committed to both strengthening and sharing existing excellence within their own institution and also to disseminating best practice across UK higher education and beyond. In this wider role they will work closely with the Higher Education Academy's Subject Centre for Geography, Earth and Environmental Sciences (GEES). The fact that GEES is based at the University of Plymouth will obviously assist communication with the CETLs on Sustainability and Experiential Learning but the Subject Centre is keen to support all four CETLs in their national work for promoting best practice.

The purpose of this particular paper is to focus on the education for sustainable development (ESD) CETL. Sustainability is an increasingly important issue for staff involved in geographical education and the design of geographical curricula. However, this is contested territory and it can even be difficult to get beyond issues of definition and terminology. So, education for sustainable development can sometimes be labelled as education for sustainability, education for sustainable futures, sustainability literacy and so on. Many governments have responded to calls for national strategies on ESD since the Rio Summit (1992), and the UN Decade for ESD 2005–2015 should precipitate more initiatives and actions.

The University of Plymouth has a particularly strong record in education for sustainability in a number of areas, including geography, environmental science, education, civil engineering, law, biological sciences and architecture. Indeed, it enjoys a national and, in some respects, an international reputation in the broad field of environmental education. As discussed later, the CETL is further strengthened by the involvement of two other internationally regarded bodies, namely Schumacher College and Forum for the Future. The CETL's aim is to transform the University of Plymouth from being a university characterized by significant areas of ESD excellence into an institution modelling a university-wide programmatic commitment to high quality ESD teaching and learning.

ESD is a holistic concept, embracing the complementary notions of environmental security, intra-generational and inter-generational equity, economic betterment, and social and environmental justice. It has accordingly been defined as "a process of learning how to make decisions that consider the long-term future of the economy, ecology and equity of all communities" and as about capacity building for 'future-oriented thinking' (UNESCO, 2003, p. 4). In its mixture of the ethical, visionary and practical it often finds a deep resonance particularly amongst young people and fosters proactive, responsible citizenship (Goldstein & Selby, 2000).

Moreover, the UK Education Secretary has recently launched a sustainable development Action Plan, and HEFCE has recently developed its first ESD strategy and sustainability features in its 2003–2008 overall Strategic Plan. The Higher Education Leadership Foundation has also identified ESD as a priority area. In an address on climate change last year, Prime Minister Tony Blair (Brown, 2004) envisaged learning institutions in which sustainability principles were built into the estate, curriculum, and teaching and learning in an interconnected and synergistic way: "students won't just be told about sustainable development, they will see and work within it: a living learning place in which to explore what a sustainable lifestyle means". This CETL programme therefore has the potential to play a path-finding role in taking forward these new national priorities.

The CETL builds upon the emerging concept of sustainability literacy, which has been defined as a skills and knowledge set enabling a proactive engagement with social, environmental and economic aspects of sustainable development allied to an understanding of the dynamically connected and nested nature of different spatial levels, local to global (Parkin *et al.*, 2004). The CETL recognizes the centrality of sustainability literacy to employability, effective professionalism, continued economic performance, social cohesion and social and individual well-being. As such, it is of trans-disciplinary significance.

It also builds upon the existing canon of ESD-related pedagogical research literature. The literature reports that, across the curriculum, the implementation of sustainability education has resulted in a progressive shift of learning approaches from the transmissive and teacher-centred towards the learner-centred, and towards collaborative learning and learning through discovery (Van de Bor *et al.*, 2000; Sterling, 2004a, 2004b). A key finding is that students' ESD-related learning is significantly enhanced if their studies are integrated in an active way into campus greening and campus environmental management and review initiatives (Rohwedder, 2004). Another is the potentially powerful effect on student skills and understandings, and their commitment to sustainability, of engaging as part of their studies in sustainability partnerships and projects within the broader community (Bowden & Pallant, 2004; Faulstich, 2004). In terms of embedding sustainability education across departments, action research suggests the effectiveness of interventions that, while providing the initial challenge and stimulus for debate, reflection and action, motivate the disciplinary professional by establishing internal departmental research and review processes harmonizing with the disciplinary culture (Appel *et al.*, 2004). Research into fostering system-wide commitment to sustainability within higher education institutions, and, hence, institutional transformation indicates that an ethos and context needs to be fostered allowing for aspects of change to be led by various stakeholder groups within the institution, including the student body (Edelstein, 2004; Jerman *et al.*, 2004; Jenks-Jay,

2004a, 2004b). The findings of ESD-related pedagogical research resonate with generic pedagogical research concerning the positive impacts of interactive and experience-based learning on student motivation and attainment (Gibbs, 1992).

The University of Plymouth has a longstanding commitment to environmental and sustainability education, dating back to 1973 when the university pioneered one of the earliest and most successful interdisciplinary programmes in environmental sciences, interlinking the physical, biological and social dimensions of sustainability. Since then, the institution's commitment to ESD has spread to many other programmes and its reputation has been enhanced by excellent evaluations by the Quality Assurance Agency (QAA), by participation in relevant QAA Benchmarking exercises and by staff research and publications. The university's reputation in environmental education was further evidenced in 2000 when it was selected to host the Higher Education Subject Centre for Geography, Earth and Environmental Sciences (GEES), which works closely with the university and has been active nationally and internationally in the ESD field.

The CETL is also enhanced by the university's ongoing partnership with the nearby Schumacher College, located in Dartington. Schumacher has an unrivalled global reputation for its courses on sustainability themes. Academics at the core of this CETL have benefited from working alongside world leaders in the field such as Fritjof Capra, James Lovelock and Vandana Shiva. A significant outcome of the existing Schumacher partnership is the interdisciplinary MSc in Holistic Science, jointly taught with university staff.

Another CETL partner of real significance is Forum for the Future, based in London. The Forum is the United Kingdom's leading sustainable development charity, with a remit to promote a positive solutions-oriented approach to building a sustainable way of life. It was centrally involved in the 2000–2003 initiative entitled the Higher Education Partnership for Sustainability (HEPS). It is a national leader in the elaboration of the concept of sustainability literacy and in its advocacy within higher education.

The CETL's principal aim will be to encourage students to engage critically with key sustainability agendas and their social, ethical, professional and personal implications. It will promote ESD across the University of Plymouth and its partner colleges and on the national and international stage. It will encourage curriculum innovation, support relevant staff development, identify and collate ESD-related resources and capitalize on the student learning opportunities created by 'greening' the university and its campus and by working with local communities.

The whole-university approach to education for sustainability envisaged by the CETL and supported by partners of both national and international reputation will enable the university to play an influential and formative role in the implementation nationally of HEFCE's new ESD strategy. The intention is that Plymouth should become a model from which other higher education institutions can learn. In practice, of course, Plymouth would be the first to recognize that it has no monopoly of good practice and therefore is keen to learn from leading exemplars elsewhere both nationally and internationally. We shall, for example, work closely with a CETL at Kingston University in London, where there is particular expertise in sustainability within surveying and related built environment disciplines.

Certainly, the Plymouth University buildings and campus are still a long way from being a model of sustainability—indeed, how many university campuses in the world can claim to be models in this respect? Such accolades as being one of the top UK universities for energy management systems are not obvious to the casual visitor to Plymouth. However, if we are to live up to being a 'Centre for Excellence' then we must ensure we work towards an exemplary model. If Prime Minister Blair's vision of "a living learning place in which to explore what a sustainable lifestyle means" (Brown, 2004) is to be achieved, it will require more than a 'green-wash makeover' and a few solar panels. As a result, a significant part of the CETL's £2 million capital allocation will be used for initiatives designed to improve the institution's overall environmental performance.

Students entering higher education probably studied recycling, waste management and energy saving at primary school; they considered sustainability in citizenship lessons at secondary school and debated issues of social justice during 'A' levels. When they come to university most do not need to be told how to recycle their beer cans and wine bottles (sadly, some still do!): instead they should be challenged with issues of sustainability commensurate with the rigour of their courses and a curriculum that both enhances their career prospects and enables them to become well informed and responsible members of society. The CETL will, of course, be keen to promote opportunities for students to participate both in its day-to-day work and in debates about its priorities and future directions.

We believe that far from being a poisoned chalice, the label of 'Centre for Excellence' is a great opportunity to influence both the institution and local, regional and national policies. We may even in a small way help wider efforts to convince world leaders that sustainability is a long-term issue that needs far more than their short-term commitment.

At the time of writing this article the Plymouth ESD CETL has just appointed its staff and is beginning to work on its key agendas. If any readers of *JGHE* would like to know more about its activities and its plans for the future, please do not hesitate to contact us at the University of Plymouth. Although the CETL's prime focus is on its home institution, it will also be operating on a broader policy stage and seeking to enhance ESD across UK higher education and more widely. Through conferences, meetings, workshops, books, journal articles and in many other ways we will be seeking to identify, develop and share good practice and to foment innovation and debate. Although important parts of our work will focus on disciplines such as geography and environmental science, which are in many ways natural allies, the CETL will also be seeking to engage with many other higher education disciplines. Indeed, part of the adventure will be working with colleagues in disciplines such as history, sociology, English and business studies in order to identify and help develop approaches to ESD that are sensitive to distinctive disciplinary cultures. We are, therefore, very much looking forward to working with a wide range of colleagues and developing links and partnerships that will enrich our contribution to the cause of education for sustainable development and justify the use of the term 'Centre for Excellence.'

References

Appel, G., Dankleman, I. & Kupers, K. (2004) Disciplinary explorations of sustainable development in higher education, in: P. B. Corcoran & A. E. J. Wals (Eds) *Higher Education and the Challenge of Sustainability*, pp. 213–222 (Dordecht: Kluwer).

Bowden, R. D. & Pallant, E. (2004) Maintaining a college–community ecotourism project: faculty initiative, institutional vision, student participation, and community partnerships, in: P. F. Bartlett & G. W. Chase (Eds) *Sustainability on Campus: Stories and Strategies for Change*, pp. 197–213 (Cambridge, MA: MIT Press).

Brown, P. (2004) Blair calls for UK to lead on climate change, *Guardian*, 15 September, p. 9.

Edelstein, M. R. (2004) Sustaining sustainability: lessons from Ramapo College, in: P. F. Bartlett & G. W. Chase (Eds) *Sustainability on Campus: Stories and Strategies for Change*, pp. 271–292 (Cambridge, MA: MIT Press).

Faulstich, P. (2004) Teaching for change: the leadership on environmental education partnership, in: P. F. Bartlett & G. W. Chase (Eds) *Sustainability on Campus: Stories and Strategies for Change*, pp. 215–227 (Cambridge, MA: MIT Press).

Gibbs, G. (1992) *Improving the Quality of Student Learning* (Bristol: Technical and Educational Services).

Goldstein, T. & Selby, D. (2000) *Weaving Connections: Educating for Peace, Social and Environmental Justice* (Toronto: Sumach).

Jenks-Jay, N. (2004a) Cultivating a shared environment vision at Middlebury, in: P. F. Bartlett & G. W. Chase (Eds) *Sustainability on Campus: Stories and Strategies for Change*, pp. 293–310 (Cambridge, MA: MIT Press).

Jenks-Jay, N. (2004b) Integrating education for the environment and sustainability into higher education at Middlesbury College, in: P. B. Corcoran & A. E. J. Wals (Eds) *Higher Education and the Challenge of Sustainability*, pp. 263–276 (Dordecht: Kluwer).

Jerman, P. L., Coull, B. C., Elzerman, A. W. & Schmidt, M. G. (2004) South Carolina Sustainable Universities Initiative, in: P. F. Bartlett & G. W. Chase (Eds) *Sustainability on Campus. Stories and Strategies for Change*, pp. 243–270 (Cambridge, MA: MIT Press).

Parkin, S., Johnston, A., Buckland, H., Brookes, F. & White, E. (2004) *Learning & Skills for Sustainable Development: Developing a Sustainability Literate Society* (London: Higher Education Partnership for Sustainability).

Rohwedder, R. (2004) A pedagogy of place: the environment technology center at Sonoma State University, in: P. B. Corcoran & A. E. J. Wals (Eds) *Higher Education and the Challenge of Sustainability*, pp. 293–304 (Dordecht: Kluwer).

Sterling, S. (2004a) An analysis of the development of sustainability education internationally: evolution, interpretation and transformative potential, in: J. Blewitt & C. Cullingford (Eds) *The Sustainability Curriculum: The Challenge for Higher Education*, pp. 43–62 (London: Earthscan).

Sterling, S. (2004b) Higher education, sustainability, and the role of systemic learning, in: P. B. Corcoran & A. E. J. Wals (Eds) *Higher Education and the Challenge of Sustainability*, pp. 47–70 (Dordecht: Kluwer).

UNESCO (2003), United Nations Decade of Education for Sustainable Development (January 2005–December 2014): Framework for a Draft International Implementation Scheme. Available at http://www.jeef.or.jp/esdj/JF%20DESD%20Framework3.doc (accessed July 2005).

Van de Bor, W., Wals, A. E. J. & Filho, W. (2000) *Education for Sustainability—From Rio to Johannesburg: Lessons Learnt from a Decade of Commitment* (Paris: UNESCO).

Sustainability Education in Scotland: The Impact of National and International Initiatives on Teacher Education and Outdoor Education

PETER HIGGINS & GORDON KIRK

Introduction

The United Nations (UN) has declared 2005–2014 to be the Decade of Education for Sustainable Development. With senior political figures from many nations now openly describing global warming as a major—or even the greatest—threat, to humankind, such a UN declaration seems timely. The issue of 'sustainability' and the educational response to it have been features of academic life and discourse in aspects of higher education (HE) (e.g. geography, earth sciences, life sciences, education) for some years, as exemplified in the first instalment of this symposium (Higgitt *et al.*, 2005). Such interest has been institutionally idiosyncratic and the responses patchy, and it remains to be seen whether this new interest amongst policy-makers will precipitate a more focused and concerted approach to the issues.

The current situation in Scotland, and to a certain degree the rest of the UK, exemplifies the tension between national and international policy (in this case on environment and sustainability), national educational responses (in teacher education, local educational authorities and schools), existing subject domains and boundaries and the potential for traditional subjects (e.g. geography) and informal subjects (e.g. outdoor education) to respond. The structural and local issues associated with these circumstances warrant discussion, particularly in light of the perceived urgent need to encourage more sustainable living.

National Policy on Sustainable Development in Scotland

In July 1999 a Scottish Parliament convened in Edinburgh for the first time in almost 300 years. Whilst Scotland remains a part of the UK, a wide range of responsibilities and powers have been devolved to this parliament, which include a number of policy areas central to sustainability education (SE). These include environment, education, transport and health. However, some important policy areas such as energy and some fiscal measures are not devolved and this gives the parliament less room for manoeuvre.

As a signatory to Agenda 21, the UK government (and hence Scotland) is committed to its principles. These have been promoted in Scotland through publications such as *Down to Earth: A Scottish Perspective on Sustainable Development* (Scottish Office, 1999a), which endorses the social, economic and educational aspects of sustainable development; and also through the report of the Secretary of State for Scotland's Advisory Group on Education for Sustainable Development (Scottish Office, 1999b), which focuses specifically on education.

In February 2000 the Scottish Parliament passed a motion committing itself to placing sustainable development at the core of its work and in August 2000 the Scottish Minister for the Environment published a draft comprehensive environmental strategy. Although given credit by commentators for its attempt to open up discussion on sustainability issues, it was roundly criticized for a 'business as usual' approach and a lack of practical ideas. Since then the UK government stance and plans were presented in *Securing the Future – The UK Sustainable Development Strategy* (UK Government, 2005), and in Scotland the equivalent plans are outlined in *Choosing Our Future: Scotland's Sustainable Development Strategy* (Scottish Executive, 2005). These are broad ranging overviews of the national context and whilst education has been a feature it has been a minor element in policy and planning, at least as far as seems evident in these documents. This is not to suggest that until now there has been no policy on sustainable development, rather that it has been piecemeal rather than integrated. Consequently, the general public has remained largely unaware of public policy in this area.

Structure of the Education System at National Level

Although in Scotland's education system there is no national curriculum prescribed by statute, there is nevertheless a national framework that is published by the Scottish Executive Education Department (SEED), which is generally acknowledged to constitute an appropriate curriculum (5–14 Guidelines). This curricular framework in the primary school covers language studies, mathematics, expressive arts, environmental studies, and religious and moral education. In the secondary school the curriculum framework covers language, mathematics, social studies, science, technology, physical education, and religious and moral education. These areas of study are not legally binding on schools; nevertheless, there is a strong professional consensus that these represent the major domains of human enquiry and reflection, into which all pupils, as a matter of right, are entitled to be initiated.

The true drivers of education policy in Scotland are *standards* and *inclusion*. There is concern that the educational achievements of school students in Scotland are not as high as they might be and consequently there is a publicly stated government commitment to raising standards of achievement. As a result, the first Act to be passed by Scotland's parliament was concerned with raising educational standards.

Uniform standards for the achievement of a given award are established by ensuring that there is a single examining body—the Scottish Qualifications Authority—which sets on an annual basis the examinations that are taken by all pupils at age 16 and at age 17/18. Performance in these end-of-school examinations (Standard, Intermediate, Higher and Advanced Higher Grades) provides the basis for entrance to higher education.

Education, Sustainability and National Sustainable Development Policy

There is no explicit linkage between the education system and the national sustainable development policy, and although in general terms the importance of education for the success of the policy is recognized, there is no mention of its role in the priorities for sustainable development in Scotland (Scottish Executive, 2002). Similarly, teacher education has no explicit recognition in the national sustainable development policy. This is somewhat paradoxical as in numerous policy statements the importance of education is fully acknowledged in enabling government policies to be realized. Nonetheless, whilst stopping short of imposition, the Scottish Government has recommended (Scottish Office, 1995) that, for example, schools should formulate their own environmental education policy and address these principles. Local Authorities are also encouraged to consider appointing environmental education officers. As might be expected these recommendations have not been implemented consistently.

Although aspects of education for sustainable development are to be found in a number of places in curricular guidance in Scotland, these neither permeate the curriculum nor are they gathered together into a single integrated sustainability education (SE) theme. Although not included in the primary aims of education in Scotland as defined by the 'national priorities' for schools (Scottish Executive Education Department, 2000), sustainable development education is a second level aim within 'citizenship and values'. In the case of the 5–14 Guidelines (Scottish Office Education and Industry Department, 1992, 1993; Scottish Executive, 2000a, 2000b), there are numerous opportunities outlined briefly in Table 1. These components clearly provide opportunities to deal with sustainability but the lack of explicit guidance on SE leaves the examples taught and emphasis adopted to individual choice. All the issues in the table could be taught well and perfectly responsibly without any emphasis on sustainability.

Whilst there are opportunities for sustainability education in a range of curricular areas (for ages 15 to 18) these are perhaps most evident in geography. At Standard Grade components such as the physical environment/human activities, competing demands/land use, trade and environmental protection lend themselves to discussions of sustainability.

Table 1. Opportunities for sustainability education in the Scottish 5–14 guidelines

5–14 curriculum area	Associated knowledge/attainment targets
Environmental Studies	
Social subjects component:	
• People in society	• People and needs in society
• People and place	• Human–physical interactions
• People in the past	• Change and continuity, cause and effect
Science component:	
• Earth and space	• Earth in space, materials from Earth
• Energy and forces	• Uses, conversion and transfer of energy
• Living things	• Interaction with environment
Technology component:	
• Technological capability	• Meeting needs/managing resources
Personal and Social Development	
	• Personal relationships and conflict resolution
	• Inter-dependence
Health Education	• Environmental effects on health
Religious & Moral Education	• Personal search/the natural world
	• Discussion of moral values

Similarly in Higher Grade geography, opportunities exist in the study of atmosphere, hydrosphere, biosphere, rural land resources/degradation, river basin management etc.

As the modern notion of sustainability rests on the relationship between environment, economy and society, it is widely accepted that values and attitudes are central to any such educational agenda. Separately in Scotland and the rest of the UK, 'Citizenship' has been developed and promoted as a vehicle for dealing with a wide range of social, community and global issues relating to values, attitudes, rights and responsibilities. Whilst the debate in Scotland has not yet been concluded there seems to be an expectation that sustainability could feature in the guidelines. At present it is not envisaged that Citizenship will become a new curricular area, rather that it will be an aspect of both teaching and other facets of the school. To demonstrate how this might be done Meldrum (personal communication) has linked a range of the components of geography (for ages 15 to 18) to knowledge, skills and attitudes proposed for Citizenship, and has emphasized the areas offering particular opportunities for sustainability education. For example, 'rural land resources and degradation' in geography Higher Grade are associated with 'economic, environmental and cultural and social aspects of needs and wants' in the Citizenship documentation. Whilst this is to be applauded as a positive interdisciplinary and holistic approach, it should be noted that such a tactic is necessary because of the absence of space in a crowded curriculum for any 'new' topic, no matter how worthy of inclusion.

Evidently the flexibility in the school curriculum noted earlier at least allows the inclusion of SE. However, despite the fact that many individuals in schools and higher education institutions are committed to SE, the lack of policy direction leaves the area vulnerable. Research on Scottish schools shows that in practice subject boundaries are often tightly maintained, making any cross-curricular or permeation approaches likely to lead to only modest change (Nixon *et al.*, 1999). The lack of a coherent curricular basis often leaves the impetus for environmental and sustainability education to voluntary or charitable organizations (e.g. RSPB, Grounds for Learning) that seek partnerships with schools (Kandemiri, 2004). Whilst on the face of it such an arrangement may seem to benefit all parties it raises questions concerning the motivations of such organizations and the consistency and quality of the educational experience for school pupils. Further, Shallcross *et al.* (2000) emphasize the need for 'whole school approaches' to sustainability, concluding from their study that schools which adopt such a strategy are more likely to deliver these educational messages.

However there are signs of change and the Scottish Executive has appointed of a Sustainability Education Development Officer at Learning and Teaching Scotland (for the Primary and Secondary sectors). This and associated appointments in citizenship education and outdoor education are oriented towards a new approach to the school curriculum. It seems likely that 'A Curriculum for Excellence' (http://www.acurriculumforexcellencescotland.gov.uk/) will become the core of work in schools, particularly up to the age of 13 or 14 years of age. Its focus on personal decision-making within a community and societal context has already been signalled as the most promising way to encourage thoughtful decision-making about sustainability issues.

The situation in England and Wales is in marked contrast, with 'environmental change and sustainable development' being specified in the new curriculum as a requirement for geography at Key Stage 3 for pupils aged 11–14 (DfEE/QCA, 1999). Implicit in the specifications is the notion that this issue is closely linked with attitudes and values (Reid, 2000) and here too a link with Citizenship has been made with geography teachers taking a significant role (Meldrum, personal communication).

Teacher Education in Scotland

In Scotland teacher education is based in six centres, all of them with a considerable tradition of specialist work and all now formally part of universities as departments or schools. Each centre offers a full range of training opportunities for work in both primary and secondary schools, although there are some areas of specialist provision (e.g. physical education) at just one or two centres.

All programmes of teacher education in Scotland have to comply with national guidelines issued from time to time by the First Minister, who is responsible to Scotland's Parliament for the quality of education in Scotland. Also, they are all required to be accredited by the General Teaching Council for Scotland. That body, which has as members the majority of practising teachers, has been the voice of the teaching profession in Scotland since 1965. It, in effect, controls entry to the teaching profession in Scotland. While teacher training programmes must show compatibility with the national guidelines before they can be delivered, there is scope for some variation between institutions in the nature of the curriculum they provide.

Structure of Teacher Certification

Teaching qualifications in Scotland are of three types: primary, secondary and further education. The national guidelines stipulate programme length and general content. There are two routes into primary or secondary education:

- a student may take a four-year degree leading to a Bachelor of Education (BEd) resulting in a qualification to teach in a primary or a secondary school (the *concurrent* route); or

- a student can first complete a degree programme and subsequently take a one-year programme of professional education called a Postgraduate Certificate of Education—PGCE (the *consecutive* route).

Whilst the former route has the advantage of a specialist training in education, the structure severely limits the extent to which students can take subjects from other parts of their university. Those who take the consecutive route will have had the opportunity to sample a number of university subjects prior to their professional training, but their studies will not have been focused on preparing for the teaching profession.

Teacher Education Programmes and Sustainability Education

Whilst the structure of teacher training programmes is determined by the regulatory bodies, teacher education institutions can be as innovative and flexible as they wish, so long as their programmes are fully compatible with the national guidelines. Nonetheless, education for sustainable development does form part of the *guidelines* for teachers published by the Scottish Office Education and Industry Department (SOEID, 1998). These include two specific references to teachers being knowledgeable about sustainable development and competent to contribute to education for sustainable development (ESD).[1] Although environmental studies is one of the areas listed for study, this is, as will be apparent from the preceding discussion, an umbrella term for a range of subjects which are taught between the ages of five and 14 and which deal, in very broad terms, with knowledge *about* the environment rather than with ESD per se. 'Education for sustainable development' is, however, listed as an *option* module that teacher education institutions may make available. Therefore, it is left to individual teacher education institutions to determine how much emphasis is to be given to ESD, either as a separate element or as part of 'environmental studies'. As a result, ESD components take different forms in different teacher education institutes. In some, there is a full programme relating to sustainability education; in others it forms part of a wider programme of, for example, environmental studies or geography. As will be obvious from the flexibility within the National Guidelines for ages 5–18, the degree to which emphasis is placed on sustainability in teacher education is to a large extent a matter for the individual institutes. Whilst there appears to be no empirical study of the merits or otherwise of 'whole institute' approaches to sustainability in teacher education institutes, it seems likely that, as Shallcross *et al.* (2000) have shown for schools, such a tactic may be an important precursor to re-orientate teacher training towards sustainability.

National Developments in Sustainability Education

As a result of a national conference on the environment in teacher education in 1995, all teacher education institutions in Scotland committed themselves to the development of the BEd (Primary Education) module in ESD noted above. In practice, the application of the module and its key elements has been variable and whilst only one university (Strathclyde) has adopted the full module others have included relevant sections in their programmes or chosen a permeation approach.

For some time attempts have been made in Scotland to mobilize professional support for SE. Following the Earth Summit in Rio, the publication of Agenda 21 and specifically the 'education' focus in Chapter 36 (UN, 1992), these efforts accelerated in the 1990s (for a major review see Lavery & Smyth, 2003) and led to the highly significant publication of the *Learning for Life* report (Smyth, 1993), in which the major theme was sustainable development education. Following this publication a 'Learning for Life Group' was convened. This continues to meet periodically and consists of representatives from all of Scotland's teacher education institutions, together with individuals from a wide range of environmental agencies. The group recently prepared a document explaining the place of SE in Scottish teacher education institutions (available from the authors).

This group has developed resource materials for use in initial teacher education programmes, and also compiled other significant resources for serving teachers. The Learning for Life Group was a key member of a group of institutions and individuals that the European Union funded to develop an in-service programme and materials for Sustainability Education in European Primary Schools (SEEPS, 1997, 2004). This significant project and other resources produced are not binding on institutions. They were prepared as ways of fostering collaboration, of minimizing the duplication of work at a time when resources are scarce, and as a way of stimulating teacher education centres to devote more time to SE.

In recent years, and partially in response to the UN Decade of Education for Sustainable Development, political momentum has increased and a Sustainable Development Education Liaison Group was established by the Scottish Executive in 2004. Its role is to take a view across all education sectors in Scotland and has recently presented its initial review of the UK situation (Learning and Teaching Scotland, 2004), though it remains to be seen how its work will impact on educational policy.

Teacher Education and Sustainability Education at the University of Edinburgh

At the University of Edinburgh aspects of SE noted above are included in the general training of teachers. However, there are several courses that have a particular emphasis. The BEd (Primary Education) includes a first-year residential fieldwork week with an SE element and a further module in SE at the end of the fourth year. Postgraduate (PGCE) students of geography have two fieldwork weekends with the emphasis as above, and an assessed part of their course that specifically addresses the role of geography in teaching for a sustainable future.

It is clear from the outline of teacher education in Scotland that room for manoeuvre is somewhat limited. However, within these constraints, the School of Education of the University of Edinburgh has committed to a number of projects. For example:

- In the BEd (Primary Education) programme the School has undertaken an audit of the 'Environmental Studies' course to see if and how the SE element can be enhanced. One current development is the inclusion of a course on 'Technology and Sustainability' within the Year 4 Option on Science.
- The School website 'Educating for a Sustainable Future' has been updated and further developed in a collaborative project with Manchester Metropolitan University.[2]

Outdoor Education

Outdoor education has often been considered to be an approach that can permeate many curricular subject areas. It can be also seen within the teaching profession as a subject in its own right, drawing on three integrated areas, namely outdoor activities, environmental education and personal and social development (Figure 1). The general focus on 'learning outdoors' is manifest in the specific intention to provide learning experiences that develop the learner in the individual domains of the 'three circles' or to emphasize and capitalize on the integrated learning potential of guided direct outdoor experiences. Hence an outdoor educator taking a group of students on a canoe journey on a river will first ensure that the students will learn appropriate skills to descend the river competently and safely and take responsibility for their own actions (outdoor activities). Throughout this process the outdoor educator will be sensitive to individual anxieties and relationships between individuals (personal and social education). However, at appropriate times attention will shift to the environment, generating explorations and discussions of topics such as the evolution and geomorphology of the river, its ecology, and its relationship with local social history (e.g. development of associated industries and commerce, ownership patterns, recreational access issues), outdoor recreation (e.g. bird watching, angling), economy (e.g. in the UK this may include water abstraction, distilleries and outdoor recreation) and indeed modification of the river channel and pollution (environmental education). The degree of emphasis on any particular aspect of such a list will depend on the stated purpose of the journey, the interests of the outdoor educator and students, and the nature of the river and local environment. 'Serendipity' also plays a part, and the outdoor educator needs to be able to capitalize on the learning potential of, for example, an unexpected capsize or a sighting of an osprey. Perhaps for this reason an experiential approach to learning is a central tenet of

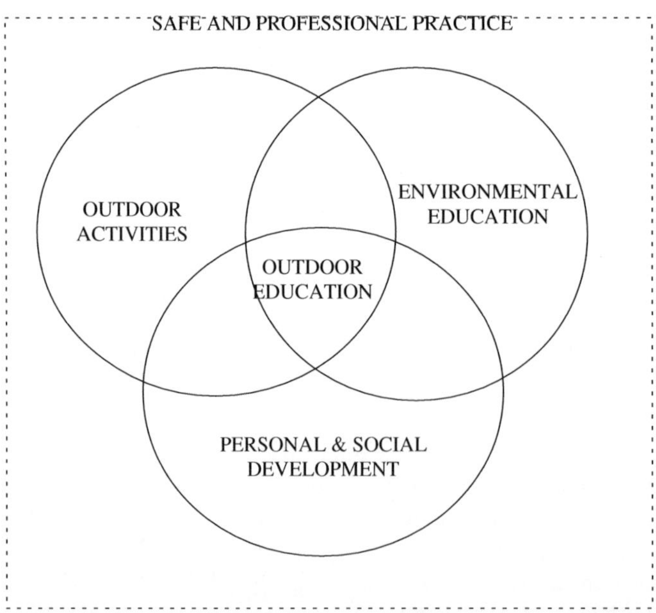

Figure 1. The range and scope of outdoor education. *Source*: Higgins (1995).

outdoor education and an element of 'adventure' is often seen as a way to maximize the learning effect of the experience (Higgins & Loynes, 1997). More detailed examples of 'integrated', 'complex' and 'interdisciplinary' outdoor experiences and their educational potential can be found elsewhere (e.g. Higgins, 2003).

Scotland was one of the first places in the world where outdoor education became formalized and as early the 1960s and 1970s there was a significant focus on the environment (Higgins, 2002). Whilst schools are traditionally the main providers of outdoor education in the UK, changes in the structure of local government and in funding have led to a decrease in the number of specifically trained and qualified staff. However, many specialist outdoor and environmental education centres continue to thrive, though many public-sector providers have lost central funding and have turned to a more commercial approach to their work. There are also a number of commercial and charitable trust centres. The majority of provision operates on a residential basis.

Outdoor Education and Sustainability Education

The natural environment is often considered in a utilitarian way as 'the workplace' for outdoor education. However, this perspective denies both the roots of outdoor education and a number of contemporary initiatives that emphasize the value of direct experiences of the natural environment in fostering a 'sense of place' and in education for sustainable development (Cooper, 1991; Higgins, 1996; Nicol & Higgins, 1998). Central to this approach is the view that developing a relationship with the environment is an important precursor to understanding sustainability (e.g. Palmer & Suggate, 1996).

For many outdoor educators understanding the environment through direct experience of it remains the focus of their efforts. For some, feeling water fall from the sky as rain, and sitting on a river in a canoe are opportunities to discuss the water cycle and perhaps develop themes to link to global climate change. Similarly, boiling water for a hot drink (using a fire or camp stove) can stimulate discussions on the storage and release of carbon from wood or oil and hence global carbon balance, embracing environmental, social and economic dimensions. As outdoor education is not a designated curricular area, there is no explicit or agreed curriculum; this can be seen as both a weakness and an opportunity (see Loynes *et al.*, 1997; Cooper, 1998; and Lemmey, 1999 for analyses of the school curriculum in the UK and the potential for outdoor education to deliver its learning outcomes). In the context of SE, there is ample opportunity to make this a key focus of outdoor programmes, and this has been advocated by a number of authors (e.g. Cooper, 1991; Higgins 1996).

Clearly there are considerable opportunities for integrated environmental and sustainability education outdoors and such experiences can meet many curricular needs. However, it is obvious that such provision is costly in terms of staff and resources and, in Scotland at least, funding difficulties have led to a reduction in provision, particularly in schools, and consequently most young people experience only a few days of outdoor education in their school career (Higgins, 2002). Nonetheless, such experiences are often claimed to be memorable and disproportionately significant (in light of their duration) by the participants. The value that schools which remain committed to such experiences place on them is evident in the overall scale of provision, and in Scotland alone 200–300 000 student days per year are spent in some form or other of outdoor education (Higgins, 2002). On such excursions the lack of a curricular 'home' provides both considerable opportunities for outdoor educators to address sustainability (or indeed other aspects of knowledge and development noted in Figure 1) or ignore it altogether.

Outdoor Education at the University of Edinburgh

The School of Education of the University of Edinburgh and its predecessor, the Moray House Institute of Education, has a long tradition of involvement in outdoor education. For many years it has provided formal courses, both pre-service and for practising teachers. The original purpose was largely to ensure the safe conduct of parties on school excursions. However, the broader responsibilities of outdoor education teachers soon became recognized and the emphasis in training has settled on the structure represented by Figure 1 and hence on the academic learning and personal development that can be achieved.

Whilst there are a number of colleges and universities offering outdoor education programmes in the UK, the 35-year tradition and wide range of courses available at the University of Edinburgh place it in a unique position in the field. Current courses all have a strong emphasis on the environment and SE. These include postgraduate (Certificate, Diploma, MSc) pathways in Outdoor Education (with substantial environmental and SE components), and in Environmental Education (see Higgins & Lugg, 2006). Recent developments to these programmes and an increasing number of Doctoral (PhD) students in these fields reflect a commitment to extend provision.[3]

International Developments: University of Edinburgh and UNESCO

Many of the above activities must be seen in the context of international environmental policy initiatives. A number of conferences in Europe led to exhortations to national governments to adopt environmental policies (e.g. Stockholm, 1972; Belgrade, 1975; Tbilisi, 1997; Moscow, 1987) and were precursors to the first 'World Summit' in 1992. This United Nations Conference on Environment and Development (UNCED) held in Rio de Janeiro resulted in the agreement of participating nations (including the UK) on a number of environmental issues that all would address. A central commitment was the adoption of Agenda 21 (UN, 1992), an action plan for progress. The importance of education to this plan is indicated in its presence as a theme in all chapters of the document, as well as in a particular chapter devoted to it (Chapter 36). In the document as a whole, 'education' appeared only second in frequency to the word 'government' (Smyth *et al.*, 1997, p. 173).

Under Agenda 21 one of the four priorities identified was 'Education, Public Awareness and Training for Sustainability'. As a result, UNESCO was asked to address teacher education, which it sees as one of the most significant areas for action (UNESCO, 1999). Hence, the task of 'reorienting teacher education to address sustainability' is a direct result of decisions taken by governments at Rio. Ten years on from Rio in 2002, commitments to place emphasis on 'Education for Sustainable Development' in primary, secondary and higher education were re-affirmed at the second 'World Summit' in Johannesburg.

However, somewhat frustrated by the lack of substantive action on sustainability education following the two 'World Summits', the Swedish Prime Minister, Goran Perssons, stated his government's belief that this was of pressing importance and offered to host an international consultation on the issue in Göteborg in Sweden in May 2004. Almost 300 delegates from 78 countries were invited because of their experience in education or responsibilities in policy-making, and these included ministers of national governments, senior representatives of the EU, UNESCO and the UN.[4]

Since the UK became a member of the European Community there has been a growing trend to harmonize European legislation relating to environmental protection, biodiversity etc. It is not the purpose of this paper to review such agreements but rather to note that such legislation has not had a consistent Europe-wide impact on environmental or sustainability education, arrangements for this being seen as a national rather than European prerogative. However, there seems little doubt that raising the profile of environmental and sustainability issues has had some impact on educational provision in many European countries. The European Union has consistently funded environmentally focused European educational projects such as the SEEPS Programmes noted earlier and a substantial project on environmental learning through landscapes (Higgins & Nicol, 2002). In 2002 the European Union held its first 'Green Week' in Brussels. This annual event invites delegates from all over Europe to meet and discuss environment and associated educational issues.

Perhaps as a result of Scotland's reputation for commitment to SE, (see Lavery & Smyth, 2003 for a major review) a representative of Moray House Institute (now the School of Education of Edinburgh University) was invited to a UNESCO meeting in Thessaloniki in Greece in 1997 (UNESCO, 1997). There were 10 universities/teacher education institutes from around the world present at that preliminary meeting, and around 30 at the subsequent meeting in Toronto in 2000.

All participating institutions attending the Toronto conference agreed subsequent actions, the principles of which are described by Hopkins & McKeown (2001). Although each institution is free to decide on its own actions, there is a shared commitment to the short- and long-term objectives of the UNESCO project. The short-term objective is 'to undertake research and experimentation on different approaches to reorienting teacher education towards sustainability, using a common research framework to allow comparison of results'. The long-term objective is 'to develop suggestions and guidelines for reorienting teacher education and associated realms of pedagogy, curriculum and evaluation'. To this end the group met again in South Africa in 2002 (to coincide with the Johannesburg Summit) and in Sweden in 2004 (to attend and coincide with the Göteborg Consultation). Each participating university has conducted its own investigation (within a commonly agreed structure) into its efforts to incorporate sustainability into education. The resulting report is wide ranging but demonstrates a remarkable consistency in the findings from various nations. It seems that other than in a few particular cases the main difficulties experienced are constraints due to competing national priorities in education, institutional change, dominance of a research agenda, administrative load and financial limitations (Hopkins & McKeown, 2004). The report addresses ways in which institutions have nonetheless managed to develop SE/ESD, and these range from successful lobbying to change national educational priorities, to devising modest changes to a curriculum that are effected solely through personal commitment. This report should prove valuable in sharing international practice. However, its main function is to report to UNESCO on progress made in this programme, and should form the basis for any efforts UNESCO might make to encourage national governments to develop policies that stimulate and integrate sustainability within the education system in the forthcoming UN decade on Education for Sustainable Development (2005–2014).

Broadly speaking, the University of Edinburgh's commitment is to review the status of SE in its provision for teacher education and outdoor education. A brief outline of the actions taken has been provided earlier in this paper, but this process is ongoing with, for example, the recent Göteborg consultation currently acting as an additional stimulus for further sustainability education developments. Notwithstanding such progress, attempts continue to raise the profile of SE at university and at national level. For further details see Higgins *et al.* (2001).

Concluding Comments

The inter-institutional collaboration between teacher education institutes and the environmental agencies noted earlier, which led to the establishment of the 'Learning for Life Group', has underpinned a number of national and international initiatives at both pre-service and in-service levels. Successful bids have been made to Scottish and European funding agencies to develop SE resources to support initial teacher education and continuing professional development programmes for teachers. In this context Shallcross *et al.* (2000), presenting the results of the SEEPS study, warn that both a whole-school approach to SE and commitment to continuing professional development of teachers are necessary to effect this change.

However, a teacher education curriculum that is 'full' already and weak political commitment at a national level militate against a decisive advance of SE in Scottish education. Although the fact that school education follows national guidelines rather than a definitive syllabus allows some room for manoeuvre, many requirements are stipulated and this makes extended provision in SE difficult to achieve. Outdoor education, free from many of these curricular constraints, provides one avenue for development, but it too lacks enthusiastic political (and hence structural and financial) support.

There can be little doubt that SE is finally moving up the political agenda in Scotland and must eventually become an imperative for the work of teacher education institutes. Some advances have been made though progress to date has depended primarily on individual and institutional commitment and, in the case of the University of Edinburgh, participation in the UNESCO project.

Notes

[1] The term 'Education for Sustainable Development' (ESD) is used in the Scottish Office documentation and so it is retained here. However, the term has been the subject of much debate, and 'Sustainable Education' (SE) is used in preference elsewhere in this article.

[2] School of Education, University of Edinburgh and Institute of Education, Manchester Metropolitan University: *Educating for a Sustainable Future.* This site is dedicated to providing online supported self-study materials for courses in Education for Sustainability in teacher education. The URL is: http://www.education.ed.ac.uk/esf

[3] For further details see the University of Edinburgh Outdoor Education Website: http://www.education.ed.ac.uk/outdoored

[4] The outcomes of this consultation are intended to inform educational policy in countries throughout the world and are summarized in reports on the project website (http://www.learning2004.se).

References

Cooper, G. (1991) The role of outdoor and field study centres in educating for the environment, *Journal of Adventure Education and Outdoor Leadership*, 8(2), pp. 10–11.

Cooper, G. (1998) *Outdoors with Young People* (Lyme Regis: Russell House).

DfEE/QCA (1999) *Geography: The National Curriculum for England. Key Stages 163* (London: DfEE/QCA).

Higgins, P. (1995) Outdoor education provision at Moray House Institute of Education, *Scottish Journal of Physical Education*, 23(3), pp. 4–11.

Higgins, P. (1996) Outdoor re-creation: connection and consequence in outdoor education, *Journal of Adventure Education and Outdoor Leadership*, 13(2), pp. 34–39.

Higgins, P. (2002) Outdoor Education in Scotland, *Journal of Adventure Education and Outdoor Learning*, 2(2), pp. 149–168.

Higgins, P. (2003) Outdoor Education: keeping learning complex, in: H. Altenberger, P. Schettgen & M. Scholz (Eds), *Innovative Ansaze Konstructiven Lernens*, pp. 49–69 (Augsberg: Zeil).

Higgins, P., Kirk, G. & Perfect, H. (2001) Teacher education for sustainable development in Scotland, *Environmental Education*, 68, pp. 25–29.

Higgins, P. & Loynes, C. (1997) Towards consensus on the nature of outdoor education, *Journal of Adventure Education and Outdoor Leadership*, 13(4), pp. 2–3.

Higgins, P. & Lugg, A. (2006) The pedagogy of people, place and activity: outdoor education at Moray House School of Education, the University of Edinburgh, in: B. Humberstone & H. Brown (Eds) *Shaping the Outdoor Profession through Higher Education*, pp. 157–165 (Penrith: Institute for Outdoor Learning).

Higgins, P. & Nicol, R. (2002) Learning as Adventure: Theory for Practice. Unpublished report for Department for Education and Skills Connexion Service, London.

Higgitt, D. L., Haigh, M. J. & Chalkley, B. (2005) Towards the UN Decade of Education for Sustainable Development, *Journal of Geography in Higher Education*, 29(1), pp. 13–17.

Hopkins, C. & McKeown, R. (2001) Reorienting teacher education to address sustainability, *Environmental Education*, 66, pp. 8–9.

Hopkins, C. & McKeown, R. (2004) Draft recommendations for reorienting teacher education to address sustainability. Unpublished report for UNESCO. Presented to the working group on reorienting teacher education to address sustainability. Göteborg, Sweden, April 2004.

http://www.acurriculumforexcellencescotland.gov.uk/ (accessed 2 May 2006)

Kandemiri, M. (2004) Environmental education in Scotland: partnerships in practice. Paper presented at the Scottish Educational Research Association Annual Conference, Perth, November 2003. Education-line, University of Leeds Available at: http://www.leeds.ac.uk/educol/documents/00003458.htm (accessed April 2004).

Lavery, A. & Smyth, J. (2003) Developing environmental education, a review of a Scottish project: international and political influences, *Environmental Education Research*, 9(3), pp. 359–383.

Learning & Teaching Scotland (2004) *Sustainable development education in England Wales, Northern Ireland and Scotland* (Dundee: Learning & Teaching Scotland).

Lemmey, R. (1999) The scope for provision of outdoor education in Primary Schools – an English case study, in: P. Higgins & B. Humberstone (Eds) *Outdoor Education and Experiential Learning in the UK*, pp. 36–42 (Luneberg: University of Luneberg Press).

Loynes, C., Michie, D. & Smith, C. (1997) Justifying outdoor education in the formal and informal curriculum, in: P. Higgins, C. Loynes & N. Crowther (Eds) *A Guide for Outdoor Educators in Scotland*, pp. 15–22 (Penrith: Adventure Education/Perth: Scottish Natural Heritage).

Nicol, R. & Higgins, P. (1998) A sense of place: a context for environmental outdoor education, in: P. Higgins & B. Humberstone (Eds) *Celebrating Diversity: Learning by Sharing Cultural Differences*, pp. 50–55 (Buckinghamshire: European Institute for Outdoor Adventure Education and Experiential Learning).

Nixon, J., Sankey, K., Furay, V. & Simmons, M. (1999) Education for sustainability in Scottish secondary schools: boundary maintenance or professional reorientation?, *Environmental Education Research*, 5(3), pp. 305–318.

Palmer, J. & Suggate, J. (1996) Influences and experiences affecting pro-environmental behaviour of educators, *Environmental Education Research*, 2(1), pp. 109–121.

Reid, A. (2000) Environmental change and sustainable development, in: K. Grimwode (Ed.) *Geography and the New Agenda*, pp. 45–60 (Sheffield: Geographical Association).

SEEPS (1997) *Sustainability Education in European Primary Schools: Creating a Better Environment in Our School* (Edinburgh: Moray House Institute of Education).

SEEPS (2004) *Sustainability Education in European Primary Schools: Creating a Better Environment in Our School* (Edinburgh: Moray House Institute of Education).

Scottish Executive (2000a) *Environmental Studies – Society, Science and Technology 5–14: National Guidelines* (Dundee: Learning and Teaching Scotland).

Scottish Executive (2000) *Health Education 5–14: National Guidelines* (Dundee: Learning and Teaching Scotland).

Scottish Executive (2002) *Meeting the needs ... Priorities, Actions and Targets for Sustainable Development in Scotland* (Edinburgh: Scottish Executive Environment Group).

Scottish Executive (2005) *Choosing Our Future: Scotland's Sustainable Development Strategy*. Available at: http://www.scotland.gov.uk/Publications/2005/12/1493902/39032 (accessed 2 May 2006).

Scottish Executive Education Department (2000) *Education (National Priorities) (Scotland) Order 2000* (London: HMSO).

Scottish Office (1995) *A Scottish Strategy for Environmental Education* (Edinburgh: Scottish Office).

Scottish Office (1999a) *Down to Earth: A Scottish Perspective on Sustainable Development* (Edinburgh: Scottish Office).

Scottish Office (1999b) *Scotland the Sustainable: The Learning Process*, Report of the Secretary of State for Scotland's Advisory Group on Education for Sustainable Development (Edinburgh: Scottish Office).

Scottish Office Education and Industry Department (1998) *Guidelines for Initial Teacher Education Courses in Scotland* (Edinburgh: SOEID).

Scottish Office Education and Industry Department (1992) *Expressive Arts 5–14: National Guidelines* (Edinburgh: SOEID).

Scottish Office Education and Industry Department (1993) *Personal and Social Development 5–14: National Guidelines* (Edinburgh: SOEID).

Shallcross, T., O'Loan, K. & Hui, D. (2000) Developing a school focused approach to continuing professional development in sustainability education, *Environmental Education Research*, 6(4), pp. 365–382.

Smyth, J. (Ed.) (1993) *Learning for Life: A National Strategy for Environmental Education in Scotland* (Edinburgh: Scottish Office).

Smyth, J., Blackmore, C. & Harvey, T. (1997) Education for sustainability at the United Nations: making progress?, *The Environmentalist*, 17, pp. 173–179.

UK Government (2005) *Securing the Future – The UK Sustainable Development Strategy*. Available at: http://www.sustainable-development.gov.uk/publications/uk-strategy/index.htm (accessed 2 May 2006).

UNESCO (1997) *Educating for a Sustainable Future: A Transdisciplinary Vision for Concerted Action.* International Conference, Thessaloniki, December 1997. (Paris: UNESCO).

UNESCO (1999) *UNESCO and Education* (Paris: UNESCO Documentation and Information Sector).

UN (1992) *Earth Summit 1992, the United Nations Conference on Environment and Development*, Rio de Janeiro 1992 (London: United Nations, Regency Press Corporation).

Promoting Environmental Education for Sustainable Development: The Value of Links between Higher Education and Non-Governmental Organizations (NGOs)

MARTIN J. HAIGH

Introduction

Environmental sustainability education is not just a classroom activity (Calder & Clugston, 2005). Certainly, it is possible to teach, in a formal classroom setting, about the environment, its problems and the techniques needed to study and sustain it. It is also possible to build upon this understanding through the direct involvement of students in field experiences in the outside world (Rickinson, 2001, pp. 265–274; Robson, 2002). However, in general, most formal environmental learning is constrained by the classroom and, in higher education, by the ethos of the academy (Margulis, 1997). This aspires to treat the environment from an objective and external viewpoint (Haigh, 2005). Inevitably, the environment becomes an object of study, something outside the student in the same way that it is outside the classroom (cf. Mitford, 2000, p7). Equally, it becomes something that can be forgotten when the class or course is over, something to be packed away with the second-hand textbooks and completed essays.

Environmental education can contribute effectively to sustainable development only if it is constructed as a process that remains with the learner beyond the classroom years; if it becomes a lifelong process rather than one restricted to the few years of formal education. This suggests that the processes of higher education needs to reach out from the academy and beyond the few years of traditional college education to engage with and support the later-life learning of former students (cf. Korze, 2005). This is especially the case for education for environmental sustainability, where the ideas are new and the need to suffuse discussion of their message throughout society is urgent (Martin & Jucker, 2005).

This paper reports on one attempt to 'think outside the university box' by linking traditional university-based applied geography research and environmental sustainability education through project work constructed within the programme of a major NGO (non-governmental organization) concerned with environmental conservation.

The Need for Education for Environmental Sustainability

The notion is not uncontested but, today, there is increasing agreement that human society cannot continue to treat the world as it does at present. UN Secretary General, Kofi Annan (2001, p. 2), notes that: "We need a break with the harmful practices of the past..." He points out that sustainable development will not happen of its own accord and adds the thought that: "Every individual ...has an obligation and an interest in changing outlooks, through education and by example, thereby helping to end thoughtless or deliberate waste and destruction" (Annan, 2004, p. 1).

Idealists argue that, to succeed, education for environmental sustainability must do more than simply build the learner's critical awareness and understanding of environmental sustainability issues. It should affect the learner such that he/she changes, or considers changing, the way he/she acts in the world (Davidson, 2003, p. 235). Protagonists hope that the results will be that, having weighed up the evidence and arguments, the learner will decide to make sustainable living a part of his/her way of life and an aspect of his/her own striving for self-improvement (cf. Naess, 1987). As Gandhi proposed, education should produce not merely educated people but people who understand their social responsibilities as integral elements of the world in which they live (Patil, 1983).

The challenge for environmental sustainability education, however, is to reach beyond the subject-bound confines of a formal academic education and influence the thinking of not just all students but, ultimately, all people. Barraza *et al.* (2003, p. 350) conceive the goal of ESD (education for sustainable development) to be "to move education itself towards more participatory practices" and, they think, political rather than practical or 'self' empowerment (cf. Haigh, 2002). In particular, environmental sustainability education needs to engage and reclaim the attention of those who, long ago, have graduated from formal education. It needs to reach those who have entered into the machineries of (what its critics style) 'the corporate extractive economy' (Berry, 1999; Jackson, 2003). This is vital because effective environmental sustainability education is integral to affecting the approach of those involved in environmental decision-making, both in the corporate business world and the wider community (Evans & Birchenough, 2001; Martin & Jucker, 2005).

From UNCED and beyond, the duty handed to environmental sustainability education has been to expand consciousness of the need to live, not just within the outer limits of natural tolerances, but more generally in non-destructive harmony with natural systems. Of course, to achieve this, those who would be educated need to understand what are 'the limits of Nature', what 'living within Nature' actually involves, and what action may be taken (cf. Volk, 1990). This is best achieved by direct experience—but such experience can be hard to come by in the technologically insulated life that most people lead—locked into city streets and office buildings (Margulis, 1997).

Unfortunately, at this point, a major problem afflicts formal environmental education. As Hudson (2001, p. 7) writes:

> Learning more about the environment generally means learning more about what we have done to the environment rather than what we have done to care for it. Although environmental education certainly requires learning about the resilience of nature, it is the catalog of harm that will seem most evident to educators and students over the next several decades. The danger is that this catalog of harm will contribute to a psychology of despair—a loss of hope for the future and a sense that we as individuals cannot make a difference.

NGOs in Environmental Education

NGOs are non-governmental organizations. They have been defined as "non-profit groups concerned with social justice and/or environmental protection" (McCoy & McCully, 1993, p. 66), but this description does little to encompass their great diversity (Pincen & Finger, 1994; Palmer & Birch, 2003). However, the NGO movement as a whole is devoted to the contradiction of Hudson's notion of hopelessness. If they stand for anything, NGOs stand for the belief that they can improve the world by 'thinking globally and acting locally' (cf. UNCED NGO Forum, 1993; Pincen & Finger, 1994; Holliday *et al.*, 2000, p. vi; Madgwick, 2000, p. 62; Mitford, 2000, p. 9). A decade or so ago, at UNCED (Rio), the NGO Forum produced a set of alternative treaties, which also set out a prospectus for this enormous and disparate group of organizations. The NGOs recognized "the central role of education in shaping values and social action" (UNCED NGO Forum, 1993, p. 5). They worried about the "erosion of basic values and the alienation and non-participation of almost all individuals in the building of their own future" (UNCED NGO Forum, 1993, p. 5.4). In respect of this, they committed themselves to a universal process "of educational transformation aimed at involving ourselves, our communities and nations in creating equitable and sustainable societies" (UNCED NGO Forum, 1993, p. 5.1). Environmental education was conceived as "a continuous learning process based on respect for all life" (UNCED NGO Forum, 1993, p. 5.2). Its purpose would include developing "an ethical awareness of all forms of life with which humans share this planet" (UNCED NGO Forum,

1993, p. 5.2). It should include “a respect for all life cycles and impose limits on humans’ exploitation of other forms of life” (UNCED NGO Forum, 1993, p. 5.21).

NGOs are self-created social groups that unite people in a shared mission (cf. Haigh, 1998). In general, NGOs are about direct action, which may be political, religious, social or environmental. Action is instructive. Experience can be a great tutor and perhaps the greatest. The process, termed ‘natural learning’ by Moore & Wong (1997), which addresses the learning of very young children, follows the path of experiential inquiry demonstrated, for the older learner, by Leopold among others (Leopold, 1949). Awareness of the power of the kinds of informal environmental understanding that involvement in NGO action may impart is now recognized by UNESCO as one of the two key sectors of environmental education. In UNESCO’s definition, non-formal environmental education includes any organized educational activity that occurs outside the established formal educational system and particularly that which is developed in groups that assemble themselves for reasons other than learning (Fortner, 2001).

Of course, NGOs are most famous for their work against destructive developments: international campaigns against pollution and environmental exploitation spearheaded by Greenpeace, Friends of the Earth, Sierra Club and their kin (Pincen & Finger, 1994). However, the work of these NGOs may be dwarfed by that of the NGOs that work in less media-headlining ways and on the harder, slower tasks of environmental conservation, education and reconstruction (cf. Holliday *et al.*, 2000). Many NGOs, like Belize’s Greenreef (Greenreef, 2002) and Uttaranchal’s Uttarakhand Seva Nidhi (Jackson, undated), try to weave action research and formal educational programmes into a consciousness-raising, ultimately policy-changing wholeness. Many NGOs seek to involve the community, and sometimes outsiders—often students, in programmes that try to empower communities to take control and management of their own habitats (such as World Neighbours in Central America (Bunch, 1982), the Association for Better Land Husbandry in Kenya (Shaxson *et al.*, 1997) and others (Cambray, 2000; Hellin & Higman, 2003). Some, like Coral Key and Earthwatch, try to involve the community and policy-makers in applied research, arguing that problem-solving research is the best way to awaken participants to a holistic appreciation of the characteristics and dimensions of an environmental and sustainability challenge.

Case Study: Earthwatch, Brookes University and the ‘Reclaiming the Land’ Project

This study focuses on one major NGO, Earthwatch, which is based near Boston, USA and has branches in England, Australia, Japan and, formerly, Russia. In June 2003, Oxford Brookes University, represented by its Chancellor Jon Snow, signed a memorandum of understanding with the European Branch of Earthwatch (Anon., 2003). The agreement vowed that the two organizations would try to work together to promote environmental education and the cause of sustainable development. This case study reviews some of the motivations for this unusual affiliation, screened through an analysis of the educational role for NGO volunteers on the community-based land reclamation research project that provided the original point of contact between the two organizations (Eisner, 1992; Haigh, 1998).

Oxford Brookes University, one of the leading members of Britain’s generation of new universities, constructed its reputation on innovations in teaching and learning, including the pioneering of modular course structures and the establishment of the *Journal of Geography in Higher Education*. Among recent claims to attention, Brookes became the first university in the world to be awarded Fairtrade status by the Fairtrade Foundation (Anon., 2004).

Earthwatch has claims to rank among the world's largest NGO provider of funds for field research, especially long-term conservation research. Currently, it supports more than 135 research projects in around 50 countries and it has sustained some of these projects for more than a decade. Earthwatch's most distinctive feature is the way that it provides support for research. It does not, for example, provide cash or equipment in any great measure, nor does it fund professional staff or laboratory-based work. It provides volunteers as field assistants, people who want to help with the 'leg-work' of data collection in the field, and it funds the costs involved in enabling these volunteers to function effectively and safely. Since its foundation in 1971, Earthwatch has recruited over 65 000 volunteers for 2800 field research projects around the world (Earthwatch Institute (Europe) 2001a, p. 2). In the process, Earthwatch has provided more than 5 million hours of field labour and £50 million in research funding (Earthwatch Institute (Europe), 2001b).

Earthwatch (Europe) emerged from the late 1980s. In its early days, the NGO emphasized field research and struggled to build a portfolio of research projects that was distinct from that of the main US organization. This had been criticized for being too populist—too oriented to the marketing of 'furry dolphins' in the succinct words of a local director. In the early 1990s, a key target was the development of a cadre of local supporters, a process inhibited by European tax rules that did not allow participants to claim allowances for project participation in the way that had been the life-blood of the US operation. In the later 1990s, the main development involved corporate programmes and sponsorship. The NGO attempted to market its products to large corporations for staff development, tax and corporate public relations purposes. During this third phase, the European branch grew large—becoming nearly 40 per cent of the whole organization—and it became increasingly corporate in its demeanour. The cost included some ethically challenged corporate partnerships and, during the new millennium, goal displacement, organizational dysfunction and increasing neglect of both its scientific mission and its ordinary members. In sum, during the course of this case study, Earthwatch (Europe) transformed from an enthusiastic shoestring NGO something more like into a mid-sized ecotourism business devoted to the provision of staff-development services to corporate customers.

Earthwatch's 'Reclaiming the Land' project ran from 1991 until 2005, mainly in Wales but, for two years, also in Bulgaria (Eisner, 1992). The project tackled an international problem, the degradation of environmental quality on lands that have been 'reclaimed' after surface coal-mining (Haigh, 2000a). It dealt with research towards the self-sustainable reconstruction of these lands and it strove to build upon the ancient technology of forest-fallowing for the reconstruction of soils (Flege, 2000; Haigh, 2000b). In 15 years, the project recruited more than 450 volunteers from 23 different nations along with sundry sponsored scientists, schoolchildren and delegates from commercial sponsors (Haigh, 1998). From the mid-1990s, the project was driven by a team of about 10 'regulars', many of whom had 'graduated' from the volunteer programme to management roles. In its later phases, the Earthwatch contribution declined from a two-week programme to one or two three- to five-day field camps each year. Traditionally, these were divided into a short camp devoted to the planting of trees for forestation trials and a second to the collection of data on the conditions of trees and soils (Haigh, 1998).

Methods

The present study attempts to focus on those things that the Earthwatch volunteers engaged in this project feel that they gain by way of environmental sustainability education. Information is being gathered at three points in the process:

- the application stage, when the volunteer signs in to a project;
- the operational phase, during which the volunteer is involved in project work;
- the project evaluation phase, when the volunteer reports back to sponsors, usually some weeks after the project experience.

Project application and registration forms from volunteers are received by Earthwatch and forwarded to the project team. These application forms include small spaces, enough for two or three handwritten sentences, for two relevant questions. One asks the volunteer to take 50 words to: "Please introduce yourself..." and thus to tell her/his own story (cf. Tilbury *et al.*, 2002, p. xii). Another asks them to "tell us why you chose this project? What are your expectations? What do you hope to contribute?" These responses have been analysed by classifying their content into general themes and epithets, then scoring the number of times each epithet or theme occurs. In practice, this has meant that each record has generated about 2.5 scores.

Earthwatch projects are usually the occasion for lively exchanges of views between volunteers and for reflections on their past experiences of similar events within Earthwatch and outside. In fact, until 2004, the project devoted one evening session to volunteers' reflections and descriptions of their other fieldwork and field project experiences, which they illustrated by photographs and anecdote.

Phase 2 of this study attempted to direct some of these discussions into a consideration of the role of the project in environmental sustainability education by the stratagem of an 'open-book' focus group. This involved gathering a group of 6–10 volunteers and asking them to consider what, exactly, they gain from this kind of work in the way of environmental sustainability education. During the discussion, speakers and non-speakers were encouraged to write their thoughts and insights in the 'open book'. This is an empty hard-bound notebook on the first page of which is written: "The Earthwatch Experience—What Value for Environmental Sustainability Education?"

The technique was piloted on a small field camp of 10 volunteers in April 2002. On this occasion, the 'open book' was introduced through a focus-group meeting near the start of the camp and kept 'open' for the duration. Subsequently, the 'open book' exercise was held back until the later stages of the camp, when the volunteers were more familiar with the character and purpose of the project and had more time to experience what was involved. On all occasions, the 'open book' remained open with unrestricted access for at least two days.

The 'open book' approach attempts to expand the benefits of formal focus-group discussion in two ways. First, the book remains open when the discussion has finished. This means that, in addition to the spoken comments, individuals are able to record their thoughts—possibly at a later time, hopefully after some further reflection. Second, if someone says something particularly interesting, controversial or insightful during the discussion session or later, they can be passed 'the book' to record their thoughts. Of course, this recording process often also involves the writer in greater explanation and justification than would be normal for a spoken comment. The disadvantage is that the open book is a public record and this may inhibit some contributors, especially those with views that they conceive to be in conflict with the general zeitgeist. Thus far, it has been possible to organize four 'open book' focus groups. These involved the teams of April 2002, July 2002, July 2003 and August 2004; in total, 87 potential volunteer contributors. Overall, there was a 2 or 3:1 female-to-male gender ratio among the participants.

Finally, after each field camp, the volunteers are asked to send an evaluation of their experiences back to Earthwatch. This questionnaire is an extensive four-page document that elicits both fixed and open-format responses. Examining these latter returns, the Likert-scale responses are, in the main, strongly positive, which is good to behold but actually provides little useful information. However, later, the form asks the volunteers to describe their most positive experience on the project and also their least positive. A later version of the questionnaire also asks volunteers to describe the personal, professional and educational impact of the project. These comments have been classified in the same fashion as the registration forms using, as far as possible, the same categories.

Results

Although more than 450 volunteers have supported this project since its inception, not all were involved, directly, in the scientific and philosophical aspects of the work. For more than half, involvement was restricted to a short weekend event, usually 1.5 working days and 2 evenings, which was convened for tree-planting. This group includes many of the Earthwatch volunteers and also almost the entire number of 'conscripts'. These are a group of 50–70 people who came to the project through high-school or corporate team-building programmes, for which the tree-planting work was a vehicle not the main objective. In recent years, a second division has appeared in the team of volunteers, which separates those who have contributed their own funds to joining the work from those who have won a competition sponsored by a corporate donor (such as ARCO, Marks & Spencer, Amerada Hess *et al.*), and have been given entry to an Earthwatch project, not necessarily the Earthwatch project they most wanted to join, as their prize. This second group has been dominated by secondary school teachers, whose listed motivations often include aspects of career development and it included several that did not request to be sent to this particular project. The incidence of external sponsorship is not always identified on the forms but is greater in the <40 age ranges. The social breakdown of participants is predominantly female with the >40 age range strongly represented (Table 1).

Results 1: Project Application Forms Analysis

Earthwatch policy includes sending project leaders the application, next of kin and health forms for each volunteer that joins the project. Unfortunately, this does not happen every year or for every event, nor are all the records that are received complete. For example, application forms were received for only one of the tree-planting events, which was that in November 2000, and for none of the 'conscripts' on corporate events. It is also likely that some application forms that were sent to the field have not survived. This analysis is based on the 140 summer camp application forms that remain with the project papers.

Table 1. Analysis of project registration forms (1991–2004)

"Please tell us why you chose this project? What are your expectations? What do you hope to contribute?"

1. Interest in subject (environmental reconstruction/'healing the Earth') (42)
2. Build technical understanding (38)
3. Broadly environmentally concerned (30)
4. Enjoy company of like-minded/interesting people (25)
5. Hope to be personally involved in a 'worthwhile' activity (24)
6. Work as part of a team (22)
7. Enjoy outdoor activities (19)
8. Commitment to local area of project (19)
9. Learn new things—useful for career (17)
10. Seeing progress of project (>2nd visit) (14)
11. Interest in practical nature/wildlife conservation (11)
12. Personal satisfaction/enjoyment (11)
13. Ecotourism/adventure (10)
14. Working with nature (spiritual aspects) (10)
15. Habitual Earthwatch volunteer (8)
16. Change from normal routine (7)
17. Allocated to the project by someone else (7)
18. Learn new things to apply in own home area (7)

Sample size: 140
Female: 91; Male 49
Age: <20: 7; 20–40: 49, 40–60: 68, >60: 16
Nationality: UK: 97; USA: 24; W. Europe: 10; E. Europe: 2; Australia: 2; Canada: 3; Africa: 1, S. America: 1

Notes: The table details the frequency of all categories identified by more than 7/140 (5%) of respondents. Those identified by more than 14 (10%) of respondents are emboldened. Most respondents listed two or three reasons (total 336; average 2.4) for their wish to join the project and all are included. There are also several broad classes of reason. These range from altruistic wishes to improve the world to technical interests in the problem, often expressed in career- or vocation-related terms. There is also an array of social and personal reasons, such as the wish to meet interesting people, enjoy camaraderie, and work outside in a common cause that is both worthwhile and a pleasant experience.

Results 2: 'Open Book' Focus Group

The 'open book' strategy was introduced to the 10 volunteers on the April 2002 field camp. The book remained open through two evenings of discussion in the lounge at the project's residential centre at Hill College, Abergavenny. The exercise was repeated in the July camps of 2002, 2003 and August 2004, with teams of 24, 30 and 23 respectively. A total of 51 unsigned responses were received. These range in length from a half-dozen words to around 300 words. In 2002, the volunteers were asked only to reflect on the contribution Earthwatch makes to environmental education. In 2003 and 2004, some supplementary questions were appended to the survey. Two of these focused on whether this kind of project was really the best way of learning what they learnt about research methods and land-reclamation theory. The third asked them to reflect on the differences between learning through a research project and through a formal taught class. A total of 21 additional responses were collected (Table 2).

The comments express the participants' metacognitive awareness of their role as opinion formers, especially the schoolteachers (Table 2: 1–5). The next group details aspects of experiential learning and its affective and transformative educational role (Table 2: 6–9 and 14–15). The third cluster concerns inspiration and empowerment for environmental action, converting learning into practice (Table 2: 9–12 and 16; cf Barraza *et al.*, 2003, p. 350). The last four comments (Table 2: 13–16) provide the best summary of the 21 brief responses to the subsidiary questions. These concur that you have to be involved in an environmental issue to truly appreciate it and you have to use a research technique to truly appreciate its strengths and weaknesses. It adds that many feel powerless to become involved—so projects like this one provide both an opportunity and an incentive for personal action.

Results 3: Post-project Evaluation Returns

Since Earthwatch engages volunteers, there is no compulsion upon participants to return their evaluation forms and apparently few do, unless they have a particularly strong feeling to express. Consequently, comparatively few evaluation returns get back to the project.

Table 2. Earthwatch: What contribution to environmental education?

Method: an open book headed by this question was handed to volunteers relaxing after field work during four 'Reclaiming the Land' Field Weekends between April 2002 and August 2004. They were invited "to add their comments". The following selected responses are transcribed.

1. "Ripple Effect involvement influences co-workers and friends"
2. "Allows people from many countries to meet under a common scientific ideal and then spread the word/work back to their own country..."
3. "Teachers—act as a role model—showing what can be done—using acquired knowledge to enhance teaching"
4. "I have used the project as an example ... for teaching"
5. "Teach me ... and I'll tell everyone"
6. "It provides real-world experience, not stuff straight out of a book"
7. "... get involved and learn more about the things that everyone should (and most people really do) care about"
8. "you only really relate to important issues when all your senses—touch, smell, sight, hearing, taste—come into contact with them. The more people who get hands on experience of important environmental problems—the more chance you have of changing the mind-set of the next generation"
9. "helped me appreciate that I own skills I never knew I had" (self-empowerment)
10. "helped me appreciate that I own skills I never knew I had" (self-empowerment)
11. "My global foot-print may be large but I will use my skills to give something back to Nature"
12. "To truly understand the environmental issues that need to be considered in any decision about planning development ... can only occur by immersing the decision makers in considering the effects of past decisions"
13. "Provides an object lesson in different approaches to solving problems ... also demonstrates that the answer to a question is often a raft of a whole lot more questions..."
14. "Provides an opportunity for adults to rekindle their sense of curiosity and wonder... When immersed in a project with people from other parts of the world and other walks of life—volunteers participate in education at several levels ... (not just) the hard science and project goals and methodology ... but also more lasting is the revaluation of the shrinking global community. This last encourages participants to rethink what is known and to look deeper into things we can change..."
15. "Connects people with the outdoors, which many wish to do but feel disempowered to do..."
16. "Tell you what, its made me think what someone can do..."

The records hold just 67—a rather small self-selected sample. Their content is summarized as Table 3.

Once again, in Table 3, respondents generated multiple responses, commonly listing two or more reasons (total 181; average 2.7) in the positive section and one (total 81: average 1.2) in the negative. The strongest themes in the evaluation returns are social, they concern participation and the mutual reinforcement found in successful team working (Table 3: 1–5, 9, 13, 14, 18; cf. Delors, 1998). The volunteers greatly valued the meeting, working with and receiving enthusiasm-based support from those with shared or similar interests. Subject-based learning is the second major theme (Table 3: 7, 13–17). Behind them, the negative issues are dominated by the bad weather, which

Table 3. Analysis of Post-Project Evaluation Returns (1991–2003)

Responses to the questions: "What were your most positive experiences during this project?" "What were your least positive experiences during the project?"

What was your most positive experience?

1. Enjoyed company of like-minded/interesting people (41)
2. Working as part of a team (15)
3. Sense of achievement (14)
4. Optimistic/shared enthusiasm for the project (12)
5. Being a valued part of the project (11)
6. Involvement with local community/heritage (9)
7. Learning new things - increased technical understanding (9)
8. New experience (7)
9. Seeing progress of project (2nd visit) (7)
10. Well planned (7)
11. Worthwhile project (7)
12. Working with Nature (6)
13. Being able to help the research (5)
14. Fired up own enthusiasm (4)
15. Guided reconnaissance walk (3)
16. Strong introductory briefing (3)
17. Doing fieldwork (3)
18. Inspirational will to do own project (3)

What was your least positive experience?

1. Bad weather (14)
2. Logistic and organizational problems (12)
3. Wanted more time to spend with the project (9)
4. Poor time-keeping (8)
5. Wanted more instruction in field (6)
6. Hard work (4)
7. Accommodation (4)
8. Wanted more variety in activities (3)
9. Wanted more free time (3)
10. Inadequate field equipment (3)
11. Un-interested person sponsored onto project (3)

Sample $n = 67$
Female: 40; Male: 16; Don't Know: 1
UK: 55; USA: 6, W. Europe: 2; Don't Know: 4

Note: The frequency of all categories mentioned by more than 3/67 (5%) respondents is included and those identified by more than 6 (10%) respondents are emboldened.

blighted the 2003 season, and a cluster of academic-environmental and logistical-organizational issues. A clear difference emerges between those who joined the project from commitment and a minority of those who received this project as a gift and who wanted more time off and sight-seeing.

Discussion

Education for environmental sustainability concerns promoting the understanding and implementation of sustainability, reconciling human activities and environmental welfare, and moving education into a more participatory and empowering mode (Barraza *et al.*, 2003). In previous research, the author undertook a stakeholder analysis of this project. This was based on semi-structured focus-group meetings held during the course of several field camps and examined the motivations of volunteer participants alongside those of the project's other stakeholders (Haigh, 1998). It concluded that the volunteers' motives covered a range that included a genuine wish to help conserve the quality of the environment, through a wish to meet others with similar beliefs, through camaraderie and meeting new friends, to 'ecotourism'—a recreational escape from an office job. For many, the field camps provided them with a holiday experience that was less vacuous than a conventional beach experience and some found within it a new hobby or cause to support (Haigh, 1998, p. 67).

Similar ideas emerge from the testimonies of volunteers on the Earthwatch Millennium Fellowship Programme, which sponsored 600 fellows from the over-50 age group onto a wide array of projects (Tordoff, 2001; cf. Tilbury *et al.*, 2002, p. xii). A special feature of this programme was that volunteers were asked to include, with their fellowship application, an indication of how they would build upon their experience on their return. Testimonies from 22 volunteers have been published by Earthwatch (Holliday *et al.*, 2000). Fellows report that through writing articles, speaking engagements and teaching, for many were teachers, they had managed to spread enthusiasm for environmental action (Mitford, 2000, p. 9; Roberts, 2000, p. 66), and affected the choices made by other individuals (Clark, 2000, p. 28). In other cases, while some were content to leave their thumbprint, figuratively or literally, on the work that was being done (Bowey, 2000, p. 20), others became actively engaged in the long-term development of the project's work (Riddell, 2001, p. 98; Turner, 2000, p. 103).

The analyses of this Earthwatch 'Reclaiming the Land' project's application and evaluation forms broadly support these findings. The volunteers signed up for the project because they had a general concern for environmental sustainability. Although few of their written comments on either application or evaluation forms contain explicit reference to atonement, the wish to address the damaging effects of the human impact on Nature seems to have been a strong motivation. Many volunteers expressed the desire to be part of a 'worthwhile' activity. A significant number of, mainly UK-based, people volunteered for the project out of a sense of duty towards resolving the problems of the South Wales valleys. Others, mainly those from further afield, sought an ecotouristic adventure—a route to understanding a new land and its people. For some volunteers, participation was conceived as a vacation from normal paid work and for some it was their main annual holiday. The logical follow-through of this aspect of volunteer engagement was the importance to the volunteers of who they worked with, which for many was as critical as what they were doing. Many volunteers hoped to meet and mingle with other like-minded people, both in the team and in the local community. Volunteers sought the opportunity for the camaraderie of teamwork, the opportunity to work with Nature and to conduct physical labour out of doors (cf. Haigh, 1998). Above all, they sought reinforcement for their own enthusiasm for environmental action and learning. Enthusiasm, as Bunch (1982) has proposed, may be the major driver for successful NGO engagement in environmental conservation and education. UNESCO's Delors Commission also stressed that teamwork, bringing people of different groups together, 'in an egalitarian setting' where 'common aims and projects are pursued' is a route to enhancing learning and engagement and also something curriculum developers should promote (Delors, 1998).

Another major theme, largely expressed by volunteers who were professional teachers, was a desire to learn something of the techniques and methods of land-reclamation research. A few mentioned some intention to emulate this work elsewhere. However, there was a real sense of a wish to spread the word and make others more aware of what could be done. A majority of the participants saw themselves as opinion leaders. Part of their engagement in the project aimed to gain sufficient understanding of the technical issues in order to lead others more effectively (see Table 2).

This theme was echoed strongly during the open-book discussion sessions. Here, volunteers talked openly of themselves as role-models, spreading the message, showing the way for others. They also talked about the personal benefits they gained from shared immersion in real-world problems, the rekindling of their sense of wonder at the processes of Nature and the recharging of enthusiasm to engage in their own local action. They emphasized that conducting 'research' into a problem was a powerful route to learning (cf. Volk, 1990; Rickinson, 2001). Research by Gerber *et al.* (2001) confirms that enriched informal learning environments, like enquiry-based formal classroom instruction, have significant benefits for students' reasoning capabilities. It was also clear that the volunteers felt that they learnt as much from discussions amongst themselves as from the specific project. They share, with the author, 'the buzz' that develops from working with other people who are 'passionate about what they are doing and extremely appreciative of our efforts' (cf. Haigh, 2002). They also recorded a delight in having the opportunity to be involved in something that aspired to effect a long-term improvement to the human habitat.

The evaluation returns are dominated by these same issues. Overwhelmingly, the volunteers regarded the greatest positive benefit of their involvement, the opportunity that it gave to meet other like-minded people. They enjoyed being part of a team, part of a project and the sense of achievement that this brought (cf. Delors, 1998). They also enjoyed learning more about the local heritage of the study area, the techniques employed by the research and the project's constructive approach to environmental challenges. They liked working with Nature, except when it rained, which it did on about 30 per cent of all field-study sessions. The negative comments include the positive wish to spend more time with the project and frustration with the organizers' logistics.

In sum, then, the field-project experience had benefits to its participants that are similar to those generated by successful fieldwork (cf. Robson, 2002). However, unlike much fieldwork, this kind of project has an added intensity. This arises from the fact that this is not an educational problem-solving exercise or simulation but the real thing. It also arises from the hot-house interactions between the community of activists, enthusiasts and believers that can quickly create a very powerful and influential ambience that affects everyone involved (Haigh, 1998, p. 70 *et seq.*). The result is an experience that can be emotionally affective and well as informative.

Kofi Annan's Dhaka speech argued that "Our biggest challenge in this new century is to take an idea that sounds abstract—sustainable development—and turn it into reality for all the world's people" (Annan, 2001, p. 2). Self-realization (from the personal to the ecological), personal empowerment and fulfilment may be the main potential educational benefits of engagement in this kind of NGO field project (Haigh, 2002).

The main tangible outcome, however, may be the further activities of the participants. These include teaching classes, giving public talks, writing articles for the media, joining similar projects elsewhere and even founding their own projects, both within and beyond the umbrella of Earthwatch's 'Reclaiming the Land' project (Eisner, 1992; Brady, 2005; cf. Holliday *et al.*, 2000).

Thinking about Education for Environmental Sustainability

In January 2005, the United Nations' Decade of Education for Sustainable Development was launched (UN, 2003; IEF, 2004; Haigh, 2005). The hope is that this will encourage a greater number of people to reflect on the consequences of their actions and begin the work of constructing more self-sustainable lifestyles across the world (Tilbury & Goldstein, 2003, p. 1). The United Nations University Rector Ginkel comments:

> Universities are increasingly called upon to play a leading role in developing an inter-trans-disciplinary and ethically-oriented form of education in order to devise solutions for the problems linked with sustainable development. They must, therefore, commit themselves to an on-going process of informing, educating, and mobilizing all the relevant parts of society concerning the consequences of ecological degradation, including its impact on global development and the conditions needed to ensure a sustainable and just world (Ginkel, 1998, pp. 13–14).

In truth, the recent record of UK universities, including most of the environmental subjects, is not encouraging (Martin & Jucker, 2005). Nonetheless, some progress has been made towards the promotion of sustainable higher education, as manifested by publications in the *International Journal of Sustainability in Higher Education*, interest in the USA's Talloires declaration (>200 universities in >40 nations), the COPERNICUS University Charter for Sustainable Development (>250 signatories) and Britain's Forum for the Future co-sponsored HEPS initiative (Higher Education Partnership for Sustainability) (HEPS, 2002). However, today, most universities focus on producing graduates who are employable and who will oil the machineries of economic growth (Berry, 1999). Some outsiders see religious fervour in the Western world's widespread belief in the wisdom of 'the market' and its economic forces (Korten, 2000; Loy, 2000). However, objectively, around the world, economic progress remains near synonymous with ecological regress and both proceed at great pace (Berry, 1999).

Meanwhile, environmental education still strives towards 'understanding the objects of the global environmental system and their interrelationships'. Theses concerns are mapped, in different ways, within every textbook of physical geography and environmental science. Traditional environmental sustainability education struggles when it tries to convey the understanding that the environmental system is the ultimate and only life-support system on this planet, and that humanity is a part of this system and intimately dependent upon it (Sterling, 2001). It also fails to support the notion that each human has a personal role in this interaction and, arguably, ethical responsibilities too (Berry, 1999).

While reductionist, dualist and passive styles still dominate contemporary teaching about the environment, the real priority for environmental education should be to make the environment personal (cf. Greig *et al.*, 1989; Schultz, 2000; Sterling, 2001; Bonnett, 2002). Binn and Wright (2002, p. 82) note that "sustainable development requires citizens who understand and care for the environment and play an active role in its management". The need is for an active approach that recognizes the dynamism and indeterminacy of natural processes and also the fact that humans are personally involved and that their decisions and choices can affect the state of the world around them (Berry, 1999, pp. 84–85; Jackson & Pande, 2000; Fien & Tilbury, 2002).

When contemplating the state of the environment and the state of higher education, it is easy to fall prey to feelings of helplessness and disempowerment. However, the fact is that, self-referenced, inward-looking and corporate though they be, higher education institutes can be changed. Arguably, much of the impetus may have to come from outside, perhaps passed upwards from primary and secondary schools, perhaps downward from governments, but change is possible (Haigh, 2005; Martin & Jucker, 2005). Meanwhile, some of the organizations that are best placed to make a difference are those for whom 'making change' is their reason for existence. The hydra-like foment of the NGO adhocracies that, in sum, form the environment movement can provide a new dynamism to the ways in which higher education interacts with Nature and society (Martin, 2000).

NGOs tend to be dedicated to problem-solving, action and change. Indeed, the success of certain NGOs in influencing environmental policy has earnt them a difficult reputation amongst developers and administrators. NGOs emerge as social pressure groups. Inevitably, their environmental interventions arise from, and sometimes integrate, a wide range of social, political, religious and ethical as well as economic contextual issues. However, in general, they incline towards both physical and spiritual holism and they espouse improvement in terms that are not driven by the economic balance sheet (cf. Lal, 2000). Instead, they are expressed in terms of quality of life, which is evaluated either in anthropocentric or in more radical ecocentric terms (Naess 1973, 1987; Stern & Dietz, 1994).

Of course, NGOs face many problems. In 1996, See-Jae Lee surveyed the NGOs of Korea. Most of these ran (or used to run) environmental education programmes and many of these had shifted from formal classroom training to informal sensitivity training in the field. However, they shared many difficulties, often financial, including the costs of activities, instructors and educational materials (Lee, 2001). The situation is not so different elsewhere. It unusual to find a campaigning NGO that is not financially stretched, which means that they need and depend on sponsorship—public, private and corporate.

The rise of Earthwatch (Europe) was constructed upon winning corporate sponsorship from large multinational companies. This contrasts with its American parent, where individual subscriptions remain a core financial stream. In April 2002, Oxford Brookes University hosted a workshop with Earthwatch, which focused on the ethical problems of who could be accepted as a donor and under what conditions sponsorship could be accepted. This debate featured Earthwatch fund-raisers and focused on its Corporate Environmental Responsibility Group (CERG), which is supported by an array of multinationals, several of them in 'ethically challenged' areas of business.

The conclusion reached was that while there was a need for sponsorship and while cash from any source would go to good works, there were limits to which multinationals might be acceptable as donors. Earthwatch (Europe) recognized that it had both an opportunity and a duty to work with its corporate supporters in an attempt to help them 'Green' their own activities.

At present, NGOs distance themselves further from the economic system than most organizations and are better able to resist the current dangerous trend to sacrifice, as a matter of routine, long-term environmental welfare to short-term economic rewards. Palmer & Birch (2003, p. 650) comment: "The very fact that NGOs are not-for-profit organizations leaves them accountable to no one." However, as the NGOs grow, so they begin to assume the characteristics of the corporate establishment and Earthwatch itself is a useful exemplar of this process. As economic needs expand, so each NGO's tendency towards compromise with its sponsors grows and the organization becomes, gradually, more 'corporate' in style, attitude and organization and less radical in thought, word and deed. Some organizations, like Earthwatch, believed that they could build partnerships from corporate links and so influence the thinking of large corporations and agencies. However, the greater likelihood is that an NGO would become compromised by these institutions, seduced by their approach and ethos, and so reduced to being public relations providers or corporations in their own right. The extent to which, inadvertently, the 'Reclaiming the Land' project in this case study has been employed as 'greenwash' for corporate sponsors has been debated in the media (Cook, 2002). Equally, similar problems could afflict those NGOs that form ties too close with higher education institutes (HEIs) and so absorb their objective, dispassionate and 'research-for-research's sake' attributes.

If forces exist that resist such changes, they emerge from each NGO's individual supporters. These are concerned people, who are motivated less by the organization's economic necessities than by a belief in its mission. In this case, they really do recognize that the world needs better environmental sustainability education, for themselves and for others, and they really believe that by 'acting locally' they can contribute towards saving the global environment.

Thinking about Links between NGOs and Higher Education

There are many examples of fruitful links between NGOs and HEIs. The four that follow illustrate some of the ways that existing links support education for sustainable development as well as the learning, teaching and research objectives of those involved from geography and sister disciplines within higher education.

Recently, the author had an opportunity to observe the workings of a link between another of the UK's leading new universities, the University of Plymouth, and a major NGO, Schumacher College, which is the international bowsprit for avant garde thinking in environmentalism and deep ecology. Previously, these two had worked together to promote a Masters Course in 'Holistic Science', which is based at Schumacher College but validated from the University of Plymouth (Schumacher College, 2004; University of Plymouth, 2004). On this occasion, the two had combined to bid for recognition of the university as a national centre of excellence in teaching and learning (CETL) in education for sustainable development, where the leading international reputation of Schumacher College and its staff would play a key supporting role (Dyer *et al.*, 2006).

The official, albeit still-born, link between Oxford Brookes University and Earthwatch was conceived in terms of joint research between staff, student placements and the incorporation of Earthwatch field expeditions in staff development and in the academic programmes of students (Anon., 2003). Here, the university moved ahead alone. In October 2004, it launched a 'U21184: Expedition' module, which provided a framework within which students could gain credit for participation in selected field-research expeditions (cf. Pawson & Teather, 2002). Subsequently, it developed a system of University Staff Development Fellowships, which allow both teaching and non-teaching staff the opportunity to join field expeditions with financial support from the staff development budget. In 2005, three Fellowships were awarded through open competition. Each carried the obligation that the participant would use the experience to promote education for sustainable development (and the work of Brookes' internal 'Environment Forum') on campus on their return.

In the Republic of Serbia and Montenegro, staff at the University of Belgrade have helped create the NGO CEKOR, 'Centre for Ecology and Sustainable Development', which aims to promote environmental regeneration in the Grdelica Klisura (Zlatić, 2003). The NGO has attracted support from REC (the Regional Environment Center for Central and Eastern Europe, Budapest), which funds small NGO projects and subsequently from government enterprises working in the same field. CEKOR strives to link the local population with local enterprises, government organizations and the media, while focusing public debate on the sustainable development of the region (CEKOR, 2004). Simultaneously, CEKOR supports the research and publication efforts of its university-based proponents.

Further east, in Turkey, colleagues at Istanbul Technical University and the University of Istanbul are allied closely with the campaigning NGO, TEMA (Turkish Foundation for Combating Soil Erosion for Reforestation and the Protection of Natural Habitats) for work on the community-based rehabilitation of damaged watersheds. The TEMA Foundation is a major, well-established NGO that aims to raise public awareness of land erosion, deforestation, declining farmland productivity and threats to the biodiversity of Turkey. It carries out model projects in rural development, rangeland rehabilitation and reforestation. TEMA has 150 000 members and a 588 strong volunteer workforce (TEMA, 2004). The benefit this link provides to its academic partners is access to TEMA's resources, infrastructure and workforce in support of their development of applied and strategic research into land rehabilitation (Haciyakupoglu *et al.*, 2004). However, TEMA's main focus is education of the public and it looks to its HEI partners for assistance in this work. Environmental education is central to its thinking about promoting sustainable development. Equally, it considers that its future depends on its success in winning over the public in order to encourage donations and to bring pressure on politicians and government agencies to adopt more environmentally sensitive policies.

There are very many similar cases from around the world and, in many cases, the themes of research, teaching, community outreach, community service, experiential and problem-based learning are very closely entwined (cf. Fortner, 2001; BSP, 2003; Kotval, 2003; Worsley, 2003; Shah & Treby, 2006). As in the TEMA case study, NGOs may provide to university scholars: resources and community support for applied field projects, opportunities for funding and for engagement in practical environmental fieldwork, an umbrella for work that might not fit easily within the run of normal university activities, and a route for communicating environmental ideas into the community (cf. Hama *et al.*, 2005). NGOs also offer a useful vehicle for building self-sustaining links between the academy and the wider community, as CEKOR does in the Grdlica Klisura. Their project focus often provides roots in particular communities or field areas, which offer a grounding and springboard for academic research as in Turkey.

Today, the importance of voluntary work in the community is recognized by both governments and HEIs. In both North America and the European Community, citizenship education and 'service learning' education have strong support (Kozeracki, 2000; Council of Europe, Division for Citizenship and Human Rights Education, 2004).

Citizenship education gives learners the capacity to play an effective role in society at local, national and international levels, and helps them to become informed, thoughtful and responsible citizens who are aware of their rights and conscious of their duties (Institute for Citizenship, 2004). These duties include responsibilities to environmental sustainability. The Committee of Ministers of the Council of Europe proclaimed 2005 'European Year of Citizenship through Education' (Council of Europe, Division for Citizenship and Human Rights Education, 2004). Previously, the Council's Education for Democratic Citizenship (EDC) project sought the answer to three issues: what set of knowledge, skills and attitudes will individuals need to be able to be active citizens in Europe in the twenty-first century, how can these be developed and how can people learn to transmit this body of knowledge, skills and attitudes (Council of Europe Division for Citizenship and Human Rights Education, 2004)? Alun Michael, the first 'First Secretary' of the National Assembly Government in Wales (NAW), declared volunteering "the first act of citizenship" (Michael, 2000, p. 1). He also urged NAW agencies to "make compacts with relevant voluntary sector groups", NGOs, to facilitate the development of opportunities for voluntary engagement in community projects (NAW, 2000, p. 17).

In the USA, more than 80 per cent of Community Colleges and many other HEIs are engaged with 'service learning' (Kozeracki, 2000). Service learning is defined as an "instructional methodology [that] integrates community service with academic instruction as it focuses on critical, reflective thinking and civic responsibility 'activities'" (American Association of Community Colleges, 1995, p. 1). These include activities, traditionally considered extracurricular, such as working with an NGO, and extend to experiential education and work-placement internships, such as working for an NGO.

Of course, there are also many problems with NGO engagement. These organizations tend to be smaller, more focused and much more volatile than HEIs. Many exude an aura of 'crankiness'—in all that word's several senses. More disconcerting, from an academic point of view, are an NGO's engagements with the media and governments. NGOs are always campaigning groups, even if their campaigns may be limited to fund-raising. They tend, therefore, to be media hungry, to court publicity and political attention, sometimes in high-risk ways that can be potentially harmful to any associated academic. The author recollects listening to a talk by the editor of the Earthwatch magazine during an early visit to an Earthwatch Annual Conference at Harvard University. This sought to explain how a project on the 'Population dynamics of sea squirts' might come to be publicized under the title 'Sea, sun and sex'. Ruefully, one reflects that this example was intended to be a spoof (cf. Cook, 2002).

Conclusion

For the UN Decade's lead agency, UNESCO, ESD involves:

> ... learning how to make decisions that consider the long-term future of the economy, ecology and equity of all communities. (UNESCO, 2003, p. 4)

UNESCO argues that:

> Higher education has ... a special responsibility ... to generate the new knowledge needed and train the leaders and teachers of tomorrow, as well as communicate this knowledge to decision-makers and the public-at-large. (UNESCO, 2001, p. 1)

UNESCO also calls on educators, governments and all relevant stakeholders to:

> ... review the programmes and curricula of schools and universities, in order to better address the challenges and opportunities of sustainable development, with a focus on: creating learning modules which bring skills, knowledge, reflections, ethics and values together in a balanced way. (UNESCO, 2002, p. 1)

The duty of promoting education for sustainable development has been handed to all levels of education. Higher education has its own role, not least among which is to update the understanding of its former graduates and to spread the ideas of environmental sustainability through the community. One way of achieving this is through involvement in the informal education provide by the projects developed by environmental NGOs. This case study has examined the impacts of a joint project shared between Oxford Brookes University and the NGO Earthwatch, which subsequently led to a brief formal association; the two organizations have vowed to cooperate in the promotion of both teaching and research. The argument for the link includes the observation that NGO engagement in practical project work provides a most valuable agency for non-formal environmental education. Those who become involved, especially in problem-solving, constructive work rather than politics and protest, often deal directly with the core issues of environmental sustainability. Normally, this might not impinge on the day-to-day lives of those involved, but direct and personal involvement can make a major impact on the lives of participants. Cardinal among these is the easy assumption of a role as an agent of social change, both through direct action and by introducing the understanding of the imperatives of environmental sustainability to those who have not shared the experience (cf. Holliday *et al.*, 2000).

The environmental sustainability education that NGO-style practical project work provides differs greatly from the factual, technical and objective work that is provided by most university classrooms. Informal environmental education is often much more involving and emotionally affective. Theory is often subsumed to practice, objectivity valued less than subjective personal engagement. Its learning outcomes reflect these differences. They may include the realization of a personal role and of both a personal responsibility and capacity to effect change. Participants come to learn technical skills and reinforce existing beliefs. However, they may carry away both new confidence and new enthusiasm for changes that, they hope, they may cascade outwards into the wider society.

Acknowledgements

Special thanks go to Earthwatch volunteers and co-workers: Heather Reed, Kip D'Aucourt, Susan Powell, Willemina Panhuis, Ben and Ceri Sansom, Dr Keith Pampling, Kath Blake, Dr Pat Woodruff, Frances Farrugia, Dr Alison Flege, Elizabeth Hatton, Chris Bull, Gill Wilding, and many more. Thanks also go to Earthwatch (Europe), especially Maureen O'Neill and Mark Goodhand, for sponsorship of the author's team research on community-based approaches to land reclamation and for the provision of internal documents to assist this study and to Prof Svetla Gentcheva-Kostadinova, Ms Tanya Minkovska, Dr Elena Zheleva, Dr Ekaterina Filcheva and colleagues in Sofia for their long-term scientific support and encouragement. A short preliminary version of this paper was published by the UK's Learning and Teaching Support, now Higher Education Academy, Network for Geography, Earth and Environmental Sciences (LTSN-GEES).The full citation is: Haigh, M. J. (2002) Sustaining environmental education: the contribution of NGO activism, *Planet,* Special Edition 4, pp. 22–24.

References

American Association of Community Colleges (1995) *Community Colleges and Service Learning*, ERIC Document ED 387 198 (Washington, DC: AACC)

Annan, K. (2004) Secretary General calls for break in political stalemate over environmental issues, United Nations Press Release SC/SM/7739 (15/03/01). Available at http://www.un.org/News/Press/docs/2001/sgsm7739.doc.htm (accessed April 2004).

Annan, K. (2004) Secretary General says failure to stop biodiversity loss too awful to contemplate, United Nations Press Release SG/SM/9289, ENV/DEV/780, OBV/420 (03/05/2004). Available at http://www.un.org/News/Press/docs/2004/sgsm9289,doc.htm (accessed June 2004).

Anon (2003) Watching over the world with Earthwatch, *Oxford Brookes University, Brookes Link*, 16 (Autumn 2003), p. 1. Available at http://www.brookes.ac.uk/publications/brookes_link/issue16/earthwatch & http://www.brookes.ac.uk/news/2003/may/nr_31_03 (accessed September 2004).

Anon (2004) Brookes becomes the world's first Fairtrade university, *The Oak (Oxford Brookes University)*, 22 (July 2004), p. 1, Available at http://www.brookes.ac.uk/publications/oak/issue22/fairtrade (accessed September 2004).

Barraza, L., Duque-Aristizabal, A. M. & Rebolledo, G. (2003) Environmental education: from policy to practice, *Environmental Education Research*, 9(3), pp. 347–357.

Berry, T. M. (1999) *The Great Work: Our Way Into The Future* (New York: Bell Tower).

Binn, D. & Wright, J. C. A. (2002) Wales: sustainability for real: a National Park initiative in environmental education, in: D. Tilbury, R. B. Stevenson, J. Fien & D. Schreuder (Eds) *Education and Sustainability: Responding to the Global Challenge*, pp. 81–90 (Gland, Switzerland: International Union for the Conservation of Nature (IUCN), Commission on Education and Communication) Available at http://www.iucn.cec.org (accessed October 2002).

Bonnett, M. (2002) Education for sustainability as a frame of mind, *Environmental Education Research*, 8(1), pp. 9–20.

Bowey, K. (2000) Barn owls, Bolivian grasslands and biodiversity, in: S. Holliday, P. Owen & C. Turner (Eds) *Journeys of Discovery*, pp. 17–22 (Oxford: Earthwatch Institute).

BSP (2003) *Bourne Stream Partnership*. Available at http://www.bwhwater.co.uk/bsp/ (accessed September 2004).

Bunch, R. (1982) *Two Ears of Corn: A Guide To People Centred Agricultural Development* (Oklahoma City: World Neighbors).

Calder, W. & Clugston, R. (2005) Editorial: education for a sustainable future, *Journal of Geography in Higher Education*, 29(1), pp. 7–12.

Cambray, J. A. (2000) Community involvement and the Eastern Cape Rocky (*Sandelia Bainsii*, Pisces, anabantidae) from the perspective of a researcher, *South African Journal of Wildlife Research*, 30(3), pp. 114–117.

CEKOR (2004) *Centar za Ekologiju i Održivi Razvoj/Center for Ecology and Sustainable Development*. Available at http://cekor.8m.net/srpski.htm (accessed September 2004).

Clark, A. (2000) Monkey business, in: S. Holliday, P. Owen & C. Turner (Eds) *Journeys of Discovery*, pp. 25–28 (Oxford: Earthwatch Institute).

Cook, S. (2002) Shrewd move, *Guardian (Educational)*, 27 August, pp. 1–2 & Education Guardian Weekly. Available at http://education.guardian.co.uk/egweekly/story/0,5500,780942,00.html (accessed September 2002).

Council of Europe Division for Citizenship and Human Rights Education (2004) *Education for Democratic Citizenship* (Strasbourg: Council of Europe, Directorate General IV—Education, Culture and Heritage, Youth and Sport) Available at http://www.coe.int/edc;http://www.coe.int/T/E/Cultural_Co-operation/education/E.D.C/What_is_education_for_democratic_citizenship/Genesis%20and%20developments.asp#P238_13024 (accessed June 2004).

Davidson, J. (2003) Editorial: the challenge of education for sustainable development and global citizenship in Wales, *Journal of Geography in Higher Education*, 27(3), pp. 235–238.

Delors, J. (1998) *Learning: The Treasure Within: Report to UNESCO from the International Commission on Education in the 21st Century* (Paris: UNESCO) [http://www.unesco.org/delors/highlights.htm (accessed June 2003).

Dyer, A., Selby, D. & Chalkley, B. (2006) A centre of excellence in education for sustainable development, *Journal of Geography in Higher Education*, 30(2), pp. 307–312.

Earthwatch Institute (Europe) (2001a) *Earthwatch Annual Report 2001* (Oxford: Earthwatch Institute).

Earthwatch Institute (Europe) (2001b) *Pollution, Predation, Migration: Environmental Case Studies For The National Curriculum: Resource Pack for Teaching 11–16 year olds* (Oxford: Earthwatch Institute).

Eisner, R. (1992) Saving soil in Wales: soil scientists and volunteers dig in to save the Earth, *The Scientist (Philadelphia)*, 6(2), pp. 1, 15, 18. Available at http://www.the-scientist.com/yr1992/jan/research_920120.html (accessed May 2002).

Evans, S. M. & Birchenough, A. C. (2001) Community-based management of the environment: lessons from the past and options for the future, *Aquatic Conservation—Marine and Freshwater Ecosystems*, 11(2), pp. 137–147.

Fien, J. & Tilbury, D. (2002) The global challenge of sustainability, in: D. Tilbury, R. B. Stevenson, J. Fien & D. Schreuder (Eds) *Education and Sustainability: Responding to the Global Challenge*, pp. 1–12 (Gland, Switzerland: International Union for the Conservation of Nature (IUCN), Commission on Education and Communication) Available at http://www.iucn.cec.org (accessed October 2002).

Flege, A. (2000) Forest recultivation of coal-mined land: problems and prospects, *Land Reconstruction and Management*, 1, pp. 291–338.

Fortner, R. W. (2001) Nonformal environmental education in the United States: current programs and practices, *Korean Federation for Environment Movement (KFEM): International Symposium on Environmental Education in 2001*. Available at http://english.kfem.or.kr/international/symposium.htm (accessed May 2002)..

Gerber, B. L., Cavallo, A. M. L. & Marek, E. A. (2001) Relationships among informal learning environments, teaching procedures and scientific reasoning ability, *International Journal of Science Education*, 23(5), pp. 535–549.

Ginkel, H. van (1998) Preparing for a sustainable future: higher education and sustainable human development, *World Conference on Higher Education: Higher Education in the Twenty-First Century: Vision and Action (UNESCO, Paris, 5-9 October 1998) Thematic Debate* (Paris: UNESCO, Division of Higher Education, CD-ROM).

Greenreef (2002) Greenreef: Education, Research and Natural Resource Development. Available at http://www.greenreefbelize.com/prog-environed.html (accessed May 2002).

Greig, S., Pike, G. & Selby, D. (1989) *Green Prints For Changing Schools* (London: World Wide Fund for Nature & Kogan Page).

Haciyakupoglu, S., Ertek, A.T., Oguz, I., Erginal, E.A., Hizal, A., Gokbulak, F. & Saygin, H. (2004) Community based rehabilitation case studies: Celikli and Yoguntas Villages in Turkey, in: M. Zlatic, S. Kostadinov & N. Dragovic (Eds) *Community-based Rehabilitation of Degraded Lands of Central Balkan Mountains and Northern Turkey*, pp. 87–94 (Belgrade: University of Belgrade, Faculty of Forestry).

Haigh, M. J. (1998) Working with NGO environmentalism for land reclamation research, in: P. Strachan & J. Moxon (Eds) *Managing Green Teams: Environmental Change in Organisations and Networks*, pp. 61–82 (Sheffield: Greenleaf).

Haigh, M. J. (2000a) The aims of land reclamation, *Land Reconstruction and Management*, 1, pp. 1–20.

Haigh, M. J. (2000b) Soil stewardship on reclaimed coal-lands, *Land Reconstruction and Management*, 1, pp. 165–274.

Haigh, M. J. (2002) Land reclamation and deep ecology: in search of a more meaningful Physical Geography, *Area*, 34(3), pp. 242–252.

Haigh, M. J. (2005) Greening the university curriculum: appraising an international movement, *Journal of Geography in Higher Education*, 29(1), pp. 31–48.

Hama, A. M., Seitz, M., Sansone, A. & Stötter, J. (2005) An environmental education concept for Galtür, Austria, *Journal of Geography in Higher Education*, 29(1), pp. 61–78.

Hellin, J. & Higman, S. (2003) *Feeding The Market: South American Farmers And Globalization* (London: Intermediate Technology Development Group Publishing).

HEPS (2002) Higher Education Partnership for Sustainability: Universities and colleges contributing towards sustainable development Available at http://www.forumforthefuture.org.uk">http://www.heps.org.uk; http://www.forumforthefuture.org.uk (accessed March 2003).

Holliday, S., Owen, P. & Turner, C. (Eds) (2000) *Journeys of Discovery* (Oxford: Earthwatch Institute).

Hudson, S. J. (2001) Challenges for environmental education: issues and ideas for the 21st century, *Bioscience*, 51 (April), pp. 283–288.

IEF (2004) *United Nations Decade of Education for Sustainable Development 2005–2014: Resources and Links* (International Environment Forum: a Bahá'í-inspired organization addressing the environment and sustainable development). Available at http://www.bcca.org/ief/desd.htm (accessed June 2004).

Institute for Citizenship (2004) *Speak Out! On European Citizenship* (London: Institute of Citizenship) Available at http://www.citizen.org.uk/speakout/about.html (accessed June 2004).

Jackson, M. G. (2003) Internationalising the curriculum, *Journal of Geography in Higher Education*, 27(3), pp. 41–48.

Jackson, M. G. (undated) *Our Land Our Life: A Practical Course of Environmental Studies for Classes VI–X in Schools and Intermediate Colleges of the Uttarakhand Region of Uttar Pradesh*, 5 (Almora: Uttaranchal, Uttarakhand Paryavaran Shiksha Kendra).

Jackson, M. G. & Pande, G. P. (2000) *Environmental Education in India: A Critical Assessment of Developments to Date and Suggestions for the Future* (Almora: Uttaranchal, Uttarakhand Paryavaran Shiksha Kendra).

Kent, M., Gilbertson, D. D. & Hunt, C. O. (1997) Fieldwork in geography teaching: a critical review, *Journal of Geography in Higher Education*, 21(3), pp. 67–83.

Korten, D. (2000) Sustainability and the global economy, in: H. Coward & D. C. Maguire (Eds) *Visions of a New Earth: Religious Perspectives on Population, Consumption and Ecology* pp. 29–42 (Albany, NY: SUNY Press).

Korze, A. V. (2005) Transition and transformation: the influence of a learning package on student performance in soils geography studies, *Journal of Geography in Higher Education*, 29(2), pp. 369–384.

Kotval, Z. (2003) Teaching experiential learning in the urban planning curriculum, *Journal of Geography in Higher Education*, 27(3), pp. 297–308.

Kozeracki, C. A. (2000) ERIC Review: Service learning in the Community College, *Community College Review (University of North Carolina)*, Spring 2000. Available at http://www.findarticles.com/p/articles/mi_m0HCZ/is_4_27/ai_63132416 (accessed September 2004).

Lal, V. (2000) Too deep for deep ecology: Gandhi and the ecological vision of life, in: C. K. Chapple & M. E. Tucker (Eds) *Hinduism and Ecology: The Intersection of Earth Sky and Water*, pp. 183–212 (Cambridge, MA: Harvard University, Center for the Study of World Religions).

Lee, S. J. (2001) Social education for environment and environmental NGO in Korea, *Korean Federation for Environment Movement (KFEM): International Symposium on Environmental Education in 2001*. Available at http://english.kfem.or.kr/international/symposium/2001/leeseejae.doc (accessed May 2002).

Leopold, A. (1949) *A Sand County Almanac and Essays on Conservation from Round River* (Oxford: Oxford University Press).

Loy, D. (2000) The religion of the market, in: H. Coward & D. C. Maguire (Eds) *Visions of a New Earth: Religious Perspectives on Population, Consumption and Ecology*, pp. 15–29 (Albany, NY: SUNY Press).

Madgwick, S. (2000) There is no such thing as a free lunch, in: S. Holliday, P. Owen & C. Turner (Eds) *Journeys of Discovery*, pp. 61–64 (Oxford: Earthwatch Institute).

Margulis, L. (1997) Science education in the USA: not science, not yet education, in: L. Margulis (Ed.) *Slanted Truths: Essays on Gaia, Symbiosis and Evolution*, pp. 317–320 (NewYork: Copernicus-Springer Verlag).

Martin, P. (2000) The contribution of the non-institutional sector, *Environmental Education and Training in Europe, Proceedings of the Conference, Brussels, 3–4 May, 1999*, p. 92 (Brussels: European Commission) (Quoted in Palmer & Birch, 2003, op. cit.).

Martin, S. & Jucker, R. (2005) Educating earth-literate leaders, *Journal of Geography in Higher Education*, 29(1), pp. 19–30.

McCoy, M. & McCully, P. (1993) *The Road from RIO; An NGO Guide to Environment and Development* (Utrecht: International Books).

Michael, A. (2000) Foreword, in: *A Sustainable Wales – Learning to Live Differently: Consultation Document*, pp 4–5 (Cardiff, National Assembly for Wales) Available at: http://www.wales.gov.uk (accessed June 2002).

Mitford, H. (2000) Back to basics, in: S. Holliday, P. Owen & C. Turner (Eds) *Journeys of Discovery*, pp. 17–11 (Oxford: Earthwatch Institute).

Moore, R. & Wong, H. (1997) *Natural Learning: Creating Environments for Rediscovering Nature's Way of Teaching* (Berkeley, CA: MIG communications).

Naess, A. (1973) The shallow and the deep, long range ecology movement: a summary, *Inquiry*, 16, p. 95, (Reprinted in: A. Drengson & Y. Inoue (Eds) (1995) *The Deep Ecology Movement, An Introductory Anthology* (Berkeley, CA, North Atlantic Books).

Naess, A. (1987) Self-realization: an ecological approach to being in the world, *Trumpeter*, 4(3), pp. 128–131. (Reprinted in: A. Drengson & Y. Inoue (Eds) (1995) *The Deep Ecology Movement, An Introductory Anthology* (Berkeley, CA, North Atlantic Books).

NAW (2000) *A Sustainable Wales – Learning to Live Differently: Consultation Document* (Cardiff: National Assembly for Wales). Available at: http://www.wales.gov.uk (accessed June 2002).

Palmer, J. A. & Birch, J. C. (2003) Education for sustainability: the contribution and potential of a non-governmental organisation, *Environmental Education Research*, 9(4), pp. 447–460.

Patil, V. T. (1983) Gandhi's concept of basic education and its current relevance in India, in: V. T. Patil (Ed.) *Studies on Gandhi*, pp. 177–196 (New Delhi: Sterling).

Pawson, E. & Teather, E. K. (2002) 'Geographical expeditions': assessing the benefits of a student driven fieldwork methods, *Journal of Geography in Higher Education*, 26(3), pp. 275–291.

Pincen, T. & Finger, M. (Eds) (1994) *Environmental NGOs in World Politics: Linking the Local and the Global* (London: Routledge).

Rickinson, M. (2001) Learners and learning in environmental education: a critical review of the evidence, *Environmental Education Research*, 7(3), pp. 207–320.

Riddell, A. (2000) Snake in the grass, in: S. Holliday, P. Owen & C. Turner (Eds) *Journeys of Discovery*, pp. 95–98 (Oxford: Earthwatch Institute).

Robson, E. (2002) 'An unbelievable academic and personal experience': issues around teaching undergraduate field courses in Africa, *Journal of Geography in Higher Education*, 26(3), pp. 327–344.

Schultz, P. W. (2000) Empathizing with nature, the effects of perspective taking on concern for environmental issues, *Journal of Social Issues*, 56(3), pp. 1–13.

Schumacher College (2004) MSc in Holistic Science. Available at http://www.schumachercollege.org.uk/HolisticScience/HolisticScience.html (accessed September 2004).

Shah, A. & Treby, E. (2006) Using a community-based project to link teaching and research: the Bourne Stream Partnership, *Journal of Geography in Higher Education*, 30(1), pp. 33–48.

Shaxson, T. F., Tiffen, M., Wood, A. & Turton, C. (1997) Better land husbandry: re-thinking approaches to land improvement and the conservation of water and soil, *Overseas Development Institute, Natural Resource Perspectives*, 19, pp. 1–4. Available at http://www.odi.org.uk/nrp/19.html (accessed July 2003).

Sterling, S. (2001) *Sustainable Education: Revisioning Learning and Change* (Bristol & Dartington: Schumacher Society (Schumacher Briefings 6) & Green Books).

Stern, P. C. & Dietz, T. (1994) The value basis of environmental concern, *Journal of Social Issues*, 50, pp. 55–84.

TEMA (2004) *Türkiye Erozyonla Mücadele Ağaçlandırma ve Doğal Varlıkları Koruma Vakfı*. Available at http://www.tema.org.tr/ (accessed September 2004).

Tilbury, D. & Goldstein, W. (2003) *Supporting the United Nations Decade of Education for Sustainable Development, 2005—2014* (Gland, Switzerland: International Union for the Conservation of Nature (IUCN), Commission on Education and Communication) Available at http://www.lut.mah.se/nms/forskarnatverk/ESDstatementdoc6.pdf; and http://www.iucn.org/cec/documents/ACF8B55.pdf (acessed September 2003)..

Tilbury, D., Stevenson, R. B., Fien, J. & Schreuder, D. (Eds) (2002) *Education and Sustainability: Responding to the Global Challenge* (Gland, Switzerland: International Union for the Conservation of Nature (IUCN), Commission on Education and Communication) Available at http://www.iucn.cec.org (accessed May 2002).

Tordoff, M. (2001) Millennium programme news, *Earthwatch: News Magazine for Members*, Summer, p. 21.

Turner, C. (2000) Food for thought, in: S. Holliday, P. Owen & C. Turner (Eds) *Journeys of Discovery*, pp. 99–103 (Oxford: Earthwatch Institute).

UN (2003), *Resolution 57/254: United Nations Decade of Education for Sustainable Development*. Resolution adopted by the General Assembly. United Nations General Assembly, 57th Session, 21 February 2003, Agenda item 87 (a) 02 55612; Document: A/RES/57/254 (New York: United Nations). Available at http://www.unesco.ch/pdf/UNDekade.pdf (accessed August 2003).

UNCED NGO Forum (1993) Treaty on environmental education for sustainable societies and global responsibility, in: R. Pollard (Ed.) *The NGO Alternative Treaties from the Global Forum at Rio De Janeiro June 1–15, 1992* (revised ed). Available at http://www.igc.org/habitat/treaties/ (accessed June 2002).

UNESCO (2001) *The Lüneburg Declaration on Higher Education for Sustainable Development of 10 October 2001* (Paris: UNESCO) Available at http://www.unesco.org/iau/ghesp/LuneburgDeclarationFinal.html (accessed June 2004).

UNESCO (2002) *Ubuntu Declaration on Education and Science and Technology for Sustainable Development* (Paris: UNESCO).

UNESCO (2003) *United Nations Decade of Education for Sustainable Development* (January 2005–December 2014): Framework for a Draft International Implementation Scheme (Draft: July 2003). Available at http://www.jeef.or.jp/esdj/JF%20DESD%20Framework3.doc (accessed April 2004).

University of Plymouth (2004) MSc/PgDip Holistic Science. Available at http://www.plymouth.ac.uk/courses/postgraduate/taught/2216/MSc%2FPgDip+Holistic+Science (accessed September 2004).

Volk, T. L. (1990) The importance of learners doing research, *Environmental Communicator*, September/October. Available at http://www.edu.uleth.ca/ciccte/naceer.pg.pgs/alternate/pubfiles/241.trudivolk.htm (accessed May 2002).

Worsley, A. (2003) Developing external links through teaching and learning in geography and environmental science: the use of the mini-conference, *Journal of Geography in Higher Education*, 27(1), pp. 69–78.

Zlatic, M. (2003) Socio-economic aspects of degradation and soil management for sustainable development in mountainous regions, in: M. Zlatic, S. Kostadinov & N. Dragovic (Eds) *Natural and Socio-Economic Effects of Erosion Control in Mountainous Regions, Proceedings*, pp. 497–515 (Belgrade: Belgrade University, Faculty of Forestry/WASWC/CEKOR).

The Firm and Shaky Ground of Education for Sustainable Development

DAVID SELBY

Narrative

There was a large clearing in the forest, a large open area from which many footpaths led off in many directions. The people were disputatious. Some argued the merits of taking one footpath, some the merits of taking another, and yet others the merits of taking a third. They milled around in confused and contentious mood. Then they discovered what looked like a broad, firm and easy path that all might take, where all kinds of folk could walk together shoulder to shoulder. Many hurried towards it, relieved that their arguments could be brought to an end. In a sigh of collective relief, few were disposed to enquire whether the path was really heading in the right direction and whether the undemanding way it seemed to offer might discourage the further seeking and exploration of alternative pathways. Even fewer bothered to ask whether going down the path would really be good for the forest and its inhabitants.

The Firm Ground

Education for sustainable development currently enjoys huge momentum and is attracting exponential adherence. It is the educational manifestation of the concept of 'sustainable development' that first saw the light of day in the *World Conservation Strategy* (International Union for Conservation of Nature and Natural Resources, 1980), and that soared into prominence with the publication of the Bruntland Commission's report, *Our Common Future* (World Commission on Environment and Development, 1987). In the latter, sustainable development was defined as: "development that meets the needs of the present without compromising the ability of future generations to meet their needs" (1987, p. 43).

The global enthronement of sustainable development came five years later at the 1992 Earth Summit, Rio de Janeiro, where 179 governments agreed that human development aspirations and the so-called 'carrying capacity' of the environment were on collision course, and that sustainable development should become the overarching framework within which policy should be formulated and enacted. In the *Rio Declaration on Environment and Development* (UNCED, 1992a), the key principles of sustainable development were enunciated. Principle 1 lays down that "Human beings are at the centre for concern for sustainable development" while Principles 3 and 4 privilege development over environment, the former insisting that the "right to development must be fulfilled" and the latter laying down that "environmental protection shall constitute an integral part of the development process" (ibid., p. 9). The educational implications of sustainable development are sketched out in *Agenda 21: Programme of Action for Sustainable Development* (UNCED, 1992a). Formal and non-formal education, according to the *Agenda*, should conflate environmental and development education and, so conflated, ensure their integration as 'cross-cutting issues' in all disciplines using an amalgam of innovative and traditional pedagogies (ibid., pp. 264–265).

World leaders reaffirmed their Rio commitments at the September 2004 World Summit on Sustainable Development in Johannesburg, and proposed a Decade for Sustainable Development (DESD), a proposal adopted by the UN General Assembly in its December 2004 session (UNESCO, 2004, p. 11). DESD began in March 2005. A minimum list of underlying values for education for sustainable development has been flagged to guide DESD initiatives:

- respect for the dignity and human rights of all people throughout the world and a commitment to social and economic justice for all;
- respect for the human rights of future generations and a commitment to intergenerational responsibility;
- respect and care for the greater community of life in all its diversity, which involves the protection and restoration of the Earth's ecosystems;
- respect for cultural diversity and commitment to build locally and globally a culture of tolerance, non-violence and peace. (UNESCO, 2004, p. 14)

Within the UK there has been a plethora of initiatives directed towards mainstreaming education for sustainable development. In 2003 the then Secretary of

State for Education, Charles Clarke, launched a *Sustainable Development Action Plan for Education and Skills* (DfES, 2003). In January 2005, the Higher Education Funding Council for England (HEFCE) published, for consultation purposes, *Sustainable Development in Higher Education*, a draft support strategy and action plan for infusing sustainable development principles across the curriculum, teaching and learning, and estates aspects of higher education institutions (HEFCE, 2005a). In the light of the ensuing consultation, HEFCE issued a strategic statement and action plan (HEFCE, 2005b). In September 2004 Prime Minister Tony Blair, in an address on climate change, envisioned schools in which sustainability principles infused curriculum, teaching and learning, as well as school estate management, in an interconnected and synergistic way: "Students won't just be told about sustainable development, they will see and work within it: a living learning place in which to explore what a sustainable lifestyle means" (Brown, 2004, p. 9).

What explains the meteoric and seemingly inexorable rise of the idea of sustainable development and its educational outcropping, education for sustainable development? Globally, sustainable development provided a means of paving—some critics would say 'papering'—over the ongoing rift between the environmental lobby of the metaphorical North of the planet and the development lobby of the metaphorical South of the planet. Confronted by the need to act given the increasingly evident confluence of multiple environmental and social crises, it allowed for consensus around a theme persuasive enough to be attractive to both and also vague and diffuse enough to enable everyone to invest it with their own meanings.

Rio, writes Sachs (1995, p. 432), marked an "unholy alliance between development enthusiasts in the South and growth fatalists in the North". The former, "deeply hurt by the breakdown of development illusions" (ibid., p. 431) given that the plight of the majority had worsened since decolonization, called for further rounds of development in the name of social justice and "discovered environmental concessions as diplomatic weapons" (ibid., p. 432). In so doing, they implicitly embraced a development discourse "deeply imbued with Western certainties like progress, growth, market integration, consumption and universal needs" (ibid., p. 429). The South showed no inclination to abandon "the notion that the North shows the way for the rest of the world" (ibid., p. 432). Governmental representatives of Northern nations were not slow to join Southern politicians in locating environmental considerations within a framework of development goals that had, over the years, consistently reinforced the global hegemony of the North. Hence, as manifest in the *Rio Declaration*, Principle 4, cited above, environment came to be construed as a subset of development. This was not the case at the parallel Rio International NGO Forum where representatives of non-governmental organizations and educators from around the world produced 16 guiding principles offering a holistic, socially critical and transformative definition of environmental education for sustainable societies, including the following:

- Principle 1: Environmental education is not neutral but is value-based. It is an act of social transformation.
- Principle 9: Environmental education must recover, reflect and utilize indigenous history and local cultures.
- Principle 16: Education must develop an ethical awareness of all forms of life with which humans share this planet, respect all life cycles and impose limits on humans' exploitation of other forms of life. (UNCED, 1992b)

Dresner (2002, p. 1) describes the idea of sustainability as more rhetorically motivational than previous environment-related concepts in that "saying that you don't care that what you are doing is unsustainable sounds tantamount to saying that you are intellectually incoherent". He regards the Bruntland conflation of equity *within* and *between* generations in its definition of sustainable development as a 'political masterstroke' (ibid., p. 2) in that it assuaged longstanding suspicions amongst social justice *advocates* that environmentalists were unconcerned about the plight of the poor. He might have added that ongoing suspicions amongst some environmentalists that social justice advocates were lost in an anthropocentric myopia were also somewhat soothed. Hence, sustainable development not only drew strength by harnessing support from both sides of the metaphorical North/South divide but also because, in its interlinking of the quests for economic betterment, environmental protection, and intra-generational and intergenerational justice, it resonated with a wide range of socially critical interest groups who, thus, found themselves willing to sink (or, at least, fudge) their differences. In the world of education, education for sustainable development opened up the possibility of a broad coalition of environmental, development, human rights, peace and social justice educators. Educational groups that had long competed at the margins saw the prospect, under a new, common banner, of a place in the educational mainstream. For many such groups, any compromise has subsequently seemed justified as ministers of education assiduously endeavour to incorporate what has become known in shorthand as ESD into policy and practice.

In the eyes of some environmental educators, education for sustainable development was attractive in that it offered a means of loosening the clutches of natural science education on their field. Increasingly vociferous in their objections to environmental education being treated as a subset of the science curriculum (Russell *et al.*, 2000, p. 205), some saw education for sustainable development as offering leverage for bringing ethical, political, social and economic lenses to bear on the study of the environment. ESD, it was hoped, would rescue environment from the domineering and ethically and socially constraining redoubt of the science curriculum.

So, education for sustainable development seems to stand on firm ground. As an idea, it has garnered global adherence; it has brought a range of issue-specific interest groups together under a single banner; it enjoys support at the highest levels. A place in the educational mainstream seems assured.

Narrative

So, many forsook the narrow paths and took to the broad path. But is the path proving as firm as was hoped? Is it realizing its potential as a way forward? Is it benefiting the forest and the trees?

Lingering in the forest clearing are folk who have concerns about the broad path. Their concerns vary. Some know what 'development' without the qualifier 'sustainable' has meant, and continues to mean, and worry if 'sustainable development' will really be very much different. Some—environmentalists and ecologists in particular—worry that they have taken a broad path without the interpretation abilities and markers required to make sense of the path. Others worry whether the song of sustainable development can really capture the song of the Earth; whether it has been worth losing the turns, complexities and irregularities of the many paths they used to tread. Yet others worry whether the idea of 'sustainability literacy', much vaunted by ESD advocates, is a sufficient and appropriate educational response in the light of the global environmental crisis and global crisis in the human condition.

The Shaky Ground

Sustainable Development as Oxymoron

Writing in 1996, Dobson counted three hundred available definitions of sustainable development and sustainability (Dobson, 1996). The definitional range has probably increased, hydra-like, since then. For Worster (1995, p. 418), the gaining of widespread acceptance for the terms has been achieved "by sacrificing real substance". For Jickling (1994, p. 232), sustainable development "has become for many a vague slogan, a bold platitude, susceptible to manipulation and deception". "Against a backdrop of endless calls for sustainability, a hypnotic formula which has been endlessly repeated", he writes elsewhere (Jickling, 2001, p. 176), "we now have massive efforts to promote education for sustainability".

If the sustainability window is befogged, whose expertise, language and values are being given most voice as we enact sustainable development? Dobson (1996) argues that the debate about what we should be sustaining has, for the most part, been cornered by economists. Embedded within the mantra of sustainable development is a largely unquestioned embrace of the growth principle. The bulk of economists are pretty clear, even razor sharp, in their perception that sustainable development means sustained growth in the economy (Worster, 1995, p. 424). For them, the concept of sustainable development "emasculates the environmental challenge by absorbing it into the empty shell of 'development'" (Sachs, 1995, p. 433). Sustainable development "calls for the conservation of development, not for the conservation of nature" (ibid., p. 434) and is conceived of as identifying means of ensuring growth through less resource-intensive usage and through finding substitutes for increased extraction of 'natural capital', for instance, genetic engineering. The approach is managerialist and technicist, as exemplified by frequent references in *Agenda 21* (UNCED, 1992a) to 'managing resources', 'integrated environmental and economic accounting', 'increased coordination' and 'sound management'. Sustainable development as conceived by economists "by and large fails to consider any reduction of material standards of living and any attempt to slow down the accumulation dynamics. In short, alternatives to development are blackballed, alternatives within development are welcome" (Sachs, 1995, p. 436).

Environmentalists or ecologists who embrace the term ecological sustainability lack the definiteness of their economist counterparts. They see ecological sustainability as a matter of identifying and measuring the carrying capacity of an ecosystem in terms of the level of resource extraction it can bear. Unlike the economists, theirs is not an exact science and, a point to be returned to later, recent understandings of volatility within ecosystems have only served to increase their appreciation of its inexactitude (Worster, 1995, pp. 423–424). There are environmentalists, too, who resist the limitation of debate to exchanging numbers, estimates and other quantifiable data with economists. Measuring ecological footprints (Wackernagel & Rees, 1996) is not for them. Their environment is about beauty, awe, enchantment, reverence and sense of wonder (Carson, 1998; Selby, 2001).

"We need", writes Jickling (2001, p. 178), "to stop devaluing and apologizing for those values that cannot be measured or falsified by scientific experimentation".

So, we face a scenario where economists, in particular, are very certain and go about promoting development, and where environmentalists, in particular, are hesitant and unsure but go about promoting environmental sustainability. Environmentalists have embraced sustainable development and environmental educators have bought into education for sustainable development but not on a level playing field. Donald Worster (1995, p. 424) writes:

> In the much acclaimed partnership between advocates of ecological sustainability and development, who is going to lead whom? ... I fear that in that partnership it will be 'development' that makes most of the decisions, and 'sustainable' will come trotting along, smiling and genial, unable to assert any firm leadership, complaining only about the pace of travel... Sustainability is, by and large, an economic concept on which economists are clear and ecologists are muddled. If you find that outcome unacceptable, as I do, then you must change the elementary terms of the discussion.

Put another way, 'development' has become such a part of economic discourse that other renditions of its meaning we might bring to the table, renditions that would challenge and conflict with the prevailing discourse—for instance, cultural development, personal development, spiritual development—are all too easily drowned or, at best, marginalized.

If we accept the finiteness of the planet—that the planet is not an inexhaustible cornucopia—and if we interpret 'sustainable development' as 'sustainable growth', then the term becomes an oxymoron, a contradiction in terms, a "self-contained *non sequitur* between noun and modifier" (Disinger, 1990, p. 3). Sustained growth within a planet that is finite is not possible unless one limits the timeframe within which the growth intention applies and/or is selective about where the growth should happen.

Responding to such concerns, as raised by eco-theorists and environmental educators, some thinkers have sought to mollify or mount an alternative conceptualization of sustainable development. "By 'development'", writes Rigby (2004, p. 2), "we mean simply moving forward in time, rather than that the majority world has to convert to the western obsessions with competition and increasing materialism". Huckle (1996, pp. 10–11) distinguishes between 'weak' and 'strong' modes of sustainable development. He explains:

> In its weak mode it represents an emerging mode of regulation, involving forms of techno-managerialism, via which capital seeks to ensure a continued supply of the means and conditions of production on its own terms while maintaining the support of the majority of voters. In its strong form it represents a revised form of self-reliant community development which sustains people's livelihoods using appropriate technology.

The latter, in its sturdiest form, Huckle argues, involves a co-mingling of green socialist and utopian radical ideas and is marked by, on the one hand, pronounced governmental action to increase levels of social justice and to enhance quality of life and, on the other, bioregionalism, self-sufficiency, decentralization, direct democracy, and decision-making that remains mindful of the local biome. Huckle intimates that 'sustainable livelihood development' might offer a means whereby those supporting 'strong' sustainable development might capture the parent term (ibid., pp. 14–15).

Others have opted for alternative terminology that takes the development out of sustainability, such as 'education for sustainability', 'education for sustainable futures' and 'education for the development of responsible societies' (Sauve, 1999, p. 11). A powerful case for 'sustainable education' has been made by Sterling (2001) who argues that education can only contribute to social transformation if it relinquishes the modernist agenda characterized by managerial, mechanistic and transmissive approaches and comes to be informed by an ecological paradigm characterized by 'whole systems thinking', participation, empowerment and self-organization. In this way education can play a crucial role in helping foment a sustainable future.

Some critics contend that alternative conceptualizations and alternative terminologies are tantamount to window dressing in that many such initiatives continue to draw legitimization from national and international documents on sustainable development in which the growth principle is assumed (Jickling 1994, p. 235). From a developing world perspective, Padua (1993, p. 14) sees sustainable development as trapped in a "capitalistic model of expansion" that has harmed people and environments while sustainability offers potential in that it "implies changing values and setting new priorities" (ibid., p. 15). She concedes, however, that the "changing of behavior according to these new values may seem too altruistic to be adopted by privileged people".

The multiple definitions of sustainable development and ESD, the arguments surrounding them, and the emergence of alternative but related conceptualizations, speak to the process benefits of vagueness. Wals & Bawden (2005, p. 38) argue, under a sub-heading, "It is no use crying over vague definitions", that vagueness in defining ESD "has an enormous canvassing and heuristic capacity if it is systematically used as a starting point or operational device to exchange views and ideas. These ongoing discussions may generate fruitful working hypotheses for the concrete formulation of curricula, study-programmes, subject matter content and didactical arrangements."

Sustainable Development as Denial of Intrinsic Value

There has long been controversy and argument within environmental ethics over why we want to save nature (let us leave aside for now the assumption that we can save nature). A bold example concerns the tropical rainforests. 'Save the forests', some exclaim because the plants might carry the cure for human diseases such as AIDS. 'Save the forests', others say, not because of their potential usefulness to humans but because the plants and creatures there have intrinsic value—value in their own right—in that they have their own impulses, urges, motivations and life trajectory to fulfil. This argument is often put as one between those, on the one hand, adopting an anthropocentric view of nature, in which value is given according to human needs, and a bio-centric or eco-centric view of nature, in which the needs of the biosphere, including those of humans and the other-than-human, take primacy.

Definitions and explanations of sustainable development are largely underpinned by the instrumentalist assumption that the natural world is primarily there to meet the material demands of the human species. The 'Our' in the Bruntland Commission report title (WCED, 1987) clearly refers to humans exclusively, as does the reference to 'future generations' in the oft-repeated Bruntland definition of sustainable development.

Rio Principle 1 states boldly that "human beings are at the centre of concerns for sustainable development" (UNCED, 1992a, p. 9). The only substantive ethical issue that is raised in both documents concerns the equitable sharing of natural resources within and between generations within the carrying capacity of the planet. In much of the discourse surrounding sustainable development, nature is characterized as resource or *natural capital* or *ecosystem services* (Porritt, 2005, p. vi) and, secondarily, as waste container. The other-than-human is in subordinate position within a worldview that is primarily egocentric and technocentric (Sauve, 1999; Wals & Bawden, 2005).

Extending the same point, the concept of sustainable development, at least in most renditions, embraces the assumption that humans have both the ability and capacity to manage the future of the Earth. It is in our power and purview, it is assumed, to do the sustaining. The evocative images of the whole globe taken from space, inspiring in their time wonder, awe and humility regarding the delicacy, finiteness and wholeness of the planet, now whet the appetite of those bent on technological and managerialist domination of Earth (Sachs, 1995). It is interesting that some environmentalists and environmental educators enthusiastically embrace the concept of Gaia—Earth as an incredible and subtly powerful self-regulating system possessing consciousness—while also acquiescing implicitly in the hubris of human managerialism through a rather uncritical embrace of sustainable development. There is a contradiction here that needs working through.

Education for Sustainable Development as Lacking in Thematic and Epistemological Breadth

The possibility of root-and-branch challenge to education for sustainable development is reduced by a rhetoric and lexicon suggestive of completeness in formulation, when there is (and should continue to be) incompleteness.

Some critics of education for sustainable development have long argued that there is something anti-educational about an education that is *for* something, suggesting closure according to goals and outcomes before the learning process has even begun. "Is it educationally justifiable", writes Jickling (2000, p. 470), "to 'implant' a new normative system into the minds of students?". Education, such commentators argue, is about presenting the widest range of possibilities to students for critical analysis and for determination of their own position, rather than driving at preconceived outcomes. Such critics argue that we need to be wary of deterministic manifestations in the ESD agenda and should replace current tendencies to present the field as a 'package', a 'done-deal', with a view of the field as in process, contested, a provisional stepping stone in constantly shifting understandings (McClaren, 1993; Jickling, 1994, 2000). "If sustainable development is converted into an ideology rather than remaining an idea in the process of development, a working set of principles", warns McClaren (1993, p. 18), "then it will be intellectually fossilized, an insect idea trapped in conceptual amber". On these counts, it is worrying that so many statements and policies calling for education for sustainable development uncritically rehearse the Bruntland definition, now 19 years old, before moving on to the concrete implications of ESD for curriculum, teaching, learning and estates. The HEFCE consultation document, *Sustainable Development in Higher Education* (2005a, p. 5) is a case in point; a surprising case in that it would have seemed astute and in harmony with best academic practice to depict the concept as contested even if, in broad terms, desirable. Responding to objections to education for sustainable development received during the consultation, HEFCE maintained that 'a high-level definition such as Bruntland' was sufficiently inclusive to embrace multiple viewpoints, postponing 'more informed discussion' for 'a couple of years' (HEFCE, 2005b, pp. 9, 10), and, thus, tacitly embracing an 'in process' understanding of the concept.

Education for, Jickling (1994, p. 237) holds, is generally held to connote a training orientation. We train for some predetermined, frequently instrumental, goal. It is something less than education. As a term informing our educational prioritizations, education for sustainable development thus aligns with the technical and economic emphasis discernible within the unfolding of the concept of sustainable development.

On the other hand, as we move inexorably towards a cliff edge, do we argue about the evenness of the remaining ground and the nature and trajectory of the drop? If education for sustainable development or its younger sisters, such as education for sustainability and education for sustainable futures, are valid and urgent responses to social and planetary trends that threaten the global environmental and human condition with disaster, *educating for* (and *educating against*) may be seen as eminently justifiable and realistic responses. After all, education has long been characterized by educating for something in preference to something else that is undesirable, whether *for* health in response to smoking or the AIDS pandemic, or *for* peace in anticipation of, or in the aftermath of, war. It is also the case that setting educational goals within a broad values framework does not preclude argument or student self-determination; the scope for disagreement remains as both values understandings and practical implications are worked through, while space still exists for deep challenge to the values framework itself. We can educate *for* sustainable development, sustainability or sustainable futures while, at one and the same time, recognizing and flagging the contested nature of the field in question.

In this context it is important to identify significant areas that education for sustainable development and sustainability discourse tend to exclude or incorporate on their own terms. Here we are talking about a range of distinctive philosophical responses to the question of humanity's relationship with the environment, each response offering its own challenge to the learner on how to live ethically and responsively on the planet. The inclusion of each response not only problematizes and thereby extends the concepts of sustainable development and sustainability but also all other responses. In the list of such responses would be, inter alia:

- animal liberation philosophies, which claim that animals have rights, and offer a philosophical basis for the claim (Singer, 1983; Regan, 1988);
- bioregionalist philosophies, which call for humans to live simply and convivially within the place they have inhabited since birth or, if they have moved, reinhabited, i.e. through conscious processes have become native to (Traina & Darley-Hill, 1995);
- deep ecology, which calls upon us to think deeply about the human–nature relationship and to renounce the anthropocentrism of much of our thought and behaviours in favour of biospherical egalitarianism (Naess, 1995; Sessions, 1995);
- ecofeminist philosophies, which, running counter to the thinking of many deep ecologists, identify the problem as patriarchy rather than anthropocentrism, and argue that oppression and exploitation of women, minorities, peripheralized groups and nature are mutually reinforcing as well as intersecting in their dynamics (Warren, 1990; Hessing, 1993);

- environmental justice theories, which identify environmental problems as social justice problems whenever class, race/ethnicity and gender are significant factors in determining who experiences the effects of, and who controls the causes of, environmental degradation (Warren, 1996; Lousley, 1998);
- social ecology theories, which argue that environmental degradation is the outcome of inequalities and injustices within human society and that, if the latter are properly addressed, environmental degradation will go into reverse (Bookchin, 1998; Clark, 1998).

Placed alongside sustainability, these fields would raise critical issues surrounding the intrinsic or instrumental value of nature, the intersection of exploitation and oppression of the human and exploitation and oppression of the other-than-human; the moral status of humans, animals and environments, a growth-orientated versus no-growth society, human embeddedness in nature, the nature/culture dialectic, and the respective merits and pitfalls of local, bioregional and global frameworks for determining environmental and social futures. By oftentimes reciting a seductive mantra that can be all things to all interest groups, education for sustainable development has tended to flatten out contradictions, mollify tensions, and blur nuances and distinctions. As such it has acted as a somewhat diversionary device that has lessened the potential for deep learning arising from deep environmental debate. We stunt the potential of the broader fields of environmental ethics and philosophy by an over-concentration on sustainable development and sustainability that, by definition, do not in and of themselves lead us to consider what we may need or want to know about beauty, culture, the spiritual (Kumar, 2005) and life purposes.

In this regard, it is interesting that ESD advocates give centre stage to the concept of 'sustainability literacy'. In a publication emerging from its Higher Education Partnership for Sustainability with 18 UK universities (Parkin *et al.*, 2004, p. 9), Forum for the Future defines a 'sustainability literate person' as one who would be expected to:

- understand the need for change to a sustainable way of doing things, individually and collectively;
- have sufficient knowledge and skills to decide and act in a way that favours sustainable development;
- be able to recognize and reward other people's decisions and actions that favour sustainable development.

Such a definition raises a number of issues, beyond its probably unintended but nonetheless implicit signal that closure now applies to conceptions of the goals of education for sustainability. First, the employment of the term 'literacy' is unexplained and appears arbitrary. Is this literacy in the originally understood sense of the ability to read and write (to decode and encode text)? If so, it has very limited application within education exploring human–environment relations. Is this literacy in the extended sense offered by semiotics, the science of signs, under which we can learn to 'read' visual texts or even social events or interactions? Are we being asked to treat the environment as 'text'—which semiotics says we can do? If so, we have more problems in that the above definition of sustainability avoids reference to active semiotic engagement with the environment (within which there is human culture and society). Nor does it refer to the application of multiple ways of finding or reading meaning in trees, ecosystems or other biophysical phenomena. It seems that the term 'sustainability literacy' is being employed indiscriminately and, maybe, counter-productively. The definition above does not seem to align with what semiotics theorists call a 'strong' conception of environmental literacy employing a multiplicity of analytical and synthesizing modes of knowing 'text' and one's relationship to 'text' (Stables & Bishop, 2001, pp. 93–94). Additionally, does sustainability have a 'text' in the sense that elements in the environment, as well as the environment taken as a whole, have a 'text' that can be interpreted?

Forum for the Future has this to say about a 'sustainability literate person':

> A sustainability literate person will be equipped with a number of intellectual and practical tools that enable them to take decisions and act in a way that is likely to contribute positively to sustainable development. They will be able to make decisions on specific matters, such as advising on financial investment, buying food or writing new policy for prisons, by applying the 'at the same time' rule—that is, taking environmental, social and economic considerations into account simultaneously, not separately. (Parkin *et al.*, 2004, p. 9)

The word 'literate' is close cousin of 'literal' (taking words in their usual or primary meaning or, as we say, at their face value). Looking at definitions and conceptions of 'sustainability literacy', we may wonder where awe, enchantment, mystery, reverence, wonder, the oceanic and spiritual sense of connectedness we feel when we climb a mountain, or weave the waters of a difficult river in a canoe, have gone. To borrow from Jane Austen, such definitions and conceptions are too much about sense and not enough about sensibility. If we restore *environmental sensibility* to our sustainability aspirations, we can add radically new, and liberating, dimensions to our epistemology; dimensions that, given their current abandonment in education, will initially feel startlingly counter-cultural.

Education for Sustainable Development as Falling Short of its Promised Scope

While conceptions of sustainable development have from the outset embraced the issues of intra-generational and intergenerational justice, environmental security and peace, it appears that the respective issue-related 'educations' have not been equally represented in the discourses of education for sustainable development. It has been, for the most part, development and environmental educators who meet under the sustainability banner. Education for sustainable development, holistic conception though it is, has not attracted peace, social justice and anti-discriminatory educators to its courses and conferences to anything like the same extent. While the introduction to a recent UNESCO document extols indigenous peoples as exemplars of sustainable living and indigenous systems of education as worthy of emulation (UNESCO, 2002, p. 3), indigenous voices are still seldom heard within Northern sustainability discourse. The voice of the South, where non-accumulative sustainable living is still the day-to-day reality for many communities, is likewise rarely heard. There is a need to "investigate, interrogate, make visible and validate other knowledges and ways of knowing" in sustainable development and sustainability discourse, particularly those that have served such communities well (Okolie, 2003, p. 255).

It is also noteworthy that the future is less than strongly represented in sustainable development curricula. While it is obvious that the future is a vital consideration for education for sustainable development, the field has not overly drawn upon the curricular models and pedagogies of futures education so that learners are given the opportunity to consider, discuss and reflect on probable futures (futures that are likely to come about), possible futures (future visions, often emanating from the countercultural fringes, that cannot be ruled out as unrealizable) and preferred futures (futures, given our values and beliefs, that we would like to see realized), and to envision a range of alternative futures (Hicks, 1994; Selby, 2000).

Sustainable Development as inheriting an Outdated 'Orderliness' Conception of Ecosystem

When ecological science emerged in the second half of the nineteenth century, scientists drew on their experience of a well-ordered industrial process to depict ecosystems as well ordered and enduring assemblages of plants and animals with stable and rarely deflected relationships (Worster, 1995). Advocates of sustainable development have inherited this 'steady state' or stability disposition, ecosystems being depicted as essentially orderly, waltz like, mirroring a well-oiled and purring machine. The reference to machine is deliberate—out of the mechanistic worldview that has dominated Western culture for three hundred years comes the notion of nature and environment as machine (Selby, 2001, 2004). Out of such a conception of nature flows the notion that humans have the capacity and understanding to steer social and economic development along the safe side of the limits of nature. Sustainability "is a matter of accommodating the human economy to ... constancy and orderliness" (Worster, 1995, p. 421).

The pack of cards collapses, however, if we take on board more recent ecological thinking that nature, while seemingly still for periods, is inherently disorderly and liable to bouts of disturbance and chaotic turbulence. As the 2004 Asian Tsunami so tragically illustrated, nature is full of flux, instability, unpredictability and uncertainty. The mass extinction of species, writes Harding (2005, 2006), has also lowered the robustness of ecosystems so that they are less able to withstand turbulence. Any system, suggests Prigogine (1989), inevitably moves towards disequilibrium followed by wholesale and radical reconfiguration, a process that is productive of a new but more complex state of balance that itself will sooner or later tilt towards disequilibrium. Abrupt climate change, now predicted by a range of leading meteorological authorities as relatively imminent (IPCC, 2001; US National Academy of Sciences, 2002), would leave us witness to the deep turbulent potential of nature.

Shelving arguments around educating *for* something for the sake of argument, it would seem both wise and prudent to complement and, hence, enrich education for sustainability by also exploring and enacting *education for ephemerality*, *education for elusiveness* and *education for ineffability*. Recognizing the power and persuasiveness of the sustainability case, we can sidestep and compensate for the mechanistic residues within the concept by also fostering an ethic valuing the short-lived, the unfathomable, the unquantifiable, the indefinable; that which we feel and intuit but which defies easy description. An understanding of the ephemeral nature of things, in turn, connects to an appreciation of the vulnerability of things and this, in turn, connects to an ethic of humility, respectfulness and precaution. In this way, paradoxically, an ethic of sustainability is strengthened by also embracing an ethic of ephemerality, and vice versa. We are more likely to achieve the transformations that sustainability processes and goals require if we have a disposition that embraces transience in everything. There is a dynamic unity of opposites here. An understanding of the elusiveness of things is central to the re-enchantment of the Earth (Berman, 1981) and the concomitant reunification of science and spirituality (Griffin, 1988; Green, 2005), both, in the aftermath of centuries of hegemonic mechanism, also vital for realizing a sustainable future. A lived appreciation of ineffability, suggests Naess (1990, 1995, 1998), promotes creativity, diversity and inclusiveness, a sentiment somewhat echoed by Wals & Bawden (2005) in their apologia, cited earlier, for loose definitions of sustainable development.

The transience of things oftentimes invests them with beauty. T. S. Eliot's intensely transcendental yet elusive moment in the rose garden (Eliot, 1963) comes to mind in this regard. As another poet, William Butler Yeats, wrote so strikingly in *The Second Coming*: "Things fall apart, the centre cannot hold" (Hayward, 1968, p. 407). Has sustainability come to be too much about trying to hold the un-holdable, seeking the steady state but disregarding the ubiquitousness of transience, casting as potentially durable what, in the nature of things, is ephemeral? Confronted by a world in increasing disarray and dislocation, has it sought to apply a culture of permanence to nature and society when both are characterized by the impermanence of flow, the elusive and ineffable dance of things?

Narrative

So some stayed in the clearing bemused and troubled. Were their worries big enough and deep enough to avoid the broad path? Should they look for an alternative path that would be more congruent with what they valued? Or, should they be pragmatic, join the throng on the wide path, and seek every opportunity to make gains even against the give and camber of the path?

Some wrestled and wrestled in their minds with what to do. But the application of reason was not enough. Others smelt flowers, watched the busy-ness of insects, the silk of a butterfly's wing (the flap of which could touch off a weather cataclysm thousands of miles away) and touched the smooth bark of beech and the rough bark of oaks. Feeling the flow of life through themselves and what they witnessed, they declared that the key was to embrace a fundamental change in our attitude to nature based not on what we can extract from her but on what we can learn from her. Her lessons of cycles, flows, networks, partnerships, diversity and, yes, unpredictability, uncertainty and turbulence can and should infuse both the curriculum and process of our learning and teaching, as well as the way our learning institutions work. As long as we are sure that our way is deeply informed by the dynamics and processes of nature, we can walk the firm and shaky ground of any path.

Acknowledgements

The author is indebted to Donald Worster (1995) for inspiring the title.

References

Berman, M. (1981) *The Reenchantment of the World* (Ithaca, NY: Cornell University Press).

Bookchin, M. (1998) Social ecology versus deep ecology, in: J. Pojman (Ed.) *Environmental Ethics. Readings in Theory and Application*, pp. 155–163 (Belmont, CA: Wadsworth).

Brown, P. (2004) Blair calls for UK to lead on climate change, *Guardian*, 15, September, p. 9.

Carson, R. (1998) *The Sense of Wonder* (New York: HarperCollins).

Clark, J. (1998) A social ecology, in: M. E. Zimmerman, J. B. Baird Callicott, G. Sessions, K. J. Warren & J. Clark (Eds) *Environmental Philosophy: From Animal Rights to Radical Ecology*, pp. 416–440 (Upper Saddle River, NJ: Prentice-Hall).

Department for Education and Skills (DfES) (2003) *Sustainable Development Action Plan for Education and Skills* (London: DfES).

Disinger, J. F. (1990) Environmental education for sustainable development?, *Journal of Environmental Education*, 21(4), pp. 3–6.

Dobson, A. (1996) Environmental sustainabilities: an analysis and typology, *Environmental Politics*, 5(3), pp. 401–428.

Dresner, S. (2002) *The Principles of Sustainability* (London: Earthscan).

Elliot, T. S. (1963) *Collected Poems 1909–1962* (London: Faber & Faber).

Green, K. (2005) A heart full of wonder, *Resurgence*, 231, July/August, pp. 10–13.

Griffin, D. R. (1988) *The Reenchantment of Science* (Albany, NY: SUNY Press).

Harding, S. (2005) Halting mass extinction, *Resurgence*, 228, January/February, pp. 8–9.

Harding, S. (2006) *Animate Earth. Science, Intuition and Gaia* (Totnes: Green Books).

Hayward, J. (Ed.) (1968) *The Penguin Book of English Verse* (Harmondsworth: Penguin).

Hessing, M. (1993) Women and sustainability: ecofeminist perspectives, *Alternatives*, 19(4), pp. 15–21.

Hicks, D. (1994) *Preparing for the Future: Notes and Queries for Concerned Educators* (London: Adamantine).

Higher Education Funding Council for England (HEFCE) (2005a) *Sustainable Development in Higher Education: Consultation on a Support Strategy and Action Plan* (London: HEFCE).

Higher Education Funding Council for England (HEFCE) (2005b) *Sustainable Development in Higher Education: Strategic Statement and Action Plan* (London: HEFCE).

Huckle, J. (1996) Realizing sustainability in changing times, in: J. Huckle & S. Sterling (Eds) *Education for Sustainability*, pp. 3–17 (London: Earthscan).

Intergovernmental Panel on Climate Change (IPCC) (2001), *Third Assessment Report: Climate Change*. Available at: http://www.ipcc.ch/pub/reports.htm. (accessed January 2006).

International Union for the Conservation of Nature and Natural Resources (1980) *World Conservation Strategy* (Gland, Switzerland: IUCN).

Jickling, B. (1994) Studying sustainable development: problems and possibilities, *Canadian Journal of Education*, 19(3), pp. 231–240.

Jickling, B. (2000) A future for sustainability?, *Water, Air and Soil Pollution*, 123, pp. 467–476.

Jickling, B. (2001) Environmental thought, the language of sustainability, and digital watches, *Environmental Education Research*, 7(2), pp. 167–180.

Kumar, S. (2005) Spiritual Imperative, *Resurgence*, 229, March/April, pp. 6–12.

Lousley, C. (1998), (De)politicizing the Environment Club: Environmental Discourses and the Culture of Schooling. Unpublished MA thesis, Department of Curriculum, Teaching and Learning, Ontario Institute for the Studies of Education of the University of Toronto.

McClaren, M. (1993) Education, not ideology, *Green Teacher*, 35, pp. 17–18.

Naess, A. (1990) *Ecology, Community and Lifestyle: Outline of an Ecosophy* (Cambridge: Cambridge University Press).

Naess, A. (1995) The deep ecological movement: some philosophical aspects, in: G. Session (Ed.) *Deep Ecology for the 21st Century*, pp. 64–84 (Boston, MA: Shambhala).

Naess, A. (1998) The shallow and the deep, long-range ecological movement, in: L. P. Pojman (Ed.) *Environmental Ethics: Readings in Theory and Application*, pp. 134–137 (Belmont, CA: Wadsworth).

Okolie, A. C. (2003) Producing knowledge for sustainable development in Africa: implications for higher education, *Higher Education*, 47, pp. 235–260.

Padua, S. (1993) Sustainability versus sustainable development, *Green Teacher*, 35, pp. 13–16.

Parkin, S., Johnston, A., Buckland, H., Brookes, F. & White, E. (2004) *Learning and Skills for Sustainable Development: Developing a Sustainability Literate Society* (London: Forum for the Future/Higher Education Partnership for Sustainability).

Porritt, J. (2005) How capitalism can save the world, *Independent Extra*, 4 November 2005, pp. i–vii.

Prigogine, I. (1989) The philosophy of instability, *Futures*, 21(4), pp. 396–400.

Regan, T. (1988) *The Case for Animal Rights* (London: Routledge).

Rigby, W. (2004) The Decade of Education for Sustainable Development 2005–2015, *Jesus College Newsletter*, Michaelmas Term, p. 2.

Russell, C. L., Bell, A. C. & Fawcett, L. (2000) Navigating the waters of Canadian environmental education, in: T. Goldstein & D. Selby (Eds) *Weaving Connections: Educating for Peace, Social and Environmental Justice*, pp. 196–217 (Toronto: Sumach).

Sachs, W. (1995) Global ecology and the shadow of 'development', in: G. Sessions (Ed.) *Deep Ecology for the 21st Century*, pp. 428–444 (Boston, MA: Shambhala).

Sauve, L. (1999) Environmental education between modernity and postmodernity: searching for an integrating educational framework, *Canadian Journal for Environmental Education*, 4, Summer, pp. 9–35.

Selby, D. (2000) Global education as transformative education, *Zeitschrift für Internationale Bildungsforschung und Entwicklungspaedagogik*, 23(3), pp. 2–10.

Selby, D. (2001) The signature of the whole: radical interconnectedness and its implications for global and environmental education, *Encounter. Education for Meaning and Social Justice*, 14(1), pp. 5–16.

Selby, D. (2004) Dancing earth: radical interconnectedness and its implications for sustainability education, *Resurgence*, 226, September/October, pp. 21–24.

Sessions, G. (Ed.) (1995) *Deep Ecology for the 21st Century* (Boston, MA: Shambhala).

Singer, P. (1983) *Animal Liberation: Towards an End to Man's Inhumanity to Animals* (Wellingborough: Thorsons).

Stables, A. & Bishop, K. (2001) Weak and strong conceptions of environmental literacy: implications for environmental education, *Environmental Education Research*, 7(1), pp. 89–97.

Sterling, S. (2001) *Sustainable Education: Re-visioning Learning and Change* (Totnes: Green Books).

Traina, F. & Darley-Hill, S. (Eds) (1995) *Perspectives in Bioregional Education* (Troy, OH: North American Association for Environmental Education).

UNESCO (2002) *Education for Sustainability: From Rio to Johannesburg: Lessons Learnt from a Decade of Commitment* (Paris: UNESCO).

UNESCO (2004) *United Nations Decade of Education for Sustainable Development 2005–2014: Draft International Implementation Scheme* (Paris: UNESCO).

United Nations Conference on the Environment and Development (UNCED) (1992a) *Agenda 21* (New York: United Nations Department of Public Information).

United Nations Conference on the Environment and Development (UNCED) (1992b) *Environmental Education for Sustainable Societies and Global Responsibility: A Citizen's Treaty from the International NGO Forum of the UNCED, Rio de Janeiro* (Rio de Janeiro: UNCED).

US National Academy of Sciences (2002) *Abrupt Climate Change: Inevitable Surprises*. Available at: http://www.nap.edu/books/0309074347/html (accessed October 2005).

Wackernagel, M. & Rees, W. (1996) *Our Ecological Footprint: Reducing Human Impact on the Earth* (Gabriola Island, British Columbia: New Society).

Wals, A. E. J. & Bawden, R. (2005) Integrating sustainability into agricultural education: dealing with complexity, uncertainty and diverging worldviews, in: A. E. J. Wals (Ed.) *Curriculum Innovations in Higher Agricultural Education*, pp. 21–56 (The Hague: Reed Business Information).

Warren, K. (1990) The power and the promise of ecofeminism, *Environmental Ethics*, 12(3), pp. 125–146.

Warren, K. (1996) Educating for environmental justice, *Journal of Experiential Education*, 19(3), pp. 135–140.

World Commission on Environment and Development (1987) *Our Common Future* (Oxford: Oxford University Press).

Worster, D. (1995) The shaky ground of sustainability, in: G. Sessions (Ed.) *Deep Ecology for the 21st Century*, pp. 417–427 (Boston, MA: Shambhala).

The United Nations Decade of Education for Sustainable Development (2005–2014): Learning to Live Together Sustainably

Bernard P. Y. Combes

Sustainable development is basically about learning. It is a process that develops awareness, knowledge, and understanding of the environment and critical thinking skills. It is about respecting, valuing, and preserving the achievements of past generations. The socialization patterns of past centuries taught us to live unsustainably, thereby creating the social and environmental problems we must now address. We have to learn our way out of the dilemma. We have to learn to live sustainably.

A powerful international consensus emerged following the 1992 Earth Summit in Rio de Janeiro and became even stronger at the 2002 World Summit on Sustainable Development in Johannesburg. The international community confirmed that education is central to achieving sustainable development, and hence the 57th Session of the General Assembly resolved in December 2002 to proclaim the 10-year period beginning on January 1, 2005, as the United Nations Decade of Education for Sustainable Development (UNDESD), and designated UNESCO as the lead agency for the promotion of the Decade.

The Decade is a world programme to reorient education around the three pillars of sustainable development: economic, social, and environmental. It is clear that there can be no long-term economic or social development on a depleted planet. Education to develop the widespread understanding of the interdependence and fragility of planetary life support systems, and the natural resource base upon which human well-being depends, lies at the core of education for sustainable development.

Education for a sustainable future is about learning to:

- respect, value, and preserve the achievements of the past;
- appreciate the wonders and the peoples of the Earth;
- live in a world where all people have sufficient food for a healthy and productive life;
- assess, care for, and restore the state of our Planet;
- create and enjoy a better, safer, more just world;
- be caring citizens who exercise their rights and responsibilities locally, nationally, and globally.

DEVELOPING AN INTERNATIONAL IMPLEMENTATION SCHEME FOR THE DECADE

As the Lead Agency for the *Decade*, UNESCO was asked to develop an International Implementation Scheme (IIS) by consulting with the UN and other international organizations, governments, nongovernmental organizations (NGO), youth, and other stakeholders. It did so through consultation and wide dissemination of a basic framework, which was shared with its UN partners, governments, NGOs, civil society organizations, academics, and experts in the field whose reflections and experience were taken into account. More importantly, the Implementation Scheme has drawn on the various international educational initiatives already in process in order to strengthen the relationship between education and sustainable development. Notable examples are the Dakar Framework for Action adopted at the World Education Forum in 2000 and the United Nations Literacy Decade that began in 2003. To these must be added the United Nations Millennium Development Goals, which figure prominently in the Implementation Plan of the World Summit on Sustainable Development, and the Decade on Water for Life, which was officially launched on World Water Day 2005.

The Scheme places *people* at the centre of the Decade's goals, and speaks to the roles of stakeholders from local to global levels, and how the UN system and its partners will reach the desired outcomes. It outlines seven guiding principles for the promotion of the Decade and approaches for implementation:

- advocacy and vision building,
- consultation and ownership,
- partnership and networks,
- capacity building and training,
- research and innovation,
- information and communication technologies, and
- monitoring and evaluation.

The basic vision of the DESD is a world where everyone has the opportunity to benefit from education and learn the values, behaviour, and lifestyles required for a sustainable future and for positive societal transformation. This translates into five objectives, to:

- facilitate networking, linkages, exchange and interaction among stakeholders in ESD;
- foster an increased quality of teaching and learning in education for sustainable development;
- help countries make progress towards and attain Millennium Development Goals (MDGs) through ESD efforts;
- provide countries with new opportunities to incorporate ESD into education reform efforts.

Learning for Sustainability

Learning to change our world to make it more viable and sustainable is quite a challenge and calls for the need for learning to be personally empowering and enriching, and to respond to learners' diverse learning needs and intelligences. This basic idea initially was developed and supported by the Delors Report,[1] which highlighted four "pillars" or fundamental types of learning: learning to know, learning to do, learning to be, and learning to live together. To these four pillars, a fifth[2] can be added: learning to transform oneself and society.

- *Learning to know,* so as to acquire a taste for learning throughout life and for understanding the world. This concerns cognitive skills and reasoning.
- *Learning to do,* so as to be able to deal with many situations, and be an actor as well as a thinker. This focuses on practical skills and knowing how to act.
- *Learning to be,* so as to better develop one's personality and be able to act with greater autonomy, judgment, and personal responsibility. This relates to personal skills and dignity.

---

[1]For more details, see Delors et al. (1996). See also www.unesco.org/education/efa/ed_for_all/dakfram_eng.shtm for more information.

[2]The addition of this fifth pillar was suggested by a number of Latin American educators, as well as UNICEF during its own analytical process of the recommendations of the Delors Report; see Black (1999).

- *Learning to live together*, so as to develop an understanding of other people and their history, traditions, and spirituality, in order to participate and cooperate with others in all human activities. This has to do with social skills and social capital.
- *Learning to transform oneself and society*, so as to develop respect for the environment, for social solidarity, and for a nondiscriminatory, gender-sensitive world. This reflects a synergy of cognitive, practical, personal, and social skills to bring about sustainability.

This has been enhanced by Dr. Howard Gardner's theory of multiple intelligence, which looks at the fact that people employ several different types of intelligence, rather than one general type. There are eight types of intelligences: language, spatial, logic/math, body movement, musical, social, self, and nature.

Education for Sustainable Development Is a Dynamic and Evolving Concept

Education for Sustainable Development is a dynamic concept that utilizes all aspects of public awareness raising, education, and training to create or enhance an understanding of sustainable development, especially in terms of linking together the issues involved and stimulating changes in conduct. Education, broadly understood, is therefore inextricably linked to well-balanced development, which takes into consideration the social, cultural, environmental, and economic dimensions of an improved quality of life for present and future generations.

The concept of ESD essentially grew out of environmental education and development, and its central role was confirmed and strengthened at the World Summit in 2002. Education is a powerful motor of change for achieving sustainable development. We refer to an expanded vision of education whose holistic and interdisciplinary approach brings together the knowledge and skills needed for a sustainable future with the necessary changes in values, behaviour, and lifestyles. This means reorienting education systems, policies, and practices so that everyone, young and old, is empowered to make the decisions and take necessary actions, in their local cultures and contexts, to overcome the challenges facing our common future.

Hence the "education" in ESD embraces a wide range of learning experiences and programmes. The focus on basic education and literacy in the orientation of the Decade is important, but it also requires contributions from secondary education, technical and vocational training, and higher education, and from a wide range of other modalities of learning that may be labelled as non-formal education, professional development, and training. Thus, in our conceptualization of ESD, we have captured as wide a scope as possible so that all partners can contribute accordingly. At the same time, we believe that such an inclusive approach serves as a stimulus to improving the quality of education—an education that is relevant to the key challenges of living in the twenty-first century, an education that empowers people to exercise their rights with a sense of responsibility, an education that cultivates good citizenship locally, nationally, and globally.

Sustainable development is not a fixed goal, but rather an ever-changing concept and horizon, a mechanism for balancing different values, priorities, and opinions. Thus, ESD must achieve several things:

- develop an awareness of the concept of sustainability;
- ensure that the system is clear in its objectives by having the question of why we learn (that is, what are the expected learning outcomes) be of equal importance as what we learn, how we learn, where we learn, and who learns;
- enable learners to understand the importance of integrating among disciplines and the nature of interdisciplinarity;
- allow students to develop the skills to understand and act on both the global and local nature of the wide range of issues that are included in sustainable development; and

- instill in learners that ability and will to integrate sustainable living practices, for themselves and others, in their daily lives.

There is a growing demand for education to reflect upon its relevance to the modern world. While in the past much of the emphasis on education related to cognitive understanding and development, now there is a need to also address the social and other dimensions of learning. Education is expected to make a contribution to addressing sustainable human development, peace and security, and the quality of life at individual, family, societal, and global levels.

Building on more than 30 years of experience in environmental education, ESD must continue to highlight the importance of addressing the issues of natural resources (water, energy, agriculture, housing, biodiversity, for example) as part of its broad agenda. In particular, the links with social and economic considerations will enable learners to adopt new behaviours in the protection and use of the world's natural resources, which are essential for human development, and, indeed, survival.

A key challenge, however, is to ensure that our emphasis on environmental sustainability is no longer limited to environmental concepts alone—we have learned that it is the complex interactions among environment, society, and economy that have brought us to this unsustainable state in the world and we must work from an understanding of these interactions to learn how to live sustainably.

To learn to ensure environmental sustainability, within this larger framework, will require a reorientation of education systems, defined broadly. UNESCO is promoting educational reforms in all modalities of education, including formal and nonformal approaches, the media, teacher education, and at all levels from early childhood through higher education and lifelong learning. UNESCO also recognizes that this reorientation is essentially about the content, processes, and environments of education—about the quality of education.

Education for sustainable development is a vision of education that seeks to balance human and economic well-being with cultural traditions and respect for the Earth's natural resources. It emphasises aspects of learning that enhance the transition toward sustainability including futures education, citizenship education, education for a culture of peace, gender equality and respect for human rights, health education, population education, education for protecting and managing natural resources, and education for sustainable consumption. Pursuing sustainable development through education requires educators and learners to reflect critically on their own communities. The DESD promotes a set of basic values, processes, and behaviours that should be part of learning in all circumstances. It is these values, processes, and behaviours that will support environmental sustainability.

ENGAGE IN NEW PARTNERSHIPS

We must acknowledge that ESD is a daunting challenge for policymakers and educators alike. It is a challenge, furthermore, that is equally relevant and critical for both developed and developing countries. It is a challenge that tests stable societies and must also address post-conflict, postcrisis, and emergency situations. Thus, ESD lies at the heart of the quest to solve the problems threatening our collective future—problems such as poverty, nutrition, wasteful consumption, environmental degradation, global warming, urban decay, inordinate population growth, gender inequality, health-related issues (including HIV/AIDS), armed conflict, terrorism, and the violation of human rights.

This great endeavour calls for cooperation and collaboration from the grassroots level upward, as well as for new and creative forms of partnership. UNESCO is eager to work with educators, policymakers, governments, academia, associations, NGOs, and civil society groups to develop national action plans and to fill out the IIS.

REFERENCES

Black, M. (Ed). (1999). *Basic education: A vision for the 21st century,* Summary Report of the ninth Innocenti Global Seminar, UNICEF International Child Development Centre 25 October–3 November 1998. Florence: UNICEF.

Delors, J., Al Mufti, I., Amagi, I., Carneiro, R., Chung, F., Geremek, W., Kornhouser, A., Manley, M., Padrón Quero, M., Savané, M. A., Singh, K., Stavenhagen, R., Won Suhr, M., & Nanzhao, Z. (1996). *Learning: The treasure within* (Report to UNESCO of the International Commission on Education for the Twenty-First Century). Paris: UNESCO Publishing.

Qualifications and Curriculum Authority (QCA). (2000). *Curriculum guidance for the foundation stage.* London: Author.

UNESCO. (2000). *The Dakar framework for action—Education for all: Meeting our collective commitments (Adopted by the World Education Forum in Dakar, Senegal, 26–28 April 2000).* Paris: Author.

UNESCO. (1997). *Declaration on the responsibilities of present generations towards future generations.* Paris: Author. [On-line]. Available: www.unesco.org/cpp/uk/declarations/generations.pdf

UNICEF. (2000). *Defining quality in education* (Programme Division Working Paper Series). New York: Author. [On-line]. Available at: http://www.unicef.org/girlseducation/files/QualityEducation.PDF

ON THE WEB

- Delors Commission, www.unesco.org/delors/
- Earth Charter, www.earthcharter.org
- Education for All for Learning to Live Together: Contents and Learning Strategies, Problems and Solutions, http://www.ibe.unesco.org/International/ICE/46english/46menue.htm
- Gardner, Howard, http://www.pz.harvard.edu/PIs/HG.htm or http://www.howardgardner.com
- Göteborg consultation, www.learning2004.se/main.html
- Highlights of the Delors Report, http://www.unesco.org/delors/delors_e.pdf
- History of Education, http://www.socsci.kun.nl/ped/whp/histeduc/
- Instituto Fronesis, http://www.fronesis.org/
- Our Multiple Intelligences, http://www.literacyworks.org/mi/intro/quickreview.html or www.literacyworks.org/mi/intro/index.html
- UNESCO Education for Sustainable Development, www.unesco.org/education/desd

EE and ESD: Two Paradigms, One Crucial Goal

Rosalyn McKeown and Chuck Hopkins

INTRODUCTION

The launch of the United Nations Decade of Education for Sustainable Development (UNDESD) gives the education community opportunity to reflect on and discuss major issues that will affect the future well-being of our world. Discussions should include questions such as, "What is my discipline's contribution to a more sustainable future?" and "What are the ties and linkages between my discipline and ESD?" In this article we look at the similarities between environmental education (EE) and education for sustainable development (ESD). We also describe some lessons learned from more than 35 years of EE history. These lessons could help ESD avoid pitfalls common to nascent disciplines and to advance its efforts and chance of success.

EE AND ESD: WHERE IS THE OVERLAP?

The goals and dreams of environmental educators are similar to those of educators involved in ESD; both carry a vision for a better world. They envision a world in which business, industry, government, and citizens practice environmental stewardship, leave smaller ecological footprints, and participate in community-based decision making. They also envision a more just and equitable society, in which the well-being of the environment, society, and economy are balanced in the pursuit of development and quality of life for all members of society. Given that the goals of EE, as described in the Tbilisi Declaration, and the major concerns of ESD, as described in Agenda 21, have much in common, collaborative work to reach those goals could advance rapidly (UNESCO, 1978; United Nations, 1993).

Sustainability has three strands—environment, society, and economy. Concomitantly, ESD also deals with these three strands. It is readily apparent how EE can contribute substantially to the environmental strand of ESD and thereby to a more sustainable future. The advantage of collaboration between proponents of EE and ESD seems obvious. In fact, the similarities between EE and ESD have led to the formation of a myth among environmental educators around the world that ESD is simply EE renamed. As a result of this convergence of purpose, EE is a good entry or starting point for ESD. Given that many nations already have EE programs, they are poised to begin or substantially enhance the work of ESD.

Jaimie Cloud of the Cloud Institute for Sustainability Education in New York has identified core concepts of ESD and habits of mind. Core concepts of education for sustainability include ecological literacy; systems dynamics and systems thinking; multiple perspectives; place; sustainable economics; and citizenship, including participation and leadership. We see a great overlap between her list and EE. She also lists habits of mind inherent in education for sustainability, including understanding of systems as the context for decision making; intergenerational responsibility, mindful of and skillful with implications and consequences; protection and enhancement of the commons; awareness of driving forces and their impacts; assumption of strategic responsibility; and paradigm shifter. Many of these habits of mind are also familiar to environmental educators (Frederico, Cloud, Byrne, & Wheeler, 2002).

WHAT WISDOM AND EXPERIENCE CAN EE OFFER THOSE WHO ARE WORKING IN ESD?

Both EE and ESD have much in common. Even being largely created from United Nations Conferences (EE from Stockholm in 1972 and ESD from the Earth Summit in Rio de Janeiro, 1992), as opposed to being constructed by educators, earmarks their common heritage. Both disciplines are based on topics that the United Nations sees as essential—environment and sustainability—yet EE and ESD are relegated to the realm of "adjectival educations." (Adjectival education is a term used by the late John Smythe of Scotland to describe those disciplines that need the word "education" attached to a term to assure their roles in formal education. In this group, he included human rights education, peace education, environmental education, and development education.) Striving not only to exist but also thrive within formal and nonformal education is no easy task for either EE or ESD, especially in the face of today's budget restraints, competition for clients, and an overly full K–12 curriculum.

The field of EE has learned a great deal over its 35-plus-year history. Some of the lessons are applicable to ESD. Because both EE and ESD are multidisciplinary, in nature environmental educators can impart experience and, in some cases, wisdom to ESD. For example, environmental educators have learned how to infuse environmental themes and content into existing disciplinary curriculum.

Advocates of ESD currently are wrestling with the question of whether ESD should be infused through the curriculum or taught as a separate class. In the early years of EE in the 1970s, the debate of whether EE should be a free-standing discipline or simply infused into other disciplines was quite heated. By 1977 and the Intergovernmental Conference on Environmental Education held in Tbilisi, Georgia, the writings leaned heavily toward infusion. While this is a practical approach to delivering EE, it greatly impedes the development of EE as a discipline. Over the years environmental educators have learned to focus on the growth and evolution of EE to maintain a place in the educational discourse and to remain relevant to the needs of society. Education for sustainable development must learn from this experience and avoid the "infusion confusion" that environmental educators such as Rick Wilke and others at the University of Wisconsin–Stevens Point so adeptly identified and dealt with more than 25 years ago (Wilke, 1980). Environmental education experience and literature show that both can be effective. Circumstances and policies often lead to one or the other; nevertheless, both can be effective.

Both EE and ESD call for behavior change. Education for sustainable development, like EE, assists people to rethink their behaviors toward the environment so they may become better stewards of the environment if they so choose. In addition to this environmental stewardship, ESD also calls for social tolerance, equity, and justice, which requires cultural changes in interactions among peoples. Environmental education experience shows that knowledge and awareness are not sufficient to bring about behavior changes, but that people also must have skills and values to support that knowledge and awareness. Environmental educators also know that giving people a chance to participate in an activity that uses both knowledge and skills increases the likelihood of behavior change (Hungerford & Volk, 1990). Education for sustainable development faces deeply rooted behaviors when it addresses the issues inherent in moving toward more sustainable production and consumption in the developed world. Experience in EE shows us that here, too, awareness and knowledge are not enough.

Environmental educators have learned valuable lessons partnering with social marketing and environmental campaigns. The presence of environmental educators at the outset of planning these campaigns is important to overall programmatic success; however, creating a binder full of messages and lesson plans to give to teachers to inculcate an audience is not effective. This might be a valuable message for our ESD colleagues.

Education for sustainable development, like EE in the 1970s and 1980s, is not taken seriously by ministries of education around the world. Again, they see reading, writing, and arithmetic as core content and ESD as nonessential. This is an unfortunate mindset, because ESD has much to offer every nation. Environmental education associations have learned to work with curriculum committees, textbook publishers, and policy writers to insert EE into educational programs and materials. Education for sustainable development could profit from this experience.

Education for sustainable development, like EE, deals with thorny issues that face society. Environmental education pioneered the teaching of controversial issues as a core strategy of developing critical thinking skills in formal education at all levels. Environmental education also has developed frameworks and strategies for teaching and analyzing issues in fair and balanced ways (Clark, 2000; Pennock & Bardwell, 1994; Ramsey & Hungerford, 1998; Ramsey, Hungerford, & Volk, 1998; McKeown et al., 2002). Education for sustainable development could use and adapt these frameworks, further cementing the positive relationship between EE and ESD.

Education for sustainable development has yet to pursue the difficult issues of defining what it means to be an informed citizen in terms of sustainability. Environmental education tackled definition of environmental literacy and how to measure it in the 1990s. These assessment efforts can serve as a pattern for ESD in defining and measuring what it means to be knowledgeable about sustainability and to lead sustainable lives. Existing elements of environmental literacy and economic literacy along with key aspects and attributes of social development could contribute to the definition and construction of sustainability-related literacy.

Perhaps EE also could help support ESD in the arena of improving basic education. Chapter 36 of Agenda 21, Promoting Education, Awareness and Training, identified four major thrusts of ESD: (1) improving the quality of and access to basic education, (2) reorienting existing education to address sustainability, (3) improving public awareness, and (4) providing training for business, industry, and government. Environmental education already works in the second and fourth thrusts; it also could contribute to improving basic education. Students in many countries decry the lack of relevancy of the curriculum to their daily lives. We know from studies by the State Environmental Education Roundtable (SEER) that children from many ethnic groups enjoy school when the environment is used as an integrating concept to teach disciplinary requirements such as natural science, social science, and math. These studies showed that academic performance, attitude toward school, and attendance all improve when the environment is used as an integrating context for the curriculum (Lieberman & Hoody, 1998; SEER, 2000).

HOW CAN ESD ENHANCE THE PRACTICE OF EE?

The UNDESD offers an opportunity to revitalize EE. Collaboration with ESD would promote what EE has been working toward for years. The UNDESD calls for an alliance of existing like-minded disciplines and efforts and creates an international bandwagon to clamber for education that leads to a more sustainable future.

The need for a more sustainable future underscores the importance of balancing the economic and social disciplines with environmental disciplines. This balance would place environmental educators in conversation with economic educators and social studies/science educators. The ensuing conversations may be awkward at first, but if all persist the dialog could be rich and advance all of these disciplines.

Environmental education already has a place at the ESD table. In fact, much of the current leadership for ESD comes from the existing EE community. We know that we will not, however meet our goals for a more sustainable future by ourselves. Environmental problems are worsening faster than we as environmental educators can handle. A more sustainable future will take educators of many disciplines working together. Let's be good participants in the UNDESD, bring our rich educational history and best practices with us, and at the same time perhaps accomplish our own dreams of an environmentally sustainable future.

REFERENCES

Clark, P. (2000). Teaching controversial issues. *Green Teacher, 62*, 29–32.

Frederico, C. M., Cloud, J. P., Byrne, J., & Wheeler, K. (2002). Kindergarten through twelfth grade education for sustainability. In J. C. Dernbach (Ed.), *Stumbling toward sustainability*. Washington, DC: Environmental Law Institute.

Hungerford, H. R., & Volk, T. L. (1990). Changing learner behavior through environmental education. *Journal of Environmental Education, 21*(3), 8–21.

Lieberman, G. A., & Hoody, L. L. (1998). *Closing the achievement gap: Using the environment as an integrating context for learning*. Poway, CA: State Education & Environment Roundtable.

McKeown, R., Hopkins, C., Rizzi, R., & Chrystalbridge, M. (2002). *Education for sustainable development toolkit, version 2*. Knoxville: University of Tennessee, Waste Management Research and Education Institute. [On-line]. Available: http://www.esdtoolkit.org

Pennock, M. T., & Bardwell, L. V. (1994). *EE toolbox—Workshop resource manual: Approaching environmental issues in the classroom*. Ann Arbor: University of Michigan.

Ramsey, J. M., & Hungerford, H. R. (1998). So . . . you want to teach issues. In H. R. Hungerford, W. J. Bluhm, T. L. Volk, & J. M. Ramsey (Eds.), *Essential reading in environmental education*. Champaign, IL: Stipes Publishing L.L.C.

Ramsey, J. M., Hungerford, H. R., & Volk, T. L. (1998). A technique for analyzing environmental issues. In H. R. Hungerford, W. J. Bluhm, T. L. Volk, & J. M. Ramsey (Eds.), *Essential reading in environmental education*. Champaign, IL: Stipes Publishing L.L.C.

State Education & Environment Roundtable (SEER). (2000). *Californian student assessment project: The effects of environment-based education on student achievement*. San Diego: Author.

United Nations. (1993). *Earth Summit Agenda 21, The United Nations Programme of Action from Rio*. New York: Author. [On-line]. Available: http://www.un.org/esa/sustdev/documents/agenda 21/index.htm

UNESCO. (1978). *Final report of the Intergovernmental Conference on Environmental Education*. (UNESCO publication Ed/MD/49). Paris: Author.

Wilke, R. (ed.). (1980). Avoiding infusion confusion, unpublished manuscript. Stevens Point: University of Wisconsin.

Some Systems Thinking Concepts for Environmental Educators during the Decade of Education for Sustainable Development

Jaimie P. Cloud

The goal of education for sustainability (EFS) is "to develop in young people and adults new knowledge and new ways of thinking needed to achieve economic prosperity, participate democratically, secure justice and equity, and all the while regenerate the health of the ecosystems, the gift upon which all life and all production depend" (The Cloud Institute, 2005). The environmental education (EE) movement has been instrumental in bringing awareness, knowledge, heart, and political capital to the plight and to the beauty of our natural systems and has forced many of us to think more deeply and profoundly about our relationship to nature. What then can the Decade for Education for Sustainable Development and, more specifically, what can we as Educators for Sustainability, contribute to the EE community?

Recognizing that EE and EFS are not the same, but do share a common interest in achieving a quality of life for all within the means of nature, I think one of the greatest opportunities that EFS can offer to EE that will strengthen its capacity over the next 10 years is the contribution of the tools, concepts, archetypes, and "habits of mind" of systems thinking and system dynamics education—a core content area of EFS. Although one can teach systems thinking and system dynamics without teaching about sustainability, one cannot do the reverse.

Systems thinking and system dynamics education encourage us to look at the relationships between and among the parts of a system—not just at the parts themselves—and they help us to understand the implications of those relationships over time. We know from ecologists that everything is interconnected to everything else on this planet, and systems theorists and educators have a great deal to teach us about how to prepare young people (and ourselves) to think and act in light of systems as the context for decisions making. One (of seven) of the dimensions on our "Rubric for a "Whole Systems Thinker" (The Cloud Institute, 2005) entitled *Understanding of Systems as the Context for Decision Making*[1] measures the extent to which one sees both the whole system and its parts, as well as the extent to which an individual can place one self within the system. This kind of thinking and acting is critical to environmental educators from an instructional point of view as well as from the point of view of developing partnerships and plans to strengthen the field of EE over the next 10 years. (For more on systems thinking/system dynamics education got to www.clexchange.org and www.watersfoundation.org.)

I will highlight two examples of concepts of systems thinking and system dynamics education—entry points and mental models—to illustrate their usefulness.

[1]A rubric is a tool that communicates what quality looks like, and what accomplishment or mastery means in a particular context. Rubrics generally appear in the form of a matrix. Down the left-hand column are the dimensions (the ingredients of quality) of the rubric, and across the rows are descriptions of the degrees of quality (1 = the poorest degree of quality and 4 or 5 = the highest degree) of that dimension.

ENTRY POINTS: WHERE DO WE BEGIN?

One very useful concept of systems thinking/system dynamics education is the concept of *entry points.* The basic idea is this: A system is made up of two or more parts that interact with one another over time. Systems are "nested" in other systems. A relationship, a body, an engine, and a rain forest are all systems. A system is not linear, rather it is more weblike. It is dynamic. There is no one way into a system. For example, if a person is feeling ill, and your goal is to assist in making that person feel well, you might enter into a diagnosis by asking, "Where does it hurt?" On the other hand, another friend might enter by asking, "What did you eat this morning?" Then again, another might ask, "What kinds of materials have you used to renovate your new apartment?" All of those questions are generated by certain experiences, expertise, and interests, and all are interconnected to one another and to the person who is not feeling very well.

If one takes a holistic or "whole systems" approach to the diagnosis, any one of those questions will lead you to the others and to a more comprehensive understanding of the situation.

For many environmental educators, the entry point to their involvement with local, regional, or global sustainability/sustainable development is their love for and connection to the flora and fauna of nature, their understanding of the significance of the natural systems to life on the planet, or all of these. For others, their interest in sustainable development comes from their love for and connection to the issues of mental and physical human health. Still others are drawn to the entrepreneurial challenge that unsustainability poses to our survival. There are people whose entry point into sustainability is their desire for economic well-being, justice and equity, issues such as human rights, poverty, or climate change, and their sense of intergenerational responsibility, place, or self-efficacy. For some, the entry point is simply and profoundly spiritual. All of those entry points are connected to and interdependent upon one another, and all are critical to the move toward sustainability.

If your ultimate goal is to achieve sustainability—either because of your interest in or passion for something or because of your perspective ("where you stand depends on where you sit" (Banyai 1995), it is critical that you understand the concept of entry points. There is no "right place" for an entry point. There is no hierarchy or preferred sequence for an entry point—no "first here and then there." No matter what your interest, perspective, or entry point, you and your interests are inextricably interlinked to all the other interests, perspectives, and entry points. We are all interdependent on one another and on the natural systems. This way of thinking binds all of us through our common interests, affords us many more allies (in some cases seemingly strange bedfellows), and does not require us to convince one another which entry point is the "right" or "most important" one. The pursuit of self-interest must be considered in light of the context of interdependence.

How might it be beneficial for environmental educators to make use of the concept of entry points? Is it being done by some already?

MENTAL MODELS

Another interesting concept of systems thinkers and system dynamicists and educators is that of mental models. A mental model is made up of your values, your assumptions, your education, and your experience. It is a paradigm—a frame through which you understand the world around you. Transcending paradigms requires an experience or set of experiences that compels you to think and see things differently. Another dimension in our "Whole Systems Thinker's Rubric" is entitled, *Paradigm Shifter.* That dimension measures "the extent to which one recognizes mental models and paradigms as guiding constructs that change over time with new knowledge and applied insights." If you "accept that things are the way they are because that is the way they have always been" (a description of the poorest degree of quality of a *paradigm shifter* "1" [lowest level] on our rubric), then you are possibly working with some dated mental models. "Resources are unlimited on Earth and nature is a stock of resources to be converted to human purpose" is a mental model that many economists and "strip" miners are still employing today. "Everything revolves around the Earth—and by extension, us" was the mental model of the Church of Rome before Copernicus proved otherwise in 1543 AD (or until 1992 when the Church of Rome conceded that Copernicus *might* have been right).

Mental models give rise to goals, structures, rules, delays, and parameters (Twelve Leverage Points to Intervene in a System, Donella Meadows). They are the sources of human systems, and open-minded people can update/shift their mental models when the need arises, thus allowing the possibility of new, more elegant systems to emerge. The pedagogy of paradigm shifting is rooted in experiential, learner-centered approaches to teaching and learning. Master paradigm shifters are:

- able to expose and examine mental models;
- able to evolve/alter/improve mental models and paradigms when proven necessary;
- skilled at communicating the value of the new mental model and paradigm;
- able to demonstrate vigilant attention paid to our habitual patterns of thinking (mental models, paradigms, unquestioned assumptions, resignation, etc.); and
- able to hold the tension of paradox and controversy without trying to resolve it quickly, and will be decisively influential on our ability to "be on the turn" toward a sustainable future (The Cloud Institute, 2005).

Shifting paradigms "when proven necessary" is the work of educators for a sustainable future. A few of the germane mental models that we have uncovered in our work, and those that have proven to be "necessary to shift" in order to move toward a sustainable future, include "the Titanic syndrome," "the zero sum game," and "the social trap."

The Titanic Syndrome

This mental model goes "We are going down anyway—so I [and my family] might as well go first class." If you imagine the kinds of goals, structures, rules, and behavior that arise out of this mental model, you can begin to understand the problem. If, on the other hand, you value "intergenerational responsibility" and you understand the necessity of:

- taking responsibility for the fact that the well-being of future generations is largely dependent upon the choices and decisions you make (as well as the choices and decisions of others) during your lifetime; and
- choosing, designing, planning, making decisions, and acting in ways that will benefit the "7th generation" (The Cloud Institute, 2005),

then you can also imagine the kinds of goals, structures, rules, and behaviors that will arise from that mental model.

What is the goal? Which mental model(s) will drive the structures, rules, and behaviors designed and applied to reach it?

The Zero Sum Game

The "zero sum game" (Stahl, 1999) is the type of game in which there are winners and losers. If your mental model for a game, (even the "big enchilada" game of life), is based on the winner/loser paradigm, then, when playing a game, any game, you will play to win. Who wants to be a loser? If, however, your mental model for a game is the "nonzero sum game" in which the players are interdependent and with their life support systems, for example, then you know that the only way to win that game is if everyone wins. The structure is different, the rules are different, and, therefore, if you want to "win" the game, the behavior is different.

The Social Trap

This mental model goes: "It doesn't make any difference what I do—because "*nobody* else is doing it" or "*Everybody* else is doing it, so why shouldn't I?" You stand on your chair at a concert to get a better view, but before you know it everyone is standing on a chair. You have the same view as before, but now you work harder for it. This social trap, like the Tragedy of the Commons, arises when what holds true for the members of a group, taken separately, does not hold true of the group taken together. The opposite of a social trap is collective action. Just as locks are made to keep honest people honest, we live in communities in which we are mutually responsible for one another and for the group, of which we are a part.

CONCLUSION

In 1949, Aldo Leopold wrote in *A Sand County Almanac* that "All ethics so far evolved rest upon a single premise: that the individual is a member of a community of interdependent parts. His instincts prompt him to compete for his place in the community but his ethics prompt him to co-operate (perhaps in order that there may be a place to compete for."

Given the goals of EE, which mental model(s) will drive the structures, rules, and behaviors designed and applied to reach them?

Whether you are a sustainability educator, or an environmental educator, or both, these and many, *many* other concepts, tools, and archetypes of systems thinking and system dynamics education and the other core content, competencies, and habits of mind that characterize EFS will improve, enhance, and contribute to your work and your life. Come on over, the water is fine.

REFERENCES

Banyai, I. (1995). *Zoom.* New York: Viking Books.

Cloud Institute for Sustainability Education. (2005). Available: www.sustainabilityed.org.

Leopold, A. (1949/1966). *A sand county almanac,* New York: Oxford University Press.

Stahl, S. (1999). *A gentle introduction to game theeory.* American Mathematical Society.

Costanza, R. (1987). Social traps and environmental policy, *BioScience, 37*(6), 407–412.

Jaimie P. Cloud is the founder and president of the Cloud Institute for Sustainability Education (formerly the Sustainability Education Center) in New York City. Ms. Cloud teaches extensively, and writes and facilitates the collaborative development of numerous interdisciplinary instructional units, courses, and programs that are designed through the lens of sustainability.

Challenging a "Closing Circle": Alternative Research Agendas for the ESD Decade

Lucie Sauvé and Tom Berryman

CORE QUESTIONS

The object of our professional work is the reconstruction of the complex web of personal and social relations to the environment, considered as a crucial educational issue. We conceptualize and practice EE (or "environment-related education," following Paul Hart's expression, 2003, p. 3) as an essential dimension of education that emphasizes the close relationships between the human and the "more-than-human-world," woven in the same life matrix. It interprets culture and nature as two intertwined dimensions of our living milieu. It considers environmental matters as socio-ecological realities and examines the links between eco-logy and eco-nomy: the *logos* (logic, theory and discourse) and *nomos* (rules, custom) of *oikos* (our shared habitat or house) in light of a critical and constantly evolving eco-sophy (knowledge, wisdom). In our professional practice—mainly centered on educators' professional development—research, teaching, and social involvement in field projects are closely interconnected reflexive activities.

Through our projects, one of our observations is that students, colleagues, teachers, and other educators often are attracted to all sorts of "new" concepts and language (they have recently "discovered" through their readings or encounters), ranging, for example, from "place-based education" to "community-based social marketing to foster sustainable behavior." Facing the seductive attraction of what is "new"—"new" seen as "better"—and also facing the large range of theoretical and practical possibilities for environmental education, we keep co-learning with them through simple questions, so as to challenge or double-check what too often appears self-evident:

- What do I mean when I talk about the "environment"?
- What is "education" to me? Where does this meaning come from?
- What is my understanding of "environmental education"? How did I construct it?
- What does "development" mean to me?
- What about the meaning of this other idea called "sustainable development"?
- And then what about "education for sustainable development"?
- Where do these ideas come from?
- Upon which type of reasoning or arguments do they rest?
- What are the various foundations upon which my own educational endeavors rest?
- What are some of the possible blind spots of my own educational theory and practice?

These are not rhetorical or abstract or useless questions. We ask these questions and many others to educators and to ourselves in the hope of continuously improving the meaning and relevance of our educational practice, both to widen and to deepen its prospects. Because of its complexity, educating about the relation with the environment calls for diversity, for the recognition and exploration of the many diverse ways of conceiving and practicing EE. The questions we raise aim at creating a reflexive distance with one's own educational history, thinking, and practice and also help to historicize the field.

HISTORICIZING THE FIELDS OF EE AND ESD

Our reading of the history of the field of EE is paradoxical. On the one hand, through our exploration of the richness, the depth, and the importance of educational writings concerning the ontogenic dimension of our human relation with the environment, through examining philosophically and ethically inspired "environmental" literature and also documenting some of the currents (models and strategies) of EE as they are theorized and practiced in different parts of the world and diverse cultures, we realized the field of EE was potentially and actually much more fertile and diversified than the formal proposals that stemmed from the Belgrade and Tbilissi conferences of 1975 and 1977, centered on environmental problem solving. On the other hand, we grew more and more wary as we witnessed a rising tide of almost purely instrumental views of EE where, as an example, education is reduced to a means of implementing a globalized mix of (highly questionable) developmental and environmental agendas, such as in *Agenda 21.*

We undertook a research project to analyze international proposals for EE that arose through the past 30 years, starting from the Stockholm conference of 1972 to the Johannesburg one of 2002. Through a content analysis of these proposals, notably focusing on the representations of "education," "environment," "development," "environmental education," and "education for development" they carry, we were staggered to see how the range of approaches to the environment have somehow been constantly narrowing. Even though the rhetoric of the proposals is increasingly about expanding the so-called narrow perspectives of EE and bringing about a "new paradigm," their actual content essentially presents education as an instrument for the conservation of the environment, which is reduced to the status of resource for economic development, itself seen as an essential precondition and goal for social development. In the conceptual framework of sustainable development (represented by three interrelated spheres: economy, society, and environment), economy is a driving force strangely reified and situated outside society, and which regulates the relations between society and environment. In the essentially anthropocentric ethics and occidental developmentalist evolutionary view of the world it proposes, the relations between human and nature (or society and environment) are reduced to the couple manager-resources, thus reducing both the environment (inputs for economy) and human nature (human as consumer and human capital "resource" for economic growth). This "cosmology" exacerbates the tendency already present through the 30-year story of international proposals for EE, which was born, let's recall, in the crucible of the united Nations (UN) "New world economic order" (1974), worried about the preservation of "raw materials" and the sharing of profits with "underdeveloped" countries. The "new" feature of education for sustainable development is that it now finally consecrates the shift from an environmental perspective ("a healthy human environment needs careful development") to a developmental one ("sustained economic development needs sustained environmental resources"). The claims of an expansion of the field of EE through ESD and DESD can thus rather be seen as an enclosure. More than 30 years after Barry Commoner (1971) wrote *The Closing Circle,* another closing seems to be expanding.

We are well aware that advancing the idea of education for sustainable development as part of a closing circle, as part of educational and environmental problems, is unsettling for many people. This idea is generally not welcomed for various reasons. Stakeholders associated with the advancement of these proposals (which entered the spheres of political programs) do not wish for contestation, they wish for consensus, for progress, quantifiable progress, often through indicators. Most actors in the field are convinced of the goodness, the fairness, and the soundness of education for sustainable development. But again, as educators and researchers, we need to be reflexive, we need to ponder very seriously the worldview we advance through our educational endeavors, through our choice of language, through our practice, through the themes we tend to prefer, and so on.

SOME ELEMENTS OF AN ALTERNATIVE AGENDA

The ESD Decade, a diffusion strategy entrusted to UNESCO by the UN Economic and Social Council to promote a worldwide politicoeconomic program, offers a new context in which to pursue such reflections through our research projects and teaching programs, following an alternative agenda from which we present the following elements:

- Exercise a critical watch regarding languages, discourses, and practices. Identify potentially hegemonic strategies in some lines of thought. For example, the rather usual promoting of educational activities on "water resources as the blue gold of the future" or on "biodiversity as genetic pools or reserves" fail to acknowledge how loaded these are with almost purely market economy approaches to the environment. Issues of language often are discarded as unimportant by many educators. While we recognize language as only one dimension of practice, for us, treating it disparagingly as a minor detail compared with action is dramatic. As Piaget noted, "every language contains a logic and a cosmology, and the child, while learning to speak at the same time or even before he learns to think, thinks according to the adult social milieu" (1926/1947, p. XL).
- Examine and experience various educational proposals for their heuristic potential to stimulate the search for political and economical alternatives within societies. Promote educational interventions that facilitate the exploration of and development of alternative cosmologies. Promote initiatives of social development that carry us "beyond development."
- Develop a "pedagogy of uncertainty" and of humility as an alternative to the naive assurance sometimes associated with sustainability. Learn to live with uncertainty, recognizing and dealing with the absence of knowledge. Be wary of large-scale projects for salvation and ideologies presented as monolithic driving powers, however virtuous they can be. Related to the notion of uncertainty, it is also important to associate "risk education" with an education for socioenvironmental resiliency, according to the proposal of Arturo Curiel Ballestero (2005). Such resiliency can only be lived through the multiplicity of singular projects, culturally and contextually relevant, aiming at creative "resistance" (Aubenas & Benasayag, 2002) as opposed to grand universal projects (as the one of global sustainable development) that impose themselves as "slogans" and moulds for thought, in spite of their call to "local agendas," which are, in fact, small-scale replicas of the same planetary project.
- Celebrate the diversity of theoretical and practical possibilities in EE: at least 15 trends regrouping a very large diversity of models and strategies have been developed through the last decades (Sauvé, 2005). Education for sustainable development in only one of the many referential frameworks in which EE (or environment-related education) can be theorized and practiced. The possibilities of other referential frameworks also should be examined: political ecologies (which strive to integrate issues of nature and society so as to overcome the dualism between culture

and nature), ecodevelopment (which integrates cultural anthropology), ecosocialism, ecofeminism, social ecology, and so on.

- Reappropriate our history of EE, as Edgar González Gaudiano (2002) invites us to do. Exert a vigil with regards to the historical reconstructions made through deforming prisms. Reappropriate our professional and cultural identity, without withdrawing. Keep on enriching this identity through our professional experiences, our exchanges, and the occasions of fertile interbreeding between various fields of education (like health education or peace education), social sciences, environmental sciences, and others.
- Pursue diagnostic assessments. Where EE seems "defectively oriented" or too limited in some particular application, as sometimes decried by ESD proponents, let's colearn with participants in these projects, possibly through the "core questions" mentioned above, as ways to enrich these initiatives rather than change them for a whole "new" educational project whose foundations remain eminently debatable and that, on the practical level, has not yet proven reliable.

While doing this, we can take up the challenge of trying to meet zones of educational intervention that ESD cannot meet as Bob Jickling (2004) signals, working both in wider and deeper ways to rebuild how we relate to the world. Environmental education can suggest paths allowing us to move beyond "sustainable development," to travel other paths and to seek breaches in this new closing circle.

REFERENCES

Aubenas, F., & Benasayag, M. (2002). *Résister, c'est créer.* Paris: La Découverte.

Commoner, B. (1971). *The Closing Circle: Nature, Man and Technology.* New York: Alfred A. Knopf.

Curiel Ballestero, A. (2005). Le territoire comme milieu d'apprentissage et de construction de la résilience sociale en Mésoamérique. *Éducation relative à l'environnement—Regards, Recherches, Réflexions, 5.* In Press.

González Gaudiano, E. (2002). Revisitando la historia de la educación ambiental. In L. Sauvé, I. Orellana, & M. Sato, (Eds.), *Textos escogidos en educación ambiental* (pp. 23–37). Montréal: Les Publications ERE-UQAM.

Hart, P. (2003). *Teacher's thinking in environmental education.* New York: Peter Lang.

Jickling, B. (2004). *Sustained poverty and sustainable development: The role of environmental education.* Paper presented at the Second World Environmental Education Congress, Rio de Janeiro, September 2004.

Piaget, J. (1947). *Les représentations du monde chez l'enfant: avec le concours de onze collaborateurs.* Paris: Presses universitaires de France. Originally published in 1926.

Sauvé, L. (2005). Currents in environmental Education. *The Journal of Environmental Education, 10.*

Education for Sustainable Development and Global Citizenship—The UK Perspective

Douglas Bourn

INTRODUCTION

Learning and understanding more about sustainable development had become a feature of policy initiatives and programmes by a number of countries prior to the decision at the Johannesburg Summit to promote a Decade on the subject (Scott & Gough, 2004a; Huckle & Sterling, 1996). But research and evaluation of programmes on sustainable development education over the past 10 years have, in the main, highlighted the initiatives as being little more than an extension and development of environmental education (Reid, 2002).

The aim in this article is to remind readers that development education is an important root of sustainable development education. The launch of the Decade of Education for Sustainable Development (DESD) provides an opportunity to ensure that international and national programmes are closely linked to understanding the world in which we live, the divisions between rich and poor, and the need to engage people in working for a more just and equitable world. Furthermore, by reviewing progress to date in England, this article will suggest there has been a distinct lack of clarity and debate about what is particular about education for sustainable development (ESD). As a consequence, many of the national policy initiatives have been little more than an extension of environmental education (EE) with limited objectives.

DEVELOPMENT EDUCATION AND EDUCATION FOR SUSTAINABLE DEVELOPMENT

Development education has moved on from being about learning about development to encouraging an understanding of how the global and the local are interconnected. In the United Kingdom and most of Western Europe, it is seen as giving people the skills and knowledge to engage in society to secure global as well as local and national change in order to create a more just and equitable society (Bourn, 2003; Osler, 1994; see also www.deeep.org and www.dea.org.uk).

For example, development education practice in England is closely linked to debates and programmes around areas such as active citizenship, human rights, improving the quality of life, and understanding of cultural diversity (Development Education Association [DEA], 2001). The main national policy document for schools produced for the Department for Education by the DEA refers to global issues being part of "young people's everyday lives," and the national curriculum for schools in England makes direct reference to education as a route to "understanding society all levels and a commitment to sustainable development at personal, national and global levels" (Department for Education and Skills [DfES], 2005). In addition, one of the eight concepts of the Global Dimension outlined by the Department for Education is sustainable development.

UNESCO AND UN DECADE ON EDUCATION FOR SUSTAINABLE DEVELOPMENT

In promoting the idea of the decade, UNESCO recognised the environment and development roots of ESD, but stated that it needed to have a moral and visioning perspective (UNESCO, 2002). This approach has been developed to see ESD as a dynamic concept that ... develop(s) the knowledge, skills, perspectives and values which will empower people of all ages to assume responsibility for creating and enjoying a sustainable future. It is about the way we live our lives, the way we respect the lives of others—far and near, present and future—and our attitudes to the world around us.

UNESCO's vision of ESD makes explicit the links to "education for all" and social justice, not necessarily a key feature of programmes to date in leading industrialised countries. Their implementation plan refers to the need to reformulate national education policies; ensure there are appropriate financial resources, engagement of broader stakeholders and civil society; and above all the need to promote debate and dialogue about the importance of the decade.

EDUCATION FOR SUSTAINABLE DEVELOPMENT IN ENGLAND

The United Kingdom could, from an initial reading of what is happening on ESD, be seen as one of the few countries that already has begun to implement many of the aims and goals of UNESCO's strategy. The United Kingdom Government's Sustainable Development Education Panel from 1998 to 2003 attempted to promote strategies that engaged with broader societal agendas and made connections with current educational initiatives. It defined ESD as "about developing the knowledge, skills, understanding and values to participate in decisions about the way we do things individually and collectively, both locally and globally, that will improve the quality of life now without damaging the planet for the future" (DETR, 1998).

In developing this definition within the context of the school curriculum, the following concepts were suggested as incorporating its main principles: *interdependence, citizenship and stewardship, needs and rights of future generations, diversity, quality of life, sustainable change, uncertainty, and precaution* (DETR, 1998).

Throughout the life of the panel, however, the following key issues continued to emerge as major challenges:

- lack of clarity as to what is meant by education for sustainable development related to how we communicate its key messages and principles;
- overemphasis within education policymakers and practitioners to see ESD as about the environment and green issues;
- Learning agenda not seen as central—all too often interpreted as environmental management indicators;
- recognition that closer connections to debates in society about citizenship, social inclusion, health, and quality of life matters need to be made.

The Fourth Annual Report of the Panel raised concerns about the absence of a positive vision and that all too often sustainable development was compartmentalised (DEFRA, 2002).

In September 2003 the (DfES) launched its Sustainable Development Action Plan. Two of its objectives appear to build on the work of the Panel. "All learners will develop the skills, knowledge and value base to be active citizens in creating a more sustainable society" and "We will make effective links between education and sustainable development to build capacity within local communities" (DfES, 2003). In addition and grafted onto the Plan were objectives related to environmental management and standards: *'We will pursue the highest standards of environmental management across all properties owned and managed by The Department and its associated bodies* 'and' *We will encourage and support all publicly-funded educational establishments to help them operate to the highest environmental standards'* (DfES, 2003).

In implementing the Action Plan, the UK government has reflected this duality of aims and objectives. It is easier to make progress on environmental indicators than raising new and challenging debates about the relationship of ESD to the future purpose of education; the results to date in the views of the key stakeholders in the sector have been very disappointing (for examples of draft strategies that reflect this approach, see especially Higher Education Funding Council for England [HEFCE] 2005).

The implementation strategy from UNESCO states, "ESD is fundamentally about values with respect at the centre: respect for others, including those of present and future generations, for difference and diversity, for the environment, for the resources of the planet we inhabit" (UNESCO, 2005).

What has been missing from the implementation programme in England has been values and the learning outcomes we are all trying to achieve. If ESD is not seen as connected to developing greater understanding and skills in what is happening in the world today, then what is its purpose? There are two main reasons for this: the desire by politicians to see progress and putting pressure on policymakers to deliver, and the lack of clarity about what is EfSD.

The government's action plans and strategies have been too top down and based on short-term targets and goals as though they would somehow secure some magical behavioural change (see evidence of Charles.Clarke, Minister of Education to EAC report) (EAC, 2003). The UK government's strategy for sustainable development launched in March 2005 states, "Formal education has a role to play in forming good habits at an early age." Also the examples given are all about making schools "more environmentally friendly and sustainable" (DEFRA, 2005).

Policy development and implementation on ESD in the United Kingdom, and probably in other countries, has gone ahead of debating what we are trying to achieve, taking risks, encouraging innovation, and reflecting on what is good practice.

By rushing into producing policies and plans there has been a lack of debate and dialogue as to what is meant by the terms being promoted. As a result most of the initiatives branded under DfES's Action Plan in England have been little more than a rebranding of traditional environmental awareness and management practices.

Until there is a clarity about what is meant by ESD and a recognition that it is about a long-term learning process, there is a danger it will be reduced to environmental management indicators rather than empowering people to be responsible and active global citizens.

As Juergen Rost has stated:

> Education for sustainability is to a greater extent a concept that stems from an expression of (international) political will. It could be understood as a kind of mission from the political arena, given to education professionals and academics, to design an educational concept that correctly deals with the necessary requirements for sustainable development in our world. (Rost, 2004, pp. 6–8)

Scott and Gough have (2004) stated that learning has to be at the heart of what we understand to be sustainable development education. Understanding sustainable development is complex and to many people it will seem impossible to achieve. They suggest, *"Sustainable development cannot possibly mean an 'end state' to be achieved because there are no end states. If sustainable development means anything it can only be a way of describing an adaptive approach to managing human-environment co-evolution"* (Scott & Gough, 2004b, p. 253).

Some of the key problems in England, and probably in other countries, are the following:

- Overemphasis on ESD being linked to environmental agendas and that by learning

about sustainable development, people's behaviour will magically change with regard to transport use, consumption patterns, and energy use.
- Little recognition of the development context, particularly the Millennium Development Goals.
- Reduction of ESD to a series or collection of issues such as food, transport, and energy use, with no recognition of the holistic and interconnected nature of ESD.

Huckle (2003) suggests that ESD is about understanding the social practices that shape and are shaped by different discourses. It is also about cultivating critical choice amongst discourses.

EDUCATION FOR SUSTAINABLE DEVELOPMENT AND GLOBAL CITIZENSHIP

It is therefore suggested here that any strategies for promoting ESD have to be linked to people's active engagement in society. What makes ESD potentially so exciting, and to governments and decisionmakers so challenging, is that for it to have any impact it necessitates a sense of responsibility for and involving people in decision making in new ways. If one takes the UNESCO framework, sustainable development is not about environmental economic indicators but about challenging values, attitudes, and ways of living, of proposing that to live in a sustainable society and on a sustainable planet with values of equity, interdependence, cooperation, and citizenship having a central role.

If ESD is to be really effective, therefore, it must be rooted in approaches toward learning and education that are participatory, about economic and social change, and, above all, give people the skills, confidence, and knowledge to improve quality of life for themselves and for others at local, national, and global levels. You cannot divorce global citizenship from ESD.

In Wales two government advisory panels, one on ESD and one on Global Citizenship, have come together under the following definition:

> *ESD and Global Citizenship is about:*
>
> - *the links between society, economy and environment and between our own lives and those of people throughout the world;*
> - *the needs and rights of both present and future generations;*
> - *the relationships between power, resources and human rights;*
> - *the local and global implications of everything we do and the actions that individuals and organisations can take in response to local and global issues.* (ACCAC, 2002)

If sustainable development is about the interrelationship of environment, economy, and society, it means including the agendas of citizenship, and social inclusion, combating poverty at local, national, and at global levels, and addressing general public concerns about the quality of life. It is about learning about how we can move toward a more sustainable society for all.

REFERENCES

Awdurdod Cymurysteran Curriculum ac Asersu (ACCAC). (2002). *Education for sustainable development and global citizenship.* Cardiff, ACCAC, DFID. Estyn, Welsh Assembly.

Bourn, D. (2003). Towards a theory of development education. *The Development Education Journal, 10*(1), 3–6.

Development Education Association (DEA). (2001). *Global perspectives in education—The contribution of development education.* London: Author.

DETR. (1998). *Sustainable development education panel, First annual report.* London: HMSO.

Department for Environment, Food and Rural Affairs (DEFRA). (2002). *Education for sustainable development—Learning to create quality of life. Fourth annual report of SDE Panel.* London: Author.

DEFRA. (2005). *Securing the future—UK sustainable development strategy.* London: Author.

Department for Education and Skills (DfES). (2003). *Sustainable development action plan for education and skills.* London: Author.

Department for Education and skills (DfES). (2005). Developing a global dimension to the school curriculum (rev. ed.), London: DFES DFID DEA.

Higher Education Funding Council for England (HEFCE). (2005). *Sustainable development in higher education* (Higher education Funding Council for England—Consultation). Bristol: Auhor.

Huckle, J. (2003). *Education for sustainable development.* Draft paper for Teacher Training Agency, London.

Huckle, J., & Sterling, S. (1996). *Education for sustainability.* London: Earthscan.

Environment Audit Committee (EAC). (2003). Learning the sustainability lesson: Report of Environment Audit Committee, House of Commons. London: Author.

Osler, A. (1994). *Development education.* London: Cassell.

Reid, A. (2002). Discussion on the possibility of education for sustainable development, *Environment Education Research, 8*(1), 5–8.

Rost, J. (2004). Competencies for global learning. *The Development Education Journal, 11*(1), 6–8.

Scott, W., & Gough, S. (2004a). *Sustainable development and learning,* London: Routledge/Falmer.

Scott, W., & Gough, S. eds. (2004b). *Key issues in sustainable development and learning,* London: Routledge/Falmer.

UNESCO. (2002). *From Rio to Johannesburg: lessons learnt from a decade of commitment.* Paris: Author.

UNESCO. (2005). *Decade for education for sustainable development 2005–2014, International Implementation Scheme.* Paris: Author, 5.

Curriculum for the Bioregion: Learning to Live Sustainably in Our "Life Places"

Jean MacGregor

BIOREGIONALISM AND SUSTAINABILITY

As the twenty-first century begins, the media relentlessly confronts us with two complex, oppositional forces in the world: on the one hand, tribal factionalism and religious fundamentalism, and on the other, global consumerist capitalism. Benjamin Barber (1995) argues that these two forces are spawning a new cartography that transcends nation-states. Another major force, fed by globalization and population growth, is the strain on the Earth's resources and ecosystems (Kane, 2002; Worldwatch Institute, 2004, 2005). In response, UNESCO's "Decade of Education for Sustainable Development" and the Earth Charter offer promising frameworks for a world increasingly stressed yet increasingly lived in common. These proposals suggest that it is not enough simply to take "action steps." Rather, we need a more comprehensive vision for understanding the systems on which our ecological and human communities depend—visions for thinking, learning, and acting.

"Sustainable development" is one framework. "Bioregionalism" is another. Both phrases have evolved in an attempt to create a powerful, encompassing vision of planetary wellness and regeneration. The ideal of "sustainable development" grew out of important commissions and conferences on international and environmental development (United Nations Conference on Environment and Development [UNCED], 1992; World Commission on Environment and Development [WECD], 1987). "Bioregionalism" has had more humble beginnings: it emerged as a grassroots idea in idealistic, even utopian books by American practitioner-philosophers of sustainable agriculture Wendell Berry (1977) and Wes Jackson (1995), writers Peter Berg (1978) and Kirkpatrick Sale (1985), novelist Ernest Callenbach (1975), and poet Gary Snyder (1974, 1990). These thinkers argued that we must become thoughtful, responsible dwellers of our places so that all life systems might be sustained.

Whereas "sustainable development" is an abstract term subject to multiple connotations and debate over its etymology and usefulness (Corcoran & Wals, 2004; Dobson, 1996; Jickling, 1992, 2004), the term "bioregion" is quite concrete. As Peter Berg has pointed out, bioregion means, literally, a "life-place" (1978). Debates simmer here as well about definitions and about which criteria (hydrological, ecological, botanical, geographic) should be used to bound or name a given bioregion. Quite apart from the activist, political notions associated with "biogreion*alism*" that emerged in the 1970s, the idea of bioregional thought and practice has quietly taken hold as a focus of research, assessment, and planning (Bernard & Young, 1997; Johnson, Swanson, Herring & Greene, 1999; Lewis, 1996; Thayer, 2003; Wackernagel & Rees, 1996).

I see these frameworks nested within each other. *Sustainability* is the global end—global in both the literal and figurative sense—and *bioregional understanding and stewardship* offer a means toward that end. As landscape architect Robert Thayer (2003) cogently argues:

> A life-place framework will be judged not on how "warm and cuddly" it makes people feel but on whether it contributes . . . to the fulfillment of needs of life on earth: clean water and air; sufficient food, shelter, and clothing; peace from violence; a sense of meaning in life . . . and enough of all of this to sustain life for other living systems as well as for our own species. When I look beyond the pragmatic requirements of a life-place approach, I see a simple set of axioms: People who stay in place may come to know that place more deeply. People who come to know a place may come to care about it more deeply. People who care about a place are more likely to take better care of it. And people who take care of places, one at a time, are the key to the future of humanity and all living creatures. . . . Embedded in the bioregional idea, therefore, is a very general hypothesis: that a mutually sustainable future for humans, other life-forms, and earthly systems can best be achieved by means of a spatial framework in which people live as rooted, active, participating members of a reasonably scaled, naturally bounded, ecologically defined territory, or life-place. (pp. 6–7)

Learning to know and care for our places is a tall order. But not an impossible one. On January 1, 2005, the Washington Center for Improving the Quality of Undergraduate Education launched "Curriculum for the Bioregion," an initiative to prepare college students, as well as ourselves, to live in a world where the complex issues of environmental quality, environmental justice, and global sustainability are paramount. The Washington Center is a 51-college network in the state of Washington (USA). For the past 20 years, this public service center at The Evergreen State College has been a leader in higher education curriculum reform, professional development for faculty and staff, organizational change, and capacity-building.

OPPORTUNITIES

Cascadia as the Learning Site

The most obvious resource for creating bioregional curriculum is the bioregion itself. Here on the northwestern edge of North America, we reside along the Pacific "rim of fire," where colliding tectonic plates rouse earthquakes and volcanoes. Dramatic geologic forces define this region, as does a dramatic landscape: majestic mountains, towering forests, and islands, estuaries, and sounds. This region is often called Cascadia, after the major mountain range along its western edge; it spans two countries and includes British Columbia, Washington, Oregon, Idaho, and adjoining parts of three other states.

For centuries, Cascadia's ecosystems have sustained forests, salmon, and abundant wildlife. They also have sustained diverse indigenous peoples, who have sustained a rich cultural heritage in spite of devastating diseases and practices visited upon them by diverse migrants who settled in their midst. Now, the 15 million people who live in Casacadia participate in the most advanced technological practices known to humankind: high-technology agriculture, medicine, software, transportation, and trade. The region is facing rapid growth, congestion, and pressures on every resource. Within the next 20 years, demographers predict, seven more cities of 200,000 or more will grow in the Puget Sound basin alone (Puget Sound Action Team [PSAT], 2004); within the next 100 years, the region's population will quadruple. Can we act to embrace new residents and sustain healthy communities while at the same time sustain the healthy ecosystems on which so many livelihoods, not to mention our sense of place and heritage, depend? Could our collective understanding and practice of sustainability actually respond to the larger trends in the world? Influence them? These are the questions we are asking.

College as a Venue for Learning and Commitment

Post secondary education is an opportune time for introducing students to issues of sustainability and the vision of sustainable development.

College-level students are intellectually ready for the kind of integrative learning, systems analysis, and critical and reflective thought so essential for understanding issues of ecosystem health, globalization, and sustainability. College students are also at a formative stage of personal and ethical development, poised to make decisions about being and acting in the world (Parks Daloz, 2000). Engagement with meaningful questions and problem-solving can plant seeds of motivation and hope at these critical moments in students' development.

In both the United States and Canada, this bioregion has well-organized systems of publicly funded 2- and 4-year colleges and universities and many independent universities as well. Many have been leaders in establishing robust environmental studies programs. In recent years many institutions have initiated sustainability projects, involving students, faculty, and staff in changing campus practices and infusing sustainability concepts in coursework.

A Climate of Innovation in the Region

Over the past two decades, the Washington Center has introduced several curriculum reform initiatives in the region that have attracted strong networks of faculty and staff. The Center is recognized nationally as a resource for the development of interdisciplinary curricula, and also has led projects on math and science reform, cultural pluralism and diversity, and globalization. These initiatives have helped to foster a climate of innovation among colleges in the region, where interdisciplinary study, active and collaborative student learning, and education for a diverse democracy are not only shared aspirations but also expanding practices.

A Wealth of Bioregional and Sustainability Resources

Cascadia has long been known for conservation activism and interests in sustainability. Strong environmental organizations, community sustainability roundtables, and environmental justice coalitions are present throughout the region. Furthermore, a rapidly growing list of businesses and government agencies in the region are adopting sustainable practices. In many ways, college curricula need to catch up with and prepare students to join the veritable explosion of conceptual thinking and practices already underway.

CHALLENGES

The Still-Modest Scale of Environment and Sustainability Studies

Many baccalaureate-level institutions in the region regularly offer environmental studies courses. Some have well-established programs. At 2-year colleges (where the majority of students are enrolled), however, just one faculty member usually shoulders some environmental science teaching among myriad other responsibilities, and only a few teachers in other disciplines offer classes with environmental or sustainability content. Across all sectors, service-learning programs are, for the most part, fledglings searching for solid perches. As a result, while small groups of students are being exposed to environmental learning or engagement with sustainability, thousands of others gain little exposure to the bioregion in which they live, to the problems confronting it, or to the conception of a sustainable future.

Encrusted Structures and Practices

When it comes to curriculum development in place-based learning or sustainability, we in postsecondary education largely are working within an old paradigm, where knowledge is still delivered piecemeal by different disciplines. Too often in academia, theory garners more status than practice, and research that explores the exotic is favored over the local and familiar. Moreover, as David Sobel argues (2004), learning at all educational levels is too much *beside* the world, not *within* it. College curriculum and teaching practice generally run counter to what we know about holistic learning, which requires the application of ideas, the examination of values, and the integration of knowledge at a systems level.

Higher Education's Fiscal Crisis

While we have found energetic, committed partners for this initiative, we also are painfully aware that most campus leaders see "sustainability" through another lens. They face what policy analyst Jane Wellman (2002) calls the "double whammy": a surge of students demanding access to higher education and, simultaneously, a significant erosion of public resources and capacity for meeting that demand. Campus leaders' priorities entail intense competition for public and private resources. The challenge facing universities is to realize more cost efficiencies without sacrificing the quality of student learning or the quality of faculty members' work lives (Guskin & Marcy, 2003).

Our Culture of Consumption

Finally, a major challenge we all face in the overdeveloped world is the nearly universal embrace of a mindlessly consumptive lifestyle. Sooner or later, aspirations of living well in a place cannot go without questions of living equitably in the world. Of necessity, this kind of self-examination will be painful. Here is where a bioregional perspective is not sufficient, and could even have a dark side of bioregional parochialism and isolationist behavior. Bioregional understandings *must* be nested within biospheric understandings, and a global, sustainable-development consciousness. We must think *and* act locally *and* globally.

GETTING STARTED

In spite of these challenges, we believe that "curriculum for the bioregion" is a compelling idea that will capture the imagination of faculty and community members here in Cascadia. With support from The Russell Family Foundation, we are initiating this project through a process of listening and community-building with our partner campuses. Working with an interinstitutional steering committee, we are visiting campuses in the Puget Sound basin to survey and converse with faculty, staff, students, and campus leadership. We are raising visibility for the sustainable development and the potential of bioregional learning, and we are asking how campuses are responding to the global and local trends mentioned above. We are mapping the assets already in place and asking what *more* can be done to enable people to live sustainably in their life-places. These conversations are revealing not only good work; they also are raising collective aspirations about a process of more ambitious curricular transformation.

REFERENCES

Barber, B. (1995). *Jihad vs. McWorld: How globalism and tribalism are reshaping the world.* New York: Random House.

Bernard, T., & Young, J. (1997). *The ecology of hope: Communities collaborate for sustainability.* Gabriola Island, B.C./Philadelphia: New Society Press.

Berg, P. (1978). *Reinhabiting a separate country: A bioregional anthology of Northern California.* San Francisco: Planet Drum Foundation.

Berry, W. (1977). *The unsettling of America: Culture and Agriculture.* New York: Avon Books.

Callenbach, E. (1975). *Ecotopia: The notebooks and reports of William Weston.* Berkeley, CA: Banyan Tree Books.

Corcoran, P. B., & Wals, A. E. J. (2004). *Higher education and the challenge of sustainability.* Dordrecht, The Netherlands: Kluwer Publishers.

Dobson, A. (1996). Environment sustainabilities: An analysis and a typology. *Environmental Politics, 5*(3), 401–428.

Guskin, A., & Marcy, M. (2003). Dealing with the future now: Principles for creating a vital campus in a climate of limited resources. Change, *35*(4), 10–21.

Jackson, W. (1995). *Becoming native to this place.* Lexington: University Kentucky Press.

Jickling, B. (1992). Why I don't want my children to be educated for sustainable development. *Journal of Environmental Education, 23*(4), 5–8.

Jickling, B. (2004). *Education for sustainability: A seductive idea, but is it enough for my grandchildren?* [On-line]. Available: http://www.ec.gc.ca/education/ee_jickling_e.htm

Johnson, K. N., Swanson, F., Herring, M., & Greene, S. (1999). *Bioregional assessments: Science at the crossroads of management and policy.* Washington, DC: Island Press.

Kane, H. (2002). *Triumph of the mundane: The unseen trends that shape our lives and environment.* Washington, DC: Island Press.

Lewis, P. H., Jr. (1996). *Tomorrow by design: A regional design process for sustainability.* New York: John Wiley.

Parks Daloz, S. (2000). *Big questions, worthy dreams: Mentoring young adults in their search for meaning, purpose and faith.* San Francisco: Jossey-Bass.

Puget Sound Action Team (PSAT). (2004). *The state of the sound 2004.* Olympia, WA: Washington Department of Ecology Publication. [On-line]. Available: http://www.psat.wa.gov/

Sale, K. (1985). *Dwellers in the land: The bioregional vision.* San Francisco: Sierra Club Books.

Snyder, G. (1974). *Turtle Island.* New York: New Directions.

Snyder, G. (1990). *The practice of the wild.* San Francisco: North Point Press.

Sobel, D. (2004). *Place-based education: Connecting classrooms and communities.* Orion.

St. John, E., et al. (2004). *Expanding college access: The impact of state finance strategies.* Lumina Foundation Research Report. Indianapolis: Lumina Foundation. [On-line]. Available: http://www.luminafoundation.org/publications/researchreports.html

Thayer, R. L., Jr. (2003). *LifePlace: Bioregional thought and practice.* Berkeley: University of California Press.

United Nations Conference on Environment and Development (UNCED). (1992). *Report of the United Nations Conference on Environment and Development, Rio de Janeiro, Rio de Janeiro: 3–14 June 1992.* (Annex I: Rio Declaration; Annex II: Agenda 21). Rio de Janeiro: Author

Wackernagel, M., & Rees, W. (1996). *Our ecological footprint: Reducing human impact on the earth.* Gabriola Island, B.C./Philadelphia: New Society Press.

Wellman, J. (2002). The double whammy: How governing boards can negotiate a volatile economy and shifting enrollments. Working Paper for the National AGB Conference on Trusteeship. Washington, DC: Association of Governing Boards of Universities and Colleges.

World Commission on Environment and Development (WCED). (1987). *Our common future. New York:* Oxford University Press (Brundtland Report).

Worldwatch Institute. (2004). *State of the World 2004.* Washington, DC: Author.

Worldwatch Institute. (2005). *State of the World 2005.* Washington, DC: Author.

The Ahmedabad Declaration

Mary Paden

The Centre for Environment Education (CEE) in Ahmedabad, India, got a running start on the United Nations Decade of Education for Sustainable Development (DESD) (2005–2015) by hosting the first international conference of the decade January 18–20. The attendance of 900 educators from 50 countries exceeded expectations. Not only did these participants share their experiences and develop action plans in 20 topical workshops, they also offered detailed comments on the UNESCO implementation plan for the Decade and presented their own hopes for the Decade in the Ahmedabad Declaration.

On the first day of the conference, CEE Director Kartikeya Sarabhi challenged participants to come up with a declaration. He set only two conditions: it must be created in a participatory manner and it must be only one page long. Participants inscribed their thoughts on a huge writing wall. Each evening a writing committee fashioned these comments into a one-page document, which was in turn posted for comment. On the final day of the conference, the proposed declaration was read. For an hour, participants offered insightful comments. By afternoon the writing team produced a revision. It was unanimously adopted.

The declaration begins by welcoming the DESD, as long-awaited international recognition for ESD. Next, it expresses a sense of urgency to move toward sustainability. It reaffirms the participants' belief in action-oriented education as a powerful force for change because this type of education empowers people to shape their own futures. It stresses that learning doesn't stop with graduation; thus policymakers, business leaders, and the public are candidates for ESD. And it acknowledges that educators have a place alongside scientists, economists, businesspeople, and others shaping the vision of sustainability.

Finally, the declaration captured the mood of the last session, noting that the participants went forth from the conference with "a spirit of urgency, commitment, hope, and enthusiasm."

THE AHMEDABAD DECLARATION

This Declaration was made on January 20, 2005, by more than 900 learners, thinkers, and practitioners from more than 40 countries, engaged in education for sustainable development, at the *Education for a Sustainable Future* conference held at the Centre for Environment Education in Ahmedabad, India.

As the first international gathering of the United Nations Decade of Education for Sustainable Development (DESD), we warmly welcome this Decade that highlights the potential of action education to move people toward sustainable lifestyles and policies.

If the world's peoples are to enjoy a high quality of life, we must move quickly toward a sustainable future. Although most indicators point away from sustainability, growing grassroots efforts worldwide are taking on the enormous task of changing this trend.

We accept our responsibility and we urge all people to join us in doing all we can to pursue the principles of the Decade with humility, inclusivity, and a strong sense of humanity. We invite wide participation through networks, partnerships, and institutions.

As we gather in the city where Mahatma Gandhi lived and worked, we remember his words: "Education for life; education through life; education throughout life." These words underscore our commitment to the ideal of education that is participatory and lifelong.

We firmly believe that a key to sustainable development is the empowerment of all people, according to the principles of equity and social justice, and that a key to such empowerment is action-oriented education.

ESD implies a shift from viewing education as a delivery mechanism to the recognition that we are all learners as well as teachers. ESD must happen in villages and cities, schools and universities, corporate offices and assembly lines, and in the offices of ministers and civil servants. All must struggle with how to live and work in a way that protects the environment, advances social justice, and promotes economic fairness for present and future generations. We must learn how to resolve conflicts, create a caring society, and live in peace.

ESD must start with examining our own lifestyles and our willingness to model and advance sustainability in our communities. We pledge to share our diverse experiences and collective knowledge to refine the vision of sustainability while continually expanding its practice. Through our actions we will add substance and vigor to the UNDESD processes.

We are optimistic that the objectives of the Decade will be realized and move forward from Ahmedabad in a spirit of urgency, commitment, hope, and enthusiasm.

Argentina and Education for Sustainable Development

Marta Andelman

In Argentina, few groups recognize the value of Education for Sustainable Development (ESD). These are, by and large, composed of activists in environmental education who are connected to environmental issues and organizations, or teachers—or people historically interested in these matters—providing environmental education at different levels. There are also a few groups within university circles.

The Decade of Education for Sustainable Development (DESD) carries no significant weight in governmental and nongovernmental circles. So far, the issue has not been specifically mentioned. It does not appear in any agenda, or in any suggestion or recommendation for policy-making, not even in proposals for decision-making, in the public or private sector, in any public or private area.

OPPORTUNITIES

Even though ESD is not widely recognized, the country has a significant history of experiences addressing—some of them very successfully—social and environmental issues. Although these experiences are not carried out under the denomination of ESD, it could be said that they include some of the conceptual aspects of it, such as dialogue, joint learning, participation and action, reflection, negotiation, and concerted actions. These initiatives are expressed in diverse ways and have different scope according to where they originate and to the context in which they are immersed. In some cases they are carried out in an organized way, more informally in others, and there are also cases in which they have great scope but are less hierarchized.

Among many other efforts originated in 2002 in response to the great social emergency Argentina went through as a result of the rise of poverty and unemployment, the Training Strategies for Environmental Promoters in cooperatives of cardboard collectors such as *Reciclar Sur* and *El Ceibo,* and the *Fábrica Social* of the *Recuperar y Construir* project, are some of the expressions of a wide range of processes that take place locally in the country as a result of the communitarian, environmental, cultural, educational, economic, and political demands of a society that is looking for a better quality of life.

In a more formal sphere, the work of the postgraduate course Educación en Ambiente para el Desarrollo Sustentable—a course of national scope organized by the Confederación de Trabajadores Docentes de la República Argentina (CTERA), a very active and committed union, in association with the Universidad Nacional del Comahue—is also noteworthy.

There are also other efforts where environmental education becomes integrated with processes that, articulating different organizations, seek to reverse the effects of desertification processes and the loss of biodiversity in the communities in which they are immersed. For instance, both the Programa Desarrollo Sustentable en Zonas Áridas y

Semiáridas de Argentina coordinated by National Institute of Farming Technology, the Environment and Sustainable Development Secretariat, with the support of the German organization GTZ and the Proyecto Manejo Sostenible de los Recursos Naturales del Gran Chaco Sudamericano coordinated by GTZ, seek to contribute to the sustainable development of their communities through the creation of networks and the strengthening of governmental and nongovernmental institutions involved in the region.

All the movements and initiatives mentioned above, and many others, involve people, grassroots organizations, and the communities at large in a learning process and a quest for sustainable solutions toward the improvement in their quality of life and the fight against poverty, and create opportunities for sustainable development at a local, provincial, nacional, and regional level. They show that in Argentina there is a strong current of socioenvironmental and cultural activities—beyond formal structures—that thinks, drives, promotes, and builds from the foundations, generating new paths and alternatives for improvement and change.

These kind of experiences provide excellent opportunities to promote the DESD and the implementation of ESD, creating strategies based on advocacy and vision building, consultation, ownership, partnership and networks, research, and innovation as the United National DESD proposed in 2004, at the Draft International Implementation Scheme.

Another aspect to take into account is that the Argentine Republic is a federal country composed of 24 jurisdictions, with a decentralized educational and political system. Article number 41 of the National Constitution establishes that all inhabitants have the right to a healthy and balanced environment, apt for human development and for the productive activities that satisfy the current needs without putting in jeopardy the needs of future generations; the inhabitants have the obligation to preserve the environment. The authorities will provide protection of this right, national use of the natural resources, preservation of the natural and cultural heritage and of biological diversity, and environmental information and education. It is the responsibility of the Nation to dictate the rules and regulations containing the minimum budgets for protection, and of the provinces, the necessary measures to complement them without altering the local jurisdictions.

This means that in order to start the debate about ESD in Argentina, it is necessary to develop strategies at national, provincial, and local levels. At the national level, there are some issues to consider. In the educational objectives for 2003–2007 "Towards quality education for everybody" stated by the National Ministry of Education, Science, and Technology, education is outlined as a decisive space for the consolidation of national identity and a strategic channel to foster social, economic, and cultural development. The need to foster an education more in line with the national development project also is stressed. Moreover, the words of the President in his inaugural speech before Congress—"We must stop considering education, science, and technology as social policies. Understood as development strategies, it is imperative to strengthen the bridges of interchange between the educational system and the world of production and labor"—suggest a suitable arena in which ESD can find an opportunity to contribute to the consolidation of democratic processes, and give the impression that the DESD will find a favorable terrain.

These declarations of intent clear the way to the building of synergies between sectorial efforts and the validation of any attempt in this respect, allowing the move from declamation to demand. They open a road toward the strengthening of the multiple efforts already existent at different levels—national, provincial, and local—and the promotion of new enterprises, as well as the building of mechanisms of interchange and alliance among the different groups, such as the private sector, the governments, and the third sector (nongovernmental organizations [NGOs]).

CHALLENGES

Argentine society is complex—it is very fragmented, and there are enormous differences and inequalities. The situation in the City of Buenos Aires is not the same as in the city of Formosa, in Formosa province, one of the poorest in the country. These differences are associated with great social inequity, and with the concentration of income, the rise of unemployment, and the number of people below the line of poverty.

Argentina has a population of 36 million. According to the 2002 Argentine Report of Poverty and Indigence, half of the country is poor and the quality of this poverty has deteriorated enormously. The extremely poor represent a growing proportion of the total of poor people. The figures for the young are even worse. According to the National Institute of Statistics and Census of Argentina, there are 1.3 million youngsters, between the ages of 15 and 24, who do not work or study.

To foster ESD in this context means, among other things, to acknowledge that tackling inequality, inequity, and poverty requires critical thinking and reflection—questions for more than a manual of techniques. We need to create the spaces and the conditions to build a sustainable, consensual, and concerted social policy—a fundamental aspect of action for sustainable development. The fact that both the National Constitution and the General Law of the Environment take into account environmental education and the right of Argentineans to a healthy environment politically validates the actions that tend to foster social development in the context of sustainability.

On the other hand, there are many ongoing projects that do not mention ESD specifically but are slightly connected to it and represent an opportunity to promote it in different circles. An example of this is provided by the Global Environmental Citizens Program coordinated by the PNUMA and dedicated to the development of responsible citizens in seven Latin-American countries, including Argentina. This effort, shared by six civil society networks that foster sustainable development, including the UICN-CEC, constitutes with governmental support an Argentinean national board and also local boards. To promote the recognition of ESD among powerful interest groups such as radio hams, churches, local authorities, legislators, educators, and consumers is an opportunity we cannot afford to lose due to the multiplying effect that these key groups have.

THE WAY FORWARD

By promoting public recognition of ESD's strategic value in achieving a successful implementation of sustainable social, environmental, and economic policies, Argentina could take advantage of the opportunities given by the DESD.

Government organizations, national associations, and key sectors should understand that ESD does not mean teaching people about sustainable development but rather getting society involved in a process of analysis of problems and important issues that have not yet been properly addressed dealt. Sustainable development includes a structure based on questions more than on answers. Beginning a debate about what sustainable development means for Argentina is one of the major issues.

Education for Sustainable Development is a social decision, a political process based on traditions, culture, and a solid technological and scientific knowledge. Reaching sustainable social, economic, and environmental development in Argentina largely will depend on people's awareness and on their aspirations expressed through different mechanisms.

In this sense, the commitment of the different sectors of government and the NGOs is needed in order to generate a reflection process and lay the foundations of what we are trying to build today as ESD. We need an all-inclusive State policy in order to have a selfless, just, and equitable society that considers a new concept of development; that takes into account the needs and aspirations of all people; that understands pluralism and the balance and harmony between humans and the environment; that allows the creation of alternative ways to eradicate the basic causes of poverty, hunger, illiteracy, pollution, exploitation, and domination; and that deals with the crucial problems not in a fragmentary way but in a holistic manner.

It is desirable that education in Argentina, viewed as a social transformation process on our way to sustainable development, should occupy the place it deserves in public policies.

The Decade of Education for Sustainable Development: A Perspective from Australia

Josephine R. Lang

INTRODUCTION

The invitation to respond to this theme enables me to reflect on my country's efforts in grappling with the implications of the UN Decade of Education for Sustainable Development. It is a personal perspective within the contexts of the Australian society and its environment. It reflects my experiences as the President of the Australian Association for Environmental Education (AAEE) and work with government as a member of the Minister's advisory body, the National Environmental Education Council (NEEC) over a 2-and-half-year period leading up to the Decade. During this time I worked as a teacher educator, which helped me to further engage with the theories and practices of learning and teaching, focusing me to re-think and re-vision *what* and *how* education and learning for sustainability may evolve. Combined, these roles have helped me to explore and examine the intricacies of Education for Sustainability.[1]

Amidst Australia's background of ecological devastation there is hope as people and their communities search for ways to re-think and re-vision our future, moving ever so slowly towards sustainability (e.g., Australian State of the Environment Committee, 2001; Barr & Cary, 1992; Campbell, 1994; Cosgrove, Evans, & Yencken, 1994; Yencken & Wilkinson, 2000).

For me, sustainability is the intersection where humanity consciously engages with the ecological systems in ways to ensure all life is supported over time: people, plants, animals, microscopic phyla as well as life represented by genetic diversity and the complexity of ecosystem diversity. This fundamentally means that humanity has to *engage* in her social, cultural, economic, and political systems to explore and examine *how* sustainability may be achieved while maintaining the integrity of ecological systems. It places the responsibility with humanity and her imagination to re-vision and re-create a sustainable future. Such responsibility can only be supported by deep understandings of how all these dimensions (social, cultural, political, economic, and ecological) interrelate to achieve sustainability. Consequently, humanity's capacity to deliver on the goals of sustainability is critically dependent upon her ability to learn and innovate within local and global contexts. The key to achieving sustainability lies with education for sustainability where it enables humanity to respond, anticipate, create, negotiate, and participate in working and living towards sustainability.

PROGRESS TO DATE

Education for sustainability operates in Australia through a three-tiered government

[1] I utilise the term Education for Sustainability in preference to Education for Sustainable Development for a number of reasons, which largely derive from my Australian cultural context.

Table 1
Recent Australian Government key attempts for engaging in education for sustainability (adapted from Lang, 2004)

Australian Government initiative	Type of initiative
Environmental Education for a Sustainable Future: National Action Plan (2000)	*Policy*; Australian Government's Department of Environment & Heritage http://www.deh.gov.au/education/nap/index.html
National Environmental Education Council (NEEC)	*Policy & Strategy;* advisory expert group across predominantly school, tertiary, and industry sectors http://www.deh.gov.au/education/neec/index.html
National Environmental Education Network (NEEN)	*Policy & Strategy;* government (federal and state/territory) departments of environment and education to plan for strategies particularly for school sector through school communities http://www.deh.gov.au/education/neen/index.html
Australian Research Institute in Education for Sustainability (ARIES)	*Research;* initiated in 2002 and is commissioned by the NEEC & NEEN to prepare research to inform its work for policy setting. http://www.aries.mq.edu.au/
Sustainable Schools initiative	*Practice;* developing knowledge and practice locally & also to inform future policy http://www.deh.gov.au/education/sustainable-schools/index.html
National Environmental Education Statement (NEES) *(under development)*	*Policy & Strategy;* Australian Government Department Environment & Heritage and Department of Education, Science & Training to collaborate in developing and supporting implementation of curriculum policy framework that focuses on building capacity of schools to introduce implementation of education for sustainability
Industry Toolbox *(under development)*	*Practice;* developing a toolbox that business and industry sector will be able to use to work towards sustainability

structure: local government, state territory government, and national government. Local and state territory levels of government in Australia are quite active in various efforts to meet the challenges of education for sustainability. Due to my work nationally, however, this discussion will focus on national efforts.

During the past few years, the focus on environmental education by the national government in Australia has been developed by the Department of Environment and Heritage (DEH). In 2000, after a public consultation process, the DEH released its Environmental Education for a Sustainable Future: A National Action Plan. This current policy's purpose is to provide leadership in environmental education across sectors and also intends "to be a starting point for an enhanced national effort in support of Australia's ecologically sustainable development" (Department of the Environment and Heritage, 2000, p. 1).

The significance of this policy framework is that it provides the opportunity for the national government to set up important political structures and mechanisms to initiate support for education for sustainability. Key examples of these structures are depicted in Table 1. The National Action Plan has provided for a mix of policy, research, and strategies to inform practice at a local level. It probably also reflects a period of transition: a government grappling with moving from environmental education to the complexities of education for sustainability.

ADDRESSING THE FUTURE

If education for sustainability is the learning that allows for positive interactivity between humanity and ecological systems that support and underpin her livelihood and her very existence, the strategic challenges that exist in Australia are related to (i) re-visioning learning and (ii) building connectivity for sustainability.

Re-Visioning Learning for Sustainability

The call to re-vision learning for sustainability is relatively new (Fien, 2001; Hernandez & Mayur, 2000; O'Sullivan, 1999; Sterling, 2001). Re-visioning learning for sustainability should not be seen in isolation however from the current debates within "mainstream" education. I argue that education for sustainability is aligning itself with the broader issue of crisis of disengagement in education such as in the middle years of schooling that encompasses students of the age range between 8–16 years old; this is at least evident from a Western perspective. This acknowledgment of a crisis of disengagement in school education along with broader societal phenomena such as change, information and communication technologies, globalization, postmodernism, urbanization, feminism, and the environmental crisis have re-focused thinking on learning. In essence there is a confluence where new paradigms on learning are emerging. The outcome has been to identify a New learning paradigm (Simons van der Linden, & Duffy, 2000; Australian Council of Deans of Education (ACDE), 2001) that involves a shift towards transformational learning where knowledge may have multiple perspectives and is constructed and mediated for meaning not only as individuals but in collaborative participation with others.

Consequently, the issues being explored in New Learning are also those identified as crucial for change to transform communities to create a sustainable future. The pedagogies being developed for New Learning also readily apply to education for sustainability. These pedagogies incorporate, for example: authentic and active learning, discovery and experiential learning, situated learning, constructivism, reflective thinking and reflexivity, inquiry and problem-based learning, values education, critical thinking and pedagogies, negotiated curriculum, lifelong and life-wide learning, deep learning, and collaborative learning, where assessment is authentic, purposeful, and connected to the learning. Like others (e.g. Hernandez & Mayur, 2000; O'Sullivan, 1999; Sterling, 2001), I argue that the crisis in the health of the environment can be juxtaposed with the crisis in education. The major way of understanding and acting to redress the crisis of the environment is through engaging in the new ways of thinking about learning to create a sustainable future.

Building Connectivity for Sustainability

As I work with adults, and particularly in my work with teachers, I have inductively derived that people find it difficult to make connections between phenomena to reach deeper understandings of the worlds that they live in. Perhaps this difficulty is a reflection of Australia's highly urbanized society where 61% live in the capital cities on the coast, and a further 14% in smaller cities of above 80,000 people (Newton et al., 2001). This characteristic of high rate of urbanization in Australia may begin to help us to understand as educators for sustainability why the people we work with have difficulties in describing and having a deeper understanding of the connections between their lives, their lifestyles, their work, and the natural systems. Their social or human worlds do not readily coincide with the natural worlds, which seems to lead to poor understandings of connections.

For this reason I argue that educators for sustainability in Australia need to build understanding and experience of connectivity for sustainability. By this I mean building connectivity at multiple levels. We need to provide learning experiences that allow for the learners to make meaning of the world through acknowledging, respecting, and understanding the connectivity between the natural and social worlds: that one action in one world (e.g., social) will have an impact (positive or negative) on at least one other aspect in other worlds (e.g., natural or economic). Education for sustainability demands learners to seek to understand the complexities of connectivity in order to re-vision how to re-create a sustainable future. The new ways of thinking about learning engage pedagogies that support building this type of complex understanding and encourage ensuing changes of behavior.

I am also advocating, however, that educators for sustainability need to connect with other notions of building connectivity for sustainability. I am coming to understand that one key difference between environmental education and education for sustainability is the shift from a predominant focus on the individual to a predominant focus on community (Lang, 2003, 2004). I strongly believe that understanding the role of community is critically significant to sustainability with implications for education for sustainability.

The sense of community is critical to sustainability because the issues and goals of sustainability cannot be attained by single individuals (or, for that matter, single organizations); a sustainable future can only be achieved through collective wisdom, collective effort, and shared vision. This understanding of community distinctly diverges from the society I live in where the values purported by the images of consumption focus on individuality, looking after one self, and competition, which often are reinforced by political policies that privilege commerce and the individual over the common public good. This tension sets the challenge for educators for sustainability to build capacity for *social connectivity*.

Once again, the new ways of thinking about learning offer pedagogies to assist educators for sustainability in their work in this area. Collaborative learning reflects significant pedagogies that support the building of capacity for social connectivity. But I would like to call for an even greater role for learning within community than collaborative learning may offer. I believe that for sustainable learning that is lifelong and life-wide, our role as educators for sustainable is to create Communities of Practice (Lave & Wenger, 1991; Weeks Hoatson, & Dixon, 2003; Wenger, 1998; Wenger, McDermott, & Snyder, 2002). Communities of practice have learning at its core but are contextualized within the *practices* of a community. Consequently, communities of practice associate learning that is embedded in the social or cultural contexts to build coherence within the community. Etienne Wenger identifies three dimensions of communities of practice: (i) mutual engagement; (ii) a joint enterprise; and (iii) a shared repertoire (of tools for negotiating meaning) that inform the practices, understandings, and identity of the community (Wenger, 1998). Engaging with the theory of communities of practice provides educators for sustainability a framework to understand how to develop capacity for social connectivity.

ROLES FOR THE AUSTRALIAN GOVERNMENT AND AAEE

The challenge facing Australia is the need not only to *engage* communities but also to *enable* communities to work towards sustainability. In the above discussion I have isolated two areas that may provide inroads to meeting such a challenge. The Australian government has the important role to provide leadership and the strategic mechanisms to support (i) re-visioning learning for sustainability and (ii) building social connectivity. As an example in the formal education sector, the National Environmental Education Statement for schools is an initial attempt by government to lead change from a curriculum policy perspective. The Australian Government needs to support this positive educational change by enabling teachers, principals, and their school communities to understand and act for sustainability. This means providing avenues for teachers and principals to form communities of practice to address issues of professional learning, implementing change, and developing their schools with the capacity for sustainability within their communities and beyond. Meeting this challenge therefore signals the need for further social connectivity, the need for governments across the local, state, and national levels to actively seek purposeful partnerships.

This creates an opportunity for the AAEE to seek out purposeful partnerships with government for sustainability. The AAEE needs to provide leadership and strategic directions in dialogue with the governments to determine ways to engage the Australian society in sustainability. Of course this could lead to multiple pathways for partnerships, but the AAEE needs to assess its capabilities to sustain such partnerships. Importantly, the AAEE also can't be solely responsible for education for sustainability in Australia. Therefore, like governments, the AAEE should identify areas of priority to collaboratively work with other organizations to ensure that education for sustainability in Australia is infiltrating all the diverse sectors of society. This creates a role for the AAEE that is outward looking in that it not only focuses on its members but also is an advocate for educational leadership for sustainability through connecting in purposeful partnerships with other organizations (or, putting it in another way, other communities of practice).

The approach Australia uses needs to continue to work on developing multiple perspectives and pathways for working towards sustainability to be inclusive of all its citizens. Sustainability demands that there is no *one* way of doing something, that it requires negotiated practice that is shared within the community. These multiple perspectives and diverse ways of knowing and working will be fostered if learning, creativity, and innovation for sustainability are nurtured and supported. Both governments and organizations such as the AAEE have a critical role to provide leadership and strategic mechanisms that are complex, holistic and support the development of diverse sustainable communities. To provide for such engagement they will need to develop purposeful partnerships where the focus should be on designing strategic frameworks that encourage and enable communities to examine new ways of learning and living for sustainability. This approach recognizes and celebrates that knowledge is generated and contextualized locally for solutions at the local community level.

REFERENCES

Australian Council of Deans of Education (ACDE). (2001). *New learning: A charter for Australian education,* Bundoora VIC. Also available from their website on: Author. [online]. Available: http://acde.edu.au/

Australian State of the Environment Committee. (2001). *Australia State of the Environment 2001, Independent Report to the Commonwealth Minister for the Environment and Heritage.* Canberra, Collingwood, Victoria. CSIRO Publishing on behalf of the Department of the Environment and Heritage.

Barr, N., & Cary, J. (1992). *Greening a brown land: The Australian search for sustainable land use.* South Melbourne: MacMillan Education Australia.

Boud, D., Cohen, R., & Sampson, J. (Eds.). (2001). *Peer learning in higher education: Learning from & with each other.* London: Kogan Page.

Campbell, A. (1994). *Landcare: Communities shaping the land and the future.* St Leonards, NSW: Allen & Unwin.

Cosgrove, L., Evans, D. G., & Yencken, D. (Eds.). (1994). *Restoring the land: Environmental values, knowledge and action.* Melbourne: Melbourne University Press.

Department of the Environment and Heritage. (2000). *Environmental education for a sustainable future: National action plan.* Canberra: Environment Australia.

Fien, J. (2001). *Education for Sustainability: Reorientating Australian schools for a sustainable future* (*Tela Paper 8.*) Melbourne, VIC: Australian Conservation Foundation in joint sponsorship with Australian Association for Environmental Education, Trust for Young Australians. Available: http://www.acfonline.org.au/docs/publications/tp008.pdf

Hernandez, C., & Mayur, R. (Eds.). (2000). *Pedagogy of the earth: Education for a sustainable future.* Mumbai, India: International Institute for Sustainable Future.

Lang, J. (2003). No school is an island: Environment and education, *EQ Australia,* (Autumn), 7–8.

Lang, J. (2004). Environmental education, education for sustainability and UN Decade of Education for Sustainable Development. In *Quality environmental education in schools for a sustainable society,* International Workshop/Seminar, Conference Proceedings, August, 25–26 2004, Cheongju, Korea. Cheongju, Korea: Cheongju National University of Education.

Lave, J., & Wenger, E. (1991). *Situated learning: Legitimate peripheral participation.* Cambridge: Cambridge University Press.

Newton, P. W., Baum, S., Bhatia, K., Brown, S. K., Cameron, A. S., Foran, B., Grant, T., Mak, S. L., Memmott, P. C.,

Mitchell, V. G., Neate, K. L., Pears, A., Smith, N., Stimson, R. J., Tucker, S. N., & Yencken, D. (2001). *Human settlements, Australian State of the Environment Report 2001 (Theme Report)*. Canberra: CSIRO Publishing on behalf of the Department of the Environment and Heritage.

O'Sullivan, E. (1999). *Transformative learning: Educational vision for the 21st century.* London: Zed Books.

Simons, R.-J., van der Linden, J., & Duffy, T. (Eds.). (2000). *New learning.* Dordrecht: Kluwer Academic Publishers.

Sterling, S. (2001). *Sustainable education: Re-visioning learning and change.* Devon: Green Books for the Schumacher Society.

Weeks, W., Hoatson, L., & Dixon, J. (Eds.). (2003). *Community practices in Australia.* Frenchs Forest, NSW: Pearson Education Australia.

Wenger, E. (1998). *Communities of practice: Learning, meaning, and identity* . Cambridge: Cambridge University Press.

Wenger, E., McDermott, R., & Snyder, W. M. (2002). *Cultivating communities of practice: A guide to managing knowledge.* Boston: Harvard Business School Press.

Yencken, D., & Wilkinson, D. (2000). *Resetting the compass: Australia's journey. Towards sustainability.* Melbourne: CSIRO Publishing.

Is It Possible to Benefit from the Decade for Education for Sustainable Development?

Zióle Zanotto Malhadas

Sustainability does not have the same connotations for the Brazilian people as it does for many Europeans or North Americans. Besides cultural differences, economic, environmental, and educational factors also need to be considered. From the South, it seems that sustainability in the developed countries means to preserve the present status, to have the same quality of life without causing ecological impact, if possible. But for the poorest communities of Brazil, sustainability means having enough food, safe shelter, and access to health services, and these depend upon getting a job, and having a job depends on education—to be able to learn enough to be employable.

Therefore, it is important to elaborate a specific action plan for the Latin American implementation of the Decade of Education for Sustainable Development (DESD). The challenges are vast and difficult. And the most crucial challenge is a deficient educational system. The resources devoted to education and research gradually are shrinking, and low salaries and poor working conditions are reducing the motivation of the majority of researchers and educators. Therefore, we would like to see government agencies and national associations offer effective support to facilitate the DESD success by empowering all the formal and nonformal educators, and encouraging them to elaborate and implement efficient educational curricula and programs, as well as to insert efficient transdisciplinary strategies of ESD in all the courses and in all the schools. According to the Report on the International Consultation on Education for Sustainable Development, "Learning to Change Our World," Götenborg, Sweden,

> In the coming decade decisive changes must be made in education systems, from pre-school to university level, in order to achieve learning for sustainable development in all societies around the world. We all have a great responsibility in this undertaking. This work is very urgent and must start immediately. Ultimately a new social contract involving qualitatively new relations between government, business and the education sector, may be required. We find ourselves at the very beginning of a long and challenging, but also inspiring and promising, journey. The United Nations Decade of Education for Sustainable Development, due to start in 2005, is a golden opportunity and a stimulus for everyone to devote continued and wide-ranging efforts in this area." (2004, p. 59)

What are the most effective means to identify and to apply the best strategies to promote and implement education for sustainable development? In Brazil, we would like to stimulate cooperation among higher education, research institutions, and other social segments through an efficient and specific network for DESD, which would spread to all of Latin America in the near future, if we succeed in getting some financial support.

We also are seeking to create a Regional Center of Expertise on Education for Sustainable Development (RCE) in the State of Paraná (according to a UNU-UNESCO proposal), which would be the first core and starting point for the future Latin American Network for DESD, where educators will become main actors in a process to develop and disseminate state-of-the-art knowledge relevant to SD. They will work with other actors in the society, e.g., representatives of the local government, volunteer and philanthropy associations, museums, NGOs, and so on, which will enable a selection of priority regional problems and deficiencies to be tackled and solved in order to promote regional development, and exchange information and experience and facilitate collaboration among organizations providing different levels of education.

In preparation for DESD, in 2001, six Seminars on Re-orienting Education for Sustainability were developed in the six major universities of Paraná State, Brazil, to stimulate university teachers and community leaders to create new projects and programs to implement Agenda 21, when 6000 copies of the Agenda 21 were handed out to the university teachers. However, there was not the immediate positive responsive from professors that we were hoping for, although many students were enthusiastic and requested other opportunities to discuss sustainability-related themes, as well as SD strategies. Due to resources shortening, however, it has being postponed. Another attempt was made in 2004. We established a partnership between the Pontificia Universidade Católica do Paraná (PUC) and Instituto para o Desenvolvimento Sustentável (IDS) in order to develop a new project, Dialogues for Sustainability, with monthly seminars focusing on themes related to ESD and preparation for the UNDESD. Parallel to the seminars, local environment restoration projects were developed by students under academic supervision. For example, on World Environment Day 2004, the Belém River that crosses the campus was cleaned and riverbank vegetation, including many threatened native species, was planted. Our follow-up plan for students to develop educational resources for local primary schools in "favela" neighbourhoods had to be cancelled, however, due to lack of funds. This was disappointing as the project sought to develop leadership skills in young people as well as a process that could be repeated in other colleges and universities if we had obtained the necessary financial support.

The DESD can be a spark for increased cooperation and solidarity. It can be an impulse for new synergies that can help us consolidate and expand projects such as these. It also can be a motivation to accelerate the university reform process and insert ESD as a priority theme to be implemented effectively in all courses. Therefore, we would promote the formation of positive leaders and efficient decisionmakers who can build up capacities and create opportunities to implement Sustainability. Otherwise, if the educational institutions do not change their basic structure and present research policies, they will move in the opposite direction and the result will be stagnation. And stagnation will generate the atrophy of the universities'/schools' members, wasting away their energy and creativity.

Moreover, during the DESD, the television, newspapers, and magazines should be motivated to produce positive stimulus to the youth educational formation by exhibiting ESD programs, as well as selected movies directed to praise the best examples of ethical social behavior and procedures, instead of detailed description of crimes, corruption, robbery, pornography, and socioenvironment degradation. Honest and responsible citizenship should be enhanced, while partnerships between the media and education leaders should enable continuous cooperation in order to disseminate the scientific innovations. Scientific research reports, and informative and formative articles should be published in a more simplified language, making it then accessible to common people. Meanwhile, in terms of global cooperation, some international educational materials for DESD should be translated to Portuguese and other languages spoken in the in-development countries (*like the ESD Toolkit*, www.unesco.org/esdtoolkit), otherwise these people will not be able to access them.

It is only then that we will be able to reduce the miserable conditions under which so many people live. According to Poormohammadi and colleagues (2004), education can help us to understand that

> most of the human problems today are not because of lack of development but as a result of disharmonious and imbalanced development. Some aspects of

life have been overvalued and some others, though very important and vital, have been underestimated or totally ignored. However, a sustainable development depends upon a reasonable and proper attention to all aspects of human life including ethical and spiritual values. (p. 3)

Learning to live by such values, ourselves, and helping bring others towards them, is the mission for environmental educators in the Decade.

REFERENCES

Ministry of Education and Science of Sweden. Report on the International Consultation on Education for Sustainable Development. Learning to change our world. Götenborg, Sweden.

Poormohammadi, M. R., Rashidi, F. R., & Fakhri, S. A. (2004). *The role of universities in promoting dialogue & development: A new perspective.* Tabriz, Iran: Tabriz University. *IAU 2004 Conference, 25–29 July, Sao Paulo, Brazil,* p. 3.

The Meaning of the DESD for Us in Japan: Three Years after Proposing it to the World

Sachi Ninomiya-Lim

Japan, a country poor in natural resources, has grown to be what it is today on the strength of its human resources. It has attached paramount importance to education as the basis of development. My government, together with Japanese non-governmental organizations, has proposed that the United Nations declare a "Decade of Education for Sustainable Development." We shall provide no less than 250 billion yen in education assistance over a five-year period. (Speech by Prime Minister of Japan Junichiro Koizumi at the World Summit on Sustainable Development, 9 February 2002)

In this statement at the Johannesburg Summit by Japan's Prime Minister, the meaning of the Decade of Education for Sustainable Development (DESD) for Japan was to provide "education assistance." The DESD, however, actually should mean much more than that for Japan and the people here. Japan may have succeeded in becoming one of the most "developed" nations in terms of industrialization and economic growth while valuing education as the Prime Minister stressed, and education assistance to the "developing" world is one such contribution Japan can make to the international community. But while conventional economic-oriented development itself has been claimed as the major reason for the currently "unsustainable" situation of the world, the success of Japan must be questioned. Indeed, the very meaning of the DESD for us in Japan is the opportunity it brings to question and reorient our ways and visions of development toward sustainability, integrating social, cultural, and environmental values, through all possible forms of education and learning.

As the *Draft International Implementation Scheme (IIS*; UNESCO, 2005) states, "The outcomes of the DESD will be seen in the lives of thousands of communities and millions of individuals as new attitudes and values inspire decisions and actions making sustainable development a more attainable ideal" (p. 41). Thus, the outcomes of our efforts throughout the Decade possibly will affect diverse aspects of our society and life. In this article, I particularly focus on two such outcomes that we in Japan hope to achieve—the reorientation of the formal school education toward sustainability, and the empowerment of people for the participatory policy development for sustainability. In addition, I introduce the efforts of the Japan Council on the UNDESD (ESD-J) as a civil society networking hub and discuss the challenges to be overcome to realise a successful DESD, before listing the measures that need to be taken by the Japanese government at the start of the Decade.

REORIENTING SCHOOL EDUCATION TOWARD SUSTAINABILITY

A reorientation of the current formal educational system toward sustainability is one of the important outcomes to be achieved with the DESD framework. The Period of Integrated Study (PIS), introduced in every public school in 2002, appears to be one major key to such educational reorientation in Japan. While the Japanese school curriculum has long been uniformly designed by the national government, the PIS lets each school, individual teachers, or school pupils themselves select their study subjects and contents relevant to their own circumstances, enabling interdisciplinary learning on a range of real-world issues through which students develop their abilities to understand and to seek to solve the problems faced in everyday life (see Ministry of Education, Culture, Sports, Science, and Technology, 1998). Such ideas underlying the PIS are clearly consistent with the ESD principles that value interdisciplinary and holistic learning to nurture critical thinking and problem solving abilities in a locally relevant way (UNESCO, 2004, p. 18). While many teachers are struggling to implement PIS, however, for which they have little experience or support, the value of PIS is now being questioned. We can regard the DESD as an opportunity to overcome this situation by developing an appropriate system that enables successful ESD implementation through PIS, as one of the significant approaches to Japanese educational reorientation toward sustainability.

Along with the introduction of PIS, the increased recognition in Japanese society of the need for gaining connections between communities and schools should be regarded as another key to reorienting school education toward sustainability. While the uniform control of school education by the national government has long disconnected schools from local communities, people in Japan are now realising the importance of community–school partnerships. Such links are critical to realise successful ESD at schools, making the content and process of education relevant to pupils' lives in local realities and empowering them to take part in the sustainable community development process. As local residents get involved in school education, their support also can provide a breakthrough for teachers facing difficulties in implementing PIS. Thus, the DESD provides an opportunity for us to foster the movement to strengthen school–community partnerships, which is important for the educational reorientation in Japan.

EMPOWERING PEOPLE FOR A PARTICIPATORY POLICY DEVELOPMENT FOR SUSTAINABILITY

Another outcome to be sought within the DESD framework is the empowerment of people in Japan to enhance citizen participation in the policy planning and implementation process. The importance of a participatory political process is increasingly recognised in the Japanese society. As ESD involves learning that leads to "active participation in seeking and implementing new patterns of social organisation and change, working to find structures and mechanisms more likely to reflect the vision of sustainable development" (UNESCO, 2004, p. 17), the DESD should further foster such recognition among people in Japan and empower them to take part in forming policies for sustainable development.

In order to effectively promote ESD practices for increased citizen participation in the Japanese political system, it is important to acknowledge experiences in *machizukuri* (a Japanese expression referring to community development—literally meaning "town/community creation") as a foundation for fostering further efforts. As a *machizukuri* facilitator, Shimizu (2004) claims that "human development is the eternal theme of community development" (p. 16), a praxis of action and learning that has long been emphasised in *machizukuri*. Indeed, *machizukuri* activities often need be interdisciplinary, reality-led, participatory, and empowering, reflecting important features of ESD. Thus, *machizukuri* learning practices should be acknowledged as having built a foundation on which further DESD efforts can develop.

Another emerging trend to be noted in seeking to increase citizen participation in the Japanese political process through the DESD is the rapidly increasing partnership between NGOs and government. Since the Law to

Promote Specified Non-Profit Activities was enacted in 1998 to recognise NGOs as legal entities, the government has actively sought to partner NGOs in implementing public projects and services. Such partnerships have expanded opportunities for broader sectors of society to participate in policy processes, at least to a certain extent. It is also evident, however, that such partnerships do not always promote effective citizen participation as, in some cases, they exploit the resources of NGOs and thus reduce costs of delivering services for government. Thus, it is important that the DESD provides an opportunity for Japanese NGOs to empower themselves so that they can establish a fair relationship with government to realise their true participation in the policy development and implementation process for sustainable future.

ESD-J: A NETWORKING HUB

While the Decade brings significant opportunities for us in Japan to reorient our learning and society toward sustainability, such opportunities cannot be seized effectively unless there is appropriate networking and coordination of existing practices and forces. The Japan Council on the UNDESD, or ESD-J, was launched in 2003 to take this role as a hub to network NGOs and individuals and synergise their efforts. While the establishment of ESD-J originally was led by a group of environmental educators, who also had led the proposal of DESD at the Johannesburg Summit, ESD-J members (94 NGOs and 202 individuals as of April 2005) now involve those working in various other fields such as peace, gender, development, human rights, social welfare, and multiculturalism. ESD-J sees the importance of cooperation across the many ESD-related fields, emphasising that underlying values, applied approaches, and nurtured abilities commonly evident in activities of these fields form "the very essence of ESD" (ESD-J 2004, see Figure 1). ESD-J members promote the Decade through activities in six areas: information sharing, extension and training, policy advocacy, domestic networking, international networking, and government/enterprise partnership (for more information on ESD-J, refer to its website: http://www.esd-j.org).

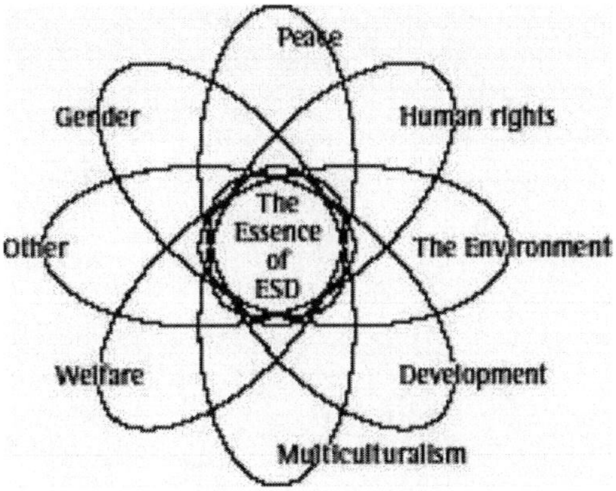

Fig. 1. The essence of ESD (ESD-J, 2004).

CHALLENGES: ACHIEVING PUBLIC UNDERSTANDING AND INTERDISCIPLINARY COOPERATION

Despite the momentum and networking generated thus far, several challenges still need to be overcome in realising the goals of the DESD. One of the greatest challenges is building wide public understanding of, and interest in, the DESD. Because the concepts of sustainability, development, and education that underlie ESD are abstract, sometimes controversial, and still evolving, our messages about the importance of ESD/DESD tend to be ambiguous and thus hard to communicate. In some cases the term "ESD" and its Japanese translation need to be replaced with other words, while some claim that the unfamiliarity and rigidity of these terms seriously hinder the public acceptance. In addition to the print materials and website that ESD-J has developed, media specifically designed for different groups of stakeholders are required.

Another significant challenge is the difficulty of connecting various fields to realise an interdisciplinary cooperation for the DESD. The conventionally vertical structure of not only administration but also civil society in Japan makes it hard to achieve such cooperation. In addition, what is even more problematic is that the holistic approach for the Decade causes the ambiguity over where responsibility lies—the claim that the DESD requires people of every field to take part in the efforts can lead to the misconception that any field has no responsibility to pour serious efforts into the Decade. To foster cooperation among different ESD-related fields for the successful Decade, the development of specific objectives and tasks need to start, to clarify the importance of interdisciplinary collaboration based on contributions by each field.

REQUIRED GOVERNMENTAL MEASURES

To effectively leverage the DESD opportunities in Japan addressing such challenges, in addition to the role of ESD-J to network civil forces, the role of the government to coordinate and synergise efforts at the national level is essential. At the DESD launching ceremony organised by ESD-J, held in Tokyo on 6 March 2005, Professor Abe (2005), President of ESD-J, proposed four measures that the government should take to fulfill this role:

- to establish a headquarter to promote the DESD within the Cabinet Office, in which all ministries and agencies participate,
- to establish a national-level DESD consortium of diverse stakeholders,
- to develop a DESD national implementation plan by March 2006,
- to develop a framework that encourages the formation of local ESD consortia. (p. 9)

The successful start of the Decade in Japan requires prompt action by the government on these measures and appropriate resource allocations. Such actions to promote the Decade domestically would demonstrate the commitment of the Japanese government to the implementation of the DESD, which it suggested to the world 3 years ago.

CONCLUDING REMARKS

Although I discussed in this article just two of the outcomes that we can possibly achieve with the DESD framework, our efforts to generate the DESD momentum can and should impact on many more aspects of our society and life. The achievement of such outcomes, however, will not be possible without committed action by every stakeholder. Now it is the time for us in Japan, living amongst unsustainable realities, to recognise the importance of interdisciplinary and intersectoral cooperation, to make the most use of the opportunities the Decade brings, and to attain a sustainable future for Japan and the world.

REFERENCES

Japan Council on the UNDESD (ESD-J). (2004). Japan too is on the move. (poster). Tokyo: Author.

Abe, O. (2005). ESD-J karano teigen: 2005nenwo minoriaru sutaatoni surutameni (Proposal from ESD-J: To achieve a fruitful start in 2005). Presentation distributed at the DESD launching ceremony in Tokyo, 6 March 2005, organised by ESD-J and the Yomiuri Shimbun.

Ministry of Education, Culture, Sports, Science, and Technology of Japan. (1998). Press Release: National curriculum standards reform for kindergarten, elementary school, lower and upper secondary school and schools for the visually disabled, the hearing impaired and the otherwise disabled (Synopsis of the Report). [Press release]. [on-line]. Available: http://www.mext.go.jp/english/news/1998/07/980712.htm

Shimizu, Y. (2004). Machizukuri waakushoppu no tenkai (Implementation of community development workshops. Gekkan Shakai Kyouiku (Monthly Community Education), *June* (584,) 11–17.

UNESCO. (2005). Draft International Implementation Scheme: United Nations Decade of Education for Sustainable Development 2005–2014. Paris: Author.

The Eastern Africa Environmental Network and the Decade of Education for Sustainable Development

George Malakwen

With a goal of increasing and intensifying public awareness on environmental and development issues in the Eastern Africa region, the Eastern Africa Environmental Network (EAEN) has been actively involved in Environmental Education (EE) networking with the objective of creating opportunities to disseminate and share information.

The EAEN adopted networking as a strategy in order to serve the interests of different groups, particularly the measures related to human relationships for improving the environment. Through networking, the EAEN has managed to bring people together, deliberate on various environmental issues, advocate and influence policies, and create learning opportunities for many.

The EAEN endeavors to provide environmental information, bearing in mind that it is only an informed society that can engage in sustainable consumption and production. This, too, enables citizens to understand the relationship between the factors of economic development and the natural environment.

Enjoying an 11-country membership with a human population of about 210 million, the EAEN has considerable opportunities of transforming the environmental ethic in the region through provision of Education for Sustainable Development (ESD).

It has the opportunity to define ESD in the African context considering the excruciating poverty that is now proving to be endemic in the region, the diminishing biodiversity that now poses challenges to human survival, and the increasing rate of environmental degradation.

Hence, the UN Declaration of 2005–2015 as the DESD lays more emphasis on the EAEN's role as an environmental education networking organization, to ensure that EE is not just an end in itself but a means to effecting changes in value systems, behavioral patterns, and lifestyles necessary in the attainment of sustainable development.

The political wars that have devastated many countries in the Great Lakes region have left a trail of environmental destruction, thus widening the EAEN's scope in terms of its EE networking. Most of these countries (Sudan, Somalia, Rwanda, and Burundi) are EAEN members and as such, the EAEN must come up with ESD programs to aid in their reconstruction. In their efforts to rebuild their social, economic, and political structures, the citizens of these countries must be equipped with the skills that guarantee wise resource utilization for the survival of current and future generations.

With a long-standing experience of providing EE through organization of successful annual conferences and workshops, the EAEN has greater chances of changing the current situation and contributing towards the attainment of Millennium Development Goals.

The EAEN participated in the Stakeholders Consultative Workshop on ESD last year organized by the National Environment Management Authority (NEMA). Seeking to raise the level of environmental awareness and building capacity that will enable all Kenyans to engage in the attainment of the goals of sustainable development, the recommendations and objectives of the workshop gave stakeholders in the environment leeway to formulate ESD programs.

The Kenyan government has demonstrated its commitment to ESD by recommending integration of ESD into learning at all levels and making it a priority in environment and development work. It also is considering establishing and supporting networks of cooperation for actors in ESD programs and projects. Hence, government support, cooperation, and commitment to ESD are another opportunity for the EAEN.

In our annual conference this year slated for May 27–28, ESD is one of the major subthemes. This is to enable participants from the region to deliberate on it in depth, bringing in their country's experiences, challenges, and recommendations. In particular, we are keen on bringing on board delegates from countries in political transition such as Sudan and Somalia so as to use their input in determining their EE needs in the formulation of appropriate ESD programmes.

Professor Wangari Maathai's achievement as the 2004 Nobel Peace Laureate is a great opportunity to expand EAEN's networking activities as it has led to increased interest in environmental issues. The EAEN is now exploiting this growing interest in furthering ESD, including reaching out to key players such as the media. The agenda-setting role of the media has to be fully utilized in the attainment of millennium development goals.

We look forward to creating more awareness of ESD through our informative environmental quarterly, *Njiwa*, which is widely read in the region especially in academic institutions.

Indeed, the EAEN has the potential to contribute immensely in the provision of ESD. The NEMA recognizes it as one of the organizations that has the potential to reduce environmental degradation through provision of more focused EE.

As such, the organization is intent on offering training in EE and environmental management. This is still in the planning and consultation stages, and, we believe, that with the support of national, regional, and international organizations and collaborators, it will be a success.

All these good intentions of transforming the environmental ethic in the region, however, might remain a dream due to social, cultural, political, and economic constraints. For EE to yield fruit, it must be practical and participatory, calling for more actors and financial resources, which the organization lacks. The poverty that is rampant in the region has led to misplacement of priorities with more focus on immediate needs, some of which are met through exploitation of natural resources. Investing in EE is a sure way of making inroads into poverty reduction.

Recent research findings reveal that in order to reduce environmental degradation, women must be incorporated in environmental programmes. This continues to pose a challenge due to the inherent gender inequalities and the deep-rooted patriarchal systems that hinder women from active participation in development issues.

Academic institutions are well placed in inculcating environmental values right from primary to tertiary levels. Getting individual governments to include EE in their national academic curricular, however, has been one of the daunting tasks.

Another major potential player is the media whose editorial policies have not favored environmental issues. Most of them are concerned with maximizing profits and more often than not, term environmental information as boring and unsellable.

Conflicting national environmental policies may also be an obstacle in the implementation of some ESD programs.

Nevertheless, with a mission to redeem Mother Earth and seal loopholes arising from lack of appropriate EE, these challenges could be turned into opportunities. We are planning to find sources of financial support from local and overseas donors and create partnerships that further enhance our implementing capacities. Research into and provision of alternative sources of livelihood, including income-generating activities, will be prerequisites.

Lobbying respective governments to encourage media organizations to promote EE in their programmes will be a step forward. It is high time that governments stopped underestimating the power of the media in promoting ESD. This could be through provision of incentives and enactment of friendly media laws and policies considering that most developing countries have not fully liberalized their information sectors.

The EAEN and other stakeholders will have to advocate for harmonization of national environmental policies, especially those that are an impediment to the furtherance of environmental efforts.

Campaigns aimed at encouraging communities to shun cultural values that do not promote ESD will have to be stepped up. Organized field trips and exposure tours to successful projects is one way of tackling cultural prejudices.

Gender equality is key to breaking the cycle of poverty and improving the quality of life of the people of the Eastern Africa region. Mainstreaming gender in environmental programmes, therefore, remains critical, as this will give girls and women the strength, information, services, and, above all, the confidence they need to navigate their way through life. This will call for enactment of policies that are gender friendly and will sensitize citizens on environmental rights and responsibilities.

Therefore, before offering any EE, the EAEN recommends that a training needs assessment be carried out. Research reveals that most EE programs have been offered haphazardly, without bearing in mind the expected outcome. For instance, Kenya has a number of colleges offering environmental studies, yet the rate of environmental degradation continues unabated.

Training programmes must be tailored to meet the environmental needs of the target group. Consequently, to have an impact, messages must be designed in a way that they are uniformly and correctly interpreted.

Further, organizations planning to offer formal training in EE should bear in mind the interplay of social, economic, cultural, and political factors that lead to environmental degradation. They must recognize the complexity of environmental issues and endeavour to embrace a multidisciplinary approach. For instance, political structures to a greater extent determine the direction and also shape solutions to environmental problems. Hence, excluding them from environmental decision-making processes is a grave omission.

Hence, the diverse sociocultural interests must be brought on board and addressed exhaustively and objectively since they directly impact the environment and development in general. The role of women in decision-making in issues that have a direct bearing on the environment and sustainable development such as population growth, poverty reduction, and natural resource use must be given priority.

They should do thorough research to ensure that duplication of efforts does not arise. Regardless of the EE programs implemented, a follow-up of those trained must be made to determine their impact.

Organizations must also guard against rural–urban biases. The tendency has been to site most EE programmes in urban centers at the expense of rural areas. In fact, the discrepancies in information, environmental awareness, and development in general between rural and urban areas are attributed to these biases. Yet it is the rural folk that are in constant touch with the environment, especially natural resources that need to be sustainably utilized. Resource centers must, therefore, be set up in rural areas where we have the majority of the population.

Above all, target groups must be well identified and constituted before any EE training commences. Otherwise, it will be an effort in futility. Offering the right information to the wrong group is as good as not offering anything. This is one of the reasons why most EE programmes have not yielded much. For example, EE needs of CBOs and nongovernment organizations are different from those of universities, middle-class colleges, and secondary and primary schools. The methods and the medium of instruction required also differ in various ways. Although different, however, the goal must be similar, to bring about positive environmental values, attitudes, and behaviors necessary in the attainment of sustainable development.

Sustainable Development by Instinct, Challenges, and Opportunities in the Decade

Gary Lim and Khaeril Zach Abdullah

INTRODUCTION

The declaration of United Nations Decade on Education for Sustainable Development (DESD 2005–2014) is an international recognition of the pivotal role that environmental education and communication (EEC) can play in enhancing sustainable development efforts.

Environmental education and to a larger extend or education for sustainable future (ESF) fosters the understanding of the interconnectedness and harmony among ecological, economical, and social needs.

Without getting into a debate about the definitions of EE in relation to ESD or ESF, our broad understanding for ESD is that it utilizes a multidisciplinary and learner-centered approach and an innovative and participatory style to sensitize and empower individuals, especially students, to think, act, and respond appropriately to the current development models. Hence, ESD may encompass EE, values education (VE), and nature education (NE).

Asian countries are charatericised by great variations in their human and economic development indices. Malaysia is no different, and before learning takes place, one has to deal with the diversity and complexity of audience and the range of environmental issues.

This brief article aims to highlight the response of citizens towards the Decade. At the same time, it attempts to examine current teachers' understanding and attitudes towards the concept of ESD and how this subjective understanding eventually affects the perceptions, effectiveness, and attitude towards ESD in Malaysia. The challenges facing the future direction of ESD in Malaysia are also briefly mentioned.

Apart from attempting to highlight visible inclinations to towards ESD, this article will also:

- discuss the opportunities in Malaysia to derive maximum benefit from DESD;
- suggest what government agencies, national associations, and civil society groups can do in response to the DESD;
- discuss availability or constraints of a support system that facilitates the adoption of ESD on a daily basis.

It is hoped that the information and insights gained would contribute to the creation of a progressive, dynamic, and practical ESD strategy applicable to Malaysia.

BACKGROUND

Communicating the important message of the environment in relation to its social, economic, and cultural dimension is a critical challenge facing us today. Environment Education is widely regarded by many planners, administrators, scientists, teachers, and learners as fundamental in spreading this message.

While EE can be a problematic process, it can be conducted as an extracurricular activity. However, there is currently no coherent framework and some limitations across the nation within which to share experiences or progress for EE or ESD.

On the forefront, the Ministry of Education (MOE), Malaysia, has tried to introduce EE into the formal curriculum through the "man and the environment module." This effort has been discontinued, however, and as a matter of principle, EE is infused across subjects. Infusing EE across the curriculum is more dependent on individual creativity, however, and in many instances it is hampered by the lack of proper training, resources, and institutional support. To make EE inclusive it has to be built into the formal curriculum.

In view of the current situation, various organizations, especially NGOs, have taken on the task of raising environmental awareness and promoting EE.

Work of the NGOs, having traditionally focused on children, has arrived at a point where it is necessary to evaluate and create more innovative approaches. Efforts that focus on specific target groups may have less impact and sustainability than activities that include the community as a whole.

ENVIRONMENTAL EDUCATION INITIATIVES

Largely focused on the urban nonformal sector, numerous EE initiatives have depended on the support and collaboration with the corporate sector as well as some government agencies.

Existing EE activities primarily target students and selected groups of communities. These initiatives are carried out in various settings such as forest and recreational parks, protected areas, schools, as well as plantations and use different methodologies. A popular method is "using the environment as a classroom" to provide valuable experiences. The philosophy of using the environment as a classroom encourages learners to focus, explore, reflect, and apply their experiences through various activities. This includes environmental games, role-play, environmental auditing, and field studies. The aim is to influence values and behavior, then sensitize people to the issues and promote sound decision making and motivate people towards positive action. Basically the methods and approaches can be divided into:

I. The *in-situ* approach through the establishment of field study centers and learning stations that offer nature study experiences; and
II. The *ex-situ* approach through outreach programmes such as school clubs, slide shows, symposia, scientific and biological expeditions, exhibitions, conferences, and public campaigns.

Activities such as organizing field trips, slide shows, symposia, and scientific expeditions are used as a key approach to encourage interest towards EE and ESD. While the effectiveness of these approaches may be deliberated further, it is regularly used to extend messages of conservation and loss of biodiversity to the public.

Several lessons emerge from the analysis of these programs and experiences, as we aim to forge stronger relationships between learners and their environment.

Community Education Program

The trend of sponsor-driven and development of EE programs with minimal participation of communities are inevitable, given the nature of the projects. Akin to the analogy of the *Cormorant and the Conflicting Interests*, implementers often have a range of "needs" with which to deal. Whereas, formerly, nongovernmental organizations (NGOs) could be assumed to be nonpartisan and apolitical, the situation today has reduced them to project consultants.

Therefore, the impact of sustainable (or unsustainable) development is most apparent at the local level. For this reason, ESD must be rooted at the community level and the power of engaging a community realized.

An example of a community-centered and a participatory approach to ESD is exemplified in the UNDP/GEF Funded Project on the Conservation of Peat Swamp Forest (2003–2007). While the project is dependent on intra-agency funding and technical expertise, efforts are already well underway to ensure that initiatives are participatory and community driven.

Finally, the aim of this project is to train and motivate the stewardship of local communities by encouraging them to participate in the development of the environment, instead of just being beneficiaries.

DISCUSSION—CHALLENGES TO ESD IN MALAYSIA

In the workshop (2000) on EE organised by the Curriculum Development Centre (CDC) and the Ministry of Education Malaysia and supported by DANCED, it was suggested that the efforts to introduce EE as a cross-cutting subject in the curriculum may not increase the competency of students to deal with environmental problems or SD.

This has been compounded by the fact that the cross-curricular approach to teaching EE has not been fully understood by many teachers who presume that EE can best be taught through a limited number of subjects like science and geography.

Subsequently, there is confusion over terms such as EE, ESD, abd conservation education (CE), which may look trivial but create communication problems between practitioners.

The broad nature of EE has to a certain degree contributed to this lack of understanding on the concept of EE, among practitioners and the public. Enviornmental education, like the concept of SD, has become more a catch phrase than a point of departure for action.

Environmental awareness tends to become an issue when environmental problems occur. Practitioners need to develop a more proactive approach, including training and capacity building of human resources, by incorporating EEC and ESD from the planning stage by instinct. Evaluation of the EE process poses another challenge due to the lack of proper baseline studies and a coherent framework for EE in Malaysia. A national policy or strategy for ESD can be designed more effectively when baseline information involving as many stakeholders as possible is available.

POSSIBLE DIRECTIONS

Due to the diversity of teaching methods and audience, there is some consensus among EE practitioners that it may be beneficial to establish an "umbrella body" to coordinate work in ESD. The umbrella body can concentrate and harness the expertise and channel resources more efficiently towards the development of an ESD strategy or policy applicable to the Malaysian scenario.

Its role could also be extended to streamline all EEC activities and act as a clearinghouse for expertise, materials, training, and funding initiatives.

Some recommendations follow:

- *Training.* There is a great need to add value to EE programs and to create a clear career path for students and practitioners of EE. Some work has begun in developing accreditation between local organizations and external universities to develop competencies through cross-training, exchange, and study visits for capacity building.
- *University leadership for ESD.* On the same level as training, encouraging action research on ESD on a multistakeholder platform between NGOs and institutions of higher learning will complement and build upon local knowledge and expertise.
- *Publications.* In relation to the gaps in training needs and research, there is strong need for publications that in turn will support growth

for ESD. Creating an EE journal may be a step in this direction.

- *Curriculum reform.* Reorientation is needed to depart from the current "cascade model" of implementing EE and developing the curriculum. This is to provide for a more open-ended and inclusive process in view of achieving learner-centered results.

Over the years, there is an increase in the number of environment-orientated postgraduate and professional courses offered by universities. However, ESD and learning for the environment should be made an integral part of higher education to increase the expertise of future administrators and decisionmakers. Partnerships such as the collaboration between the University Sains Malaysia (USM) and the United Nations University (UNU) to organize a workshop on ESD in April is very much in line with these needs. There are potential benefits to be derived in collaborating with international agencies on ESD in the areas mentioned above.

CONCLUSION

It is imperative that we continue to create opportunities for people to come together to debate and discuss issues concerning ESD. This is crucial in view of Malaysia's "young development" in the field of EE. Whether we like it or not, the process and results from the implementation, engagement of citizens in dialogue, participation, and opportunities to work towards a more open way of "doing and thinking" will be the way of the future. Education for sustainable development when properly understood should become a natural instinct to include in a comprehensive lifelong education process, responsive to changes in a rapidly evolving world.

REFERENCES

Larsen, E., & Azizi bin Muda, (2000). *Strengthening of EE in primary and secondary schools in Malaysia: 2000.*

EE Asia and Beyond Proceedings: 1999.

Lim M. H. (1998/1999). *A study of environmental attitudes and knowledge of M'sian secondary school students.*

Ismail, M. *Case study of adult learning program.*

Environmental self-governance (The 6th Pacific Environmental Conference).

Report: regional workshop on promotion of environmental awareness. (1997).

William, J., & Peters, J. R. (1997). Local participation in the conservation of the Ranomafana National Park, Madagascar: *Journal of World Resource Management. 8,* 109–135. 0261-4286.

The Decade of Education for Sustainable Development: Challenges and Opportunities in México

Edgar González-Gaudiano

The international implementation plan for the Decade of Education for Sustainable Development (DESD) identifies four elements for the achievement of sustainable development through education:

1. Recognising the challenge (learning to learn)
2. Collective responsibility and constructive society (learning to live together)
3. Acting with determination (learning to do)
4. The indivisibility of human dignity (learning to be)[1]

These four structural elements make reference to desirable principles of basic education, the realignment of current educational programmes, the raising of public awareness, understanding the meaning of sustainability, and training. The principles in turn refer to objectives that define the goals and areas of action that it is hoped will be dealt with during the Decade, namely:

1. Eradication of poverty
2. Gender equality
3. The promotion of health
4. Environmental conservation and protection
5. Rural transformation
6. Human rights
7. Inter-cultural understanding and peace
8. Sustainable production and consumption
9. Cultural diversity
10. Information and communications technologies.

What is the meaning of this for Mexico and, particularly, what are the implications for the Ministry of Public Education?

Agenda 21 recognised that profound change in lifestyles, in development styles, and in styles of thought and nowledge were fundamental to achieving sustainability. All of these changes are related to educational processes designed to raise public awareness, informed citizen participation, and the development of decision-making skills applicable to all matters affecting quality of life. However, funding for such an approach to education was not forthcoming and complaints began to be heard, such as the opinion voiced at the IUCN World Congress for Conservation (Montreal, 1996) that "education was the forgotten priority from Rio." In the 10 years between Rio de Janeiro and the World Summit for Sustainable Development (Johannesburg, 2002), the foreseeable climate remained largely unchanged. Environmental education has featured as a priority in

[1] The four kinds of learning mentioned in parentheses were also the structural elements proposed by the Delors Commission, which prepared the 1996 report on *Learning: The Treasure Within.*

institutional speeches and declarations, but very little funding has been provided to establish a strategy and a plan of action in keeping with the importance it was given in the rhetoric.

In the education field, environmental education has been seen as just one more verbose form of education, as is also the case of multicultural education, education for democratic thought, and human rights education: emerging fields, precariously established, perceived as passing fads that exist on the periphery of education and in the folds of the social attitudes of our times, but which, according to the "makers of education in the country," do not manage to impact the mainstream of educational debate and yet dare to challenge the system for a space in an already over-burdened school curriculum.

In Mexico, environmental education and related fields such as training and communications have merely played a supportive role and have been called "instruments" for environmental management. That is to say, they are seen as tools that help achieve environmental goals (renovation, conservation, etc.), in themselves considered essential ends and, therefore, superior to education's role in the creation of social values, attitudes, and aptitudes.

Why this talk about education for sustainable development now?

Precisely because it is hoped that we can transcend the limited role that has been given to environmental education, to date, in the broad context of developed countries and many others, including Mexico. Too often, the meaning of "environment" has been reduced to "nature," and "environmental education" to elementary schooling.

This is why the resolution for the Decade speaks of the Dakar Plan of Action of Education for All, because sustainability is no longer only linked to ecological policy but also to the struggle against poverty in search of greater social equality that affords better opportunities to the most vulnerable social groups (women, indigenous peoples, young people, etc.). Education for sustainable development is conceived as education in values, civil and ethical education that seeks the formation of a critical citizenry capable of stimulating an analysis of what is going on with respect to our concerns and desires for social change. And, if sustainable development implies new and different thought processes, it requires creativity, flexibility, and critical reflection in order to influence the systems of public participation in decision making. Evidently, this empowerment could never come about by simply including more course materials and didactic activities in different school syllabuses because, although it implies qualitative modifications in schooling, it transcends such considerations to become a prerequisite for our transformation into a knowledge society.

One problem that derives from all of this is that in Mexico, and in other parts of the world (Latin America and the Caribbean, and certain Spanish and Canadian institutions), we have been giving environmental education the same twist, with a socio-critical approach currently being sponsored for education for sustainable development; therefore, simply substituting the concepts, in addition to losing hard-won political assets, would add to the confusion of those who have become more and more involved in this field over recent years.

From a pragmatic standpoint, and in the knowledge that the DESD represents a window of opportunity to strengthen some of the processes and practices slowly established in Mexico with great difficulty and precious little institutional support, certain groups are beginning to talk about environmental education for sustainable development or environmental education for sustainability, which, as a matter of fact, was agreed upon at the International Environment and Society Conference, Education and Sensitization for Sustainability held in Thessaloniki, Greece, 1997.

The Decade is faced with two additional problems: The first is the conceptual opaqueness regarding the nature of sustainable development and consequently ESD. This does not permit a clear definition of target groups, practical strategies, and the scope of projects. UNESCO's definition of ESD comprises 10 topics that have to be dealt with, even though in reality it is a case of disjointed communities of educators that have gone through their own process, their own struggles. This brings us to the second problem, namely, that generally only environmental educators are aware of ESD and are discussing it. Truth be told, although other groups of educators, defenders of human rights and gender, students of multi-cultural issues, and so on, have found out that they are involved in the Decade, at least in Mexico, they do not seem to feel included. Furthermore, the seeming neglect of environmental education in discussions of ESD may undermine some of the advances made, on a regional level in environmental education, such as laws and specialist organisations and journals.

In the meantime, and to take advantage of the institutional opportunities that the Decade may offer, the Ministry of Public Education has considered environmental and sustainability issues as a backbone in the design of its National "Education for All" Programme. Moreover, it has set up a high-level internal group comprising 14 directors of the Ministry's different agencies, under the coordination of the International Affairs Directorate, to draw up an institutional plan of action in this respect that may, when the time is right, fit in with the plans drawn up by other sectors. It is producing a television series with educational goals in mind on a variety of topics in conjunction with the Ministry of the Environment and Natural Resources. In addition, a National Commitment to the Decade of Education for Sustainable Development has been signed by all local governments, principal business organisations, churches, academic institutions, and civil society organisms. Nonetheless, it would be desirable, as part of the DESD, 2005–2014, that:

a) An inter-ministerial commission should be set up to agree upon the adoption of institutional individual and group measures that would include initiating a nationwide call to all federal entities to throw their weight behind this major undertaking in an effective coordinated manner.
b) A national policy should be developed with the different social groups and sectors for the creation of Environmental Education for Sustainable Development that would involve the most diverse spaces of public life.
c) A national fund for Environmental Education for Sustainable Development should be set up with contributions from public, private, and social sectors.
d) Other education fields such as sustainable consumption, peace, population issues, health, and water conservation and energy savings, among others, should be taken into account in the creation of Environmental Education for Sustainable Development.
e) A support network should be set up that would get the entire academic community involved: universities and institutes of higher education, research centres, and professional organisms and colleges.
f) Different ways should be explored to make use of the mass media to maximise the impact of Environmental Education for Sustainable Development in the public's daily activities, placing emphasis on matters of employment, public security, and the struggle against corruption and unaccountability.
g) Mechanisms of international collaboration should be agreed upon, making special mention of those of a regional nature: North America, Latin America, and the Caribbean.

Education for Sustainable Development in New Zealand

Barry Law

The UN Decade of Education for Sustainable Development (DESD) is yet to feature in major government initiatives in New Zealand. Many opportunities for deriving maximum benefit from the DESD, however, may be noted. These opportunities are based around four key areas:

- government policy and national reports,
- formal education initiatives,
- local government, community, and business education, and
- tertiary education.

GOVERNMENT POLICIES AND REPORTS

In New Zealand education for sustainable development (ESD) is being addressed through a range of education and learning programmes that traditionally have focused on environmental education. There is a movement, however, towards using the broader term "education for sustainable development." This shift is associated with changes from the narrower biophysical ecology focus of the term "environmental education" towards the broader social, environmental, and economic focus of ESD. Furthermore, sustainable development in New Zealand is viewed as "a process rather than an end result" (Ministry for the Environment [MFE], 2000, p. 1).

Two key documents establish the government's overarching priorities for education and sustainability and potentially provide opportunities for ESD: *Sustainable Development for New Zealand Programme of Action* (New Zealand, [NZ] Department of Prime Minister and Cabinet, 2003) and *Education Priorities for New Zealand* (NZ Ministry of Education, 2003).

The *Programme of Action* notes that "sustainable development must be at the core of all government policy. It includes a vision that New Zealanders will 'cherish our natural environment [and be] committed to protecting it for future generations." The role that education could play in meeting this vision is not overtly explored, although it is noted that "fostering an appreciation of New Zealand's unique natural environment among children and young people helps to ensure its protection and enhancement for future generations."

Education Priorities for New Zealand (NZ Ministry of Education, 2003) provides a summary of the government's priorities in education. Education is seen as being at the heart of social and economic development in New Zealand. *Education Priorities* focuses on raising achievement among learners—it does not identify environment care or protection as a goal for that achievement. However, the NZ Ministry of Education has produced the document *Guidelines for Environmental Education in New Zealand Schools* (NZ Ministry of Education, 1999). The *Guidelines* does not mandate a compulsory environmental education programme or approach but does identify how the mandated curriculum in each of the essential learning areas could support such a programme.

Two reports also establish priorities for education and sustainability. They include *Curriculum Stocktake Report (2002)*, Ministry of Education Curriculum Review, and *See Change: Learning and Education for Sustainability* Parliamentary Commissioner for the Environment [PCE], 2004.

In 2002 the *Curriculum Stocktake Report* (Ministry of Education, 2002a) was accepted by the Cabinet. This report reflected a 2-year review of the New Zealand Curriculum. It recommended a number of changes. Those relevant to education for sustainability included the identification of six "future focused themes." It was suggested that these be used to audit the redeveloped outcome aims and objectives of the revised curriculum. The future-focused themes follow:

- Social cohesion (including resilience and social connectedness),
- citizenship (local, national, and global),
- education for a sustainable future (including sustainable development and environmental sustainability),
- bicultural awareness and multicultural awareness,
- enterprise and innovation, and
- critical literacy (including digital literacy).

It is interesting to note that social cohesion, citizenship, bicultural and multicultural awareness, enterprise education, and critical literacy are all key elements of education for a sustainable future. This point has been noted by the national environmental education coordinators and further highlights the importance of ESD as a major theme that should permeate the national curriculum.

The PCE released his report *See Change: Learning and Education for Sustainability* (January 2004) that explores "how societies can learn to live in sustainable ways" (PCE, 2004, p. 12). The document highlights the critical importance of education in its broadest sense and the need for redesign in education across all sector groups in New Zealand to bring about a fundamental change in thinking to achieve a sustainable future.

The purpose of the report "is to raise the level of debate about education for sustainability and to stimulate effective action so that New Zealanders can learn to live in sustainable ways" (PCE, 2004, p. 130). The document addresses the need for new thinking and a shift in how we view issues/problems in order to implement action that brings about situation improvement. This document has the potential to influence our thinking and shape future decision-making in a wide range of governmental and local body policies over the next few years. The Parliamentary Commissioners Office, however, can only influence and stimulate the level of debate: It has no ability to directly develop policy in this area.

FORMAL EDUCATION

Education for sustainable development has been recognized by innovative educators in the formal sector who are planning for the future. This is in contrast to those who seek to promote more traditional areas of study that in the past have worked. Some education officials, teachers, and teacher educators have explored the potential of introducing courses of study at the senior secondary school level and in in-service courses in teacher education.

In January 2003 a national environmental education coordination team was set up throughout New Zealand to support schoolteachers. Eleven full-time positions were allocated to the six School Support Service providers. One national coordinator was established (.5, half time of a Full time position) based at the Christchurch College of Education. The coordination team participates in two 3-day meetings a year and reports once a year to a national reference group to gain feedback and provide guidance to the Ministry of Education. UNESCO NZ have established a coordination committee responsible for overseeing the UNDESD. The Minister responsible for the Decade has agreed to a high level committee to lead, advocate for, and facilitate the New Zealand response to the Decade. Representatives from key government departments, local government, Maori and Pacific communities, civil society, youth, NGO's, business, media, and academia have been appointed.

LOCAL GOVERNMENT, COMMUNITY, AND BUSINESS EDUCATION

The MfE has also undertaken some initiatives in the environment and education area. The MfE provides guidance to local government, community, and business specifically on issues affecting the biophysical environment. Traditionally this has involved both a regulatory and educative role. More recently, however, the support for formal education has been left to other sector groups.

The MfE contribution includes establishing a sustainable management fund. Some of the projects often have a strong educational component. The MfE has provided contestable funding for some Environment Education Centres. Most recently the MfE has organised a National Youth Environment Forum, first established in 2003, cosponsored by the Sir Peter Blake Trust in 2004, and likely to become an annual event.

Local government and the MfE have helped establish the national "Enviroschools" (Enviroschools Foundation, 2003) programme and "awards scheme" (Auckland Regional Council, 2002) facilitated by the Enviroschool Foundation Trust based in Hamilton. Enviroschools is a whole-school approach to environmental education where students participate in creating a sustainable school with support from their communities. Schools form an Envirogroup, create a Vision Map, and undertake environmental action projects on the schools grounds that integrate the formal curriculum.

Sustainable business interests have become involved in supporting education for sustainability in schools. Enviroschools New Zealand is supported by way of grants for administration and staffing. Untouched World Foundation in Christchurch provides funding support for the Blumine Island sustainable futures project in the Marlborough Sounds. The Blumine Island project is a joint partnership between Untouched World Foundation, Department of Conservation, Christchurch College of Education, and South Island secondary schools and is likely to be extended to other others around New Zealand.

TERTIARY EDUCATION

In 2002 the *Tertiary Education Strategy* 2002–2007 (Ministry of Education, 2002b) was released. It includes six national development objectives taken from the Growth and Innovation Framework (*Growing an Innovative New Zealand*, Ministry of Economic Development, 2002).

The *Tertiary Education Strategy* identifies a need for research and skills:

- to contribute to international understanding of climate change;
- to sustain biodiversity;
- to manage changing patterns of land and sea use; and
- to "help all New Zealanders develop an awareness of the environment and the impacts economic and social activities have on it" (Ministry of Education, 2002b).

However, there is limited detail or mention of how this might be achieved in the document. While many universities in New Zealand provide environment-related papers, the focus of these papers is often on knowledge acquisition and awareness rather than on developing one's action competence skills.

There have been several attempts within teacher education to address the inclusion of core or optional papers in environmental education and ESD. Currently four institutions have developed either optional or core courses in ESD. The national environmental education coordination team has allocated funding to support preservice initiatives during the 2005 financial year.

SUMMARY

In summary, the opportunities for deriving maximum benefit from the Decade in New Zealand include the following.

1. The development of effective partnerships among formal education, local government, community educators, and sustainable business.
2. A shift in curriculum thinking that identifies education for a sustainable future as a key focus theme in the redevelopment of the NZ Curriculum.
3. The development of National Certificate of Educational Achievement (NCEA) courses at the senior secondary level that focus on sustainable futures.
4. A strong national coordination team (11 full-time positions) that facilitate regional in-service professional development for teachers in environmental education across New Zealand.
5. An innovative Enviroschools Foundation and awards scheme that supports the concept of sustainable schools.
6. A strong national environmental education association (NZAEE) that provides networking, an organizational structure, political support, and conference opportunities for environmental educators.
7. A developing research community in education for sustainability through the NZ Council for Education Research, the University of Waikato, and Christchurch College of Education.

CHALLENGES AND HOW THESE COULD BE ADDRESSED

One major constraint is that the government's *Programme of Action* does not specifically mention education for sustainability or ESD. (Education more generally is a focus in a number of parts of the programme including the identification of child and youth development as one of several key issues.)

A second constraint is the nature and structure of schooling. There is a need to re-examine the structures of schooling in a more critical way to address education for a sustainable future in its broadest context. Education requires a deeper critique and a broader vision to ensure a sustainable future. Thus, a whole system redesign needs to be considered to challenge existing frameworks and shift our thinking beyond current practice and towards a sustainable future. The Ministry of Education has to date not supported the role of education for sustainability as a key aspect of formal education. Political pressure is required to ensure that education for sustainable development is given higher status in our national achievement goals.

Teaching and learning in ESD poses a third constraint. Learning needs to move beyond a mechanisitic and transmissive approach and adopt a more transformational process that shifts people's thinking. Teachers and students should operate as a critical community of reflective thinkers rather than as functional learners. Meaning and understanding needs to be constructed and emergent rather than given, and learning needs to be active rather than passive.

A fourth constraint is that tertiary education providers have been slow to offer programmes that comprehensively address ESD in formal qualifications. Consequently, there are limited qualifications in the tertiary sector that specifically address education for sustainability by linking biophysical, economic, cultural, social, and political aspects together in a coherent programme of study. There are no ESD requirements or specific outcomes identified for teacher education by central government and, therefore, very few teacher education providers have developed courses or acknowledge ESD components in their preservice or inservice programmes.

Assessment issues are a fifth constraint. There are currently no achievement standards that specifically address cross-curricular standards for ESD. The national environmental education coordinators, however, have addressed this issue and developed four new draft standards for submission in August 2005.

Although indigenous perspectives of the environment are recognized as a crucial component of environmental education and ESD, a further constraint is a lack of structure within many organizations and institutions to provide support for this. More Maori environmental educators and resources in te reo Maori are required for Maori students and teachers in Kura, Maori immersion, and mainstream schools to address the cultural perspectives of ESD.

Probably the most serious challenge by far, however, is the need for coordination between individual people, nongovernmental organizations (NGOs), government sector groups, and community groups working in New Zealand. While some coordination is beginning to happen between some groups, there is a lack of coordination and direction between government departments in identifying joint national outcomes for ESD.

Presently, there are attempts to address some of the issues outlined above. They tend to be further constrained, however, by the lack of any organisational and operational framework that outlines how specific outcomes will be achieved for each sector group working in ESD in New Zealand. There is also no formal monitoring procedure to check on whether specific outcomes for ESD are being met in formal, local government, or community education.

CONCLUSION

In conclusion, What would I like to see government agencies and national associations do in response to the Decade?

1. Add ESD to the New Zealand Government's *Programme of Action.*
2. Have the government establish and coordinate a cross-sectoral strategy for ESD.
3. Request that government departments provide adequate support and funding to implement effective ESD programmes in community education, formal education, and tertiary education.
4. Link school, adult education, and tertiary based ESD programmes to local community projects so learners are involved in monitoring their own action-based skills in real environments (not theoretical ones) and contribute towards a sustainable environment.
5. Have the Ministry of Education recognize that ESD is an essential aspect of education for the future and a domain in which quality teaching and learning can flourish.
6. Enable more access to research funding to support the development of ESD action and evaluation.

REFERENCES

Auckland Regional Council. (2002). *Enviroschools Awards Scheme.* Auckland: ARC.

Enviroschools Foundation NZ. (2003). *Strategic plan.* Hamilton: Enviroschools.

New Zealand Department of Prime Minister and Cabinet. (2003). *Sustainable Development for New Zealand Programme of Action.* Wellington: Department of Prime Minister and Cabinet.

New Zealand Ministry of Economic Development. (2002). *Growing an Innovative New Zealand.* Wellington: Ministry of Economic Development. Available: http://gif.med.govt.nz/aboutus/index.asp.

New Zealand Ministry of Education. (1999). *Guidelines for environmental education in New Zealand schools.* Wellington: Learning Media.

New Zealand Ministry of Education. (2002a). *Curriculum Stockade Report.* Wellington: Author, Unpublished.

New Zealand Ministry of Education. (2002b). *Tertiary Education Strategy 2002–2007.* Wellington: Ministry of Education. Available: tertiary.strategy@minedu.govt.nz.

New Zealand Ministry of Education. (2003). *Education Priorities for New Zealand.* Wellington: Ministry of Education.

New Zealand Ministry for the Environment. (2000). *Briefing Papers.* Wellington: Author, Unpublished.

Parliamentary Commission for the Environment (PCE). (2004). *See change: Learning and education for sustainability.* Wellington: Author.

Embarking on the Decade for Sustainable Development: A Swaziland View

Irma Allen

INTRODUCTION

Tucked between South Africa and Mozambique, and usually "gowned" in green, Swaziland is one of the smallest countries in Africa (17,364 square kilometers), but it has great variation in landscape, geology, and climate. It also has great diversity of fauna and flora (846 species of vertebrates and approximately 3,500 species of flora). This diversity of flora and fauna and their gene pool and ecosystems are the natural wealth of Swaziland and provide the basis for economic development and well-being.

Nevertheless, rapid population growth (2.9%), industrialization, urbanization, increasing agricultural demands, and a declining economy, whose effects are exacerbated by poverty and an increasing prevalence of HIV/AIDS, are among factors that are fast degrading the natural resource base and this, in turn, is posing a threat to sustainable development.

In recognition of the importance that sound environmental management plays in the course of Swaziland's development, and cognizant of the country's commitment to implement international Conventions and agreements, the government has been following a steady course towards improved environmental management beginning with the establishment of the Swaziland Environment Authority (SEA) by statute in 1992 as a government department. This was followed by the development of the *Swaziland's Environment Action Plan* (SEAP GOS/MTEC) in 1997. This plan is being implemented with the assistance of four cross-sectoral committees of stakeholders. Important national environmental policies have been developed in important areas, including biodiversity, environmental education, waste management, forestry, and water.

In 2000, the Environmental Management Act established SEA as a corporate body. It continues to have four major areas of responsibility:

1. policy development and research,
2. environmental assessment and monitoring,
3. regulation and compliance, and
4. education and information.

Its mission is to:

> Ensure that Swaziland's development is environmentally, economically and socially sustainable, by means of promoting sound environmental policies, practices and development which meets appropriate national and international standards.

The SEA relies on other Ministries, government agencies, and private sector nongovernmental organizations (NGOs), CBOs, and the public at large for the implementation of its policies, compliance with legislation and regulations, and participation in environmental action.

OPPORTUNITIES

The SEA is only one of the major stakeholders of sustainable development, but it clearly has an important role to play in the Decade for Education for Sustainable Development

(DESD). In terms of the evolution of the environmental processes that it has catalyzed, it is at a critical stage, where vital national policies have been developed but need to be implemented:

- The DESD offers the opportunity for mounting a national campaign to raise awareness about national environmental policies and strategies, call people to action, and provide training for implementation.
- It also offers the opportunity to achieve the recommendations of the SEAP in the area of education, public awareness, and participation.

A Swaziland Environmental Education Strategy and Action Plan (SEESAP) has been developed with a sound plan for formal and nonformal environmental education.

- The DESD offers the opportunity for accessing resources to implement the recommended strategies and action plan of the SEESAP. This could result in a systematic integration of EE (in this case synonymous with ESD) at all levels of formal education and expand the number of stakeholders in nonformal EE).
- It offers the opportunity to take EE to higher levels of achievement as ESD becomes more sensitive to the different realities that challenge people, more community and solidarity oriented, and preoccupied with linking social, economic, and environmental equity at all levels.

In addition to the opportunities above, Swaziland is committed to achieving the UN Millennium Development Goals, one of the most significant international initiatives launched in 2000 to respond to issues of health, poverty, and environmental degradation. Some of the goals that seem to have a greater significance for the future of EE (or ESD) follow:

- eradication of extreme poverty and hunger,
- achievement of universal primary education,
- promotion of gender equality and empowerment of women,
- elimination of HIV/AIDS, malaria, and other diseases,
- assurance of environmental sustainability (Lotz, 2004),
- Swaziland (along with 190 other countries) committed itself to achieving the above goals by 2015. The DESD provides a wonderful opportunity for renewed commitment and action.

CHALLENGES

Although there are good opportunities in Swaziland for deriving maximum benefits from the DESD, there are also some formidable challenges currently facing the country that will have to be faced by any undertaking for the DESD. These include a declining economy, poverty, and an HIV/AIDS pandemic.

- Swaziland currently has the highest incidence of HIV/AIDS in the world. In 2002, HIV/AIDS affected 38.6% of the population. In 2004, the incidence rose to 42.6%. This situation impacts negatively on deriving maximum benefits from DESD mainly in three ways:

  a. A large proportion of the population will not be available to provide the manpower and energy needed to take action to ensure sustainable development.
  b. The fight against AIDS has become the highest priority in Swaziland, and requires the expenditure of a large proportion of the financial resources of the country and of those coming from donor partners.
  c. As a result of the AIDS pandemic, there are now orphans.

The country's economic status has been declining in the last few years. Among many factors, reliance on the exportation of sugar and of textiles and clothing has resulted in disappointing returns, primarily due to the devaluation of the

U.S. dollar, which now buys less Emalangeni (the Swaziland currency, which is tied to the South African rand). In the last few years, the declining economy has given rise to new priorities, such as job creation.

- In attempts to attract new investments, environmental assessment has sometimes been perceived as an "impediment" and is often not given the consideration that it merits.
- There also appears to be a great lack of awareness (or even possibly a disregard) of the environmental dimension that underpins development.

For example, a current draft of a Poverty Reduction Action Plan states that by 2020, people, in Swaziland will all have access to water and sanitation. There is no mention however, of the environmental management strategy/strategies, such as catchment protection or water conservation practices that need to be in place before this goal can be achieved. Again, some of the macropolicies in the National Development Strategy (NDS) will have a negative impact on the environment, but this was not taken into consideration when the NDS was developed and approved.

- Swaziland is classified as a lower-middle-income country with a per capita income of about US $1,350, although 69% of the population lives in extreme poverty. This classification has precluded major programming initiatives by multilateral financing institutions and bilateral development assistance agencies.

Swaziland has a highly skewed income distribution. In the 1980s, industrialization and development policies resulted in growth and creation of significant new wealth especially in urban areas. There still continues to be wide income disparity. The top 10% of the population controls 40% of the wealth, while the bottom 40% of the population control only 14% of the wealth (UNDP/GOS, 2005).

ACTION

In the ensuing decade since the international community agreed on the Rio Principles and Agenda 21, it has been acknowledged that one of the biggest challenges in meeting the commitments and obligations assumed within the various conventions continues to be a lack of capacity. These capacity issues exist at various levels, namely, individual, organizational, and systemic.

Currently, with support from GEF/UNDP's Capacity Development Initiative (CDI), which was launched in 2000, Swaziland is implementing a project to identify national capacity constraints and priorities to meet binding commitments contained in the three Rio Conventions on biodiversity, climate change, and desertification.

The results of this study on National Capacity Needs will be used to determine how best to develop this capacity to meet Swaziland's commitment to global environmental management through the production of a strategy and action plan.

- During the DESD, resources need to be accessed and harnessed by government agencies and national associations toward the implementation of the action plan to build capacity at individual, institutional, and organizational level for environmental management and ultimately compliance with international agreements and conventions.

Part of building capacity entails decentralizing environmental management activities. Most of the national strategies and action plans that have been developed were developed at the national level, with some input from the regions. Now that implementation is the next step, it is time to decentralize the process.

- To ensure the widest possible participation in sustainable development in all sectors and levels of the Swaziland community, it is necessary to establish cross-sectoral environment task forces in the five regions of Swaziland, provide them with orientation/training on the new national strategies and action plans, and assist them to develop Regional Environment Action Plans.

Another important area of action for the DESD is in formal education. The public education system in Swaziland utilizes an evaluation process based on "external" examinations at various levels, for example, Primary Examination at the end of Grade 7, Junior Certificate Examination at the end of Grade 9, and O level examination at the end of Grade 11 or 12. The curriculum is designed at a national curriculum unit and is largely academic. Computer studies have been introduced in a limited number of schools within the last few years. The country does not have free universal education.

When one examines the potential implications of the Millennium Development Goals' commitment to working for environmental sustainability in formal education, it is imperative to consider the relevant environmental issues and risks. This means that we need to adopt a contextualized approach to EE (or ESD) in the country's education programs. There is a need to reorient curriculum and policy to be more responsive to local needs and to promote social and economic development.

Furthermore, the World Summit for Sustainable Development Plan of Implementation (WSSD 2000) emphasized the major role that education plays in sustainable development, and called for "the integration of sustainable development concepts, actions and principles in all levels of education in order to promote education as a key agent for change."

- It is therefore essential that Swaziland's Ministry of Education and its partners, in light of the Millennium Development Goals and the WSSD Implementation Plan, review the existing education policies and national curriculum to ensure that environmental sustainability is contextualized in the educational programs, and to make provision for accommodating the increasing number of orphans and vulnerable children.

Swaziland is fortunate to receive donor assistance from various sources. However, these resources are limited; thus efforts are being made to ensure the best possible strategic use of these resources. Currently a UN Development Assistance Framework (UNDAF) is being prepared for the period 2006–2010. Through a consultative process, the following key priority areas for assistance have been identified:

- HIV and AIDS,
- poverty reduction,
- food security,
- basic social services (mainly health and education), and
- governance.

The overpowering priority is HIV/AIDS; that the other four areas will complement the HIV/AIDS response. The main UN agencies who will be spearheading activities in these priority areas are UNICEF, WFP, World Health Organization (WHO), Food and Agriculture Organization of the United Nations (FAO), and UNDP.

- It is essential that all projects and activities in these priority areas include an EE/ESD dimension in order to empower the stakeholders to seek their own solutions to existing problems and ultimately to mobilize and make effective use of their own resources for sustainability.

VIEWPOINT

Having looked at the current position as regards opportunities, challenges, and needed action to obtain maximum benefits from the DESD, it is impossible not to almost simultaneously feel myriad emotions, for example optimism, trepidation, enthusiasm, and frustration. But the driving force that impels us all in Swaziland to embark on this challenging DESD is the vision of how sustainable development will enhance the quality of life in the country, and faith in the noble nature, indomitable spirit, and resourcefulness of the most valuable natural resource that we have in this little kingdom.... the people of Swaziland.

REFERENCES

Allen, I. (2004). *Biodiversity conservation awareness and training needs assessment: Final report.* Mbabane: Swaziland Environment Authority.

GOS/IUCN. (2004). *Enabling environmental education in Swaziland: The lobbying and awareness-raising Component.* Mbabane: Swaziland Environment Authority.

GOS/MTEC. (1997). *Swaziland environment action plan.* (vols. I and II). Mbabane: Swaziland Environment Authority.

Obol, C., Allen, I., & Springall Bach, H. (2003). Environmental education policy processes in the Southern African Region. *Southern African Journal of Environmental Education, 20,* 22–36

UNDP/GOS. (2005). *The United nations development assistance framework for the Kingdom of Swaziland* (draft). Mbabane: Author.

Emerging Opportunities in Education for Sustainable Development

BRIAN CHALKLEY

Rather than casting an eye backwards over the various articles brought together in this volume, this final paper will instead look forwards and focus on some recent or newly emerging ideas and opportunities for advancing the cause of sustainable development education. This is not to suggest that we should abandon existing structures, procedures and curricula, but rather that we should recognise the value of being open both to strengthening what we currently do and to sharing more widely different ways of thinking and working.

This call for change is not to deny that, both here in the UK and in many other parts of the world, there are already significant signs of progress. Many Universities and Colleges are certainly doing more to inject a sustainability dimension into their teaching and their research, and also to reduce their own institution's environmental footprint. However, it is increasingly clear that issues such as climate change and energy depletion are much more pressing and urgent than was thought five or ten years ago. Higher education, therefore, needs to raise its game and to accelerate its pace if it is to make a substantial and timely contribution to addressing these national and international issues. In effect, it needs to change both more quickly and more deeply.

Amongst the evidence for this is a recently published review of sustainable development in higher education in England which was commissioned by the Higher Education Funding Council for England (HEFCE, 2008). It found that although there is now clearly more SD activity in HEIs than there was a few years ago, there is only 'slight evidence' that it is still increasing. The authors acknowledge that there is no authoritative data-base from which to derive really firm conclusions on trends, but their research, covering 93 HEIs, suggest that significant barriers remain which are preventing a wider take-up of SD. Many of these have been referred to in the previous papers in this volume but the HEFCE study points particularly to the focus on mono-disciplinarity, the conservatism of some professional bodies, the impact of the Research Assessment Exercise (RAE) and the lack of clear incentives to engage with SD. So, while there are a small number of HEIs which are seeking to become exemplar organisations, there are many for whom sustainable development remains a low priority or not priority at all.

In recognising, therefore, that there is much to be done, this volume's final paper will highlight a selection of recent developments and fresh initiatives which arguably could make a worthwhile contribution. No attempt is made here to undertake a comprehensive approach, rather the aim is to highlight a small selection of ideas which have potential, and which have yet to be widely adopted. To readers with considerable ESD expertise and experience, some of these suggestions will already be familiar. (Indeed, some are touched on briefly in earlier parts of this volume.) What they have in common is that they are currently under-utilised and deserve a higher profile and wider adoption. In this way it is hoped that this publication, with its multiplicity of papers and perspectives, will end on a note of opportunity.

The first possibilities highlighted here are for those disciplines, such as Geography and Environmental Sciences, which already have, by virtue of their subject matter, a long-established interest in this area and in the broader field of society-environment relationships. In the case of these disciplines, the aim must be to capitalise on their 'natural advantage'. This means auditing the current curricula and exploring afresh the possibilities for engaging more fully and deeply with sustainability agendas. It also means making this engagement more explicit. At present many degree programmes which do address these issues do not make this sufficiently clear in the module/unit titles or in their publicity and marketing. Paradoxically, in the UK and in many other countries too, geography and environmental science have been experiencing static or even declining higher education recruitment (Gardner & Craig, 2001). The roots of this problem lie in part in the sometimes disappointing quality of geographical education in secondary schools (OFSTED, 2008): nonetheless it is clear that in higher education too, geography and environmental science need to re-focus their curriculum, play to their natural strengths and raise their ESD colours.

Given, however, that everyone, particularly in modern societies, consumes natural resources and produces pollution, it is obviously important that all students, irrespective of their discipline background, should become fully aware of the significance of the sustainability agenda. Indeed, the breadth of this agenda, with its social, economic, scientific and technological dimensions, means that in almost all disciplines there are real opportunities for engagement. In History or Sociology it may involve exploring the role of the environment in historical or social change, in English or Media Studies it could mean students examining the coverage of sustainability issues in poetry, novels or the press; in Engineering or Architecture there are opportunities in areas such as low energy designs. In some disciplines and some departments, these kinds of opportunity have already begun to be explored but there are substantial parts of the higher education arena where it could be useful for academics such as geographers and environmental scientists to take a lead and to promote dialogue and change amongst other colleagues. In doing so, it will be important both to capitalize upon established expertise but also to respect the extent to which different disciplines have different traditions, curricula, cultures and expectations. While ESD opens up particular opportunities and obligations for geographers and environmental scientists, this should not be seen as an exercise in academic colonisation. The recent book edited by Roberts and Roberts (2007) illustrates very effectively the way in which within a single institution (in this case the University of Gloucestershire) a wide variety of disciplines can contribute. In the UK, the Higher Education Academy has established a multi-disciplinary working group whose purpose is to encourage as wide a range of disciplines as possible to engage with SD. Details of how this group is now taking forward the agenda can be found at: http://www.heacademy.ac.uk/ourwork/learning/sustainability.

In addition to pursuing ESD via the disciplines, and indeed through multi and inter-disciplinary programmes and approaches, it is important also to work through educational institutions and their policies and practices. Although many Universities and Colleges have long had environmental policies (covering, for example, buildings, energy use, waste and landscape) relatively few have fully-fledged policies on how they intend to more towards a comprehensive institution-wide engagement with sustainability, spanning not only the campus but also areas such as the curriculum, research, finance, procurement, catering, transport and relationships with local and regional communities. To date few, if any, institutions have integrated sustainability into all their strategies, plans, policies and practices. Opportunities abound, therefore, for Universities and Colleges to move towards and help create a sustainability culture. Although, inevitably, this is an ambitious goal, with many barriers and obstacles along the way, the challenge is now for institutions to develop a culture in which sustainability values permeate and play a part in all the key areas of policy design and delivery.

Arguably, of course, the key policy area to be reviewed and strengthened relates to teaching and student learning. Today almost all Universities and Colleges have learning and teaching policies which deal with issues such as promoting deep learning, using the new technologies, designing fair and appropriate assessment methods and maintaining academic standards. As yet, very few such policies give much prominence to producing graduates who are equipped to contribute to the sustainability agenda, as professionals, as citizens or in their personal lives. There are opportunities here, therefore, to initiate change in learning and teaching policies and in so doing to provide a framework for and commitment to sustainability in the curriculum. Turning such policies into practice, of course, requires winning the hearts and minds of academic staff and ensuring that, where appropriate, they are supported in developing the necessary knowledge and expertise. The provision of appropriate continuing professional development (CPD) therefore represents another emerging area of opportunity for those who may wish to lead or contribute to change in this area.

Central to the shaping of an institution with a strong sustainability commitment will be an active and engaged student community. This means working in partnership with the Students Union and achieving active student representation in policy and decision-making. It may also involve working alongside the student body through activities such as special events, articles in student newspapers, campaigns, competitions, displays, campus trails, exhibitions and the promotion of volunteering. Institutions and academics need in future to recognise more fully that students' learning does not stop the moment they leave the lecture theatre of laboratory. A key part of what students learn through their higher education derives from the 'informal curriculum'. Institutions need, therefore, to encourage students and staff to engage with sustainability by ensuring that it is a part of their routine experience and everyday life. In adopting this approach, staff in 'professional service' roles, such as estates, procurement and catering, will be encouraged to recognise that they too can contribute to student learning and awareness.

In highlighting some new and emerging agendas, it is important in particular to consider the growing links between sustainability and employability. The great majority of students entering higher education do so primarily to enhance their job prospects: and although the student experience can be worthwhile and rewarding in many different ways, for most students (and their parents!) the bottom line is career prospects. Traditionally, the world of business, corporations and the economy has often been thought of as having little interest in the environment or in related fields such as social responsibility. However, not least because of public concerns about climate change and pollution, particularly in the last two or three years, there is growing evidence of a change in attitude. Companies in all sectors, from retailing to energy supply, are suddenly keen to advertise their 'green' credentials. While some of this can be dismissed as 'greenwash', it is interesting that a recent survey by Adam Cade (2008) found that over half of UK graduate employers (54%) were looking to employ candidates who could demonstrate social and environmental responsibility. About a quarter said that their policies on Corporate Social Responsibility (CSR) or sustainable development directly affected the way they now recruit graduates. The same study found that among students deciding what job to apply for, some 37% considered the social and environmental ethos of the potential employer to be an important discriminating factor.

Of course, sceptics will point out that the Cade study (prepared for the UK Higher Education Academy) was undertaken by Student Force for Sustainability (a charity with a clear interest in this field). However, there can be little doubt that an increasing number of employers do want to attract graduates with responsible values and that more and more students want to work for organisations which genuinely are environmentally and socially responsible. There is, of course, a long way to go but the employability and sustainability agendas are starting to converge; and given the importance which today's higher education system attaches to employability, the start of this alignment has to be good news for ESD. Universities and Colleges will increasingly need, therefore, to take steps to produce 'sustainability literate' graduates for reasons of employability as well as citizenship.

Synopsis

This closing paper has, therefore, highlighted some examples of opportunities for change and innovation in the ESD arena. The ideas presented will no doubt be new to some readers and familiar to others. What they have in common is that they are not yet in common practice. They span areas such as curriculum review and enhancement, pioneering ESD in a range of disciplines, developing fresh institutional policies and cultures, using the informal curriculum and connecting sustainability and employability.

Throughout this volume, as in this final paper, the reader will have encountered a varied menu of approaches to the sustainability agenda. It is hoped that the book's contents will encourage both a sharing of ideas and a strengthening of commitment. In the past, higher education has often been portrayed as (by omission) doing more to exacerbate than to ameliorate the growing threats to society's sustainability. We have been part of the problem rather than the solution. This volume and its multitude of authors have illustrated that it doesn't have to be like this. It doesn't have to be 'business as usual'. There is another way — indeed, a multiplicity of other ways.

References

Cade, A. (2008) *Employable Graduates for Responsible Employers* (York: Higher Education Academy).

Gardner, R. & Craig, L. (2001) Editorial. Is Geography History?, *Journal of Geography in Higher Education*, 25(1), pp.5-10

Gough, S. & Scott, W. (2008) *Higher Education and Sustainable Development: Paradox and Possibility* (London: Routledge).

HEFCE (Higher Education Funding Council for England) (2005) *Sustainable Development in Higher Education* (Bristol: Higher Education Funding Council for England). Available at http://www.hefce.ac.uk/lgm/sustain/ (accessed April 2008).

HEFCE (Higher Education Funding Council (England)) (2008) *HEFCE Strategic Review of Sustainable Development in Higher Education in England* (Bristol: Higher Educational Funding Council for England).

OFSTED (2008) *The Geography in Schools: Changing Practice* (London: OFSTED) Available from: http://www.ofsted.gov.uk (accessed April 2008).

Roberts, C. & Roberts, J. (2007) *Greener by Degrees: Exploring sustainability through higher education curricula* (Cheltenham: University of Gloucestershire).

INDEX

Page numbers in **bold** and 'n.' plus note number indicate figures/tables and notes respectively.